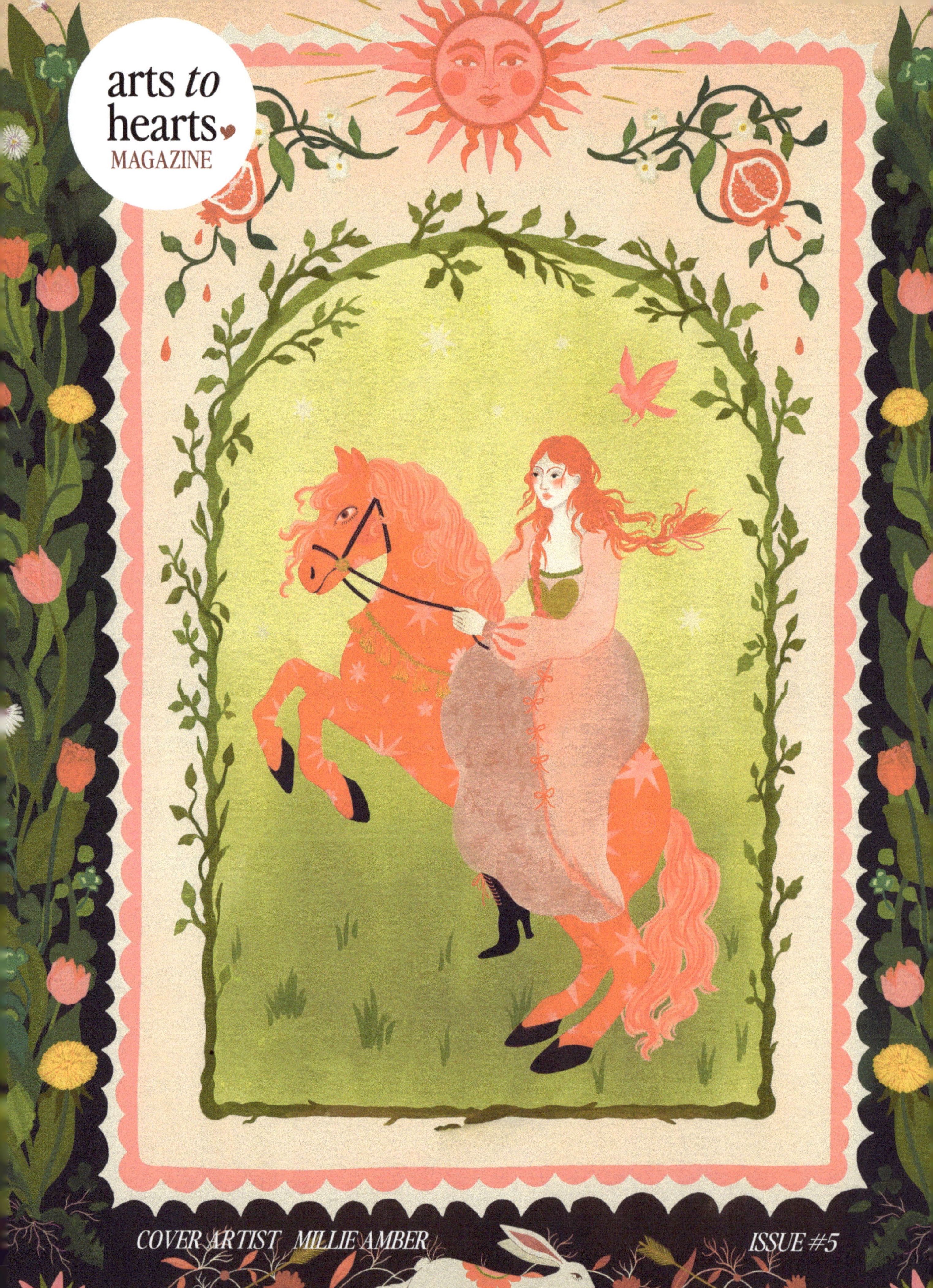

arts to hearts
MAGAZINE
COVER ARTIST MILLIE AMBER
ISSUE #5

arts to hearts ♥

MAGAZINE

We are a contemporary
Art publication on a mission to
Discover, connect, and engage with
Contemporary & emerging
Women artists from around the world.

A Product of

ARTS TO HEARTS PROJECT

We are a global creative community uniting contemporary & emerging women Artists
to build successful, fulfilling, and money-making careers via collaboration, learning,
community, networking, and peer-to-peer learning.

SUBMIT YOUR WORK

We have several opportunities throughout the year for people
interested in the global arts. From open calls to grants to exhibits,
you can stay on top of all our upcoming and ongoing opportunities
by subscribing to our newsletter on our website.

COVER ART
Persephone
2023
42 x 59cm
Watercolour & gouache on paper

ISBN CODES
E-book reader: 978-81-968407-1-6
Paperback / Softback: 978-81-968407-5-4

VISIT OUR WEBSITE
www.artstoheartsproject.com

FOLLOW US ON INSTAGRAM
@artstoheartsproject

JOIN ARTS TO HEARTS CLUB
http://www.artstoheartsproject.com/athclub

EMAIL info@artstoheartsproject.com

"You gotta be prepared for rejection

to happen continually again and again, and no matter what, you keep persevering."

-Tanmaya Bingham

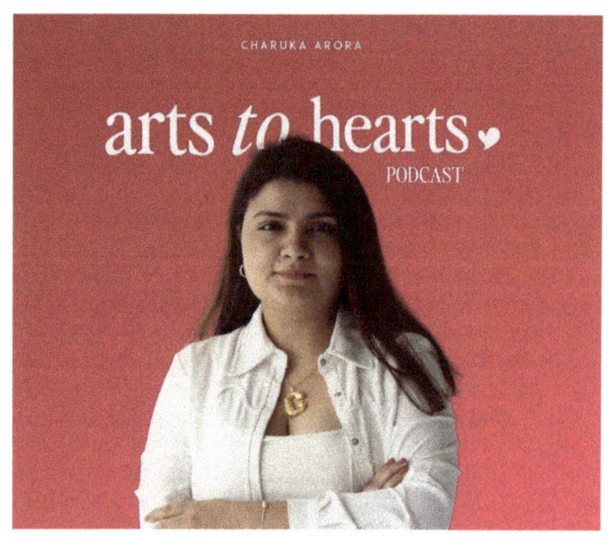

ARTS TO HEARTS PODCAST

Season 4 Episode 3

How to overcome your limiting beliefs as an artist

Scan to listen
Available on spotify, apple podcasts or anywhere you listen to your podcasts.

Editor's Note

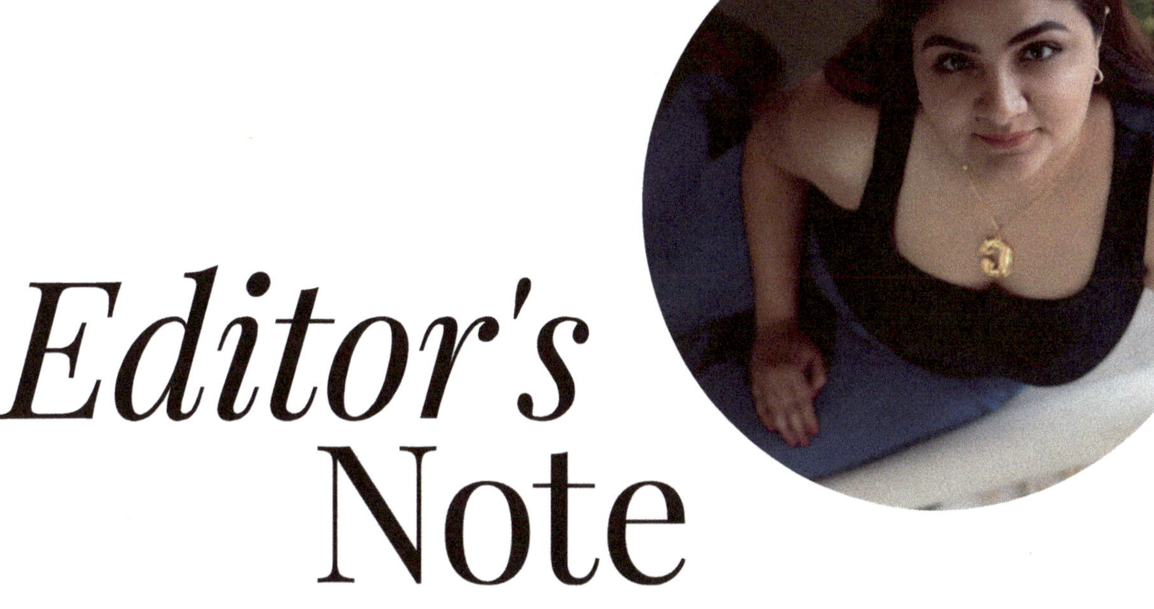

Dear Readers,

We are very excited to release the first-anniversary issue of our magazine. Honestly, today we are celebrating much more than just an anniversary; we are celebrating the very essence of what prompted us to start this journey. "Arts to Hearts Project" has always been a space brimming with sacred love, dedicated to helping, supporting, and empowering deeper conversations—and it will continue to be so for as long as possible.

In this issue, we feature some truly exciting content. As you know, we are always energized—fueled by our love for what we do. We consistently challenge ourselves in the way we present our content, from the aesthetics of the book to the design of the magazine, the features we include, and the questions we ask. It's all part of our commitment to excellence.

We're offering some great resources, spanning topics from financial success to artists we admire. It's been an extraordinary year, publishing these incredible issues one after another. Till now, we've featured Rebecca Brodksis, Rachel Burke, Rithika Merchant, and many others, each bringing a unique perspective to the world of arts through our covers.

We are incredibly happy to have Millie Amber as our cover artist in this issue, an amazing artist whose mystical creations embody the exact feeling that "Arts to Heart Project" is all about for me.

Looking forward, I continue to hope that we celebrate many more years of success and innovation. By sharing content, creating wonderful magazine issues filled with love, featuring inspiring artists, fostering more conversations, and creating a safe space for women in the arts around the world to be seen, supported, and empowered.

So, I hope that you continue to support us and share the love. May we always keep a heart in the arts. Sending lots of love from the team at Arts to Hearts Project, may we remain steadfastly committed to doing the work that we do.

Charvi

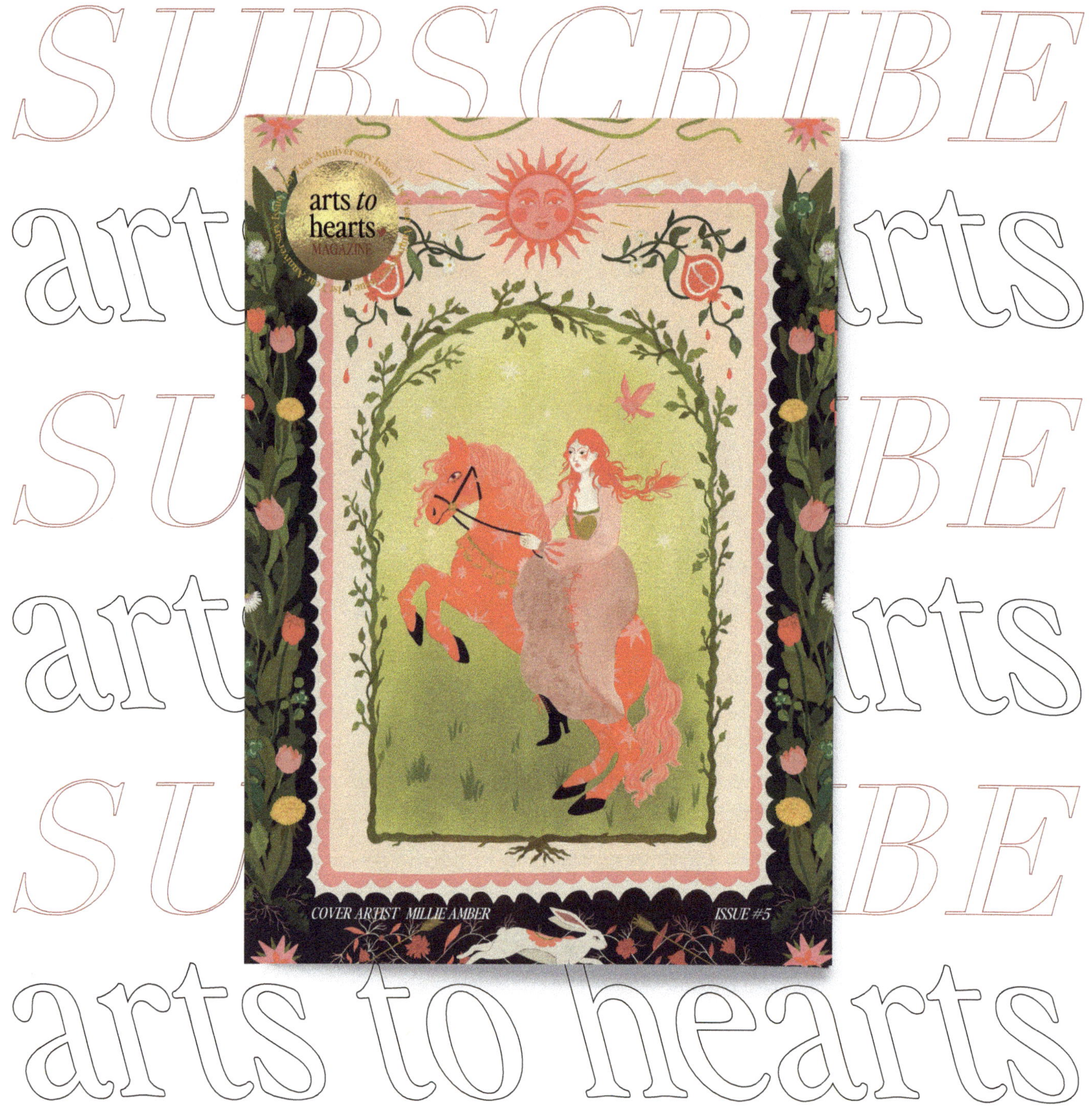
SUBSCRIBE
arts to hearts
arts
arts to hearts

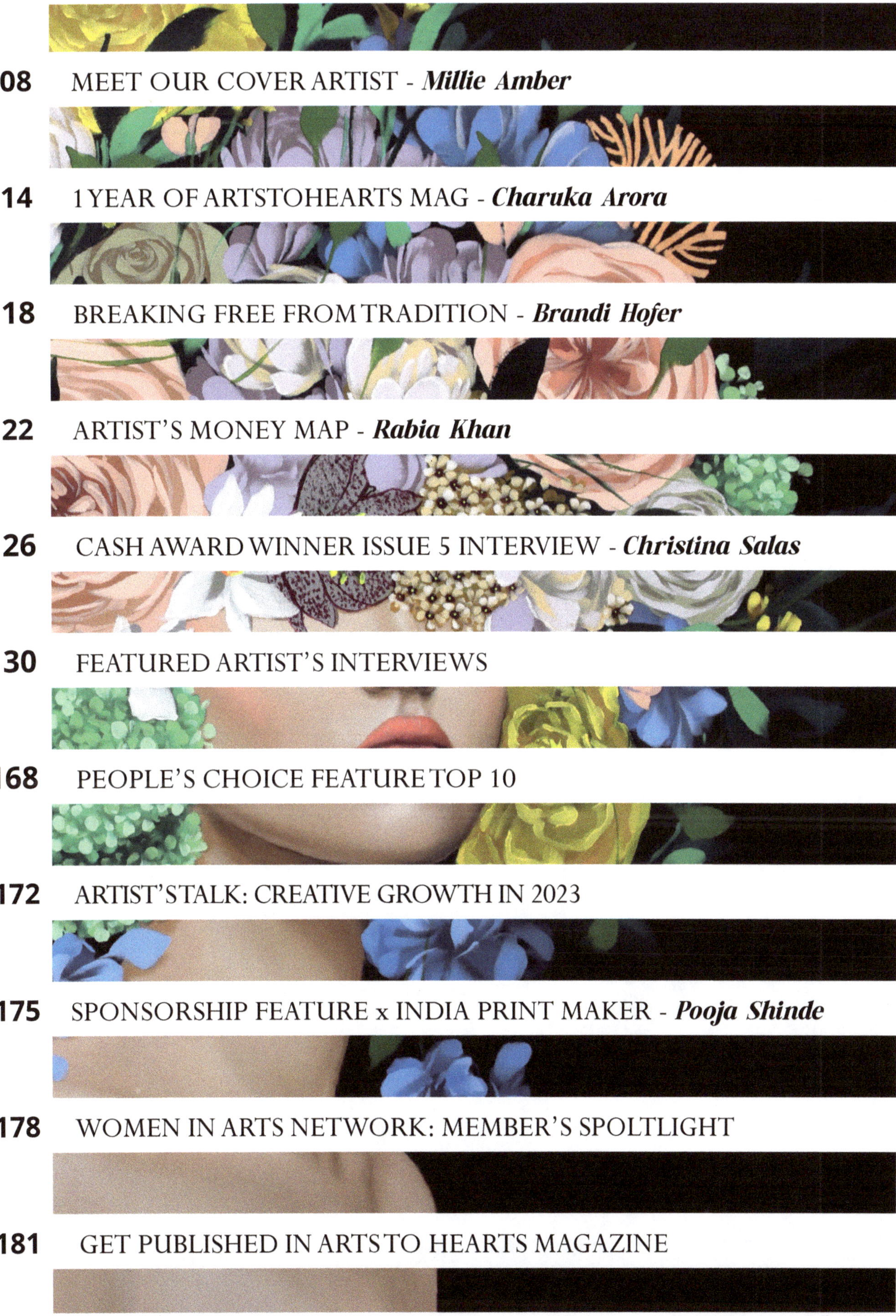

Image Courtesy : Sally Khoury

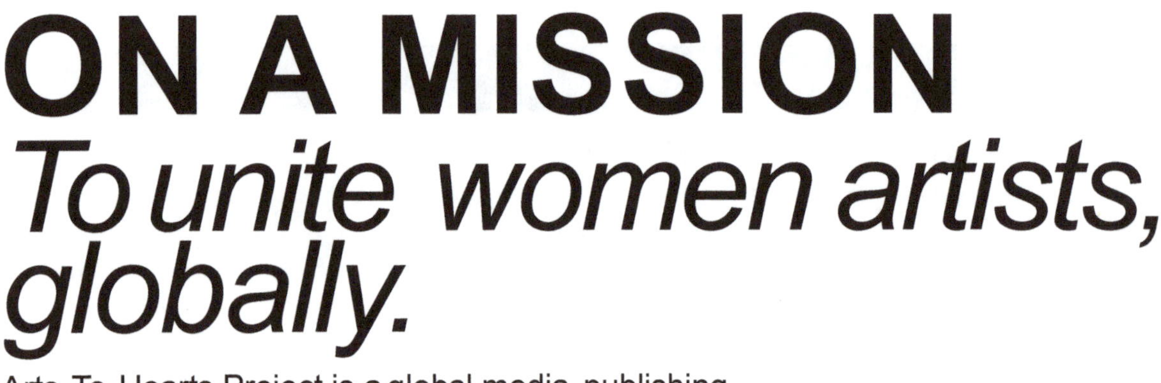

ON A MISSION
To unite women artists, globally.

Arts To Hearts Project is a global media, publishing, education, and community platform for women in the arts.

We established this platform with a mission: to create a safe and empowering space for women artists. Our goal is to foster a global community where female artists and creatives can come together, collaborate, learn, and uplift their lives and careers. Our platform serves as a one-stop destination for all their needs. Join us in celebrating the collective female voice and empowering women in the arts.

Through our diverse range of media, publications, educational initiatives, and community platforms, we create a secure and empowering space for women artists to collaborate, learn, and uplift one another. Together, we strive to make a profound impact and elevate the lives and careers of women in the arts, forging a path toward a brighter future.

In 2024, artists will have the privilege of exploring a multitude of exciting and thrilling opportunities. The year will commence with the eagerly awaited 100 Emerging Artists Project followed by releasing the much anticipated ATH Magazine Issues, Studio Visit Books, and an array of captivating ventures.

Prepare yourself for an extraordinary year ahead at Arts to Hearts Project, filled with awards, cash prizes, and endless inspiration.

We've had the privilege of collaborating with exceptional individuals in arts. From gallerists to mentors, founders to artists.

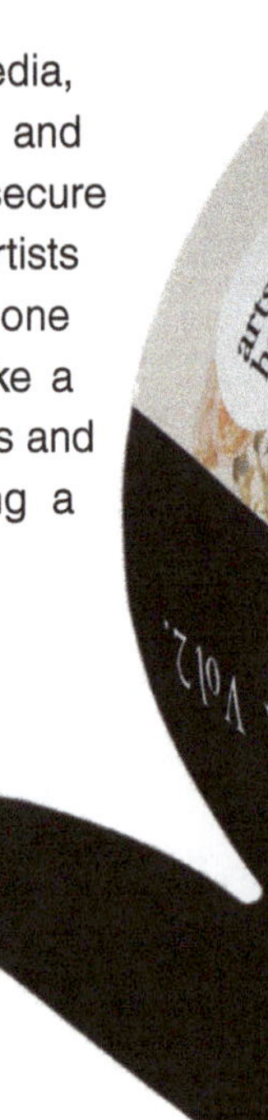

Visit our Website
Catch the freshest Articles
Updated daily
Read anytime, anywhere

Get Published
Submit to Call for Art
Showcase your Artwork
Get Global Exposure

arts *to*
hearts
PROJECT

How We Help Women in Arts

Arts Publications, Books & Magazines
Studio Visit Book, Arts to Hearts Magazine, 101 Art Books, Journals, Arts to Hearts Quest, 100 Emerging Artwork, 100 Emerging Artists

Learning and Resources
Arts to Hearts Club, Arts to Hearts Podcast

Recognitions and Opportunities for Artists
Cash Prizes, Emerging Woman Artist Award, Virtual Exhibition

Business & Creative Consulting for Artists

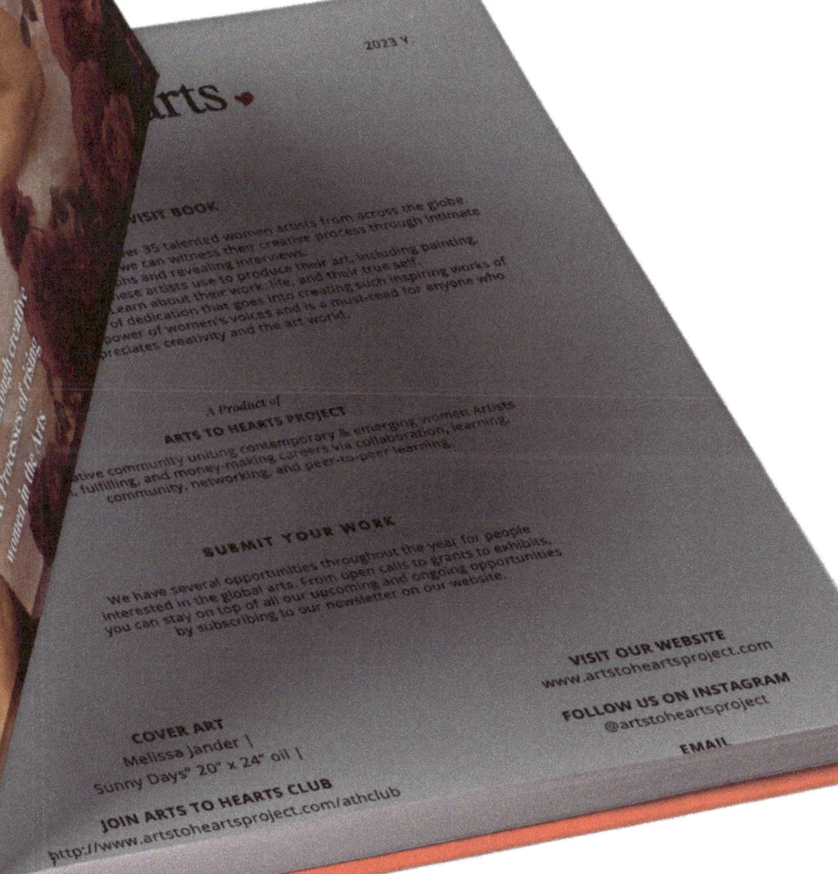

Publisher's Note

Arts to Hearts magazine spotlights emerging women artists and boosts fellow creatives. We hope that you will find joy in this creation, that it becomes a treasured part of your collection, and that it further encourages the participation of more women and creative individuals in the industry.

EDITOR IN CHIEF
Charuka Arora

ASSOCIATE EDITOR
Rabia Khan

LEAD DESIGNER
Saba Javed

ASSOCIATE DESIGNER
Asbah Gull

CONTRIBUTING WRITER
Brandi Hofer

WRITER
Sonam Bindra

WRITER
Museerah Nisar

FIND US ON
www.artstoheartsproject.com
facebook.com/groups/womenartistsworldwideath
instagram.com/artstoheartsproject

GENERAL ENQUIRIES
info@artstoheartsproject.com

READ OUR DIGITAL EDITORIALS AND RESOURCES ON
www.artstoheartsproject.com

JOIN OUR CLUB
www.artstoheartsproject.com/athclub

ISBN CODES
E-book reader: 978-81-968407-1-6
Paperback / Softback: 978-81-968407-5-4

The Mystical Folk Art World *of*

Interview by *Rabia Khan*

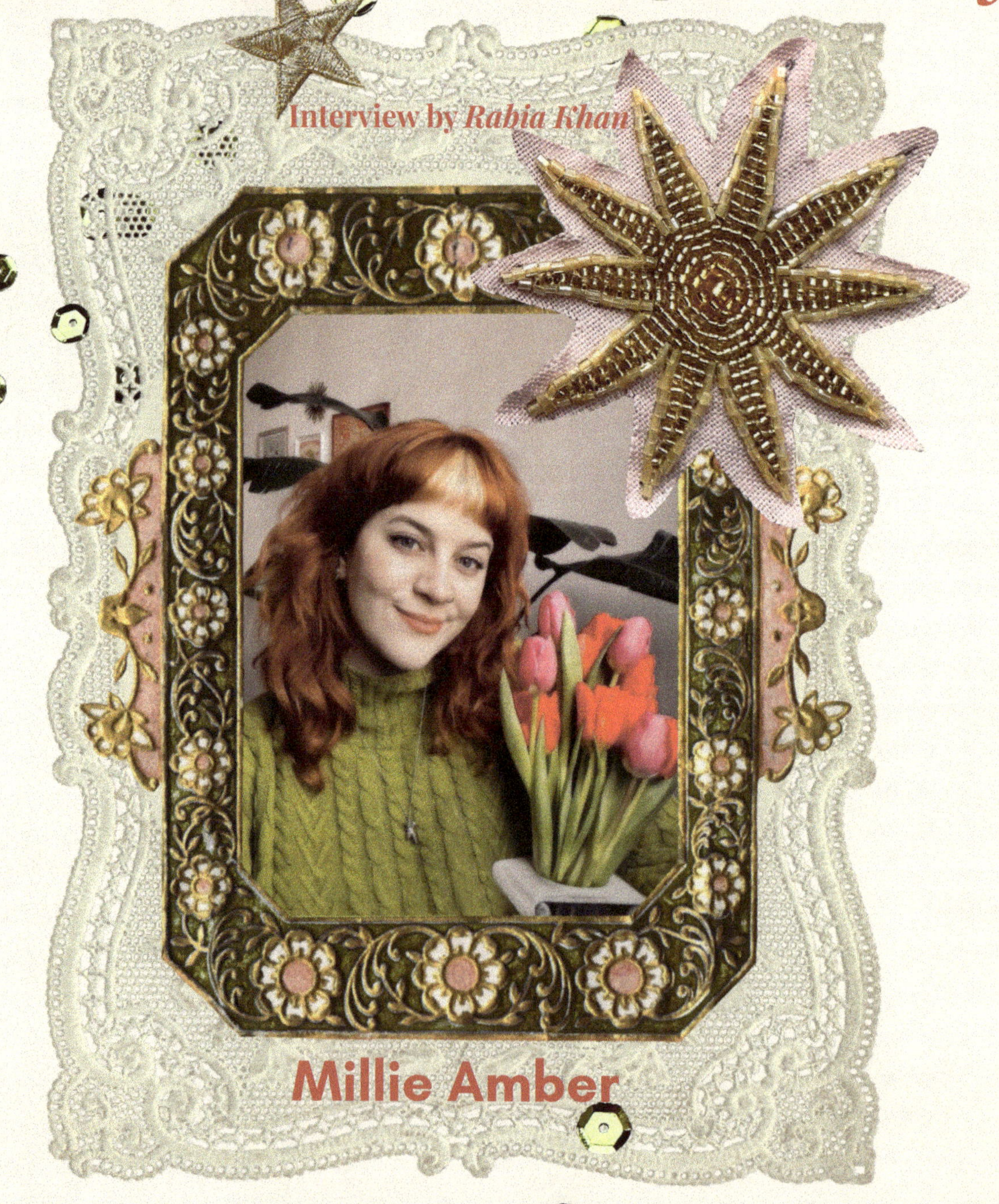

Millie Amber

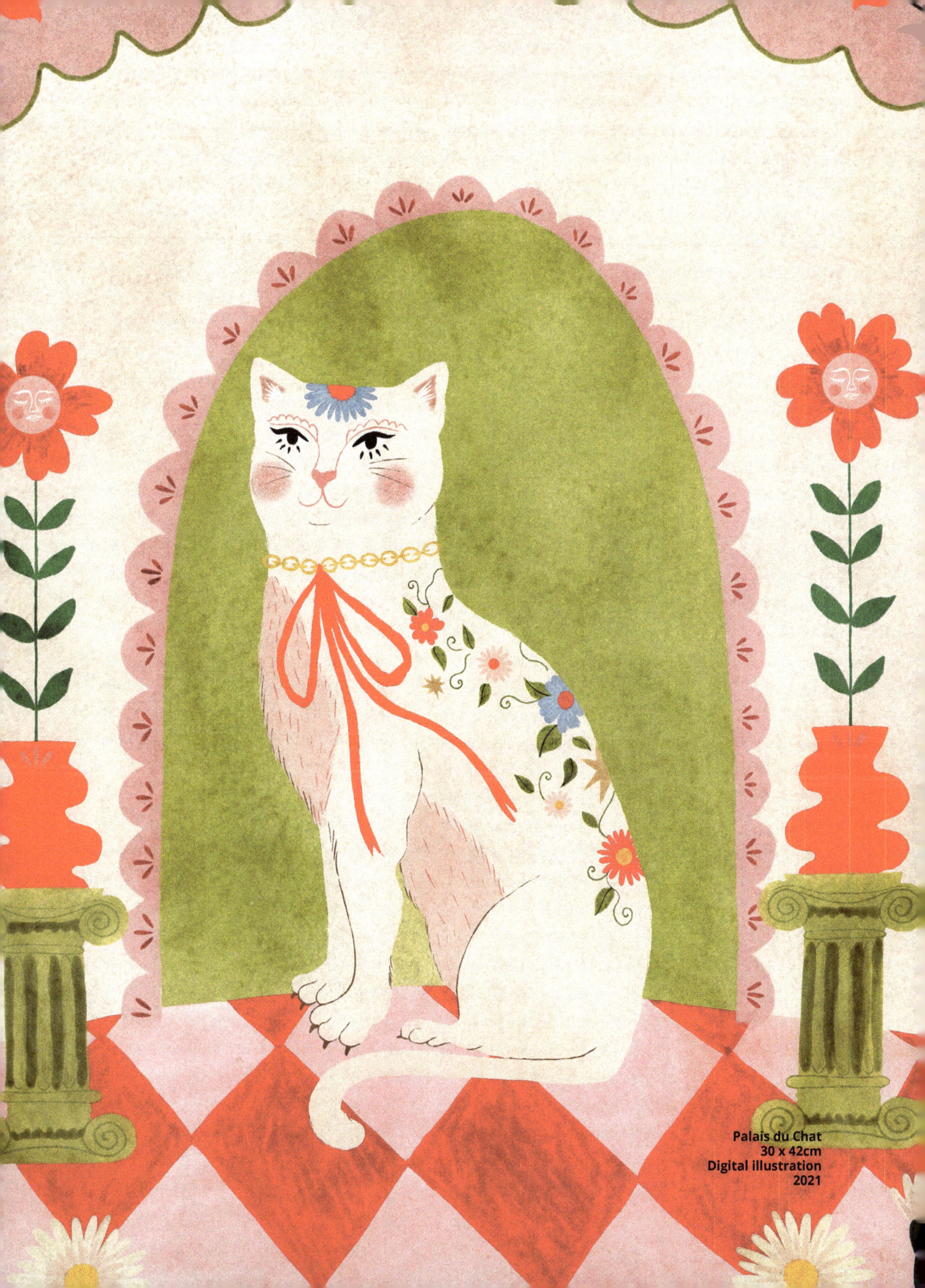
Palais du Chat
30 x 42cm
Digital illustration
2021

*I*n our special anniversary issue of ATH Magazine, we're honored to have Millie Amber as our cover artist. Millie is an artist whose creative skills extend far beyond the canvas. Known for her unique blend of art, Millie has etched a distinct space for herself in the art world. This London-based illustrator and textile artist is celebrated for her decorative, intricate, and vibrant work that revolves around romantic symbolism, folkloric motifs, and poetic narratives. Her pieces, often inspired by folk art, mythology, and ephemera, resonate with a sense of whimsy and wonder. From her illustrations to her innovative textile designs, Millie's work reflects her passion and dedication to her craft. As we delve into our conversation with Millie, we discuss her inspirations, her journey, and how she navigates the challenges of being both an artist and entrepreneur. So, without further ado, let's jump into our discussion with Millie Amber.

So, Millie! Textiles seem to play a big role in your creations. Can you share why they're important to you?

I just love the tangible nature of them. I enjoy making things with my hands and having physical artwork at the end of it. Working with textiles allows you to play with texture and there are so many techniques to learn. I love to embroider, and even though it often feels like a very slow way of working, (especially if there is a deadline involved) the end result feels so special to me. I'm also a total magpie, drawn to shiny things so working with fabrics and beads is very satisfying.

Millie, I see a lot of hearts in your work. Is there any specific reason for you to choose it as one of your subjects?

They are definitely a recurring theme! I'm not sure how that started, perhaps through my love of folk art. I guess I am a bit of a romantic and I like the universal symbolism they hold. Hearts have been used as a motif for hundreds of years and they can portray so many emotions from devotion and joy to pain and sorrow.

Artists often say their style evolves over time. Have you noticed a change in your work?

I think style evolves as you perfect your skills and pick up new techniques, my work has definitely become more refined over the years as I've figured out how I like to do things. I think my style often reflects what I'm interested in at a given time but a lot stays the same, there are certain motifs and color palettes that I am drawn to and will use again and again.

Every career has its ups and downs. Can you share a challenging time in yours and how you got through it?

The first thing that springs to mind is when a brand used one of my designs and claimed it as their own, for a collaboration with an even bigger brand that I had once dreamed of working with. This is an unfortunate downside of sharing your work online and frustratingly happens to artists too often. It was surreal going into a store and seeing the products in person and I couldn't help but feel robbed of an opportunity. Things like this can be so disheartening and knock your confidence, I didn't know how to get help and big companies often feel untouchable. I had to spur myself on to make new and hopefully better things. I'm a bit more protective of my work now and have had similar things happen on occasion. More generally though I think the challenge that presents itself the most is dealing with the quiet times. When work is slow it can be hard to stop the imposter syndrome creeping in and so easy to fall into the trap of comparing yourself to others. I have to remind myself that everyone has these moments and opportunities will ebb and flow the same way your creativity does, you have to be able to ride it out. I'm trying to reframe times like this as a chance to reflect on and develop my practice. It's the perfect time to try something new or finally start on an idea that got put to one side in the past.

I'm always curious about how artists work. Can you walk us through your creative process?

I love gathering inspiration. I am a bit of a collector and go through phases of searching for things that inspire me, vintage fabrics and trimmings, ephemera, silk scarves, jewelry! Both in real life and online. I love making Pinterest boards and trawling through archives of museum collections or reference books so I tend to start there. If I'm working on a commission/brief there is usually a clearer end result in mind and things are more planned out but with my personal work I'll start with a vague sketch and decide on the rest as I go along. I find that it less restrictive that way, to try and go with the flow of a piece and see where it takes me.

You're not just an artist, but a businesswoman too. How do you juggle your creative side with the practicalities of running a business?

This is something I'm getting to grips with and I definitely still have a lot to figure out. I've never thought of myself as a business person before! I would prefer to just lose myself

in the creative side of things for sure. It doesn't come naturally to me, my brain isn't wired for organization and admin so there are a lot of aspects that I struggle with. I think the most important thing is finding a balance so that you can make and grow as an artist and keep on top of the practical stuff. It really can feel like you are juggling multiple roles and most of the time I am learning as I go. But as much as I find the business stuff difficult, I'm so grateful that there are people interested in what I make and who appreciate my work - the joy that makes me feel far outweighs anything else.

One last question before we finish this interview. If someone's dreaming of becoming an illustrator or textile artist, what advice would you give them?

Experiment! Try out different mediums/ techniques and find what you are passionate about. Don't worry about having a particular style because that will come with time, and try to avoid following trends or making work just because you think it's what other people deem to be 'good' art. Try to find inspiration outside of the internet (as useful as it can be!) People have said this to me a lot, but it's true, keep putting your work out there because you never know who is looking and what might come along.

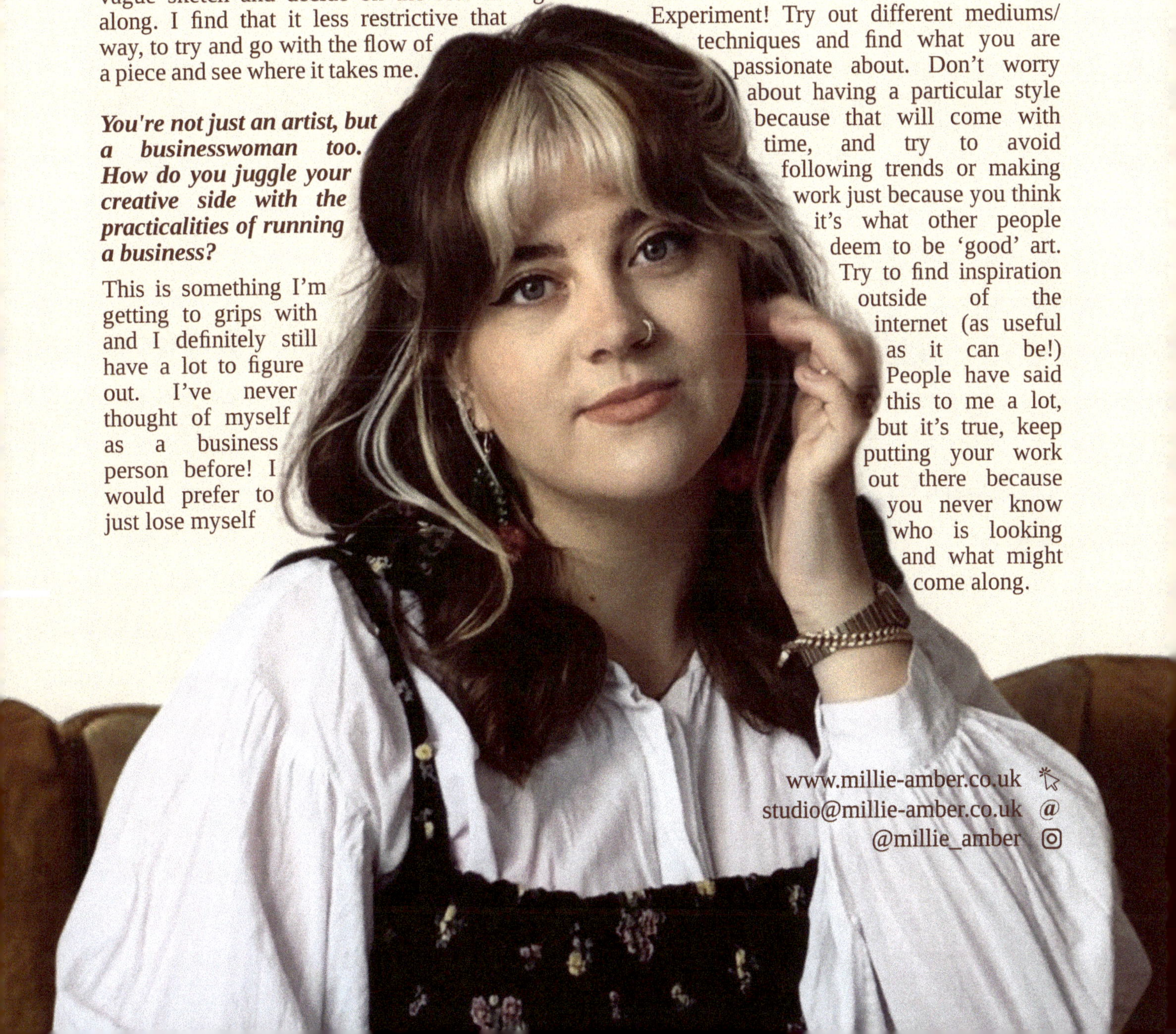

www.millie-amber.co.uk
studio@millie-amber.co.uk @
@millie_amber

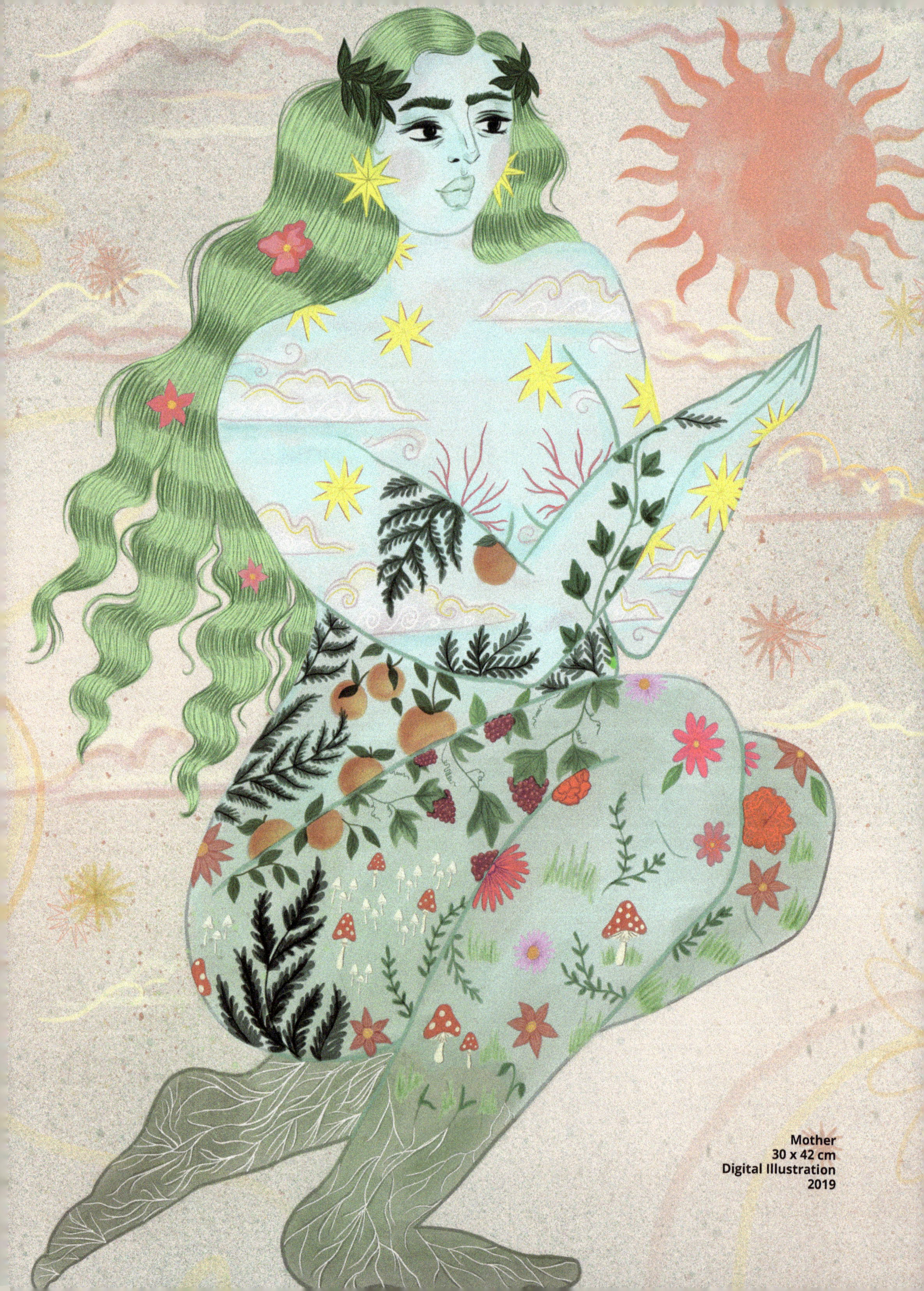

Mother
30 x 42 cm
Digital Illustration
2019

Get Your Artist Book Published

with Arts to Hearts Project

Want to publish your own artist book but don't know where to start? Arts to Hearts Project has got you covered. We offer an end-to-end solution, taking care of everything from the initial concept to the final print.

Here's how we make it happen:

Custom Designs

Our skilled designers will create a beautiful art book that shows off your unique style.

Careful Proofreading

Our proofreaders will carefully check your art book. They'll fix any mistakes and make sure everything reads well.

Smart Review

After the design is done, our art-loving team will check your art book. They'll make sure your work looks its best on paper.

Easy Publication

Once your art book is designed, checked, and proofread, we'll take care of getting it published. You won't have to worry about a thing.

Interested? Reach Out!

Getting your art book published is easy and fun. So why wait? Start your publishing journey with us today.

Celebrating
Womanhood &
Artrepreneurial
Journey of

Arts to Hearts Magazine

Interview By Rabia Khan

Step into the world of Arts to Hearts Magazine as we interview Charuka Arora about a very special milestone: the Arts to Hearts Magazine's first anniversary and three years of the Arts to Hearts Project. During the interview, we discussed how the magazine and Arts to Hearts Project has expanded into a space where women in the arts can connect, share their work, and pursue their dreams. It has been an entire year of amazing stories from creative women, and we're thrilled to hear from Charuka herself about the journey, including the highs and lows, and the plans for the future. Prepare to discover a community that is entirely dedicated to women supporting each other through their love of art.

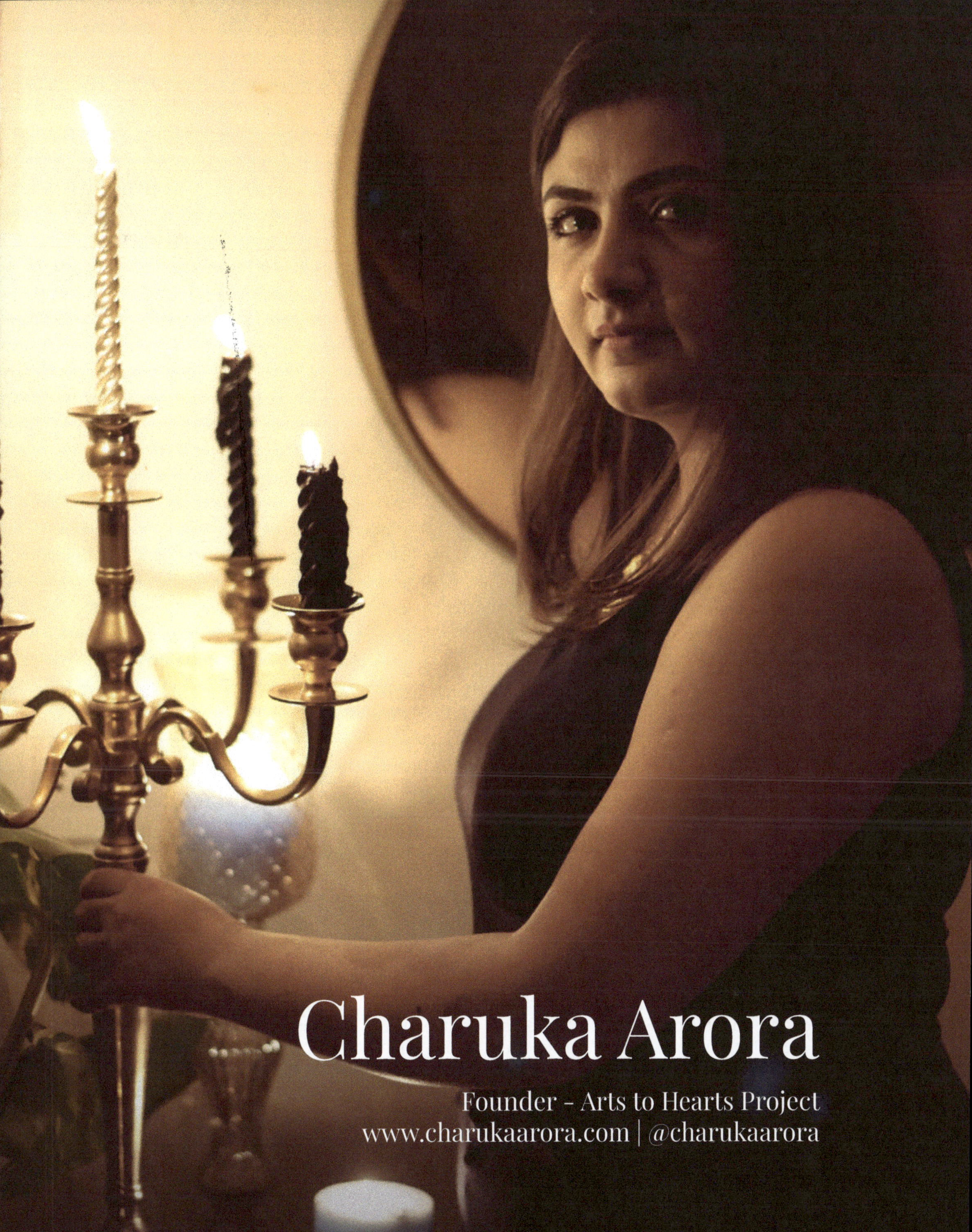

Charuka Arora
Founder - Arts to Hearts Project
www.charukaarora.com | @charukaarora

IN WHAT WAYS HAS THE ARTS TO HEARTS PROJECT IMPACTED THE LIVES OF WOMEN ARTISTS AROUND THE WORLD? CAN YOU SHARE SOME INSPIRING STORIES?

I'm excited because our project is just getting started and has so much room to grow. I want our impact to reach many more people, no matter the size. The heart of what we do is giving artists recognition, making them feel seen, and sharing their work with the world. Seeing an artist's face when they're featured in one of our books is priceless. We aim to help artists who often feel invisible by getting their art into hard-to-reach places, including galleries. This year feels extra special for teamwork and meaningful discussions.

One of my big goals is to help more women by creating jobs and giving them financial support. Soon, I plan to give cash awards to artists to open up new chances and connections for them. Even small steps can make a huge difference in someone's life. I'll never forget a great chat I had with Daniel's creator, and I hope to inspire more of these moments. We want to keep supporting both women and the arts through our hiring, customer service, and partnerships.

FROM YOUR PERSPECTIVE, WHY IS IT IMPORTANT TO HAVE SPACES LIKE ARTS TO HEARTS PROJECT AND ARTS TO HEARTS MAGAZINE THAT SPECIFICALLY CATER TO WOMEN IN THE ART INDUSTRY?

As I recognize the importance of supporting women in the arts, I find it crucial to have spaces like our Arts to Hearts Project and Arts to Hearts Magazine. There's a pressing need to focus on creating more avenues for women artists, to foster a better ecosystem. While we lack sufficient opportunities, structures, and organizations to facilitate it, I believe that in the next few years, the creative industries will significantly expand. Similarly, I envision a future where women hold influential positions, and they need all the support and resources available to them. We at Arts to Hearts Project aim to ensure that every creative woman has the means to fulfill her dreams.

LOOKING AHEAD, WHAT ARE YOUR HOPES AND DREAMS FOR THE FUTURE OF THE ARTS TO HEARTS PROJECT?

"I trust my intuition. My dream is to persevere through life's stages and transitions. I aim to conquer challenges, savor good days, make an impact, improve lives, and drive change. Witnessing others' dreams come true is vital to me. As for the future, I aspire to build a connected community where individuals can connect and share beyond the limits of religion and geography. A place where shared emotions and experiences unite us. For now, we aim to be a one-stop hub where anyone can find support, resources, and answers for their heart."

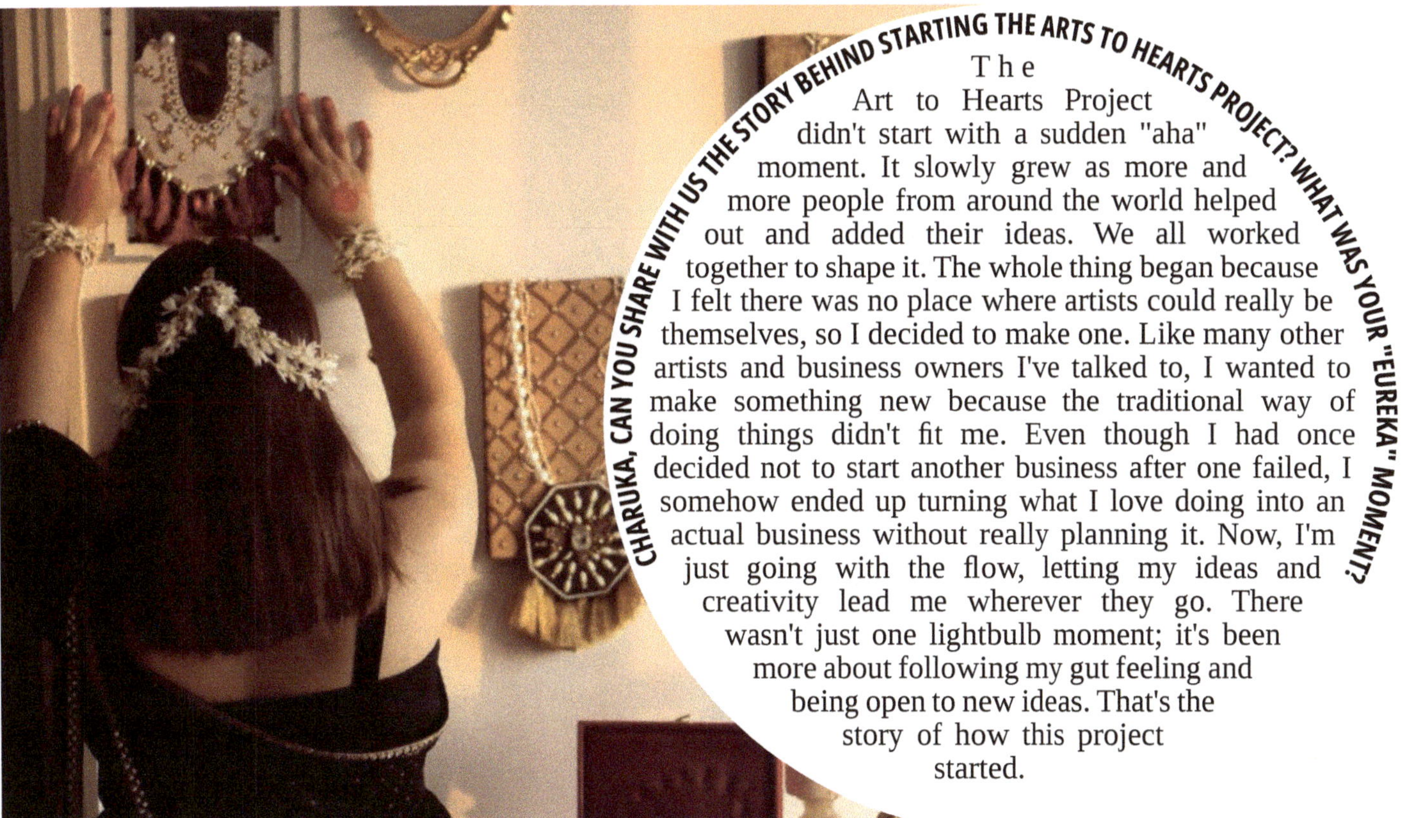

The Art to Hearts Project didn't start with a sudden "aha" moment. It slowly grew as more and more people from around the world helped out and added their ideas. We all worked together to shape it. The whole thing began because I felt there was no place where artists could really be themselves, so I decided to make one. Like many other artists and business owners I've talked to, I wanted to make something new because the traditional way of doing things didn't fit me. Even though I had once decided not to start another business after one failed, I somehow ended up turning what I love doing into an actual business without really planning it. Now, I'm just going with the flow, letting my ideas and creativity lead me wherever they go. There wasn't just one lightbulb moment; it's been more about following my gut feeling and being open to new ideas. That's the story of how this project started.

OVER THE PAST THREE YEARS, HOW WOULD YOU DESCRIBE THE JOURNEY OF THE ARTS TO HEARTS PROJECT? CAN YOU SHARE SOME HIGHS AND LOWS THAT HAVE SHAPED ITS PATH?

I can't believe it's been three years since the Art to Hearts Project began. Time flies, and even after a decade in business, this project feels like a fresh start every day. It wasn't planned; it grew from my passion to be an artist and create a space for others like me. The team I work with and the artists we support make every effort worthwhile. Despite the stress of running a business, especially the financial part, and making sure we're doing our best, the joy comes from our community. We're all about making connections and helping each other grow. Sure, there are tough days when I worry if I'm doing enough, but then I see our artists succeeding, and I know we're on the right track.

WHAT ADVICE WOULD YOU GIVE TO OTHER WOMEN WHO ASPIRE TO INTERTWINE THEIR PASSION FOR ART WITH ENTREPRENEURSHIP?

Entrepreneurship is a demanding yet fulfilling journey that requires a creative and data-driven approach. Remember to balance different aspects of your business and prioritize accordingly. Pursue entrepreneurship with the right reasons in mind, approach it with a mindset of service and responsibility, and know that it can be tremendously rewarding, teaching and changing you profoundly.

REFLECTING ON THE PAST THREE YEARS, WHAT ARE SOME KEY LESSONS YOU'VE LEARNED WHILE STEERING THE ARTS TO HEARTS PROJECT?

Persistence is key, whether you're having a good or bad day. As an entrepreneur, I've learned to take small steps forward and not let failures or successes get in the way. On tough days, I remind myself that these moments are temporary and any progress is valuable. Pursuing a greater purpose beyond money or fame is crucial, as is kindness and empathy in business. The journey is just as important as the outcome, and the growth we experience along the way is the ultimate reward.

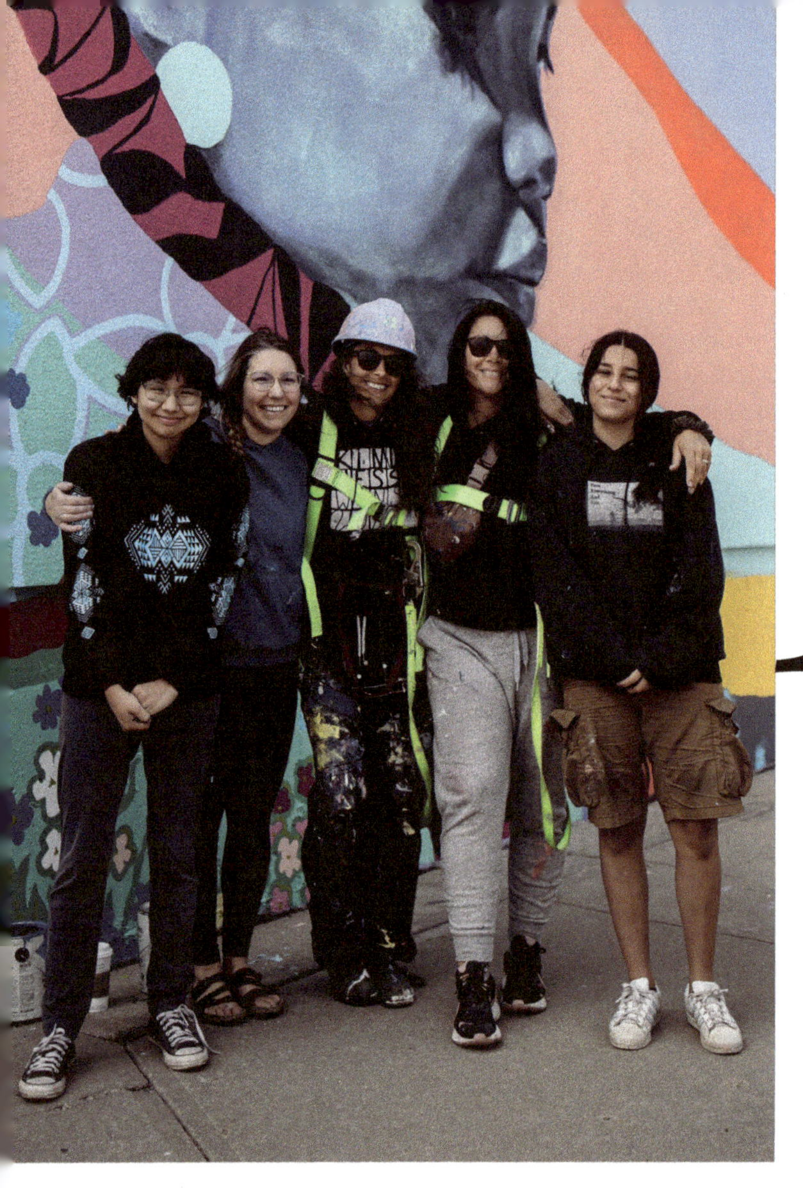

Breaking *free* *from* Tradition

Shaping a diverse artistic journey

Brandi Hofer | Contributing writer

Founder of Colour Me Happy Community/ Podcast/ Book and Brandi Hofer Studios

www.brandihofer.ca
@brandihoferstudios

Reflecting on my journey as an artist and entrepreneur, the disparities in societal perceptions of fathers and mothers in parenthood become evident. A viral video of a male artist painting with his child garnered attention, prompting me to question why such roles by men are considered anomalies. Canadian Photographer Randi Noble humorously notes, "Sometimes I show up with the confidence of a mediocre white man, which really helps!" The lack of representation for women in business and art entrepreneurship fueled my journey to overcome self-doubt. It illuminated the need for change, challenging stereotypes associated with artists. I defied traditional gender roles and launched my business at 33, highlighting gender biases in family dynamics. The need for change was undeniable. The traditional norms were slowly evolving, and womxn-identifying creatives globally shed gender roles. This shift inspired me to redefine the conventional studio practice, transforming it into a dynamic and multifaceted business. Diversification wasn't just strategic; it was a conscious effort to break free from traditional models. Giving and receiving with love and adopting compassion over competition became guiding principles. Four years of dedication and shedding limiting beliefs paved the way for transformative endeavors. This journey transcended personal success, fostering a supportive ecosystem. In this evolving landscape, the article explores the realities of motherhood, celebrating its undervalued role. Far from hindering success, parenthood instills strength, compassion, and determination, becoming a unique edge. The shared experiences of women, regardless of motherhood status, celebrate diverse paths, transparency, and the strength derived from being part of a supportive community.

All the LOVE!

Randi Noble Smith
Photographer

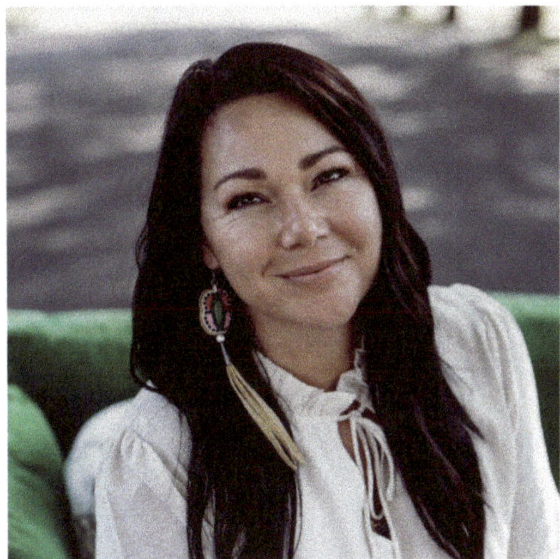

As a female identifying creative and professional in the music scene, has there been a limiting belief put on you by societal expectations? How did you overcome it?

My name is Elenee and I am a multi-award winning Canadian songwriter, artist, and producer. I am a wife, mother, and a third-generation restaurateur in the Canadian prairies and I am currently putting the finishing touches on a full length album to release Spring 2024. I think one of the biggest societal narratives that I can fall into is that I have no creative freedom over my art, because the music production space is very male-dominated. I am surrounded by males in the industry, and even on my team. Thankfully, my team works hard to abolish that narrative by allowing me creative freedom over every part of the creative process. I decided the best way to overcome this, even with the amazing team I have, was to invest time into learning music production on my own and be able to be the producer on all my music going forward. This has resulted in a passive income projects for other female artists.

In your honest observation how do you feel about the view of motherhood in the art world? And how has motherhood impacted your creative life?

I think times have changed so much and the world view on motherhood and careers is shifting. 60 years ago, women were the heart of the home - the ones who cooked, cleaned, dusted you off when you fell, and steered the energy in the room when the father was feeling temperamental (men weren't allowed to show emotion back then, and a lot of the time, the mothers would clean up after them and hush the children when times were stressful.) Nowadays, I like to think that family connection is at the heart of the home and we now give space for the kids who want to make some noise, we talk to our husbands or partners more deeply and give space for their emotions. Parenting seems more equal. We strive to balance our lives with work and home - which is not easy, but things have changed. Women want to feed their desires and show the world what we are made of. It's been a bit of an upheaval for society, as we are learning that often 9-5 jobs don't cut it.

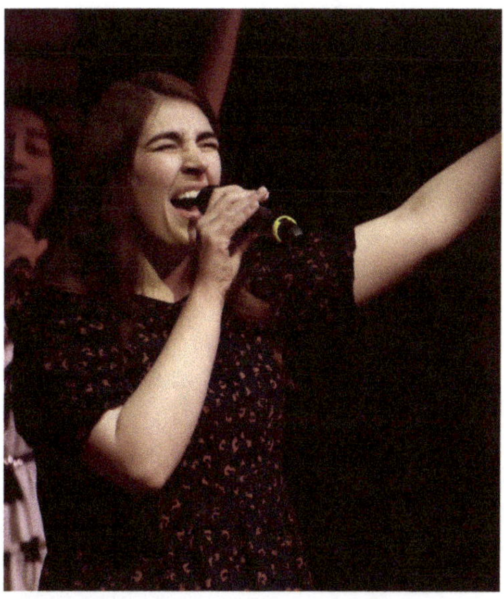

Elenee Marie Young
Songstress

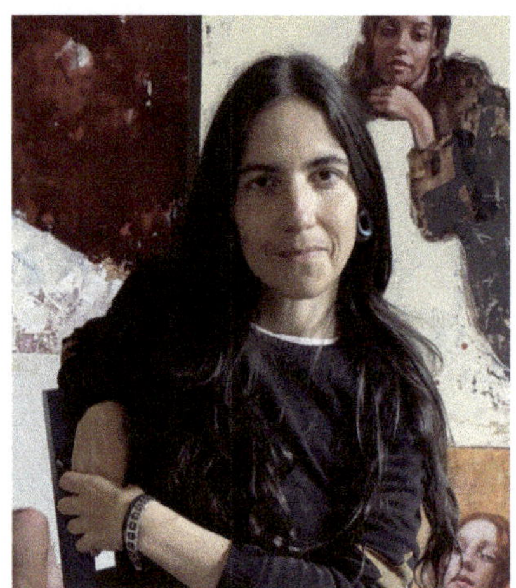

Rosso Emerald Crimson
Painter

As a female identifying creative and professional in the art world, has there been a limiting belief put on you by societal expectations? How did you overcome it?.

I started my career in my early 30s, after having worked in advertising for a few years, after graduating in Politics and International relations (yes, nothing to do with art). I was completely unaware of my 'artistic' vocation, except from some distant memories of my school days when I loved to draw portraits and caricatures of my classmates. All I knew was I could not cope with an office-life for much longer. I have not faced any societal limitations/ expectations for being a "woman", only for being an "artist". Regardless of your gender, to become a successful professional artist is still regarded as something utopic and idealistic. People just struggle to believe that is the only thing you do – creating art as your job. Oh well, sometimes I struggle with the same idea too.

In your honest observation how do you feel about the view of motherhood in the art world? And how has motherhood impacted your creative life?

I am a prairie-based contemporary landscape painter, writer, mom of 3 teenagers, RCAF veteran, former engineer, occasional runner, self-help book addict, and optimist. I paint as a means of connection, not only to nature and our physical landscapes, but to humanity, memory and hope. My own career path has been indirect, meandering and occasionally bumpy, transitioning from aerospace engineer in uniform to full-time creative while moving across multiple provinces several times. Motherhood is a beautiful component of creative living. Becoming a mom was a first shift in perspective for me and brought me back to my art. I like to think that by demonstrating and modeling the importance of creativity and expression in our daily being, we are teaching future generations of this important skill set and nurturing relationships.

Jodi Miller
Painter

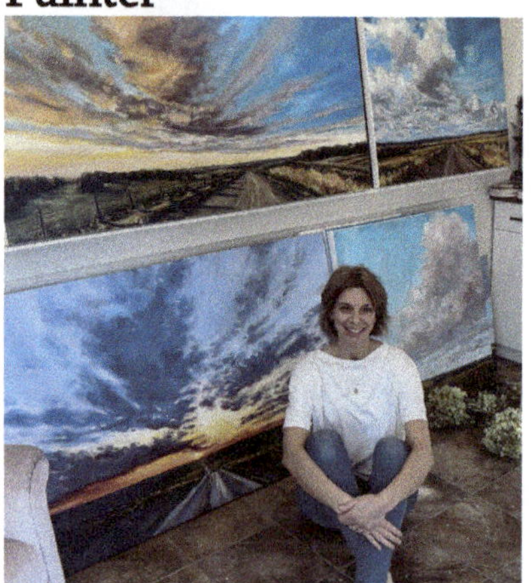

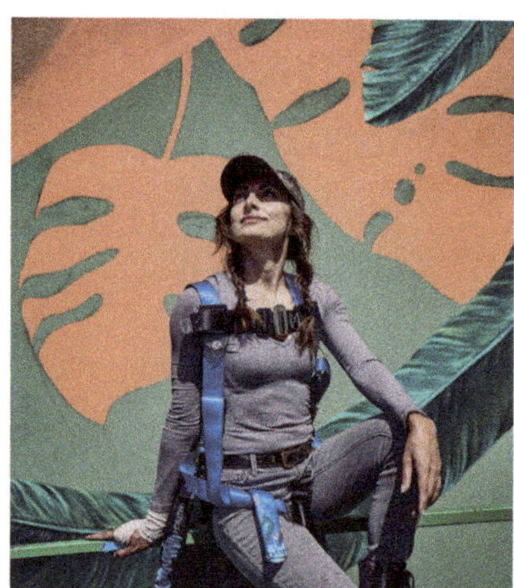

Elba Raquel Martinez
Painter, Muralist

As a female identifying creative and professional in the art world, has there been a limiting belief put on you by societal expectations? How did you overcome it?

As a high school teacher I have noticed that my Art classes are primarily filled with female students, and yet women are underrepresented in the Professional Art world. While looking at artist rosters for shows and galleries I exhibit at, I am typically astounded at the small percentage of female exhibiting artists. Where in the transition from student to professional did women get pushed out of the equation? While painting murals I get two reactions: Disbelief and Pride. Disbelief because "No, offense but, I have never seen a woman do that type of work." Pride because "You really inspire me to follow my dreams as a woman." All I can do to overcome female societal expectations is to keep following my aspirations and thrive as a professional artist to join the many other artist women who are redefining female norms for future generations.

In your honest observation how do you feel about the view of motherhood in the art world? And how has motherhood impacted your creative life?

I am the curator & co-founder of PxP Contemporary gallery, an arts writer, and the co-author of The Complete Smartist Guide and The Creative Business Handbook. I have worked in the arts industry for galleries, museums, art fairs, private collectors, and an auction house for over fifteen years in the US, the Netherlands, and Costa Rica. I've worked with numerous artists who are mothers (or have become mothers during the years I've represented their work), and it's never changed how I view or treat them professionally. I'd say many, if not most, gallerists nowadays are like this (at least outwardly). It's always hard to know what opportunities they may be holding women back from behind closed doors. But it makes sense. If you find a talented artist who's a solid match for your audience, it's in your best interest to build and maintain a relationship with them. That said, there are certainly some dealers/curators/critics/etc who would say that motherhood limits one's potential career trajectory - and we all know the statistics of how art created by women compares at auction. My hope is that these antiquated views are becoming less and less common and that we all continue to support artist mothers.

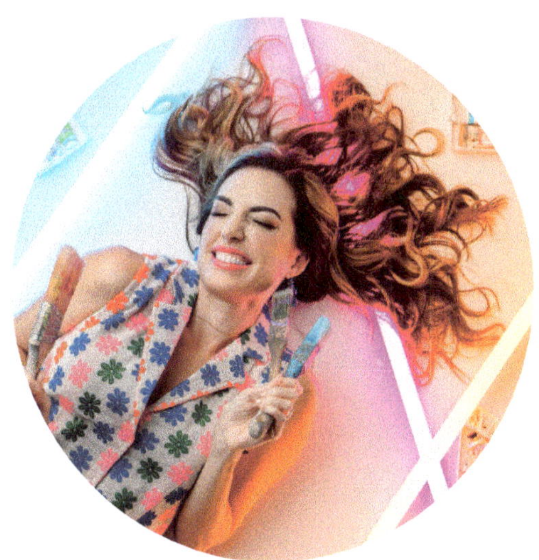

Ashley Cassens
Painter, Muralist

As a female identifying creative and professional in the art world, has there been a limiting belief put on you by societal expectations? How did you overcome it?

There weren't very many examples of female artists with families in undergrad school. The art history I grew up on was 99% male and the only women in art history that I knew about were Artemesia Gentilschi, Mary Cassatt, etc. All of the contemporary figurative artists that I loved (idols?) weren't parents. They didn't have families (or they didn't share that aspect). It was like every famous and successful artist was male and had dipped out of his wife and kids, to live out their real passion of painting and we just glaze over that. I really sought out contemporary female artists in grad school who had full lives outside of their practice. I wanted the WHOLE package and I wasn't interested in sacrificing my health and happiness for my art. I wanted to live passionately painting but also have a family and live by the ocean. I didn't think they had to be mutually exclusive or that one has to live a toxic "artistic" life to be financially successful.

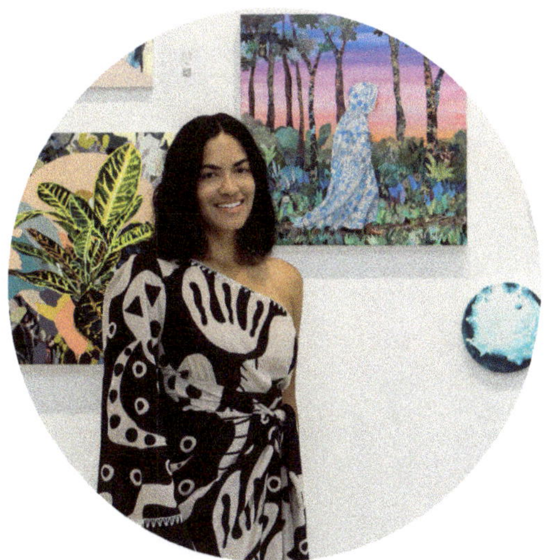

Alicia Puig
Gallerist, Curator, Author

The Artist's Money

Turning a hobby into a business is an exciting venture. It's a chance to monetize something you're passionate about, potentially making a living doing what you love. But amidst all the creating and marketing, there's a crucial aspect that often falls by the wayside: finances. Yes, the dreaded 'F-word' - but fear not! We're here to help make this less intimidating and more approachable for you.

Written by *Rabia Khan*

The idea of being 'business-minded' often contradicts the romantic notion of the 'starving artist.' However, ignoring your financial situation can lead to stress and poor decisions, which can ultimately harm your business. By taking control of your finances, you can make informed decisions that can help your business grow. This doesn't mean you have to become a financial expert overnight. Start small, learn as you go, and remember: it's okay to seek help when you need it.

So, let's start this journey together, and jump into the world of budgeting for artists. We'll explore practical steps that can aid you in your creative journey, helping you navigate the financial aspect of your passion with confidence.

Join Arts to Hearts Club

Grow your creative career with easy to consume bite size content designed specifically for you. Along with mentor-ship with experts, resources, and like-minded community with our membership.

Figure Out How Much Money You're Making

As an artist, budgeting can be a daunting task. However, it is important to understand how much money you are making to plan for the future. The first step in this process is to write down all sources of income, including art sales, commissioned work, grants, and any side jobs. Keeping a record of art sales and grants can help you monitor your progress and identify trends over time. Additionally, it is important to include any income from side jobs, no matter how small, to get an accurate picture of your financial situation. By taking the time to understand your income, you can make informed decisions and plan for a successful art career. Just like planning a road trip requires knowledge of how much gas is in the car, planning a successful art career requires knowledge of your financial situation.

Figure Out What You're Spending

After knowing how much money you're making, the next step is to understand where you're spending it. This means everything from the cost of your art supplies and studio rent to your daily expenses like food, getting around, and even fun stuff like eating out or watching movies.

Think about it like this: if you were planning a road trip, you'd need to know how much gas your car uses. Similarly, in your budget, you need to know where your 'fuel' (money) is going.

Don't forget the small stuff either - like your daily coffee or your monthly Netflix bill. Every little bit adds up and it's essential to know where every penny is going.

Now, just like you might find ways to use less gas on your road trip, like driving more efficiently or taking a shorter route, you can also find ways to save money in your budget.

For instance, buying your art supplies in bulk or when they're on sale could save you some cash. You could also save on transport by sharing rides with others or using public transport. And instead of eating out a lot, try cooking at home more or packing your lunch.

By understanding your spending habits, you can make smarter decisions and find ways to save money. This way, you'll have more 'fuel' (money) to keep your art business running smoothly.

Budget for Your Art Projects

Once you know how much money you're making and spending, the next step is to plan out your art projects. This is like planning out the stops on your road trip. You need to figure out what resources you have (like equipment, materials, and skills) and how much they'll cost.

Don't just focus on costs though, take some time to do your homework. Look around at different options, compare prices, and get quotes from suppliers. It's all about getting the most bang for your buck.

As you move forward with your project, keep tweaking your budget as needed. Maybe you need to spend a bit more on high-quality materials or you decide to hire a professional for certain services. It's all part of the journey.

Just like you'd plan for extra gas or snacks on a road trip, you should also plan for unexpected costs in your art project. Things like surprise shipping costs or needing special tools can pop up, so it's smart to have some extra money set aside just in case.

By keeping these tips in mind, you can make sure your art project stays on track and within budget while still having some wiggle room for surprises. Just like having a well-planned road trip can make for a smoother journey, having a well-planned budget can make for a smoother art project.

Keep Your Budget Balanced

Once you've planned your art projects, the next step is to balance your income with your expenses. This is like checking your road trip map to ensure you stay on track. To balance your income with expenses as an artist, calculate your total income by adding up your earnings from art sales, prizes, commissions, teaching, or residencies, and any other part-time jobs or side hustles. For example, if you sell art for $5000, earn $1000 from teaching, and receive $500 for a commission in one month, your total income for that month is $6500. Then, add up your expenses, including art supplies, studio rent, advertising, exhibition fees, and personal expenses. For instance, if your studio rent is $800, art supplies cost $500, advertising is $200, exhibition fees are $100, travel costs are $400, and personal expenses total $1500, your total expenses for the month amount to $3500.

Subtract your expenses from your income to find your net income. In this example, subtract $3500 (expenses) from $6500 (income) to get a net income of $3000. Ideally, your net income should be positive or '0', indicating you're earning more than you're spending or breaking even. If your net income is negative, review your expenses and find ways to increase your income.

Visualize and Budget Your Art Project

Once you've balanced your books and gained a clear understanding of your financial situation, it's time to dream and describe your art projects. When planning an art project, it's important to not only let your imagination run wild but also to estimate your expenses and income. This means calculating both direct and indirect costs, researching prices for all necessary materials and services, and estimating your potential income from sales, grants, crowdfunding, and personal savings. By subtracting your total expenses from your total income, you can determine how much funding you need and seek out additional grants, sponsorships, or sales if necessary. A well-planned budget is crucial to the success of your art project and can help demonstrate to potential funders that you have a financially feasible plan in place. Just like a well-planned road trip, a well-planned budget is key to a successful art project.

Reflect and Refine Your Budget

The final step in your financial journey as an artist is to regularly review and adjust your budget. Just as a road trip might need detours or alternative routes due to unexpected roadblocks or new attractions, your art business requires course corrections based on evolving income and expenses.

So, it is essential to regularly review and adjust your budget to ensure that your art business remains financially stable. Income from artwork sales, grants, or teaching, as well as expenses like material costs, rent, or marketing campaigns, can vary and fluctuate over time. By reviewing your budget monthly, you can track these changes and adjust your course accordingly. If your expenses consistently outweigh your income, you can revisit pricing or explore cost reduction opportunities.

To assist you in gaining a better understanding of your financial situation and provide guidance on art-related matters, you can add yourself to the waitlist for our Arts to Hearts Club. This club offers an opportunity for us to engage in activities together, learn from each other, and work towards ensuring the financial stability of our art business.

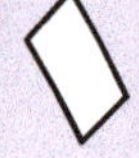

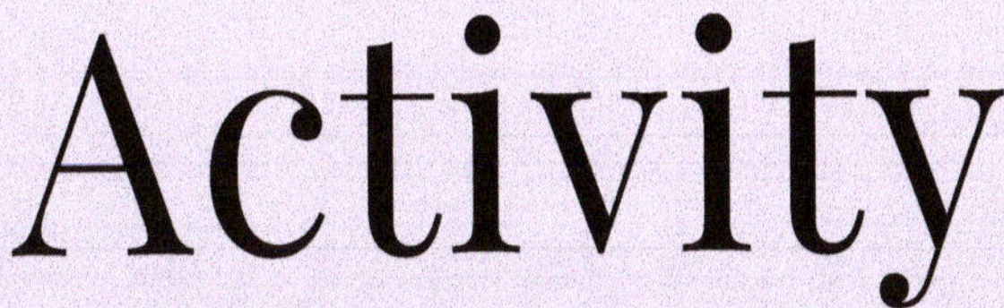

Activity

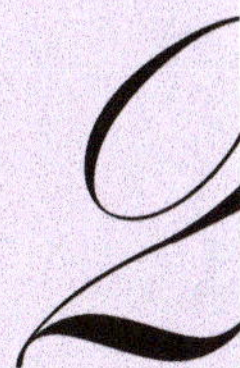

Activity 1: How Much Money Are You Making?

Instructions:

1. List all your income sources for one month.

2. Calculate the total monthly income.

Activity 2: What Are You Spending On?

Instructions:

1. Keep track of all your expenses for one week.

2. Categorize your expenses (eg. art supplies, bills, food, etc.) and calculate the total for each category.

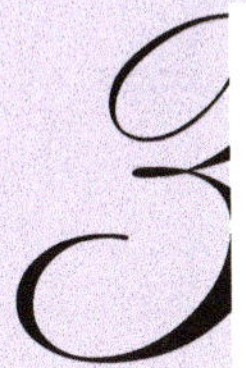

Activity 3: Budget for Your Art Projects

Instructions:

1. Outline an upcoming art project. Include all necessary materials and their costs.

2. Calculate the total cost of the project and compare with your monthly income.

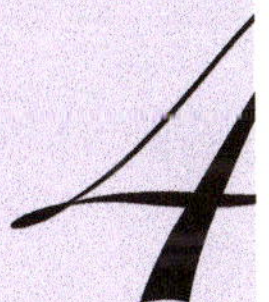

Activity 4: Balance Your Budget

Instructions:

1. Based on your income and expenses, adjust your budget to accommodate your art project. This may require cutting back on certain expenses or finding the additional income sources.

2. Repeat the process until you find a balanced budget.

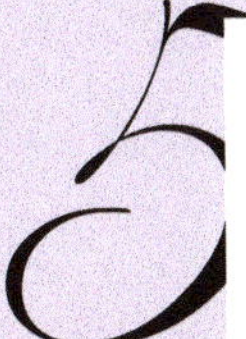

Activity 5: Visualize Your Art Project Budget

Instructions:

1. Create a visual representation (graph, chart, or diagram) of your budget for your art project.

2. This will help you visualize where your money is going and identify any potential areas for cost reduction.

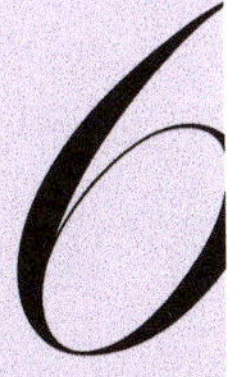

Activity 6: Reflect and Refine Your Budget

Instructions:

1. After completing the art project, reflect on the initial budget you created. Were there any unforeseen costs? Did you stay within your budget?

2. Based on your reflection, adjust your budgeting process for future projects.

At the end of this worksheet, reflect on your findings. How does understanding your finances impact your approach to art projects?

CRISTINA SALAS

AWARD WINNER

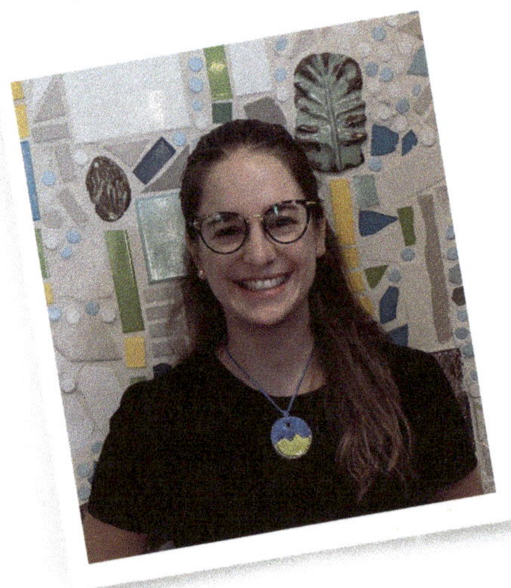

$1,000
CASH PRIZE
AND
PEOPLE'S CHOICE
FEATURE

It's not every day you meet someone who can weave a whole universe into their artwork, but Cristina Salas does just that. She's a wizard with her hands and imagination, spinning everyday materials into a beautiful creation. Her art is all about mixing it up; she plays with drawing, fibers, mosaics, ceramics, paint, and little treasures she finds along the way. And it turns out, people are loving it! Cristina has just scored a big win in ATH Magazine's 5th-anniversary issue, snagging herself a sweet $1,000 and charming her way to the top of the People's Choice award. So what's her secret? It could be the stories each piece tells, or maybe it's the spark of joy you feel when you see her work. There's something about the way she blends colors and textures that turns her art into a conversation piece. Whether it's her intricate mosaic patterns that catch the light just right or the warm, inviting feel of her fiber work, Cristina's creations have a way of sticking with you. As we unwrap the pages of this anniversary issue, get ready to be pulled into a world where every detail is a slice of magic—just like stepping into a garden where every turn shows off a new, beautiful bloom.

www.cristinasalas.com

hola@crissalas.com

@crissalas

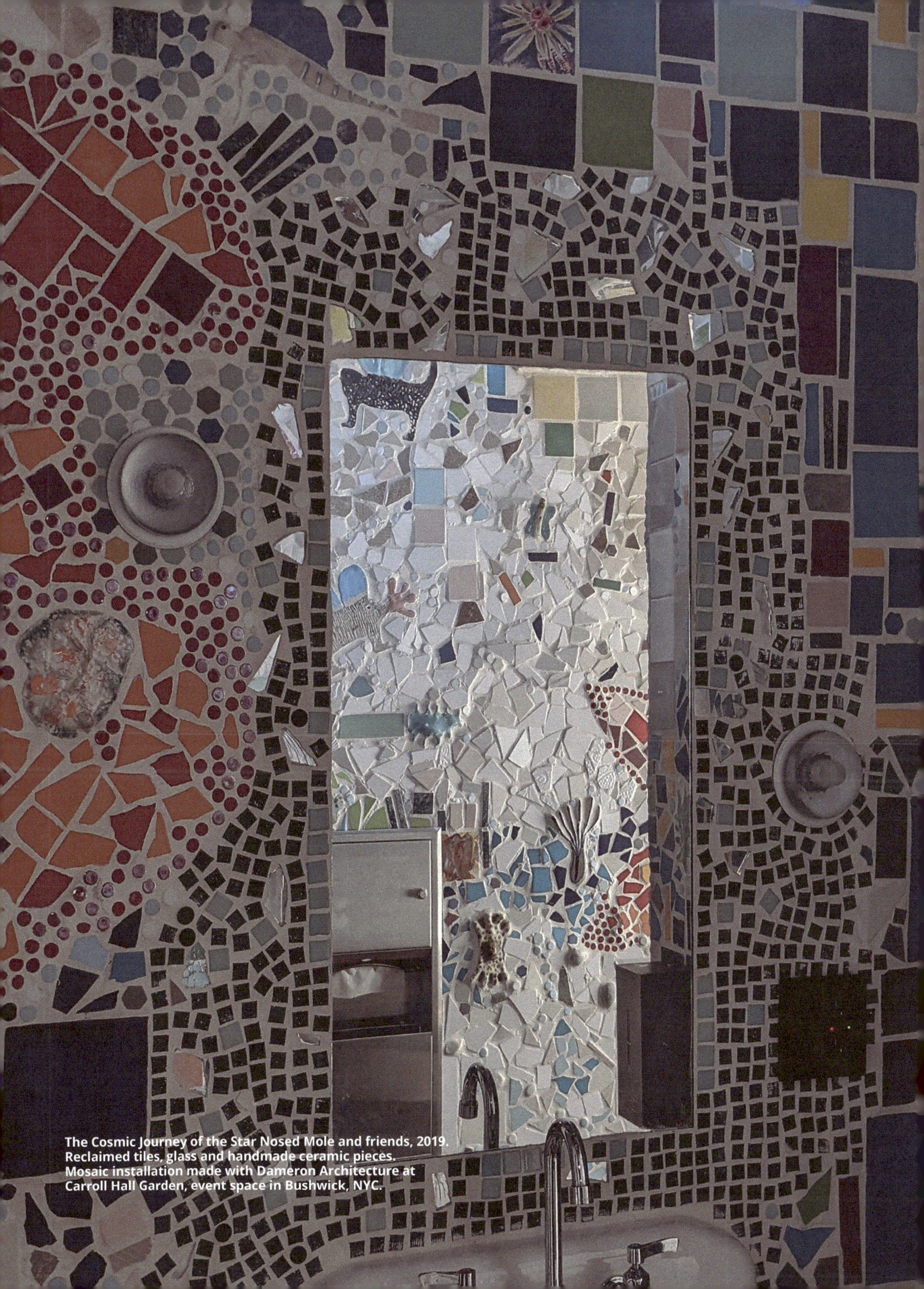

The Cosmic Journey of the Star Nosed Mole and friends, 2019.
Reclaimed tiles, glass and handmade ceramic pieces.
Mosaic installation made with Dameron Architecture at
Carroll Hall Garden, event space in Bushwick, NYC.

Can you share a moment when you felt discouraged as an artist? How did you overcome it?

In 2022 I got the opportunity to exhibit my work with Chashama. But they called me at the last minute with a huge space in Manhattan. Although this was an exciting opportunity, I felt discouraged, it seemed like a huge task that I was not prepared for and still I wanted to make the best of it. I overcame the fear by PLAYING. I said to myself: I'm going to do the best I can with what I have. I took my paper drawings in the subway and started to make compositions on the wall. People were entering the space, we were having conversations, I got feedback, sold work, gave a workshop and some of the people who came are still my friends! I let myself be SPONTANEOUS and HAVE FUN, I FELT SUCCESSFUL!

How do you cope with the vulnerability of sharing your art with the world?

The beauty of sharing art is that when it leaves the studio and it is out there, it sort of belongs to everyone else. Your name is there and that is the vulnerability because you feel judged. But I just try my best to communicate well and still remain spontaneous. I tell myself: everything is in progress.

How has your art helped you understand yourself better?

My art is a reflection of who I am and it tells me where I need to go. It is the map of my life.

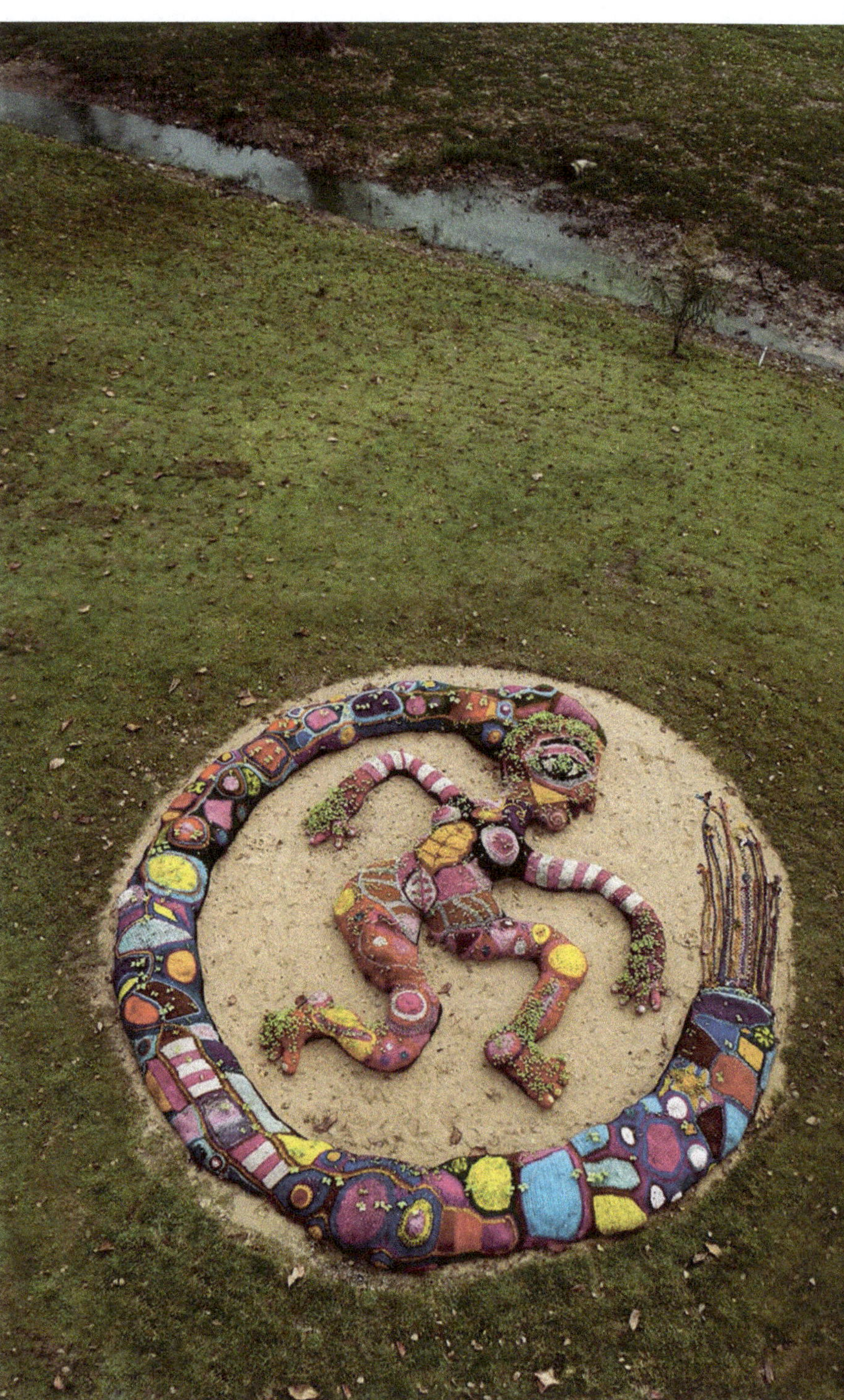

Muñeca Viajera, fibers, earth and Zinnia, Morning Glory and Moonflower seeds, (8'x8') Approx. 2013 Commissioned and installed at Arte Fits Foundation, Dorado, Puerto Rico

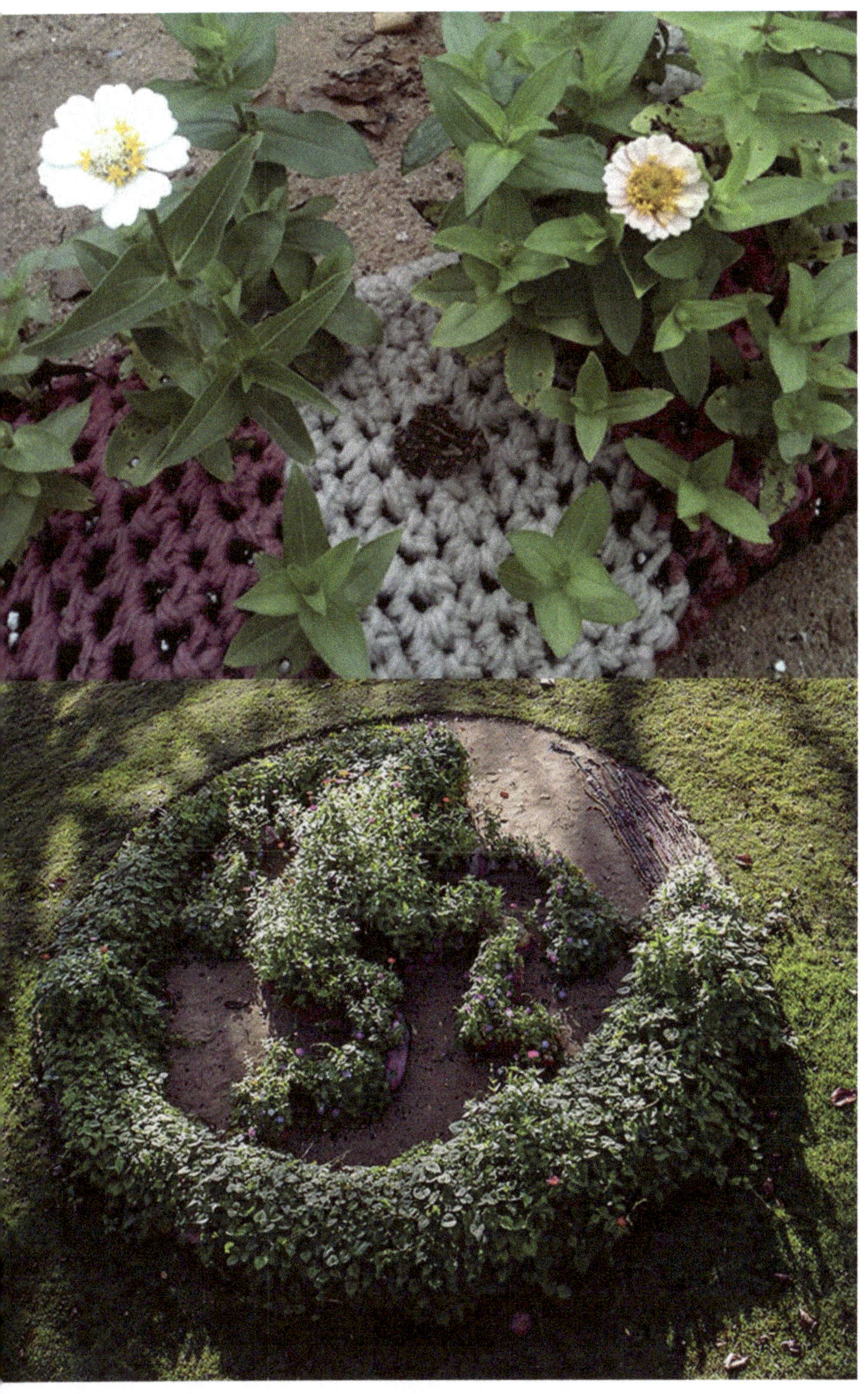

What do you want people to take away from your work?

I want to express playfulness, freedom, and the joy of taking care of each other and the planet.

How do you decide what to charge for your work?

Well, this depends on the project and it is something that I'm still learning how to do. But for 2-dimensional artworks, I use a formula where I multiply the length by the width by a number I developed depending on the technique of the piece, and then I get the price. In this way, my prices can remain consistent. For larger public works I make a budget of expenses and I pay myself an artist fee which is usually 20-25% of the project. Then I have a yearly budget for expenses and income and I try to balance them throughout the year to remain healthy.

What's one piece of advice you'd give to aspiring artists?

When I was studying architecture I thought I was becoming this other person. Like if I had to fit in and be this certain way. I was messy when I was developing my projects and felt overwhelmed by it. Luckily, one of my professors at LSU told me: Embrace your mess. This is something that until today I have to remind myself when I'm starting a project. Life and art are messy so CREATE FREELY, HAVE FUN, AND PLAY!

Curated Artists

Learn all about the work, process, and inspiration of the curated artists from all around the world by digging into their creative careers.

Alisa Teletovic
AUSTRALIA

Allison moyers
UNITED STATES

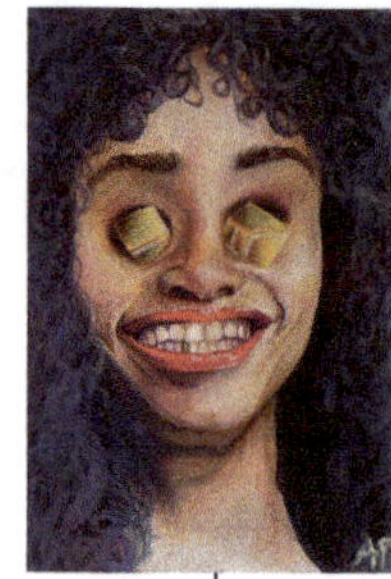

Andrea Castaneda
HONDURAS

Ann Mechelinck
IRELAND

Brady Sloane-Duncan
UNITED STATES

Alyson Petruncio
UNITED STATES

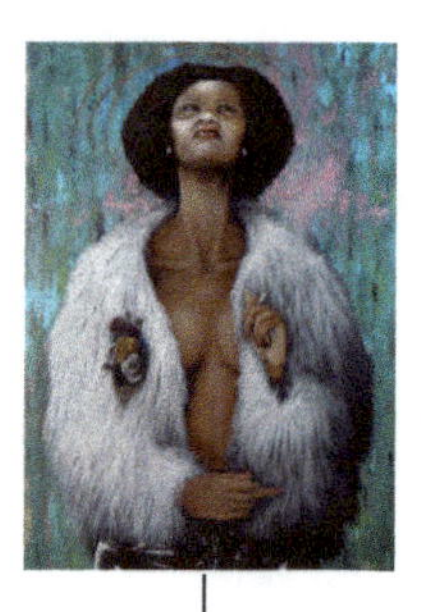

Cagla Toprak Attia
UNITED STATES

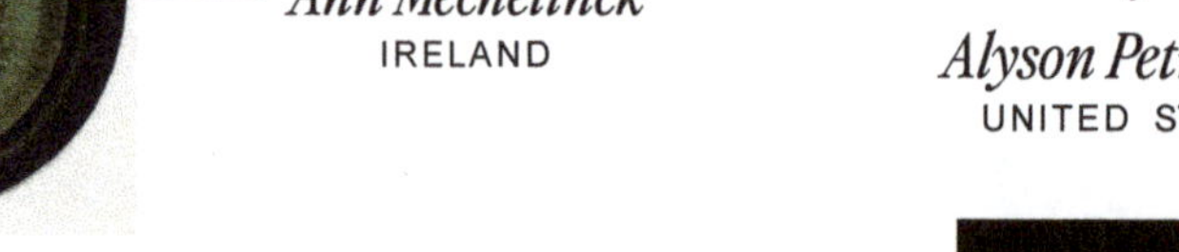

Christine Nightingale
UNITED STATES

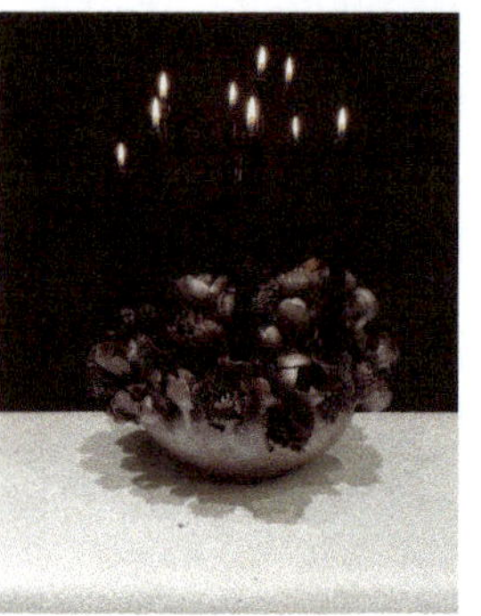

Corinne Forrester
UNITED STATES

Cristina Salas
UNITED STATES

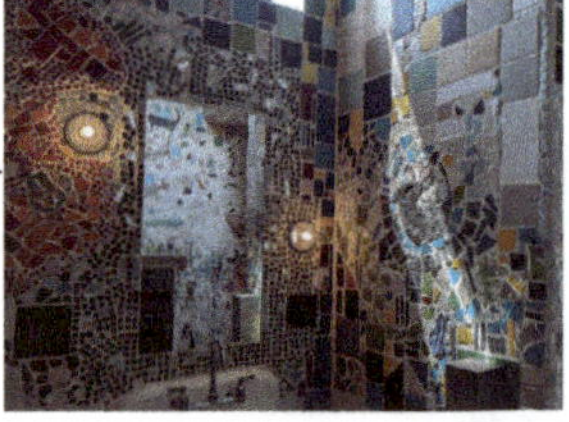

Daniella Queirolo
UNITED STATES

Freeda Kingelin
SCANDINAVIA

Elisabeth Handelsby
NORWAY

Dimelza Broche
UNITED STATES

Hannaleah Ledwell
CANADA

Hana Sebelova
FRANCE

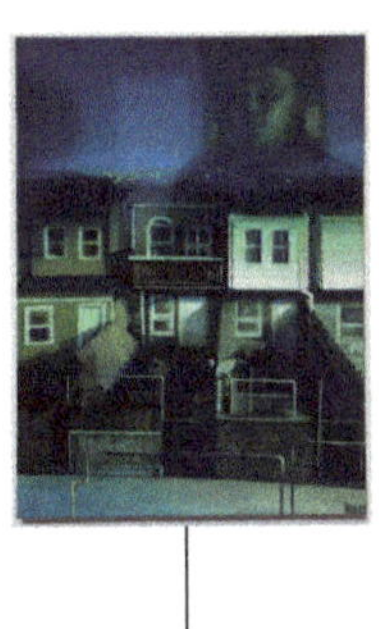

Hari Lualhati
SOUTH AFRICA

Heather Heitzenrater
UNITED STATES

Heidi Brueckner
UNITED STATES

Heather Martindale
UNITED STATES

Holly Cerna
UNITED STATES

Kate Chassner
UNITED STATES

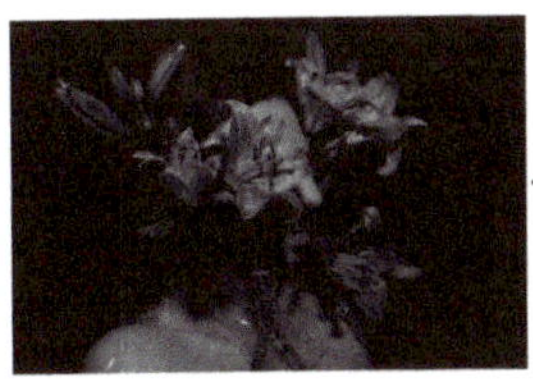

Kathrin Kolbow
GERMANY

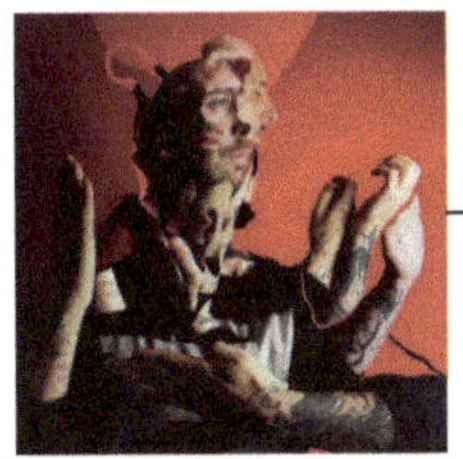

Katy Williamson
UNITED KINGDOM

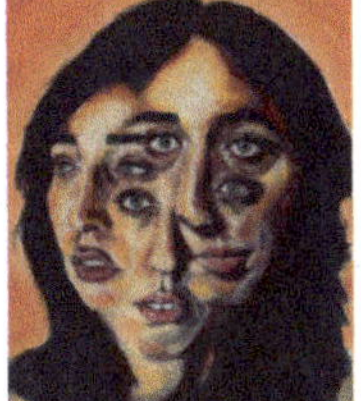

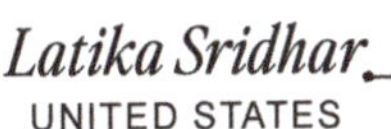
Latika Sridhar
UNITED STATES

Sally Khoury
QATAR

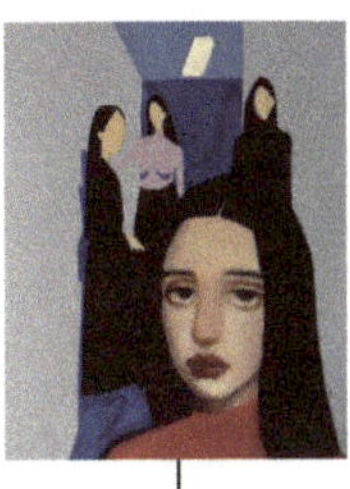

Marina Schulze
GERMANY

Molly Shivers
UNITED STATES

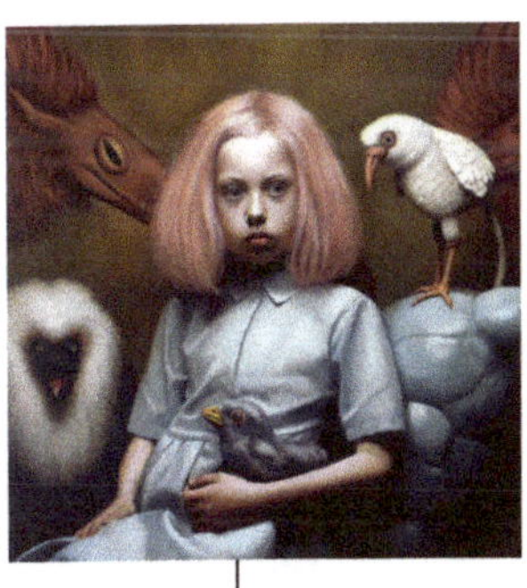

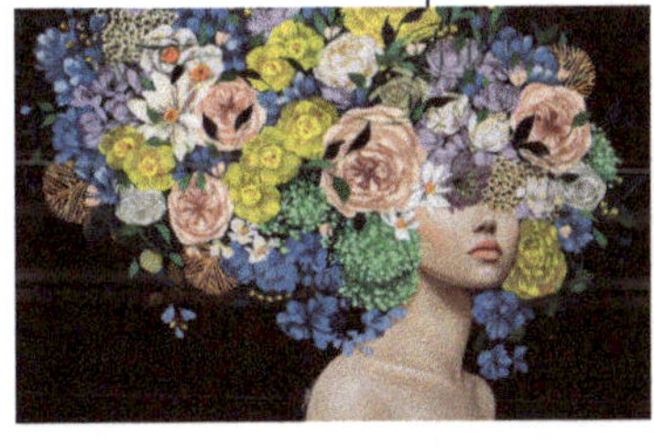

Luz Angela Medina
UNITED STATES

Megan King
UNITED STATES

Sheri Rush
UNITED STATES

Omma Moon
SWEDEN

Sofia Ruiz
COSTA RICA

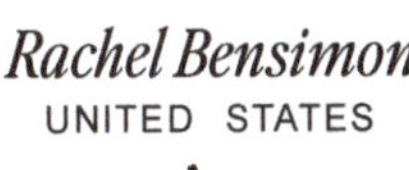
Rachel Bensimon
UNITED STATES

Teodora Stojanović
SERBIA

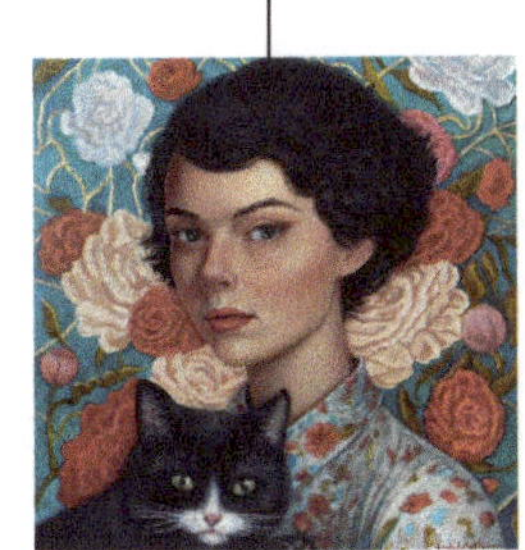

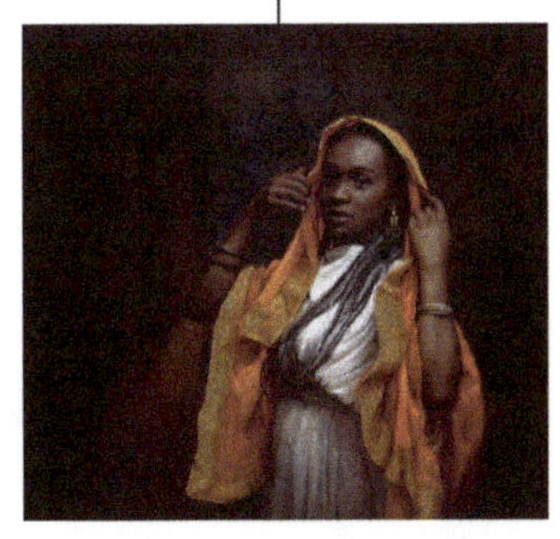

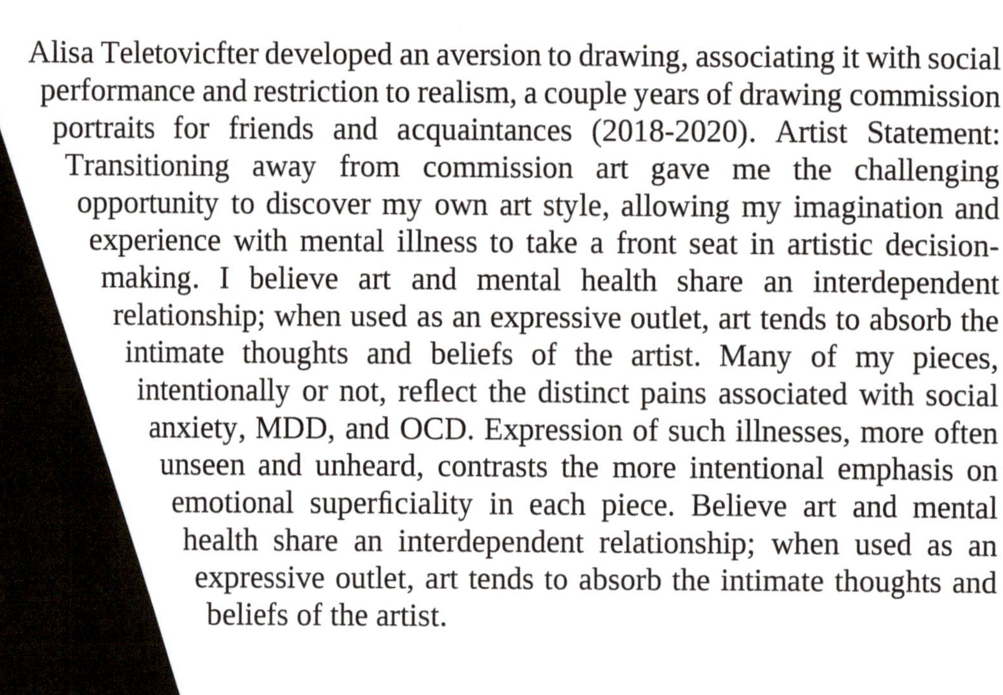

Alisa Teletovicfter developed an aversion to drawing, associating it with social performance and restriction to realism, a couple years of drawing commission portraits for friends and acquaintances (2018-2020). Artist Statement: Transitioning away from commission art gave me the challenging opportunity to discover my own art style, allowing my imagination and experience with mental illness to take a front seat in artistic decision-making. I believe art and mental health share an interdependent relationship; when used as an expressive outlet, art tends to absorb the intimate thoughts and beliefs of the artist. Many of my pieces, intentionally or not, reflect the distinct pains associated with social anxiety, MDD, and OCD. Expression of such illnesses, more often unseen and unheard, contrasts the more intentional emphasis on emotional superficiality in each piece. Believe art and mental health share an interdependent relationship; when used as an expressive outlet, art tends to absorb the intimate thoughts and beliefs of the artist.

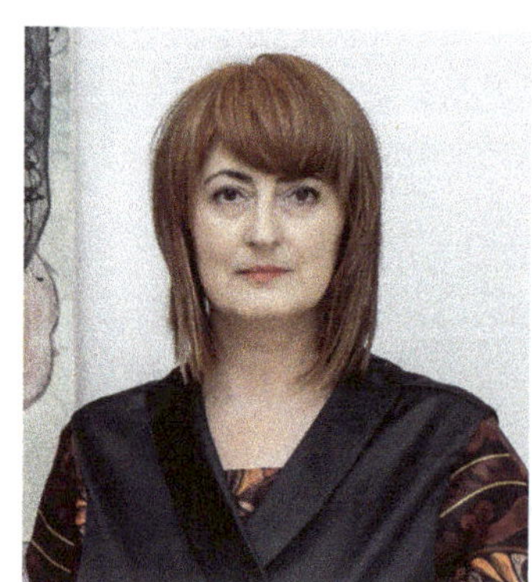

https://alisateletovicartist.com

mail@alisateletovic.com

@alisateletovicartist

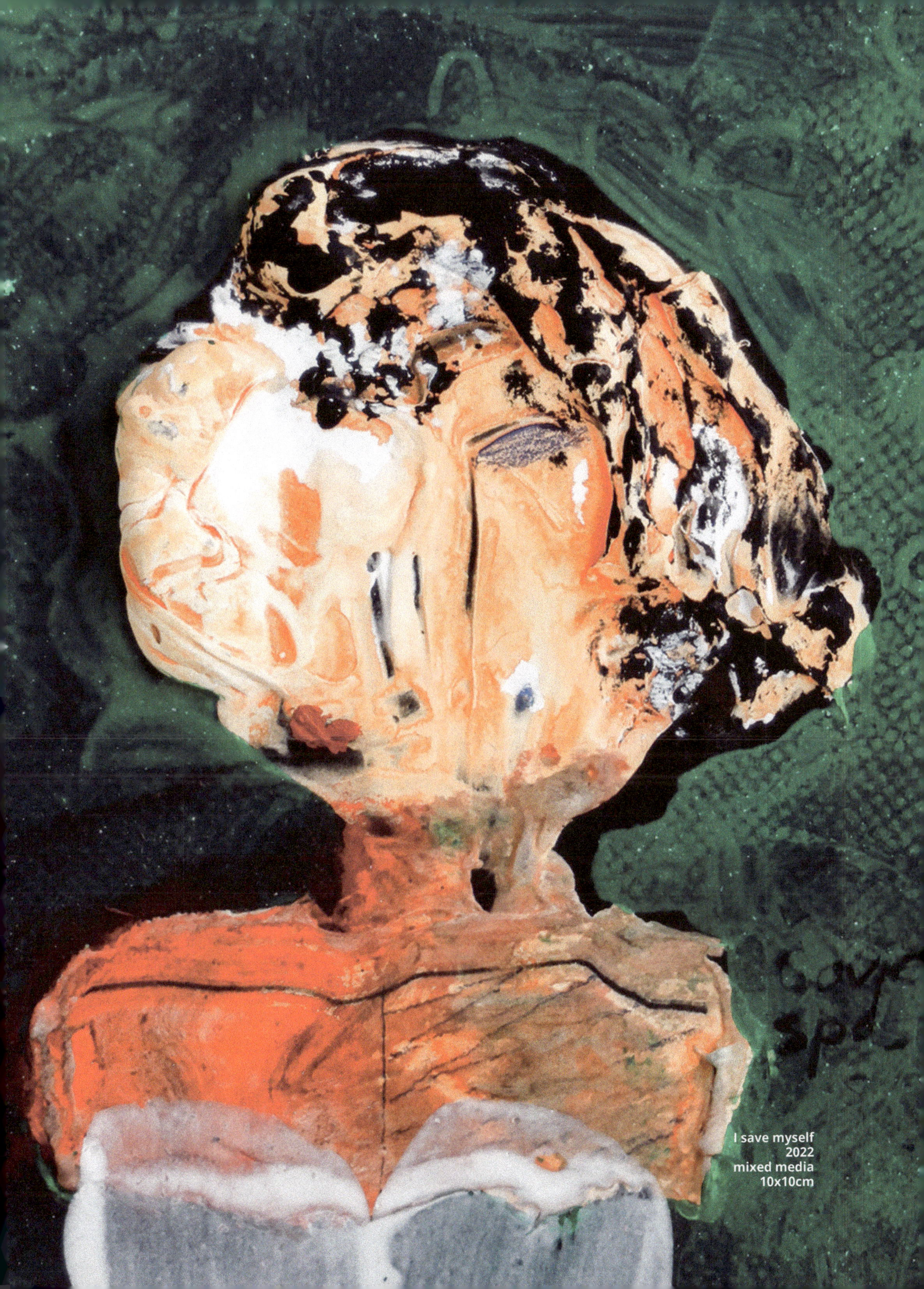
I save myself
2022
mixed media
10x10cm

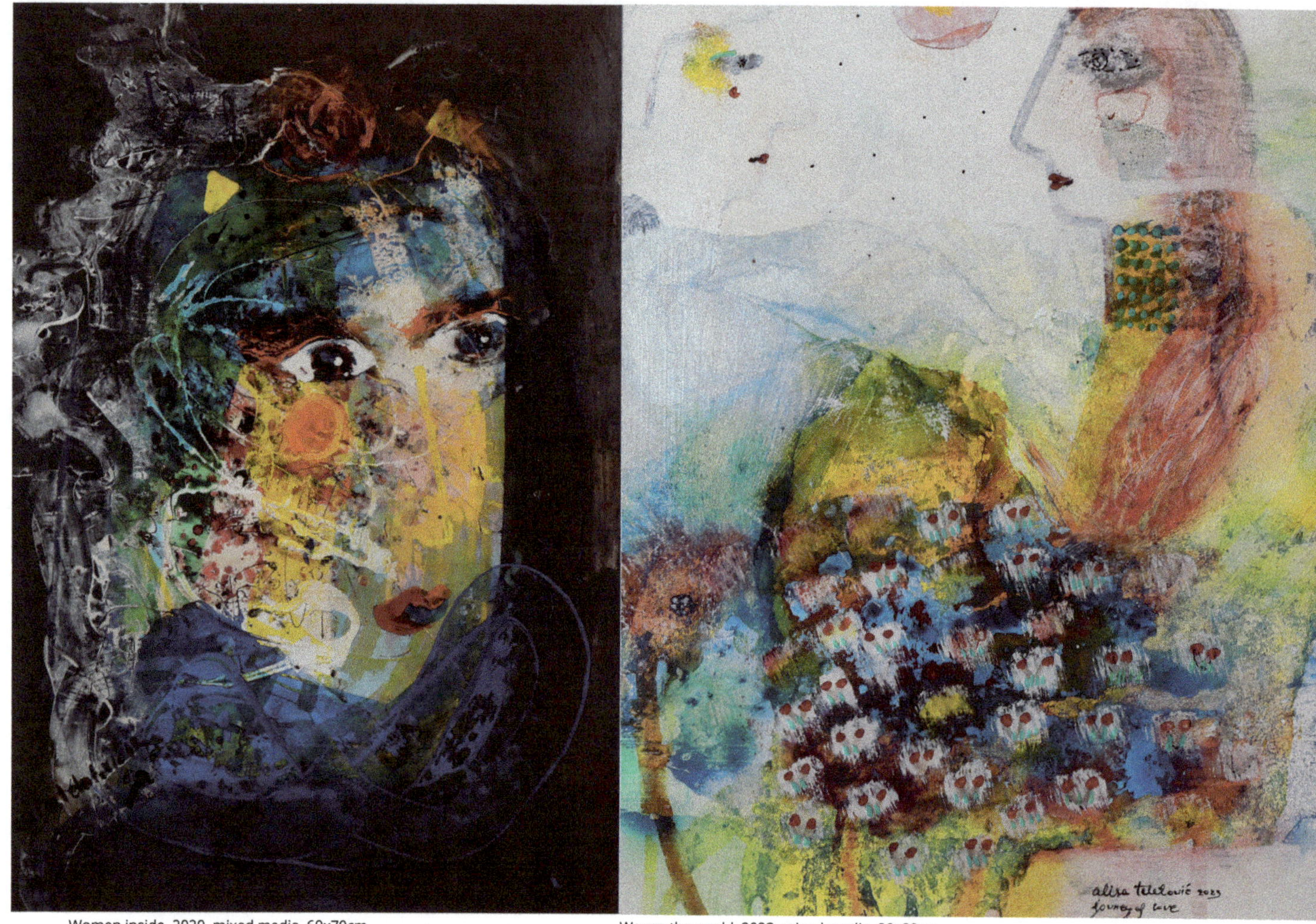

Women inside, 2020, mixed media, 60x70cm

We are the world, 2023, mixed media, 80x80cm

Can you share a moment when you felt discouraged as an artist? How did you overcome it?

I always say I have had three lives by now. I felt discouraged when I arrived in Bosnia and Herzegovina after living in Australia for 17th years. It was like I did not belong here not I belong all those years ago in Australia when I came as refugee. It was hard to adapt in place that was sleeping, and where art was still very traditional and realistic, and modern art was something that people did not understand, and did not appreciate. My art was expressive and figurative and very personal. I spoke about my own life journey. Painted trauma of war, new continent, homes, and family. When my mum died 7 years ago, I went deep into spiritual awakening, and continued to paint. Through it I answered all questions I had, I cried all tears I had, I saw myself and became my best friend in my art studio.

How do you cope with the vulnerability of sharing your art with the world?

I am gentle and intense in the same time, vibrant, loving but also a dynamic, expressive woman that wants to dance, smile and radiate love and happiness. I was very shy, but I managed to deal with that as I kept discovering my soul and my heart. I am happy and content with all I am, I am free and authentic in all I do. I want to share my art with people, as it inspires them , motivates them in a good and positive way. It is a choice, to be a woman that creates a better world. I am learning and getting better each day.

How has your art helped you understand yourself better?

Since my childhood, I painted my pain , it was called Escape from reality. Then through life, my emotions, bad and good, depressive, strange, quirky, happy they were all ending on paper, or

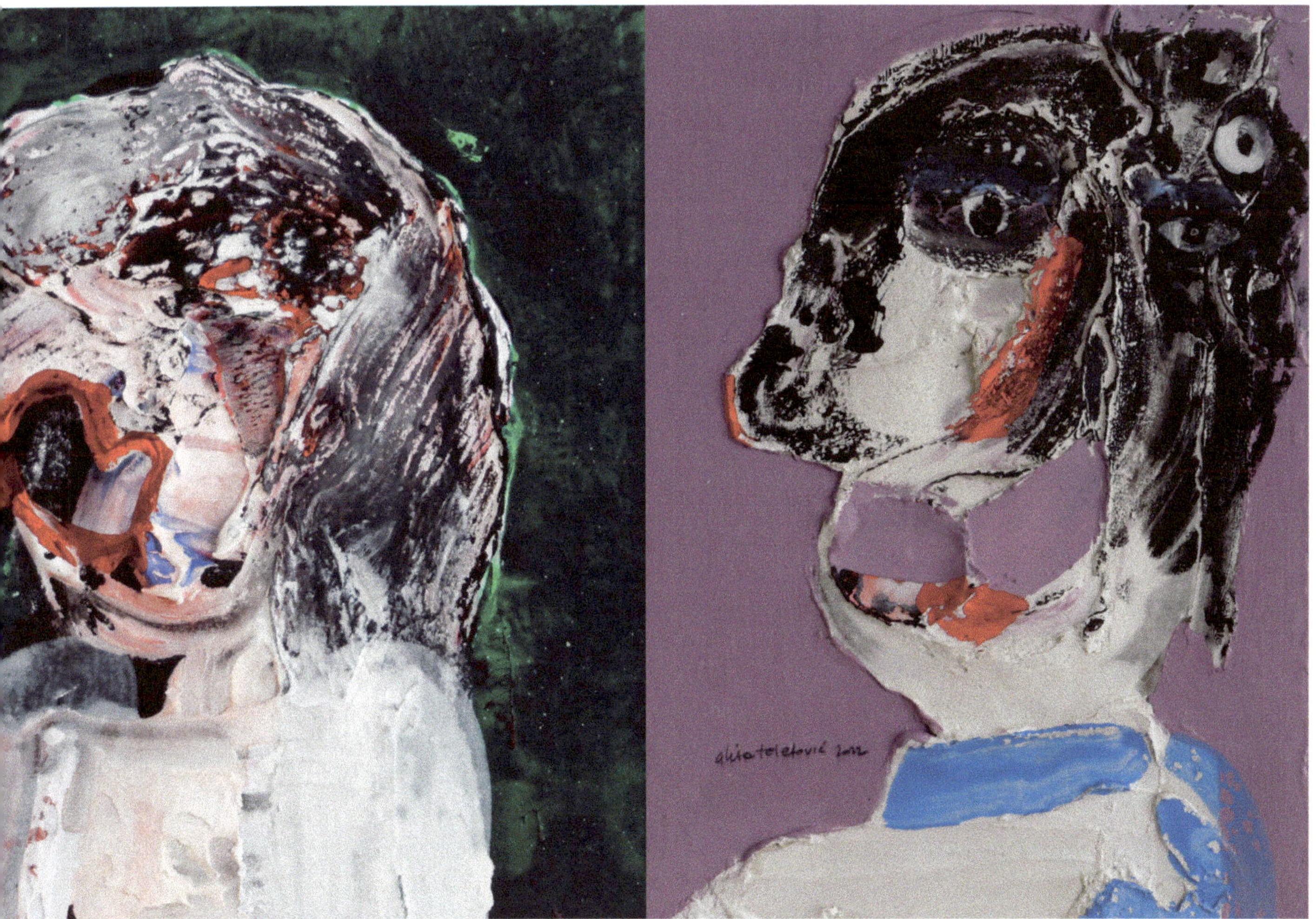

Lips that sing, 2022, 10x10cm, mixed media

Bosnian men, 2021, mixed media, 30x20cm

canvas. I am creating all the time, and will never stop. I am possessed by art hehe. When I paint I speak to myself, it is like alive meditation, I answer question in my head, give answers, I realize from inside all that I am. All energy and inspiration long time ago, you start with exhibitions, if you receive awards, you place your paintings bit higher and again if sells, you grow.

How do you decide what to charge for your work?

In Australia I learned the rules as emerging artist long time ago, you start with exhibitions, if you receive awards, you place your paintings bit higher and again if it sells, you grow. Every time you put a bit higher. Then when you value yourself as an artist, the time, energy, authenticity, all that play a big role and you reach a point when you want go below a certain line. I am comfortable now that I am in good place, although I was always told that my art should be higher in price.

What do you want people to take away from your work?

I am so humbled when people buy my work, as it is purely mine and intimate. I am so honored and proud. Those people to me are amazing souls. They support you through your good and bad. So grateful. In my art very often I choose, to became positive and have interesting messages of love, kindness, empathy, understanding of each other, togetherness, and passion. Landscapes are of the soul heart and mind. FREEDOM, self care, peace through intriguing colors that bring life into the homes.

What's one piece of advice you'd give to aspiring artists?

It is important to find a unique style. To believe in it no matter what. To paint all the time, to go through the process. It is important to find oneself in order to be comfortable with your own art.

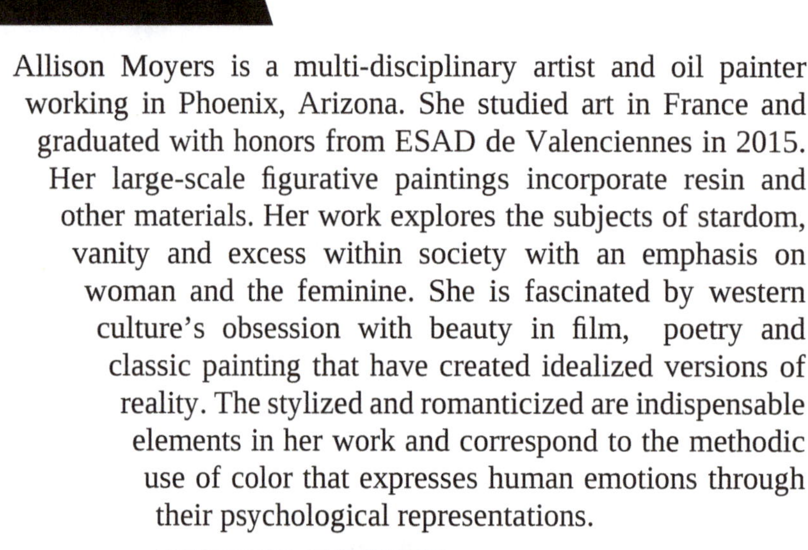

Allison Moyers is a multi-disciplinary artist and oil painter working in Phoenix, Arizona. She studied art in France and graduated with honors from ESAD de Valenciennes in 2015. Her large-scale figurative paintings incorporate resin and other materials. Her work explores the subjects of stardom, vanity and excess within society with an emphasis on woman and the feminine. She is fascinated by western culture's obsession with beauty in film, poetry and classic painting that have created idealized versions of reality. The stylized and romanticized are indispensable elements in her work and correspond to the methodic use of color that expresses human emotions through their psychological representations.

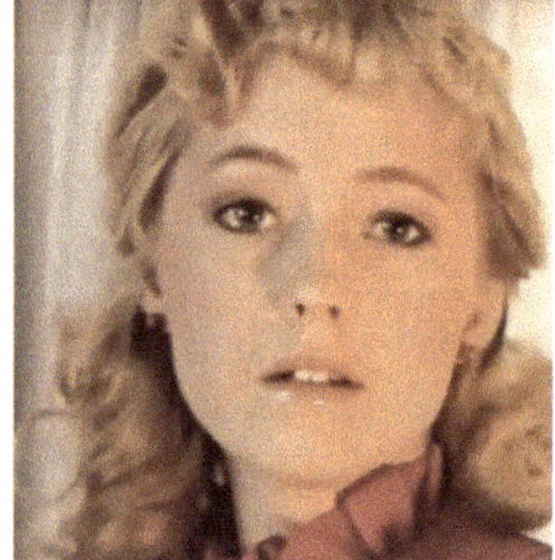

www.allisonmoyersart.com

allisonmoyers@yahoo.com

@thepoetthatpaints

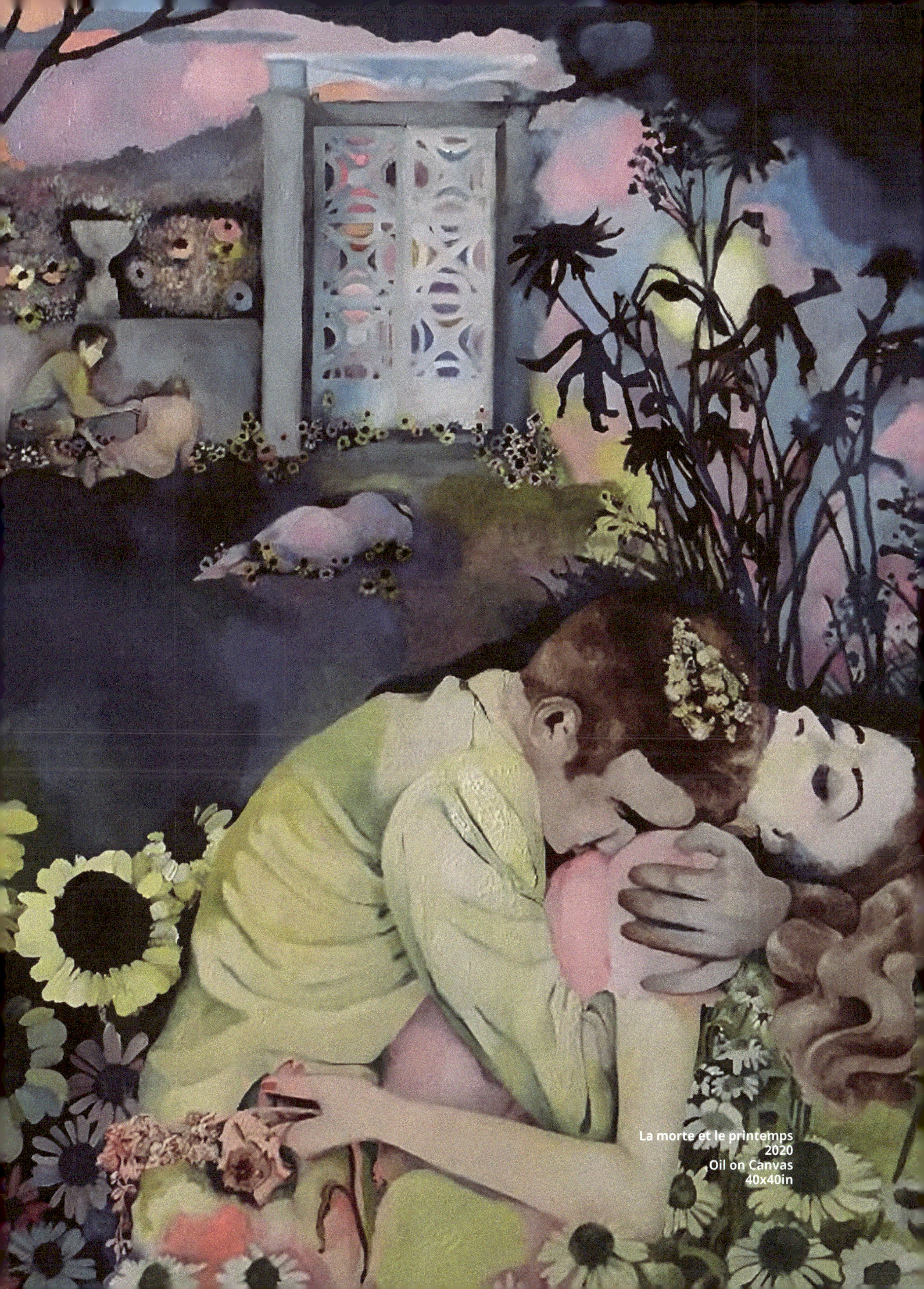

La morte et le printemps
2020
Oil on Canvas
40x40in

How do you cope with the vulnerability of sharing your art with the world?

Coping comes with sharing a lot, even when things aren't perfect. Eventually the work gets better, and the process becomes second nature. When I get overwhelmed and feel pressure to have a perfect online presence or art show, I take a step back and live in the moment. Spending time with friends and family, taking a break from social media, or going outside to clear my head are simple things that help me to focus on what is truly important.

Can you share a moment when you felt discouraged as an artist? How did you overcome it?

After graduating and moving to Phoenix, I felt lost. It was a strange transition from art student to art professional. I was searching for my confidence and voice outside of school, and the challenge was real. What helped me the most was connecting with artists on instagram, reading books by other creatives and making friends with like minded people in my local community.

The Age of Innocence, 2021, Oil on Canvas, 34x40in

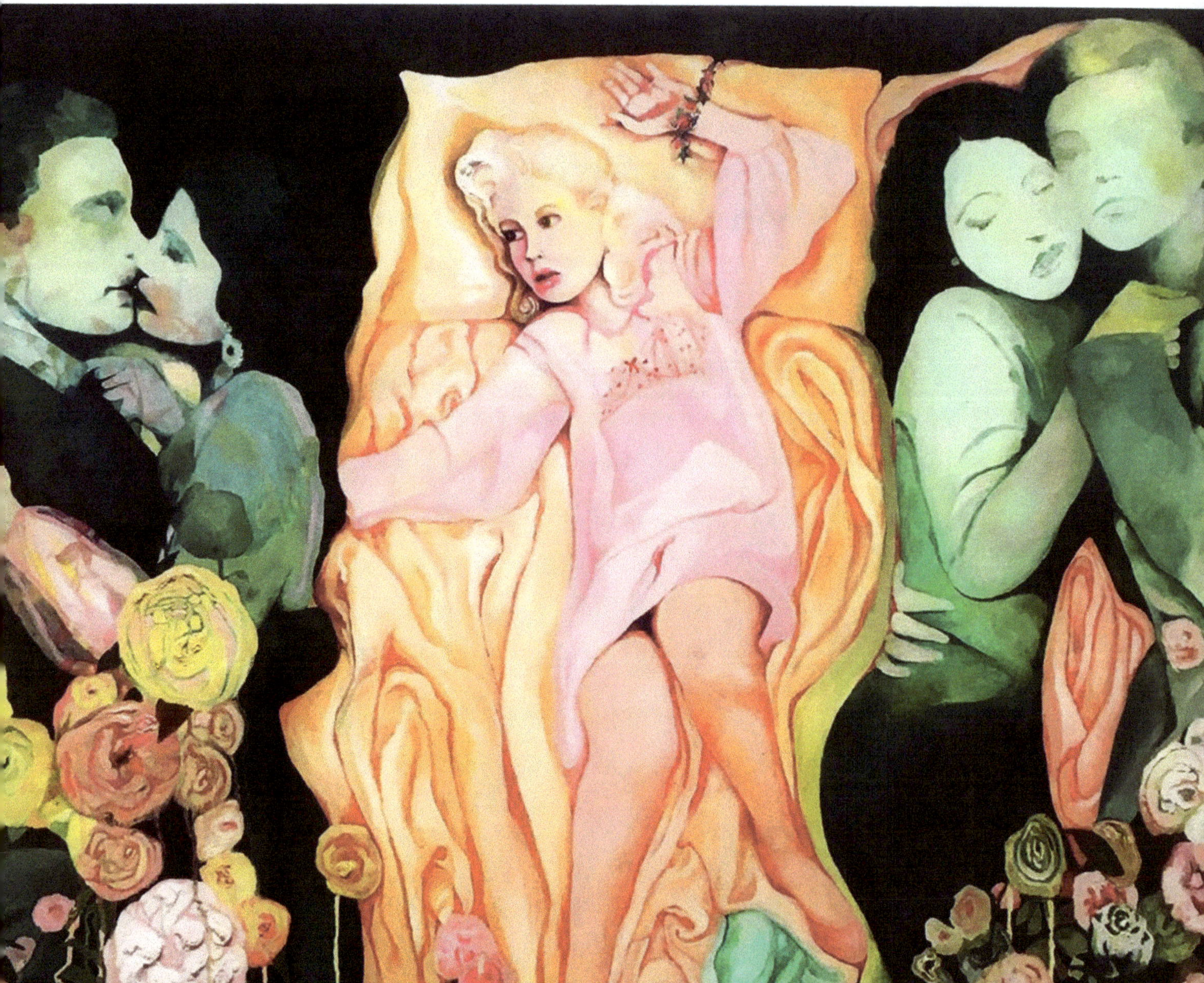

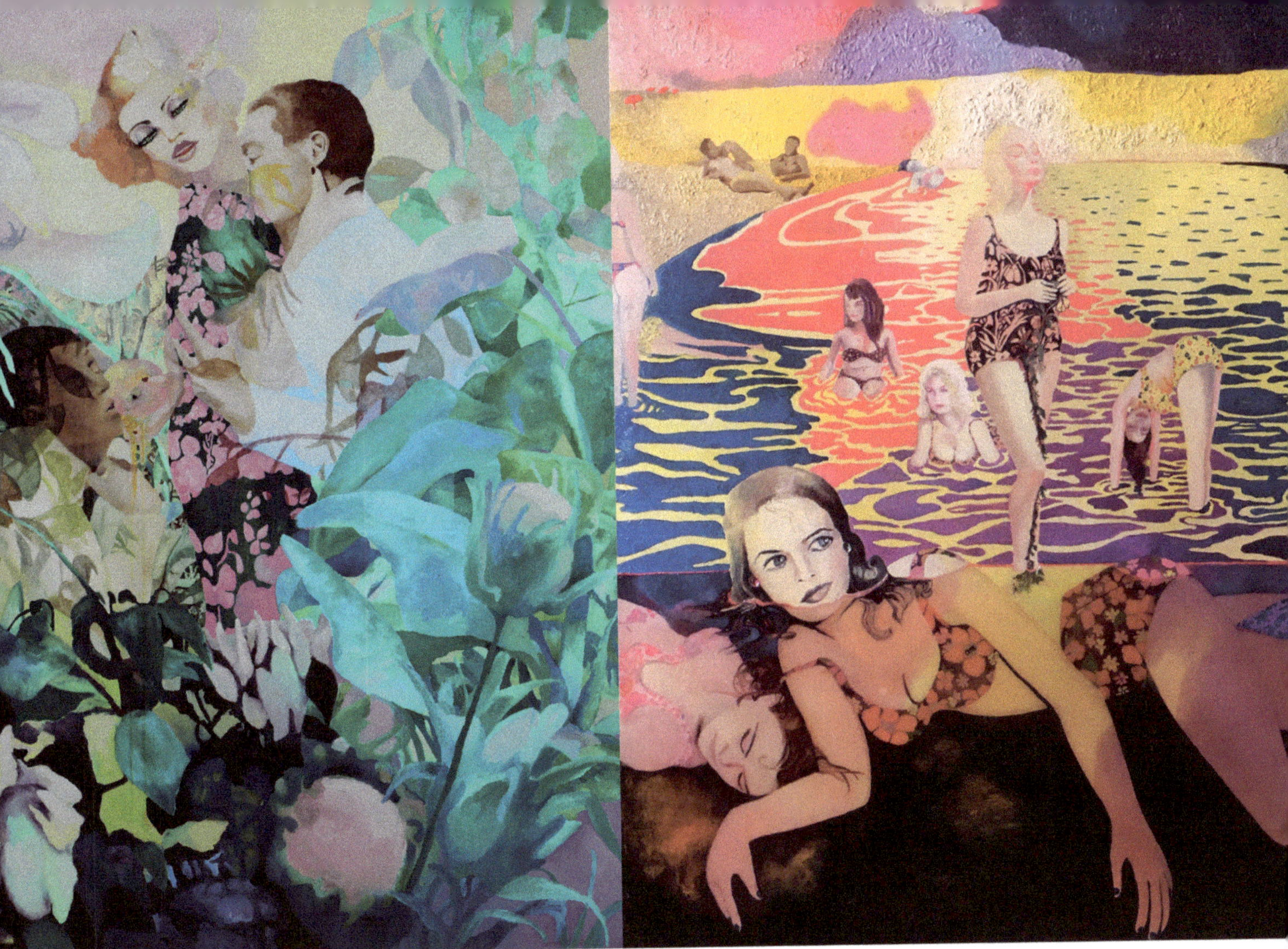

Evelyn the Garden, 2019, Oil on Canvas, 36x48in

Under the Dark Umbrellas, 2021, Oil and Resin on Canvas, 50x54in

How has your art helped you understand yourself better?

Being an artist has helped me understand my best and worst traits. I can always see in my past works when I have been lazy or motivated. It shows me what to let go of and what to focus on. My paintings reveal my emotions and the internal changes of my heart.

What do you want people to take away from your work?

I hope people can connect emotionally with my paintings and see themselves in my work by sharing the beauty in loss and heartbreak and a sense of vulnerability in being human.

What's one piece of advice you'd give to aspiring artists?

Work hard, never give up, and don't be afraid to ask for help from others who have been where you are before.

How do you decide what to charge for your work?

I have a basic price range for works based on size, material and the market in Phoenix, but I have to increase my price when I send my work out of state to include shipping and market differences. I try to price my work honestly and realistically based on where I am at/have been in my career. I do have some pieces that are more expensive because they hold personal value and they are a part of my home, but most of my work is consistently priced based on size and materials.

Alyson Petruncio is a self-taught artist who initiated her artistic career in 2018 by drawing commissioned portraits for friends and acquaintances. After a couple of years of commission work, she developed an aversion to drawing, associating it with social performance and constraint to realism. Transitioning away from commission art provided the challenging opportunity to explore a unique style, prioritizing imagination and incorporating experiences with mental illness into artistic decision-making. She believes that when used as an expressive outlet, art absorbs the artist's intimate thoughts and beliefs. Many of Alyson's pieces depict the distinct pains of social anxiety, Major Depressive Disorder (MDD), and Obsessive-Compulsive Disorder (OCD). The expression of these often unseen and unheard illnesses intentionally contrasts with the emphasis on emotional superficiality in each piece.

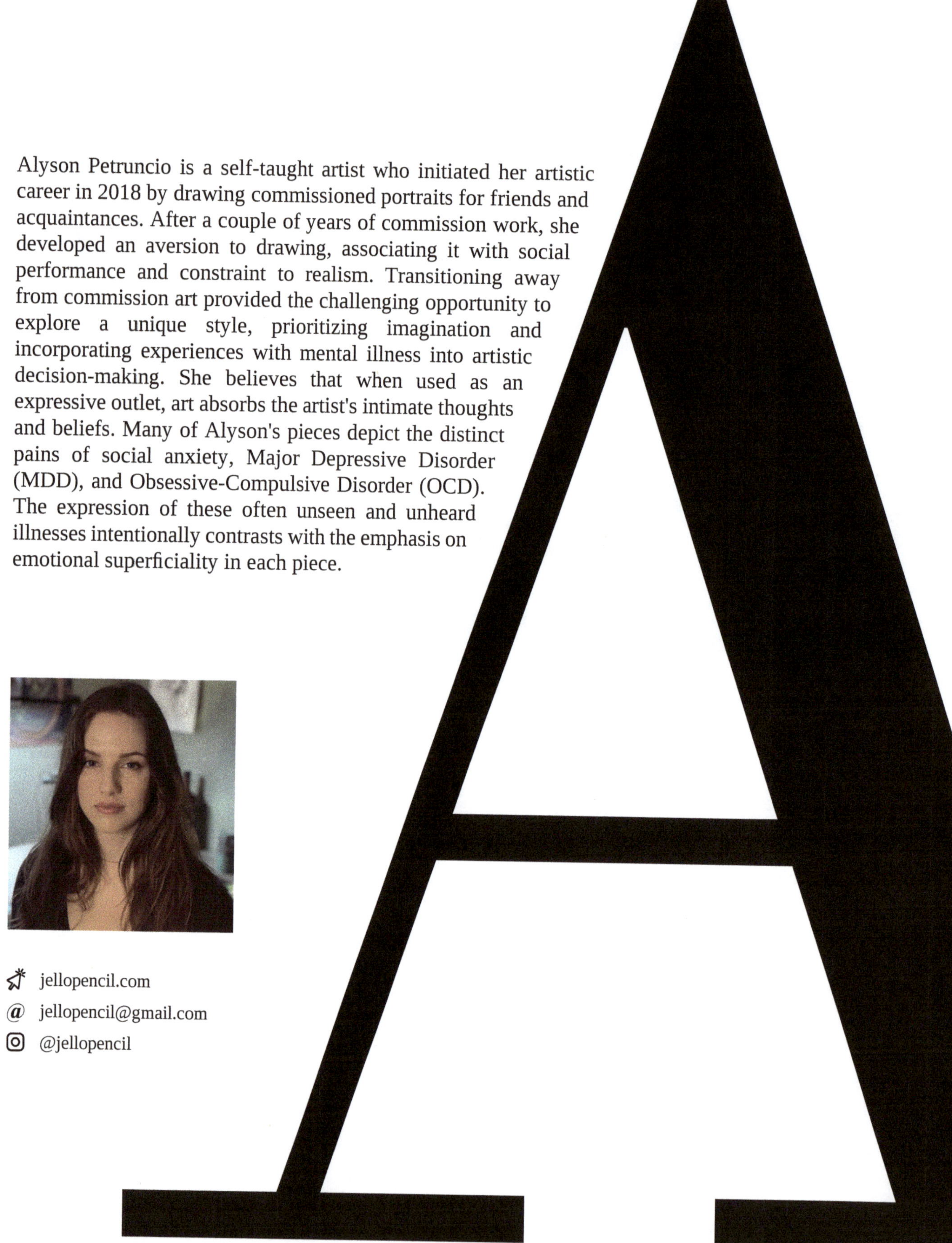

jellopencil.com

@ jellopencil@gmail.com

@jellopencil

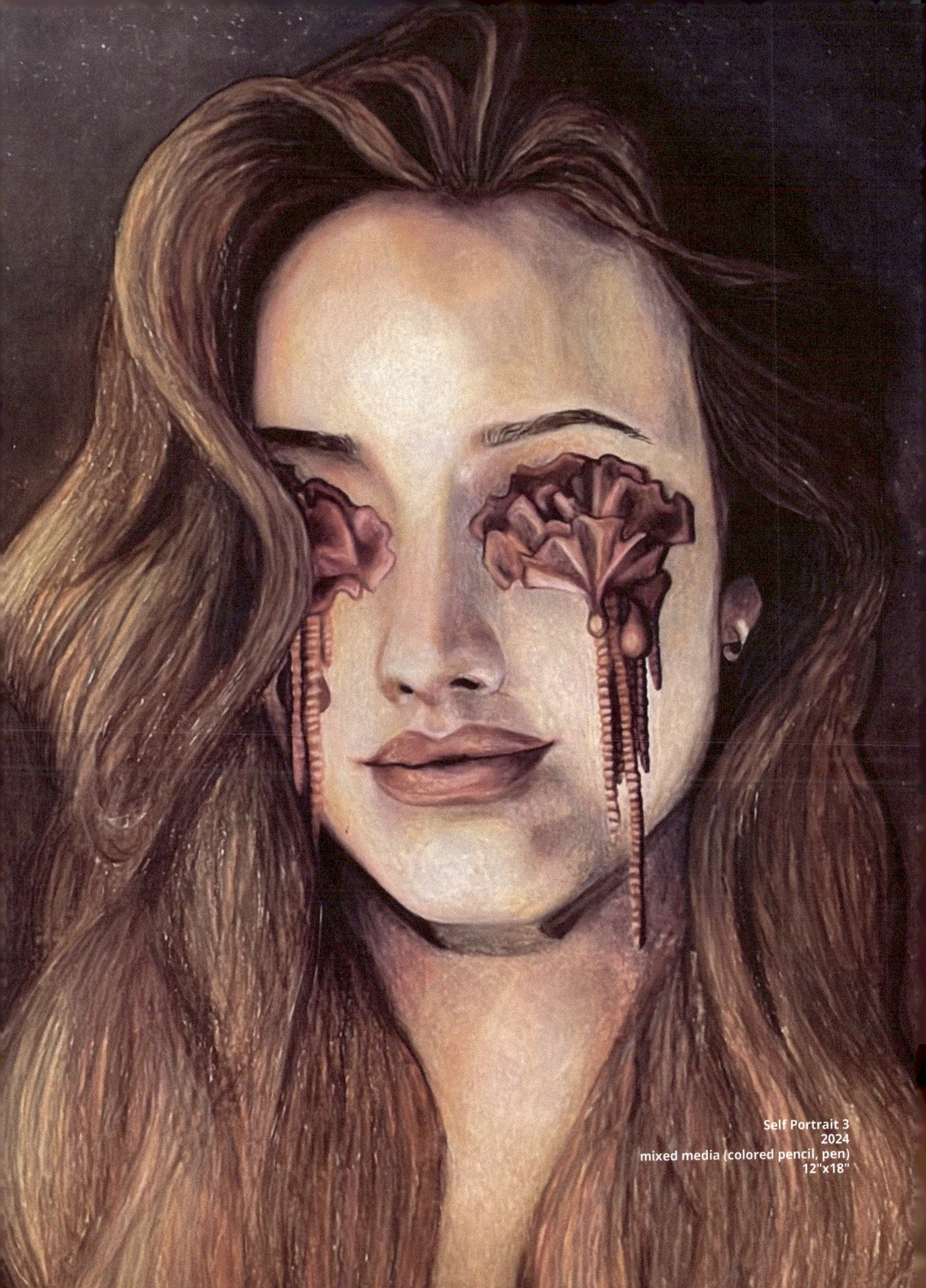

Self Portrait 3
2024
mixed media (colored pencil, pen)
12"x18"

Can you share a moment when you felt discouraged as an artist? How did you overcome it?

Standing out from the frequent moments of self-doubt, the most memorable time I felt discouraged as an artist was just several months ago. I felt like I finally settled into my personal style, but feedback from both social media and trusted sources left me considering that I may not have enough skill and insight to be an impactful artist. My art wasn't affecting viewers in the way I felt it should and my technique needed work. Before quitting entirely, I tried investing more into each drawing in the form of planning composition and value distribution, as well as putting more care into the "little things", like background and lighting. This additional effort resulted in the creation of my favorite drawings, which received some strong emotional reactions and minimal distraction by poor technique.

How do you cope with the vulnerability of sharing your art with the world?

Ironically, vulnerability in the form of sharing artwork has always felt therapeutic. My first original, non-commission piece was uncomfortable to share. The discomfort however, was refreshing in a way that was difficult to describe at the time. Looking back, I experienced a sort of emotional exhibitionism without stepping over the personal boundaries of others. The chance to express my human experience without words, all while finding others who resonate with that experience was just too good to pass up.

How has your art helped you understand yourself better?

I started to develop a personal art style partly in an attempt to better understand my struggles with mental illness. The most surprising and beautiful part of creating consistently for a few years now was looking back and realizing everyone's experiences with pain are

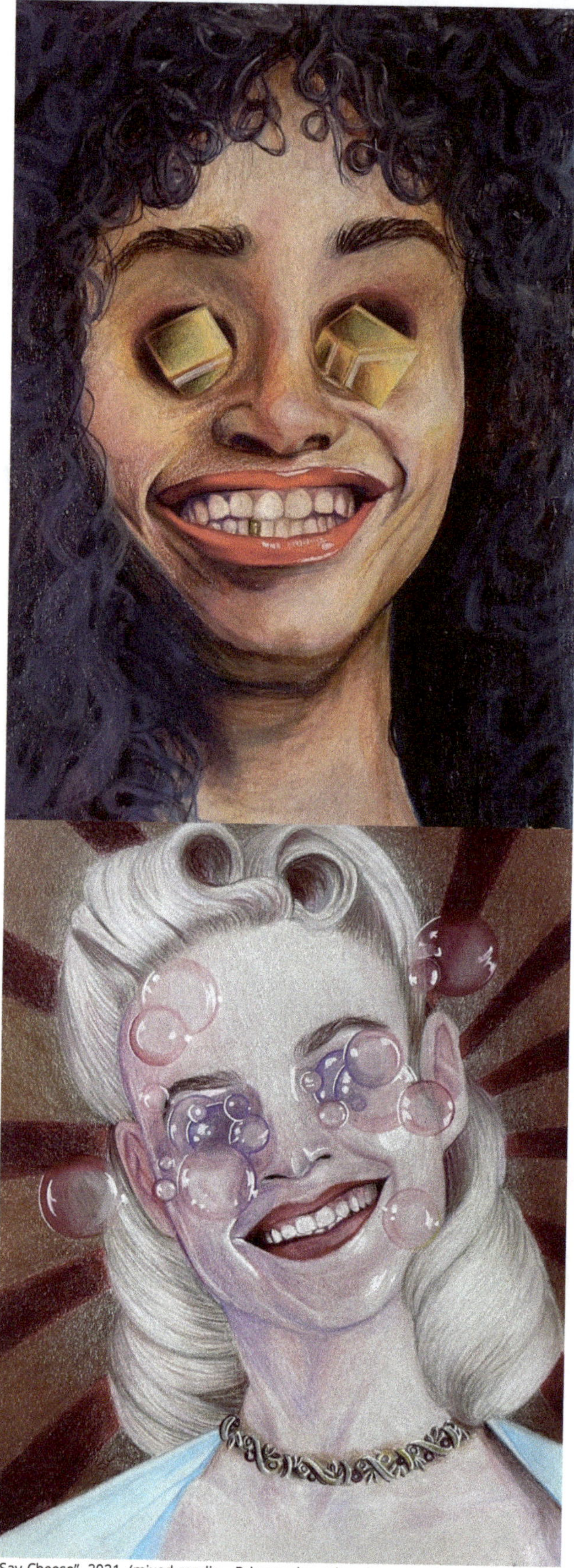

Paycheck, 2021, (mixed media - Prismacolor colored pencils, Posca white acrylic marker, pen)

"Say Cheese", 2021, (mixed media - Prismacolor colored pencils, Posca white acrylic marker, pen)

often parallel, and from an outsider's perspective, mental illness paints people in unique, often beautiful ways.

How do you decide what to charge for your work?

Ah, the age-old question... I have no idea. I'm still trying to find a pricing system for originals, and drop-shipping blank product rates generally dictate the costs of my prints. For now, I'm working on making my drawing prints as financially accessible as possible until I'm more confident in my pricing methods.

What do you want people to take away from your work?

If someone is impacted emotionally, in any way, after seeing my work, I would call that a success. Ideally, that emotional impact would not only last, but provide some comfort, provoke thought, or at the very least, spark creativity or interest. The best case scenario would be at least one struggling person feels heard and consoled.

What's one piece of advice you'd give to aspiring artists?

Keep. On. Going. I'm certainly not on the other side of this advice, so I can't fully vouch for its validity, but it's working so far. For me, 'keep on going' meant pushing myself out of some lazy tendencies, learning some new techniques, taking my time, and taking risks. I would also advise to let walls down when it comes to receiving criticism, but I'm just beginning to work on that one.

"Monday", 2023, mixed media (colored pencil, pen, acrylic marker), 12"x18"   "Dazzle", 2021, mixed media (colored pencil, pen, acrylic marker), 11"x14"

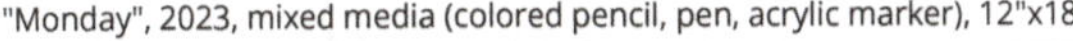

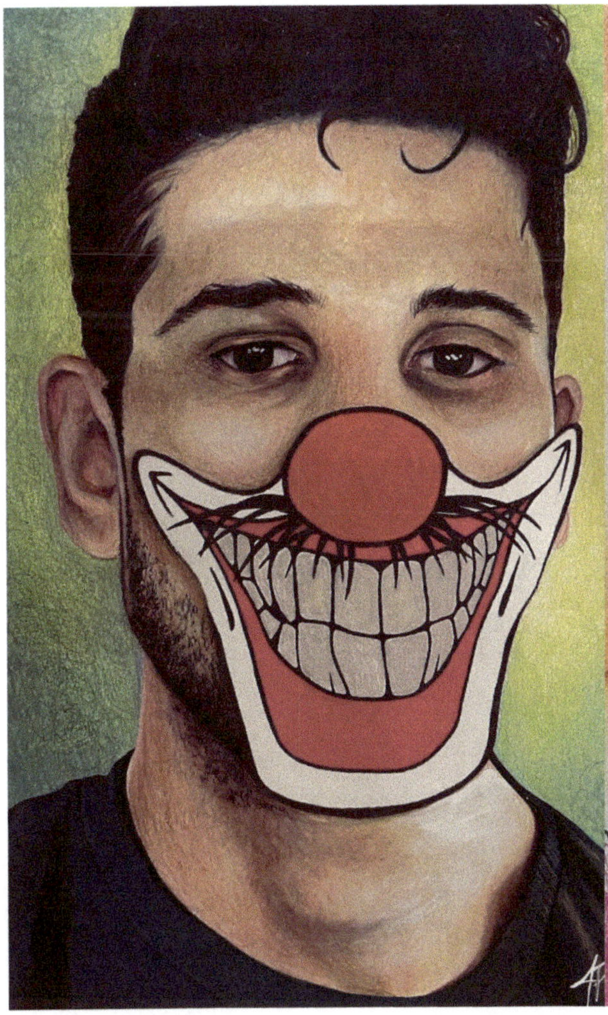

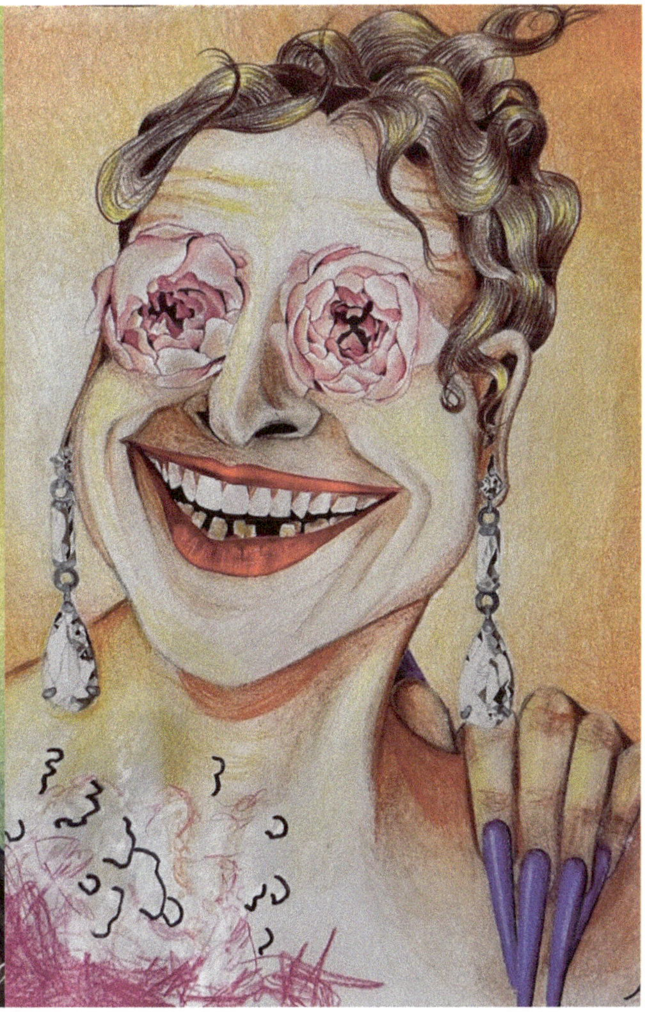

Andrea Castanda was born in Tegucigalpa, Honduras, and her beginnings as an artist were from a very young age. At 13, she worked as an illustrator at Calderon company in Honduras. Andrea sold her first painting and did her first mural at 15. Andrea continued her art career studying at Savannah College of Art & Design, where she got a 70% scholarship. After studying there for a year, she returned to Mexico and continued studying Graphic Design and, at the same time, worked as an illustrator for several foreign companies. Andrea moved back to Honduras, where she had the opportunity to work as a muralist. She painted different restaurants, bars, and Dive shops. Since then, she has continued her art career as a muralist in Mexico and the United States. This has allowed her to present her works in art galleries such as Washington DC, NY, Miami, Brevard county, Italy, Reston VA, Cocoa Beach FL, Woodbridge VA, Honduras and And murals.

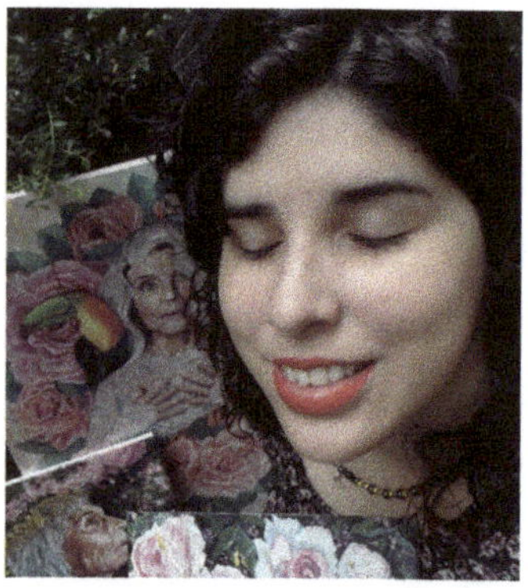

www.andreacastanedacastro.com

andrea.castaneda@ecoworkers.net

@andreacastanedacastro

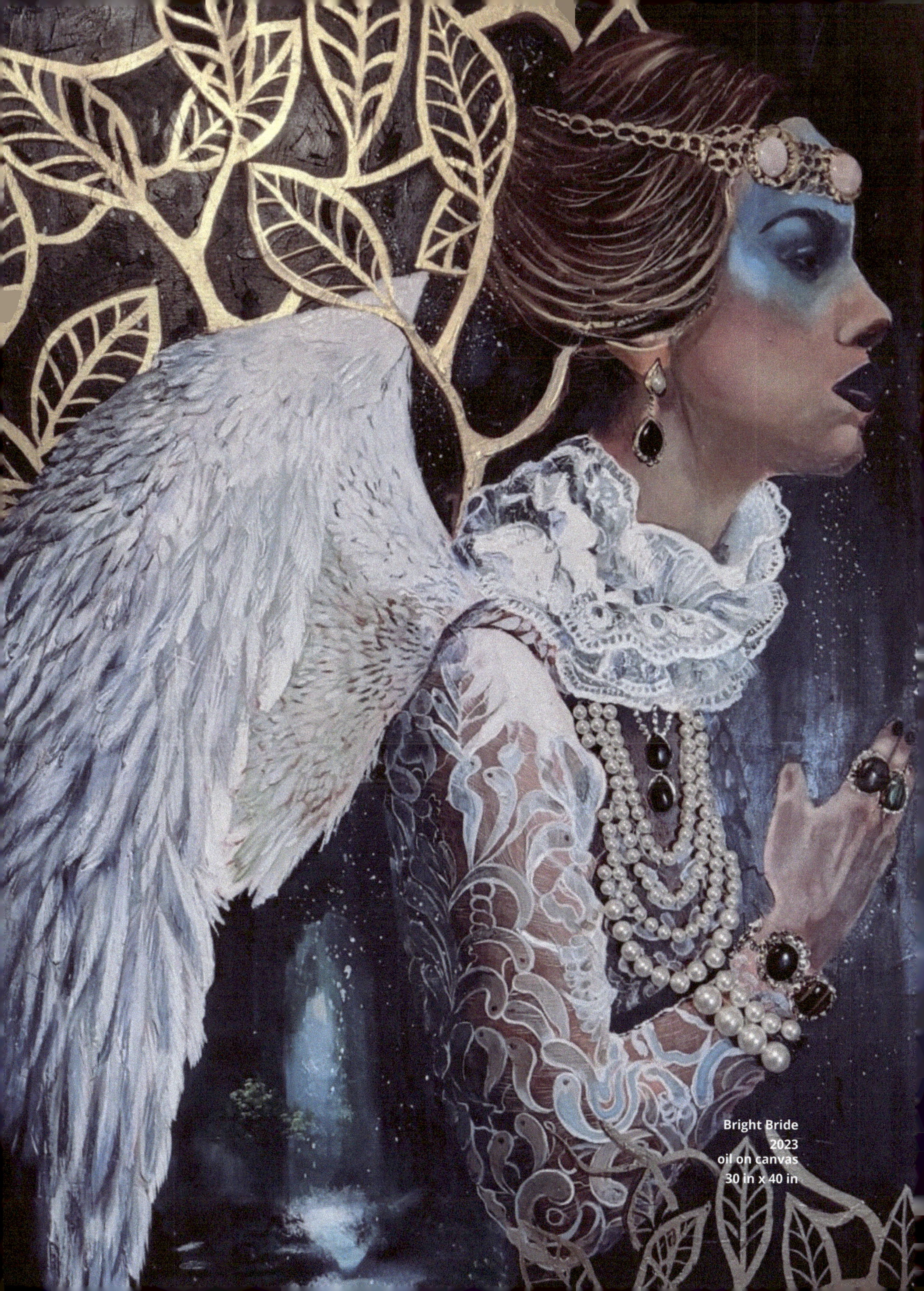
Bright Bride
2023
oil on canvas
30 in x 40 in

Can you share a moment when you felt discouraged as an artist? How did you overcome it?

Yes, I had moments in the past when I was painting, and I didn't sell any of my paintings. I thought that I was a pretty bad artist and stopped believing in myself. However, I never stopped painting, even though I was discouraged. I always woke up the next day and kept painting, studying new art techniques, marketing, and improving as much as I could.

How do you decide what to charge for your work?

Because of my experience, art materials, and size of the work.

How has your art helped you understand yourself better?

It has helped me understand my personality better and the things that I like. I now know my favorite color, the places I truly like, and why I like them. I have started knowing myself more and spending time with myself because painting from the heart has opened my eyes to the world.

How do you cope with the vulnerability of sharing your art with the world?

I believe I share my emotions, thoughts, and heart with the world. I see it as an act of strength. Sharing my art makes me believe more in myself and dispels my fears.

New Years, 2022, oil on canvas, 24 in x 30 in

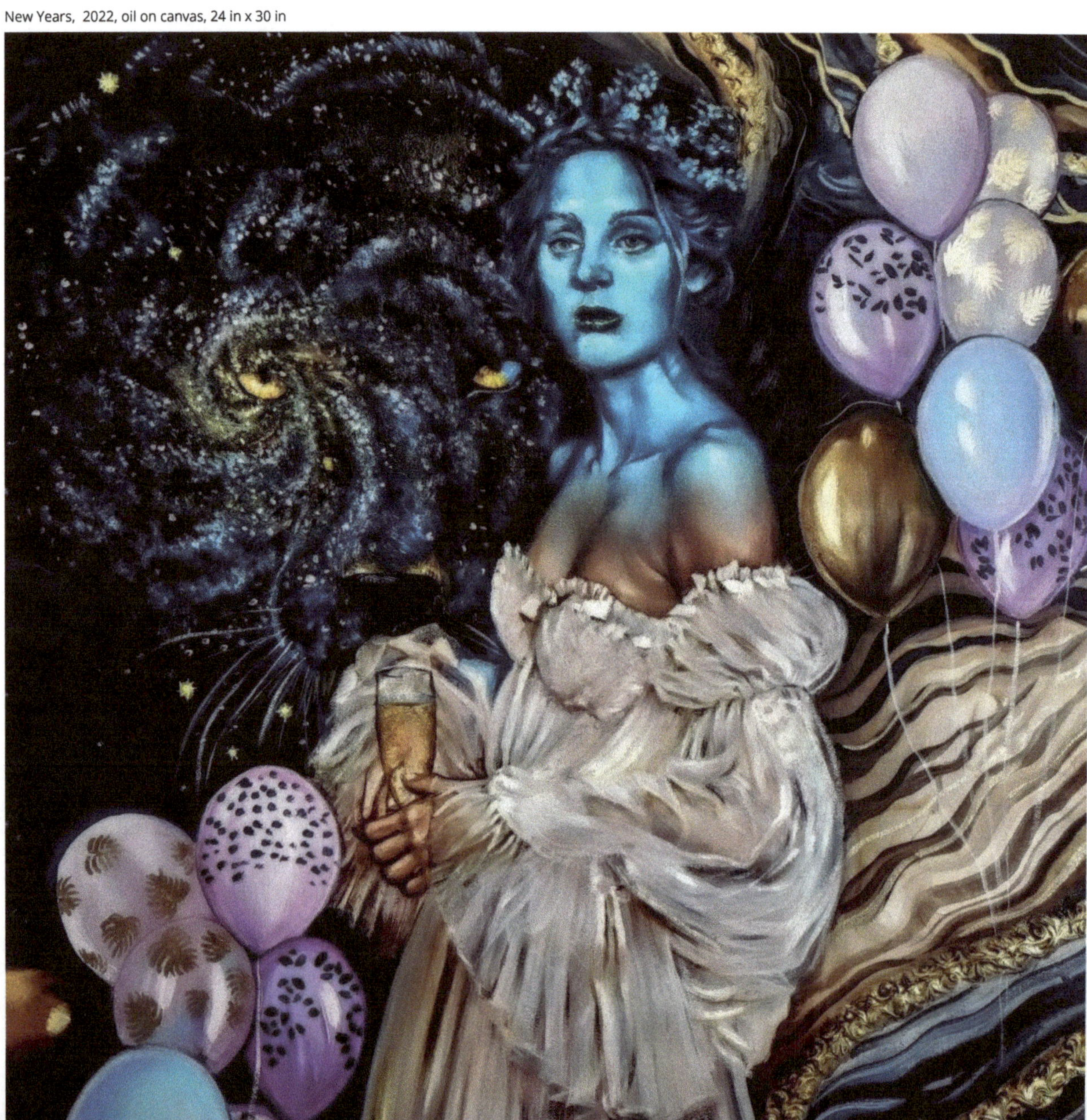

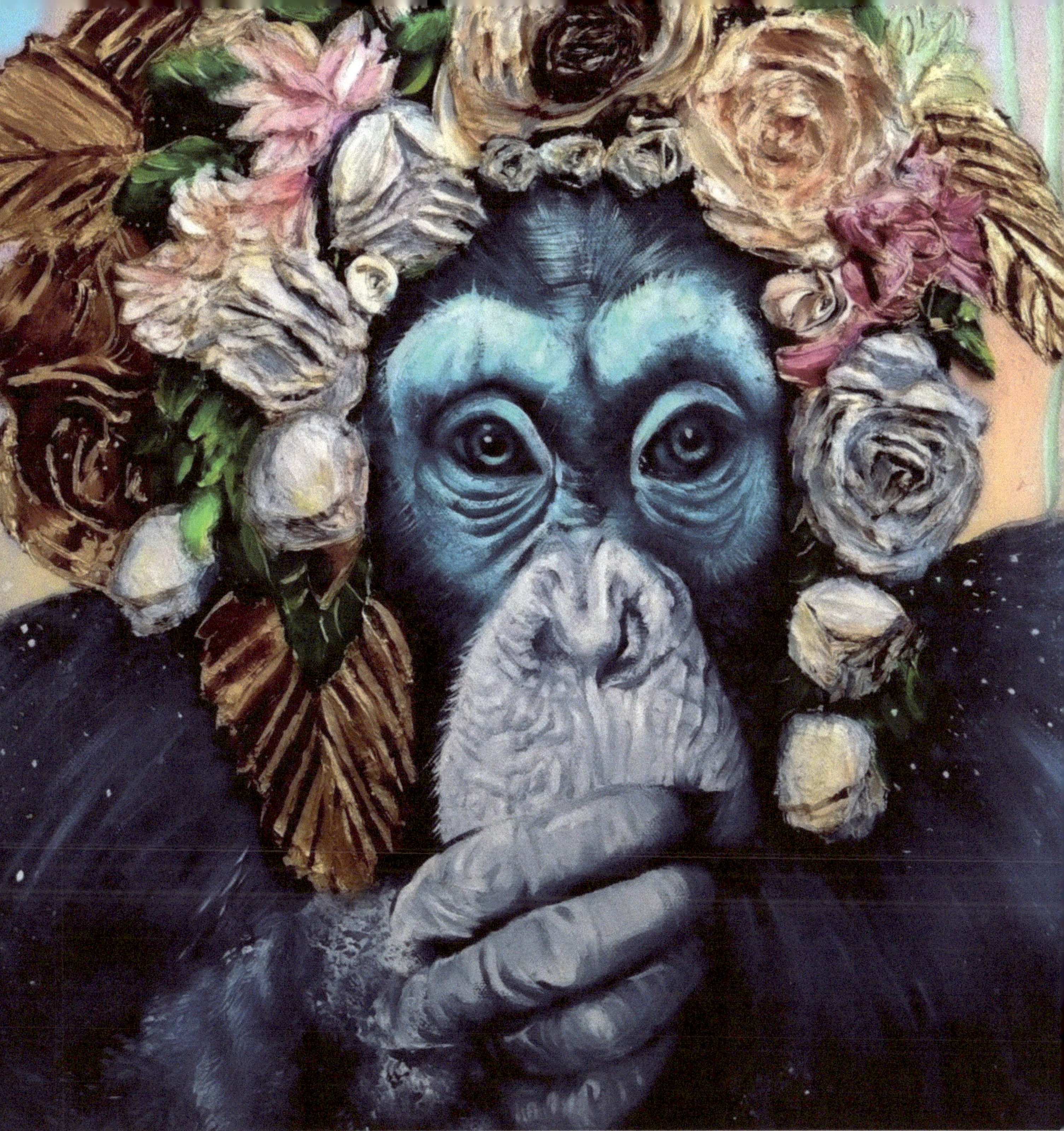

Queen, 2022, oil on canvas, 18 in x 22 in

What do you want people to take away from your work?

That my work conveys real emotions. I'm not selling just a piece of decoration; I'm selling and sharing a piece of my heart. Every painting is created with my heart, good-quality art materials, and my knowledge.

What's one piece of advice you'd give to aspiring artists?

To keep fighting for your dreams even though sometimes you feel you won't make it, just stand up and keep working on it until you achieve it. It can feel like an eternity, but if you fight, you will get there.

https://anmechelincktextileartist.com

annmechelinck@hotmail.com

@annmechelinck

Ann Mechelinck is originally from Belgium, Ann came to live in Ireland in 2005 where she has pursued a successful career as a textile artist, exhibiting national and international as far as Ukraine and Japan. Ann's latest work is inspired by moss, which became her symbolisation of positivity in a negative world, a synonym of healing, hope, and optimism, mindsets that are too often disregarded or go unnoticed in our current society. The slow and repetitive processes of weaving, crochet, and embroidery allow the artist the time to reflect and meditate, away from a world that often doesn't make sense. Ann believes that these traditional skills, passed from generation to generation, need to be kept alive in today's day and age where everything has become mechanized or computerized. For that reason, she deliberately works solely by hand, nurturing a slower pace of life and a more conscious way of living and working, merging traditional techniques into contemporary, abstract textile artworks that convey the comfort and tranquility of being in nature.

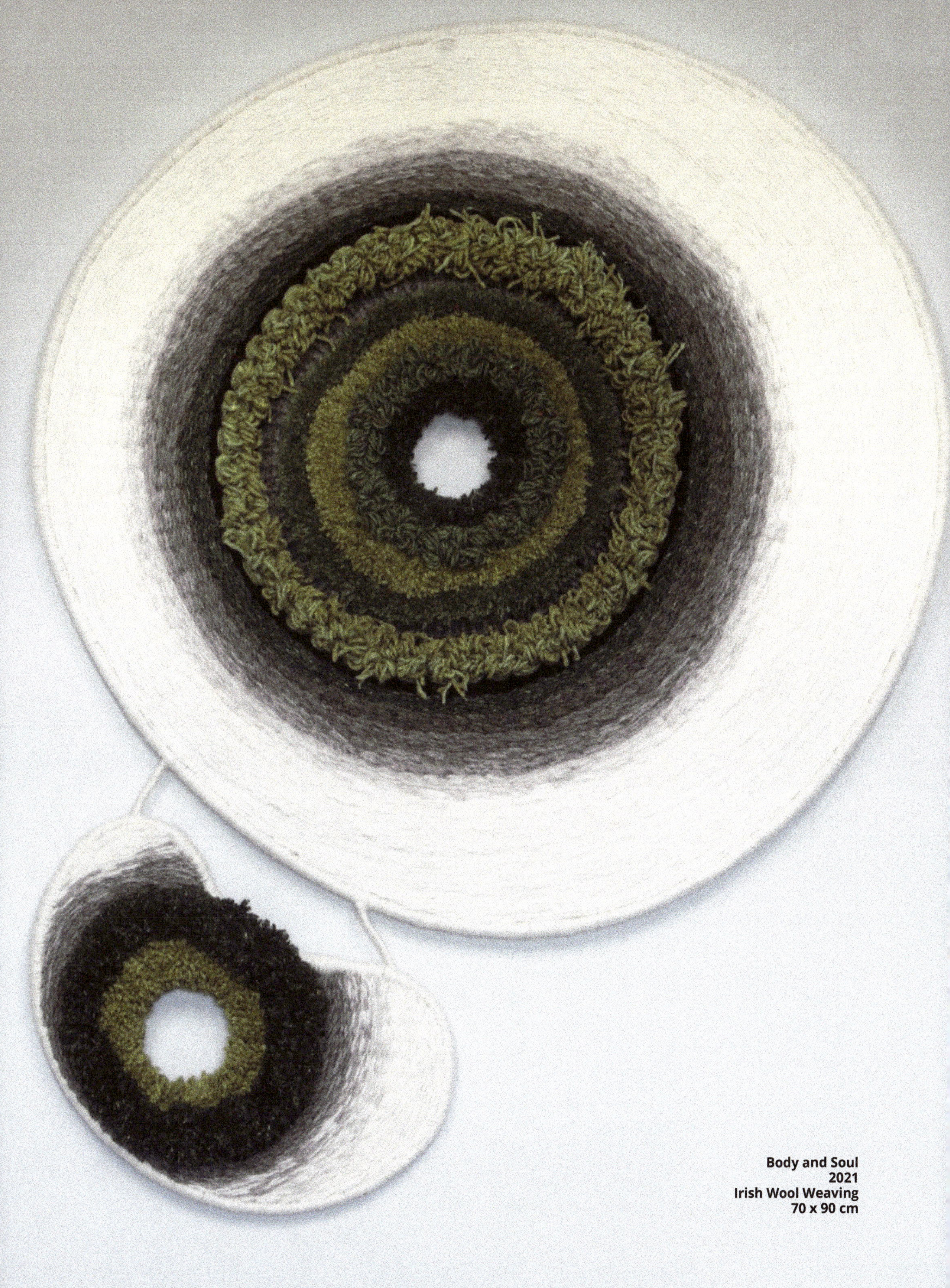

Body and Soul
2021
Irish Wool Weaving
70 x 90 cm

Can you share a moment when you felt discouraged as an artist? How did you overcome it?

After graduating from Art College I was suddenly 'on my own' in the art world. That dream of wanting to become a full-time, self-employed artist, could it become a reality? Would I continue to have inspiration? Would I be able to come up with new ideas and new work? Would I be good enough to make a living out of this path that I had chosen? By surrounding myself with a network of creative people, by becoming a member of a variety of textile organization in Ireland and abroad, those doubts and fears quickly subsided. It's so important and so beneficial to meet like-minded people and maintain those relationships, to learn from each other. It keeps you inspired, creates opportunities to get your work seen, and possibilities to collaborate with other artists.

How do you cope with the vulnerability of sharing your art with the world?

I never make work for others, or with potential clients in my mind. My work comes from my heart, my soul, my hands. It's in my DNA, it's who I am. I make because I have something to say and share. I make because I need to make, to express an inner voice. I make, and then I share my work, and with that I share myself. It's an incredible feeling and honor when people connect with my work and the concept behind it. With some of my clients, I have developed a warm bond. But I don't expect everyone who sees my work to feel a connection with it or like it. That would be quite arrogant.

How has your art helped you understand yourself better?

Making art is a catalyst. I work most of the time in silence and prefer to work solely by hand, eliminating mechanical sounds. I find it really beneficial for my mental health and well being and for my creative thinking to have periods of silence where my brain can effectively relax and allow all my thoughts and ideas to slow down and settle down. The slow and repetitive processes of weaving, crochet and embroidery allow me the time

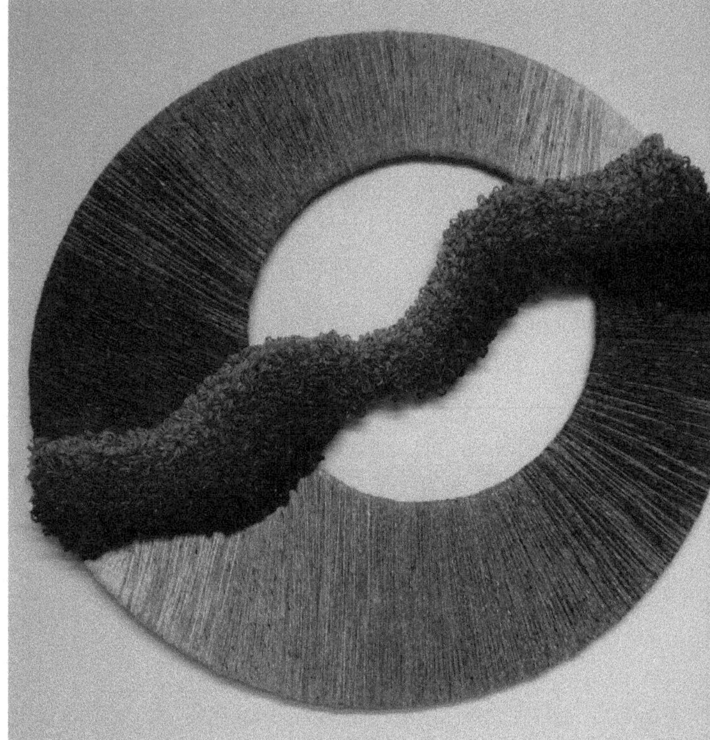

Unity I, 2023, Irish Wool, Weaving, wrapping, appr. 80cm diameter

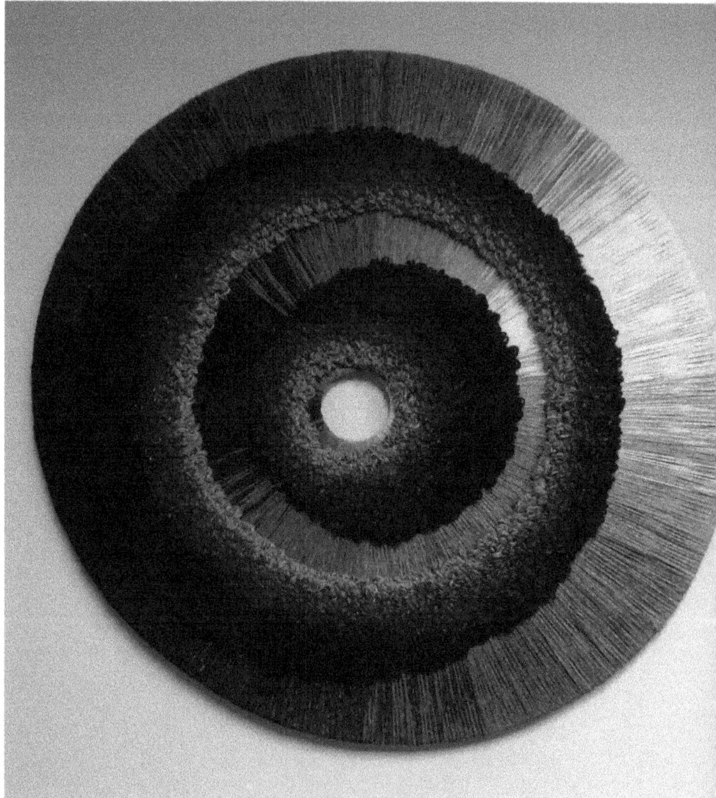

Morning Dawn, 2023, Irish Wool, Weaving, wrapping, 95 x 89cm

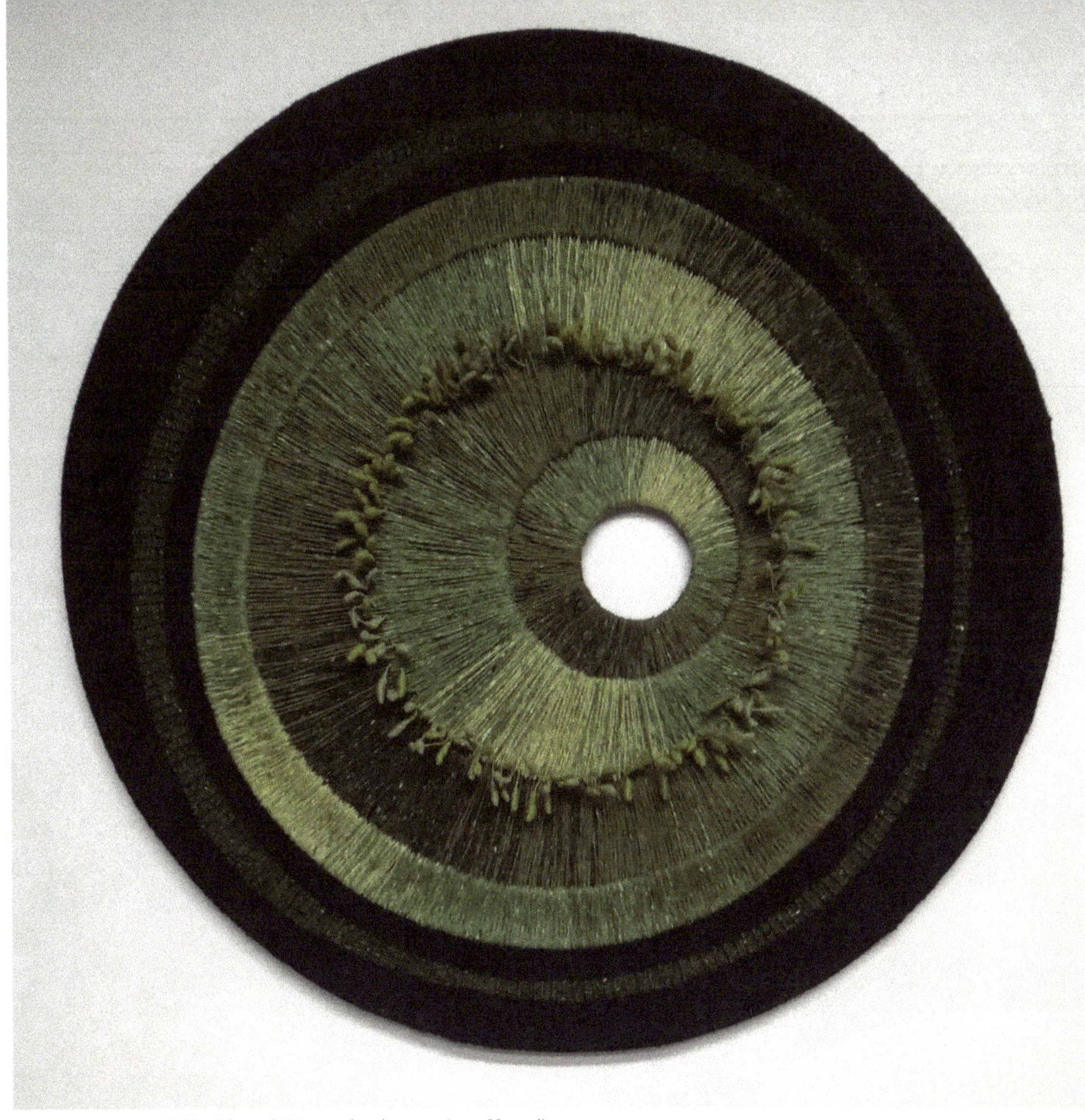

Nurture, 2023, Irish wool / Wrapped and woven, Appr. 80 cm diameter

to reflect, to contemplate and meditate, away from a world that often doesn't make sense.

How do you decide what to charge for your work?

Whether you're an established artist or an emerging one, have confidence in yourself and your prices. Take the time to properly, realistically price your work and stand behind the price, ready to justify your price. I give myself an hourly wage and include the costs of materials. I have used this formula consistently and transparently. People like to understand why a work is priced a certain way whether it's a private buyer or a gallery. And just know that not everyone is going to agree with the way you valued your work, no matter your process.

What do you want people to take away from your work?

In a world full of doom and gloom, I want my my work to bring comfort to people, moments of stillness and contemplation, allowing them to see the good, the beautiful, the wonderful in a world that often doesn't make sense. I want my work to send a message of hope in a world saturated with negativity to never ever give up believing in better times to come. I hope that through my works, people will experience the healing power of being in and with nature.

What's one piece of advice you'd give to aspiring artists?

Don't use your phone or the internet as an option for inspiration. Go to a gallery or museum, go to art events. Go out into the REAL world! You don't get that sort of connection, interaction, and immersive experiences from staring at Instagram or Pinterest, artists' websites, or virtual exhibitions, as you do from places like Tate Modern, MoMa, or The Louvre. Surround yourself with magazines and books.

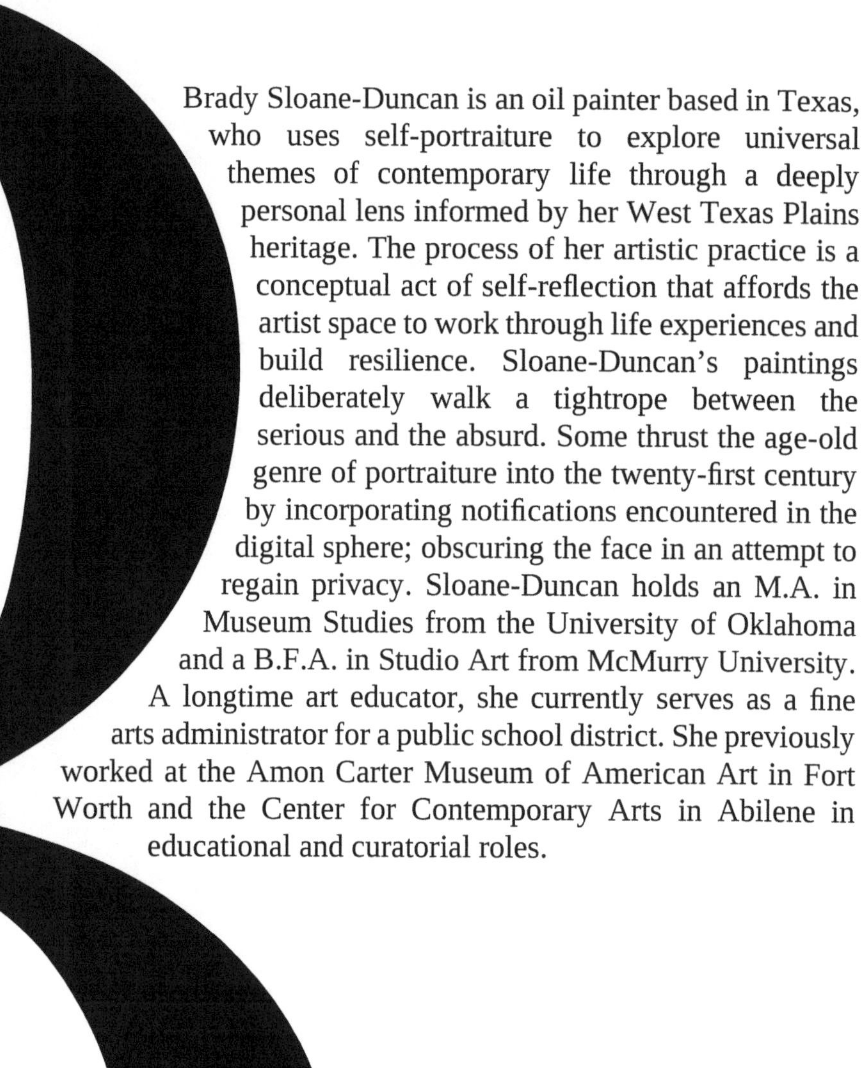

Brady Sloane-Duncan is an oil painter based in Texas, who uses self-portraiture to explore universal themes of contemporary life through a deeply personal lens informed by her West Texas Plains heritage. The process of her artistic practice is a conceptual act of self-reflection that affords the artist space to work through life experiences and build resilience. Sloane-Duncan's paintings deliberately walk a tightrope between the serious and the absurd. Some thrust the age-old genre of portraiture into the twenty-first century by incorporating notifications encountered in the digital sphere; obscuring the face in an attempt to regain privacy. Sloane-Duncan holds an M.A. in Museum Studies from the University of Oklahoma and a B.F.A. in Studio Art from McMurry University. A longtime art educator, she currently serves as a fine arts administrator for a public school district. She previously worked at the Amon Carter Museum of American Art in Fort Worth and the Center for Contemporary Arts in Abilene in educational and curatorial roles.

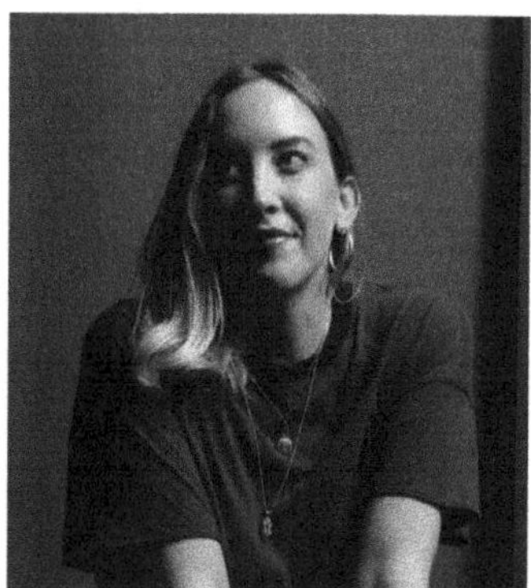

www.bradysloaneduncan.com

brady.sloane@gmail.com

@bradykinns__art

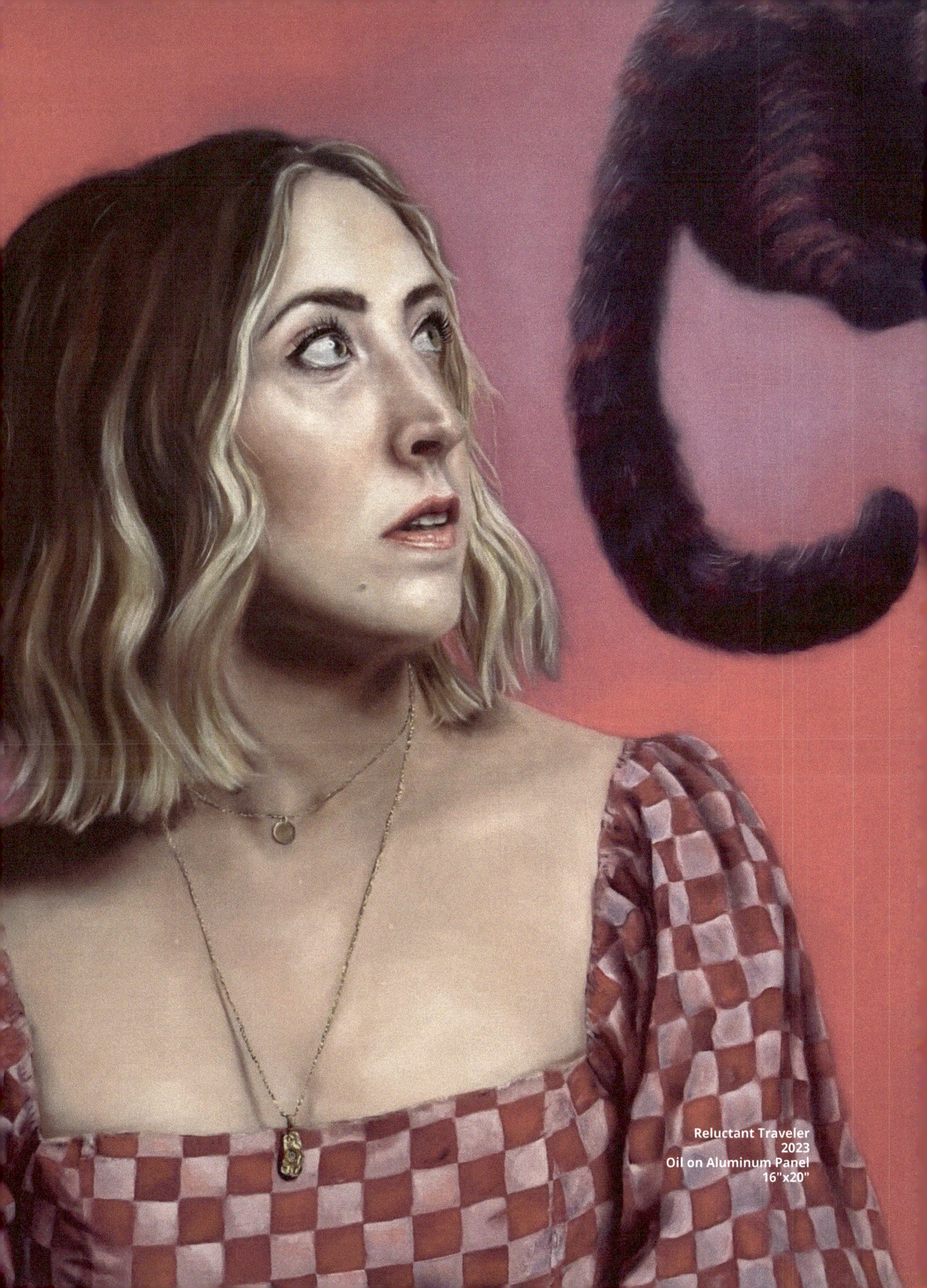

Reluctant Traveler
2023
Oil on Aluminum Panel
16"x20"

Can you share a moment when you felt discouraged as an artist? How did you overcome it?

Years ago, while working in museums and galleries, I began to question my worth as an artist because so many people were "already" doing amazing things. It led me to not creating for over a decade. I finally overcame it when going through my divorce; I attended an intense painting workshop and got back in the groove. Now I aim to reach my own personal goals and keep an active practice; and my family and children are proud of that as well. There are still many discouraging moments, but resilience is growing!

How do you cope with the vulnerability of sharing your art with the world?

This can be difficult for me because my paintings often explore the tensions between public and private and question whether we can ever fully be known by another person. I investigate the strategies we use to veil or mask our truest selves and the reasons we hold back and keep parts of ourselves private, even from those closest to us; so sharing with the public at large can be daunting. But, the more I share, the more people tell me the work resonates with them…so I keep going.

Installation Image, Camouflage, 2023, Framed Oil on Aluminum Panel over 4'x8' Wallpaper covered board

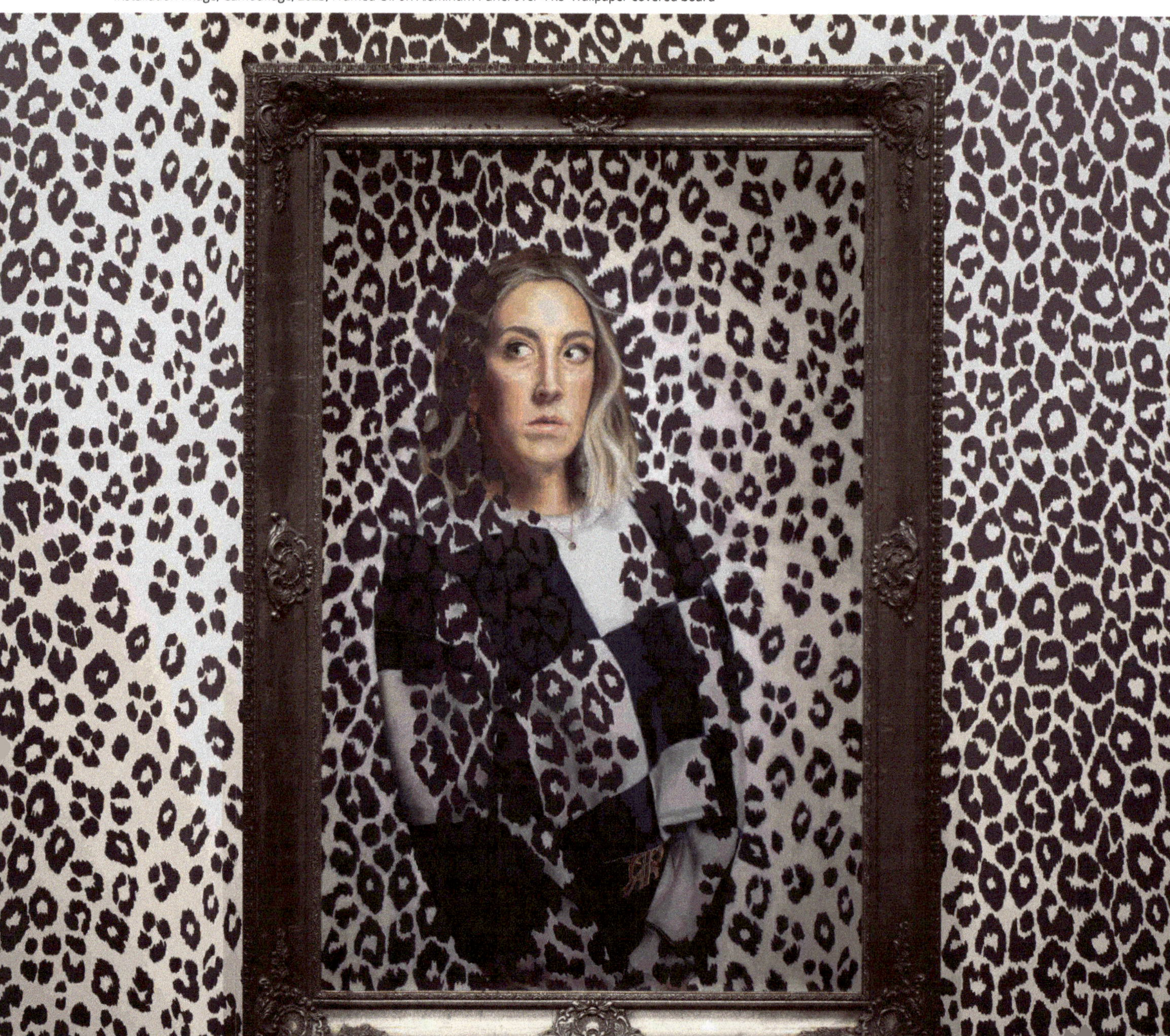

What do you want people to take away from your work?

I want my self-portraits to raise the same questions essential to my practice: How and why do we use personal embellishment to shape others' views of ourselves? I often take on a wallflower role in my paintings, positioned in front of patterned (often luxury brand) wallpapers wearing carefully selected garments to camouflage myself within the compositions to varying degrees. I want the viewer to ask themselves (especially in a commercially-driven society); are self-adornment and interior decor forms of expression or manipulation?

How do you decide what to charge for your work?

I actually work with a mentor, who is a successful painter, for guidance. She helps me understand so many aspects of the art world and gives advice concerning many areas; including pricing and how to do it depending on where you are in your career. Working with a mentor helps me stay on track, meet deadlines, and push myself to improve technically.

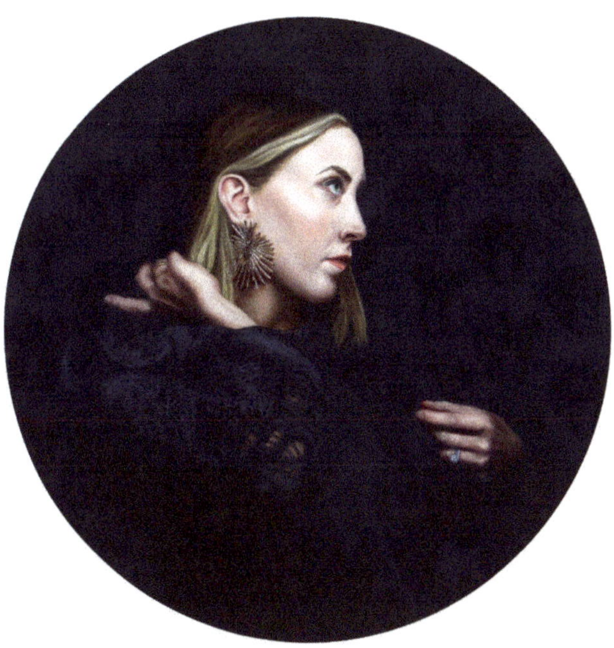

Behind the Armory, 2023, Oil on Linen on Aluminum Panel, 24" Tondo

How has your art helped you understand yourself better?

At times I can be excruciatingly self-aware, and I create paintings to navigate emotionally difficult situations. It takes me time to create a series, so the meanings and messages in my work are often from struggles of years past. One thing I have discovered is that there will always be a hint of humor and absurdity in my work-it's just who I am.

What's one piece of advice you'd give to aspiring artists?

Of course, people always say to go for it, and I agree; but I do think it is OK to determine the balance needed for your life and family. Ignore thoughts of defeat or shame because you choose to work a salaried job so your children can have medical insurance, or can be able to participate in activities regularly (not beholden to sales). Balance can be elusive, but if it is looked at in a more holistic way over the period of a year, and not in a way that demands each day to have a tight schedule, it is easier to give yourself grace.

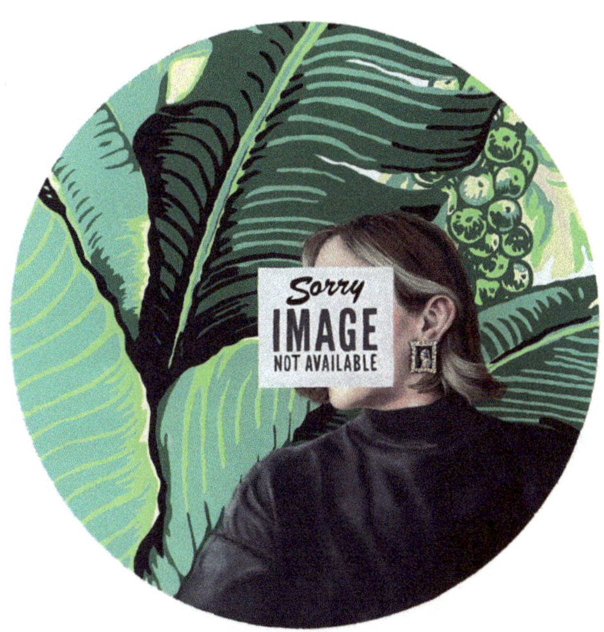

Sorry Image Not Available, 2022, Oil on Wood Panel, 18" Tondo

Cagla Toprak Attia started out as a fashion designer in her hometown of Istanbul, and after nine years craved a break from the fast pace and long nights. Swapping one metropolis for another, She found a home in Brooklyn in 2019, where she was curious to try a ceramics class. From the first moment working with clay, she knew it would become a permanent fixture in my life. Converting a corner of the apartment into a "Tiny Studio", she found solace at the pottery wheel, every day happily discovering a liberty this art form provided. What started as a hobby quickly developed into something more as she found creative freedom and felt compelled to pursue ceramics full time. She works exclusively with the highest quality porcelain because it allows her to experiment with the creative process and shape exquisite and fragile flowers. Her pieces are a testament to the celebration of life, represented by the blooms one shares with loved ones. Flowers remind us how one also can grow and blossom, each uniquely, just as each piece is hand crafted and glazed. Walking with her young son through Brooklyn, she finds inspiration everywhere from neighbors' gardens to the local park and then research the shapes and petals that catch her eye.

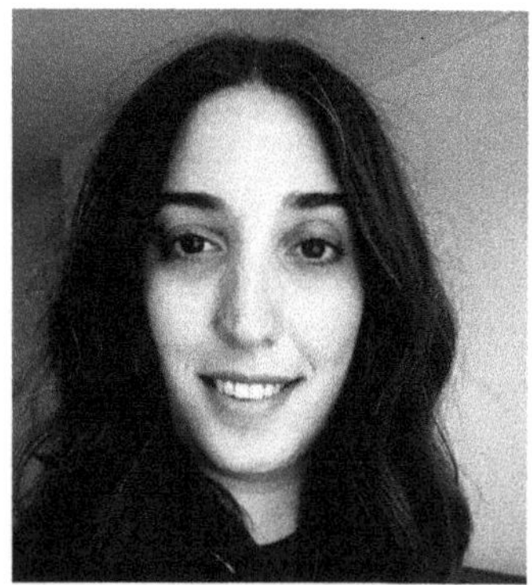

www.dearyouceramics.com

chala@dearyouceramics.com

@dearyouceramics

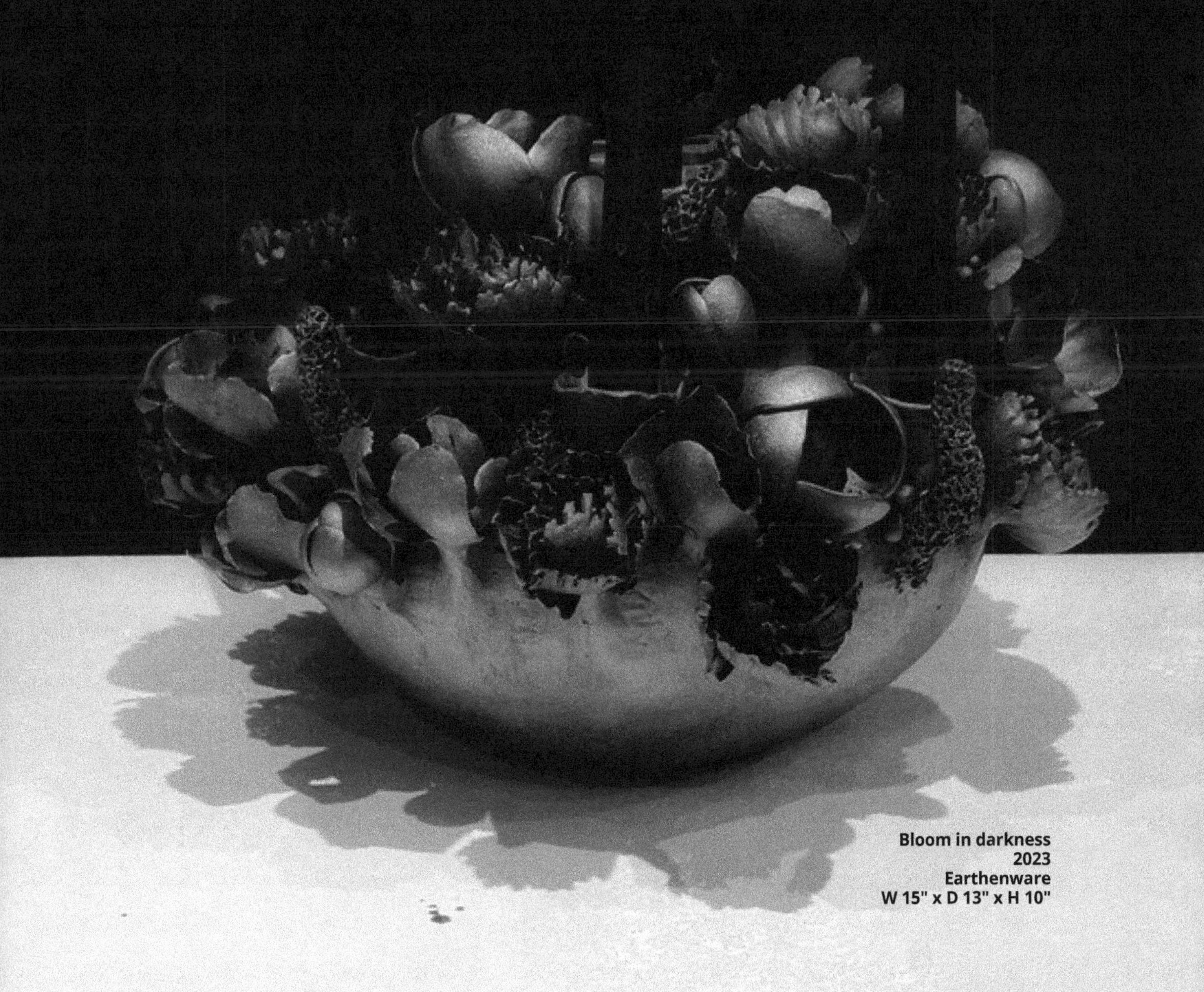

Bloom in darkness
2023
Earthenware
W 15" x D 13" x H 10"

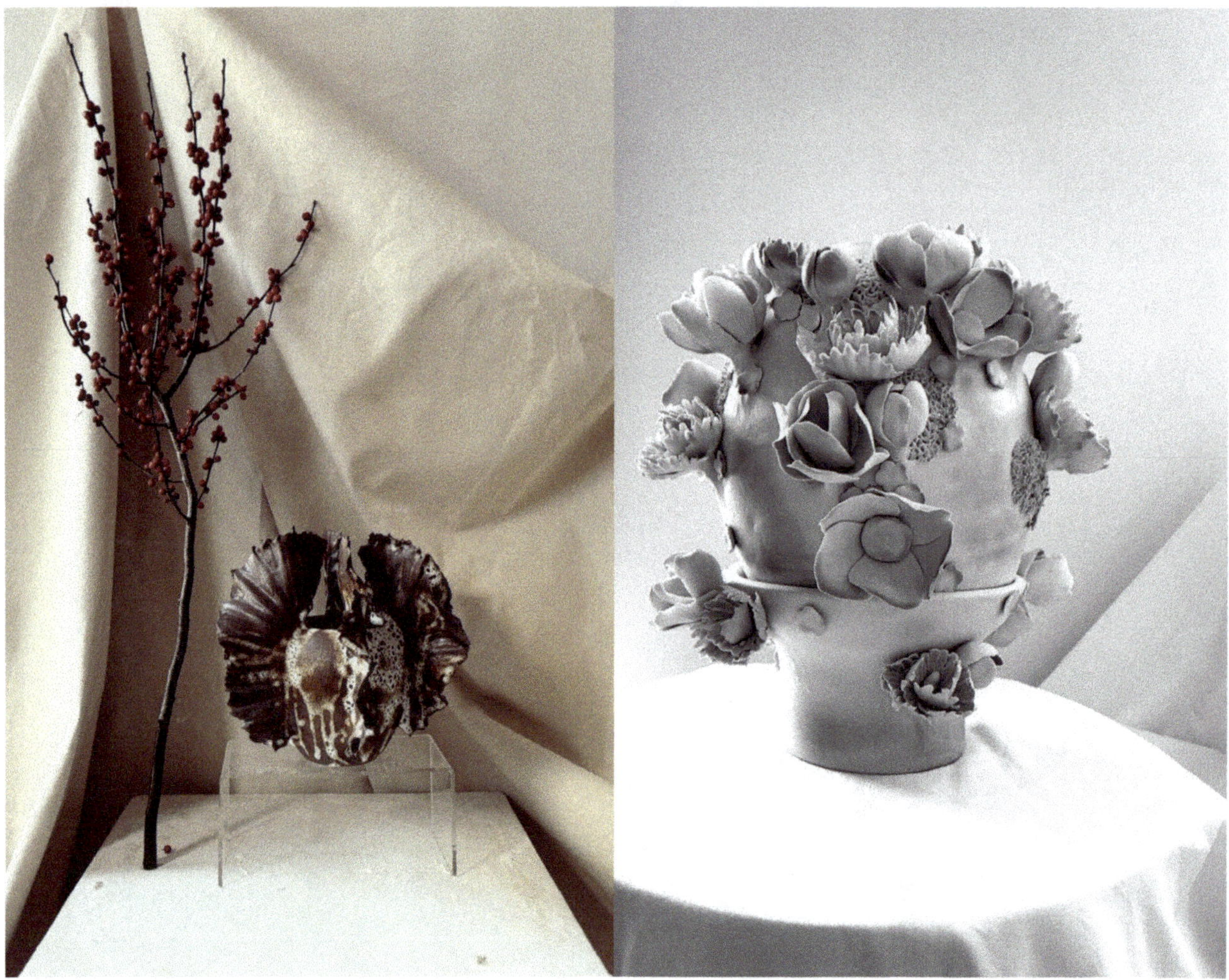

Wild Petals N.1 - Hand built, one of a kind vase with textured glaze. Earthenware, W 11" x D 11" x H 8.5"

My Wild Garden Sculpture, 2023, Porcelain, W 10" x D 10" x H 12"

Can you share a moment when you felt discouraged as an artist? How did you overcome it?

Shortly after being a mom, I started to go back to my studio with all the creative ideas that I had in my sleepless nights. When my son was less than a year old, I was feeling really productive and inspired until I started to put more time and effort for him. In other words, until he started to be more human (other than being baby)! After the age of 1, I started to spend less time at the studio and this really made me discouraged to create or focus on creating something "satisfying". Then this dissatisfaction started to get whole my mind and took me deep into a whirlpool where I didn't trust my inner voice. As an artist+parent, coping with this kind of feeling was really hard. After a while, one thing that made me feel back to my true self was meditation. I am meditating 3-4 times a week and that 15-20 minute is boosting my self confidence.

How do you decide what to charge for your work?

It's all about a feeling. It's hard to describe it; but, after spending good amount of time with same signature detail of your art, your soul starts to search for something new but still you. This feeling is not coming to me every other month or every year. When my soul shows me it needs this change, I start to seek for a new detail but still me!, Still what I love to remind people with my art is that it can take a month or a year. Only thing is to be patient until you say "this is it!"

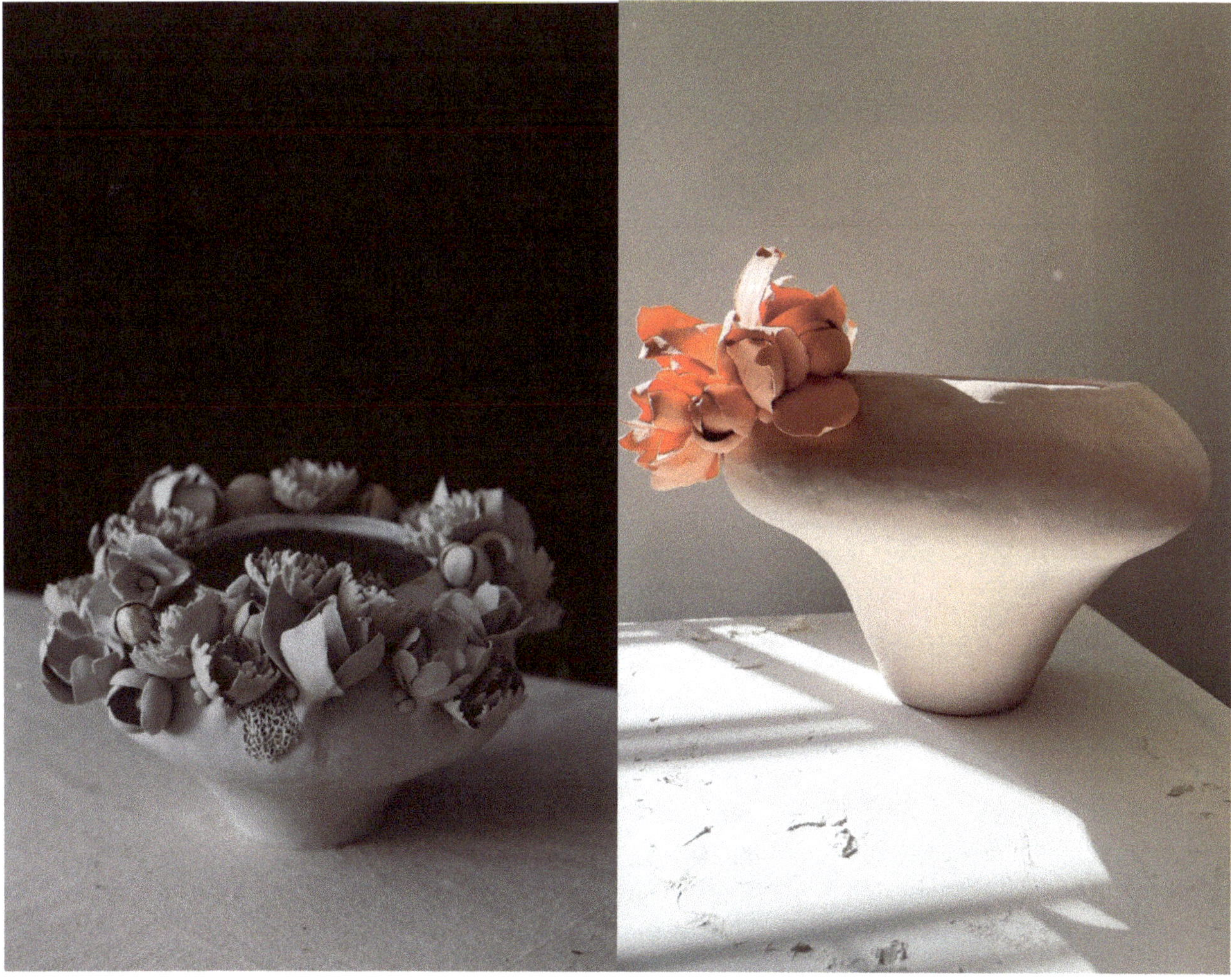

My Wild Garden Sculpture - Hand built, one of a kind centerpiece with a glazes smooth surface inside. Porcelain W 14" x D 13" x H 8.5"

Sunset Blooms, 2022, Porcelain, W 13" x D 11" x H 10"

What do you want people to take away from your work?

I want them to remember what beautiful souls they have and, no matter what happened in their life through years, be proud of themselves. Every one of us is unique like each flower on Earth.

What's one piece of advice you'd give to aspiring artists?

Do not try to do anything popular or get likes on social media. Create something that you can touch some people's hearts with it. Real success is not followers or likes or shares. Also, never forget, one idea can come to you; but, it also can come to someone else in another city/country. Keep that idea and make it yours.

How do you cope with the vulnerability of sharing your art with the world?

To be honest, sharing my art is the most exciting part of the process. Since my pieces have so much from me, when I share my art with the world, I feel like I'm inspiring many people.

How has your art helped you understand yourself better?

For me ceramics is therapeutic. Every single time I sit to work on my art, I feel like I am creating a happier version of myself with patience. The more patient I become, the happier I am. Because patience is teaching me how to deal with things and find better way to express myself in life.

C h r i s t i n e Nightingale is a Chilean figurative artist whose work is a product of her deep passion for self-expression and exploring the mysteries of the universe. As an artist, Christine is known for creating emotionally and thought-provoking pieces that are visually striking. Her art leads the viewer to awareness of self and their surroundings. She draws inspiration from ancient cultures, nature, photography, and spirituality, making her art deeply personal yet universally relatable. Christine explores themes of connection between humans, nature, and the higher self by using a variety of mediums and techniques. Her art speaks to a wide audience inspiring individuals to question their beliefs, emotions, and realities. She creates beauty to touch people's emotions through her paintings and bring awareness of what she believes to be important for us, as human beings. Christine puts the intention to heal through her art and cause curiosity, making the viewer wonder beyond what is obvious. Nightingale is a dreamer in every sense of the word. In the dream world, everything is possible, it is limitless and magic just like creating art. The world needs that magic and she wants to show it through what inspires her: connection.

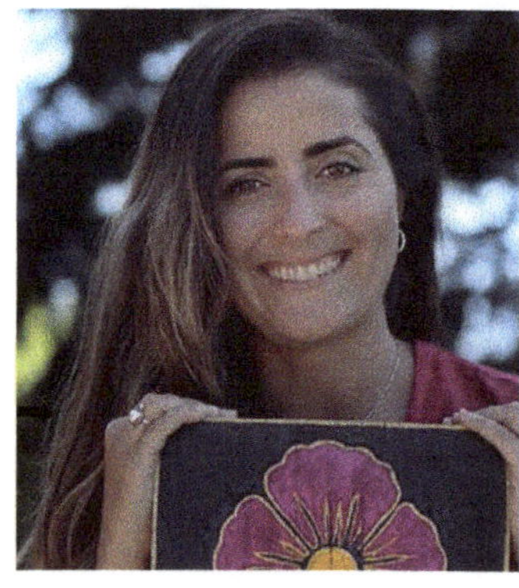

www.christinenightingale.com

chrisnightdesign@gmail.com

@christinenightingale_art

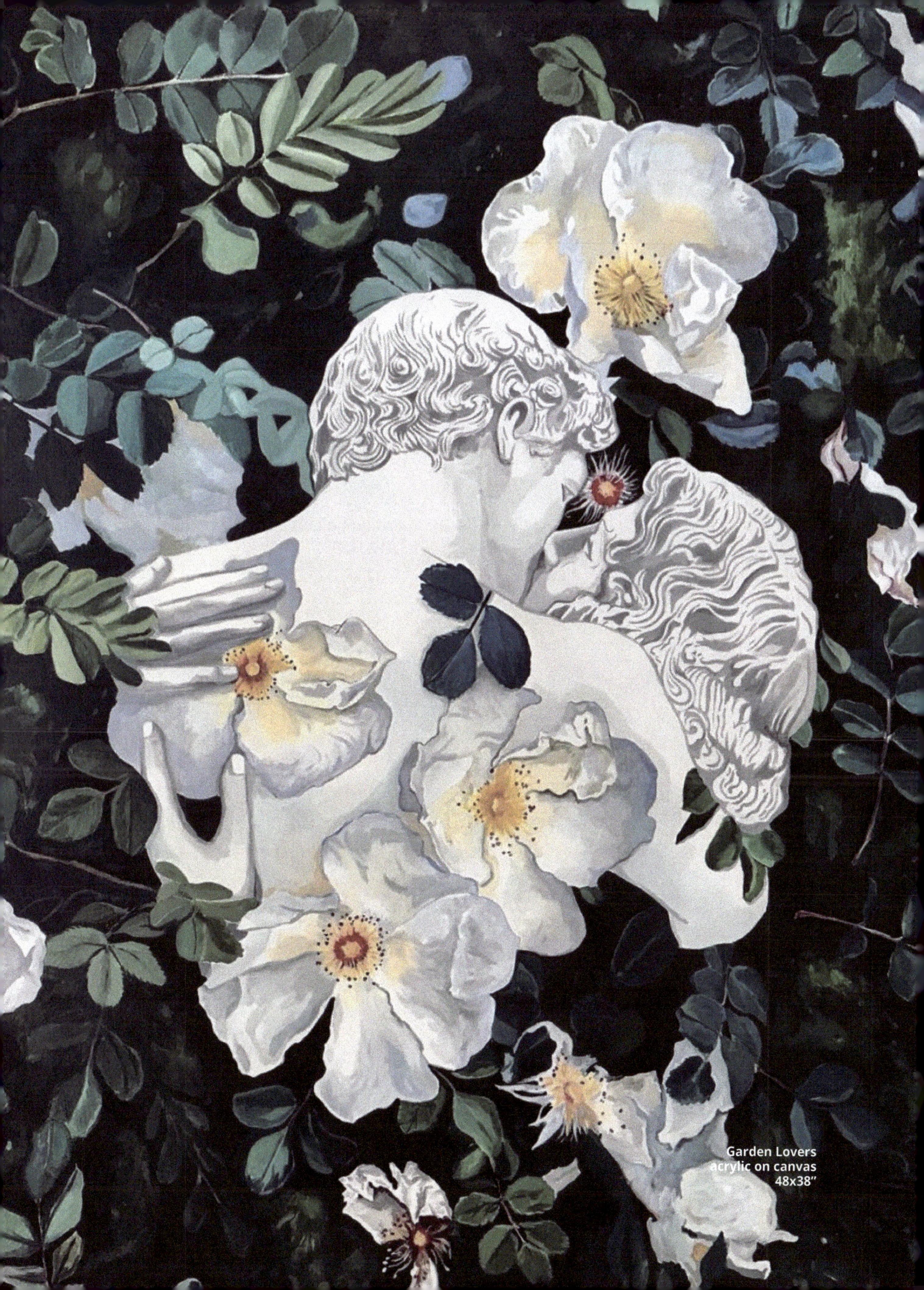

Garden Lovers
acrylic on canvas
48x38"

Can you share a moment when you felt discouraged as an artist? How did you overcome it?

Overcoming discouragement is an inevitable part of an artist's life. It can be especially disheartening when you've spent months creating art pieces but see no results in sales, for example. However, I always try to go back to my true motivation and remind myself why I paint. I understand that this moment of despair is just a part of the process, and my time will come. Above all, I remind myself to enjoy the process.

How do you cope with the vulnerability of sharing your art with the world?

Sharing your art with the world can be a vulnerable experience, but I believe that vulnerability makes us stronger. The more I show up as my true self through my art, the stronger I become as an artist and individual. It's not easy because of the fear of being judged and ignored, but I remind myself that there are different people with different opinions. I trust that the ones who resonate with me and my art will come to me when I show my truth.

How has your art helped you understand yourself better?

Creating art has helped me understand myself better. It has shown me how my mind works and how I process ideas and emotions. It connects me to a higher plane and helps me find what makes me unique. I can see my strengths and weaknesses, what brings my curiosity out, and what doesn't interest me. Art is like a visual map of my life.

How do you decide what to charge for your work?

When it comes to pricing my work, I typically charge by square foot and consider the technique I use. Oils tend to be more labor-intensive than acrylics, so that would add up to an additional price. As an artist, I want to reveal the beauty and hope in life. I want the viewer to feel connected and to sense the possibility of a better life beyond what they see.

"Sunflower Señora", 2021, Mixed media on canvas, 48" x 36"

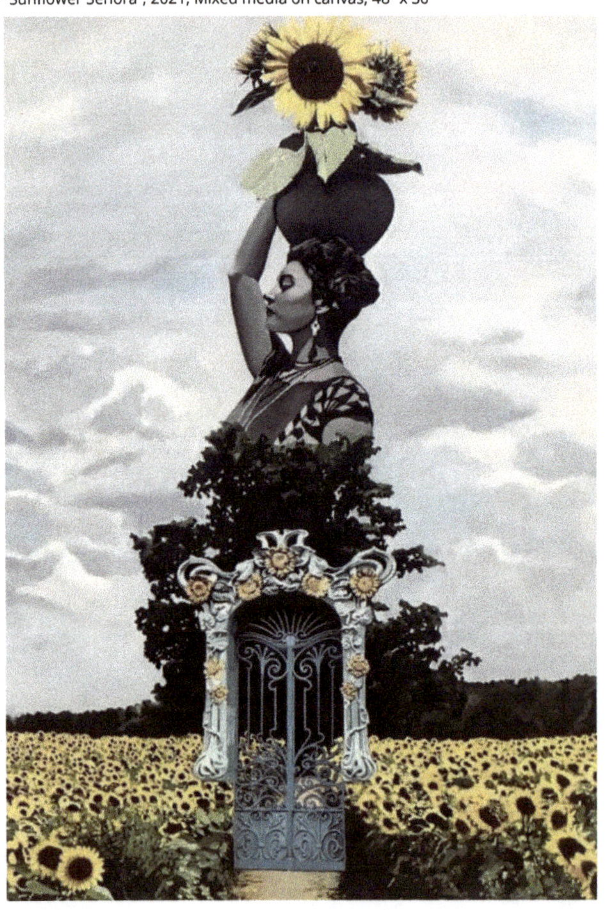

Guardians of the Forest, mixed media on canvas, 48x36"

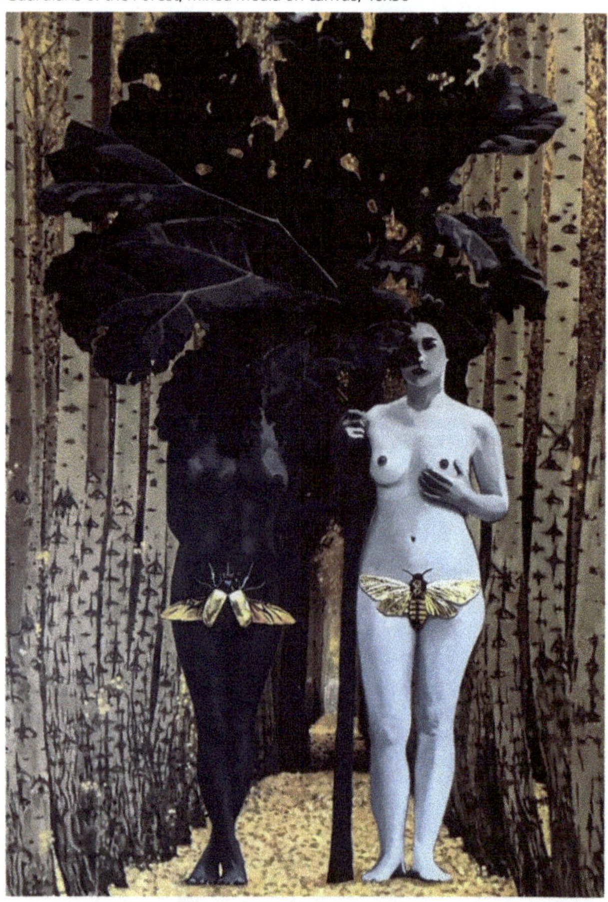

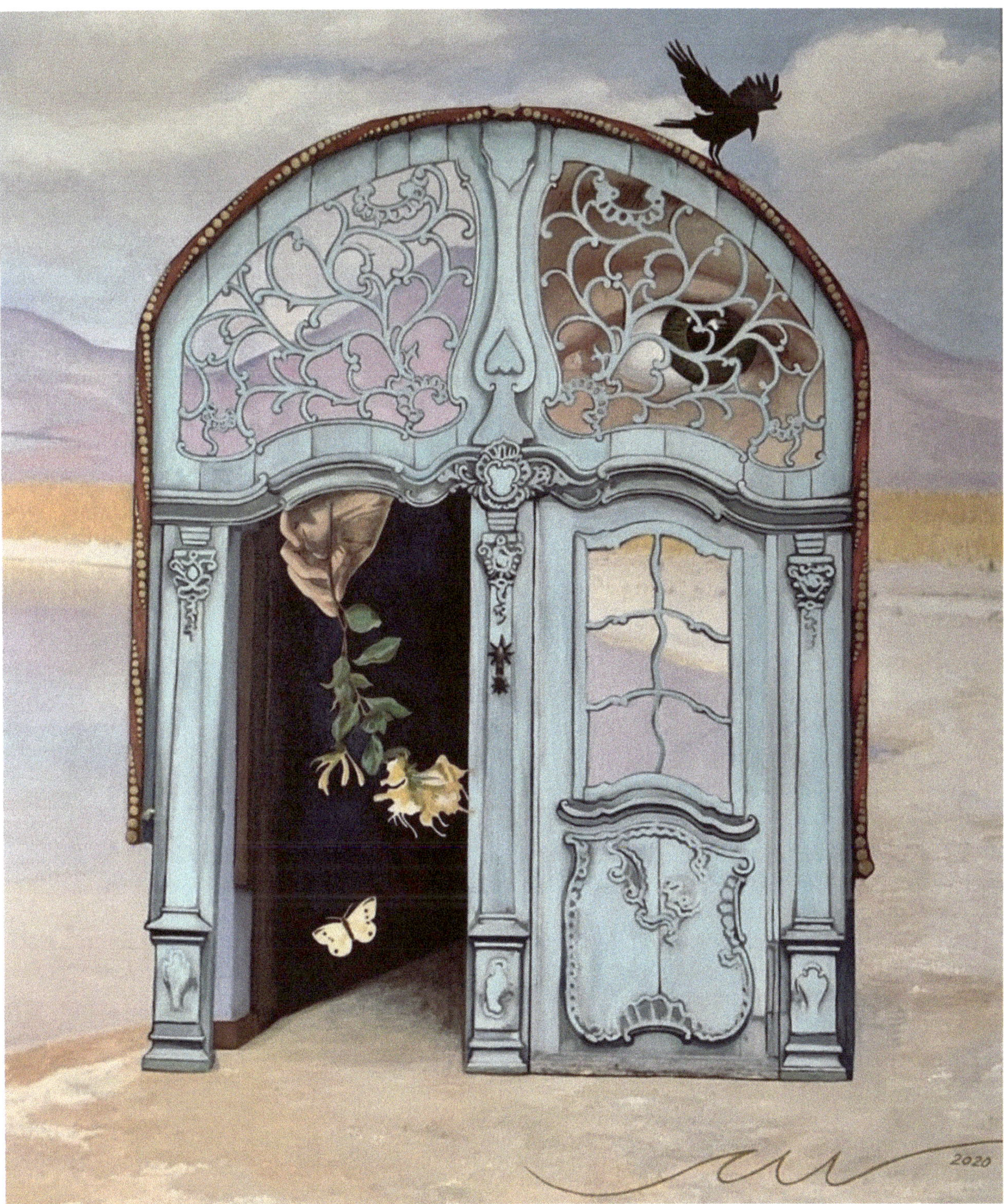

The Intuition, mixed media on canvas, 48x36"

What's one piece of advice you'd give to aspiring artists?

Believe in yourself and your unique voice. If you do so and trust that the universe or God or whatever you believe in has your back, you can achieve wonderful things! Keep that idea and make it yours.

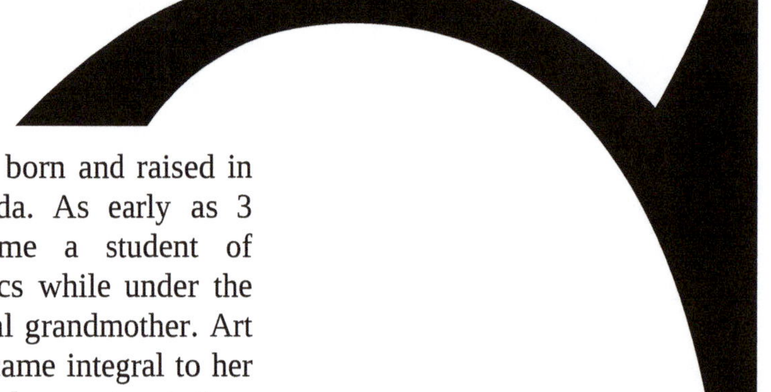

Corinne Forrester was born and raised in Daytona Beach, Florida. As early as 3 years old, she became a student of watercolors and acrylics while under the tutelage of her maternal grandmother. Art and design quickly became integral to her daily bread. Today, when not painting, she's a graphic designer/copywriter, and licensed massage therapist. Artist Statement: It's my goal in life to shine a light on the "other" and underrepresented, to linger on the beauty of "different" until it resonates elsewhere. I've always been greatly influenced by the stories of us—the complexity and simplicity of the human condition and form, femininity, body consciousness, exploration of culture and ethnicity, social constructs, history, nature, spirituality, and my personal experiences as a "tall southern biracial bbw with hair and character as wild as the day is long." My heritage is a huge source of personal pride and curiosity, as are our inner quiet storms, and how we overcome or cope. Nonetheless, these dynamic topics tend to spill over into much of my work. The pieces I'm submitting here are my quiet love songs to all of the aforementioned, but mainly to "different," to pride, to tiredness and joy, to resilience, evolution, resistance, to acceptance and love of self and others.

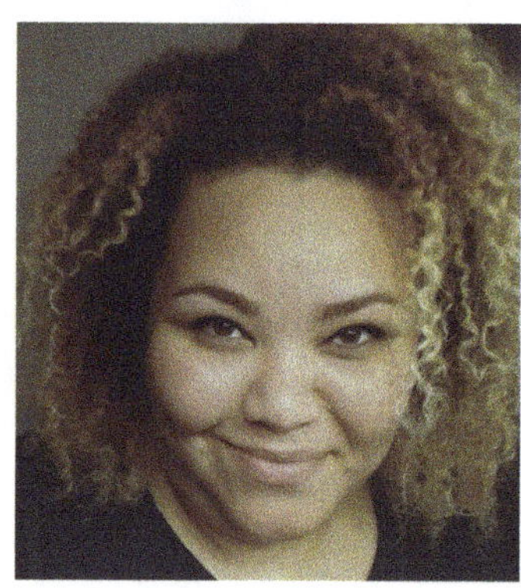

www.lucidbirdgallery.com

lucidbirdinc@gmail.com

@lucidbirdgal

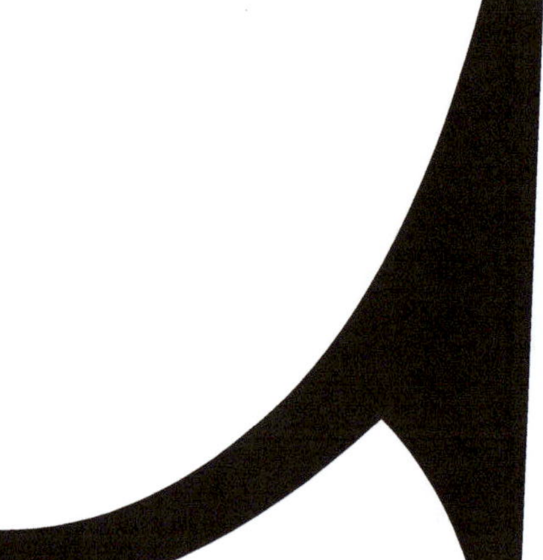

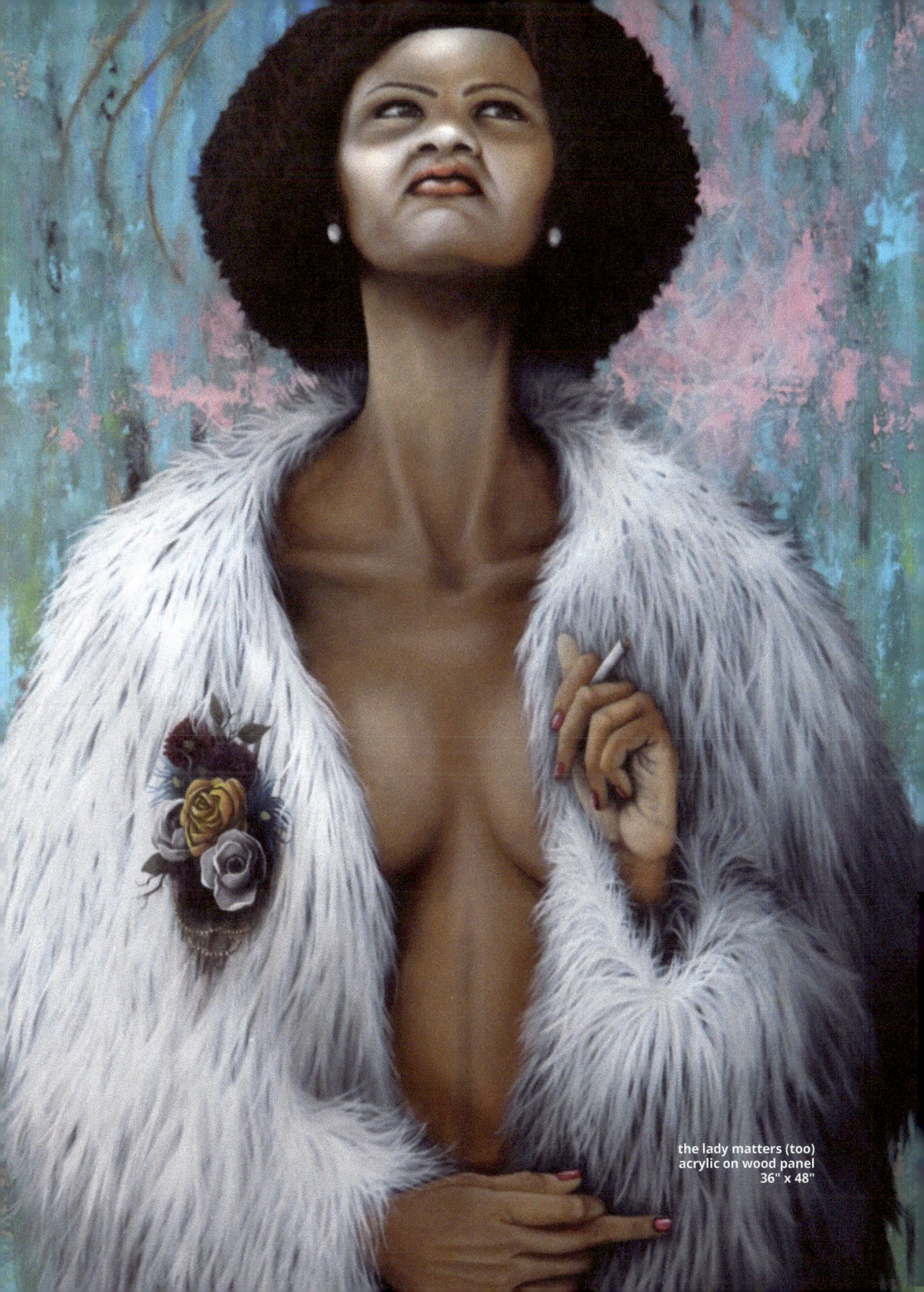

the lady matters (too)
acrylic on wood panel
36" x 48"

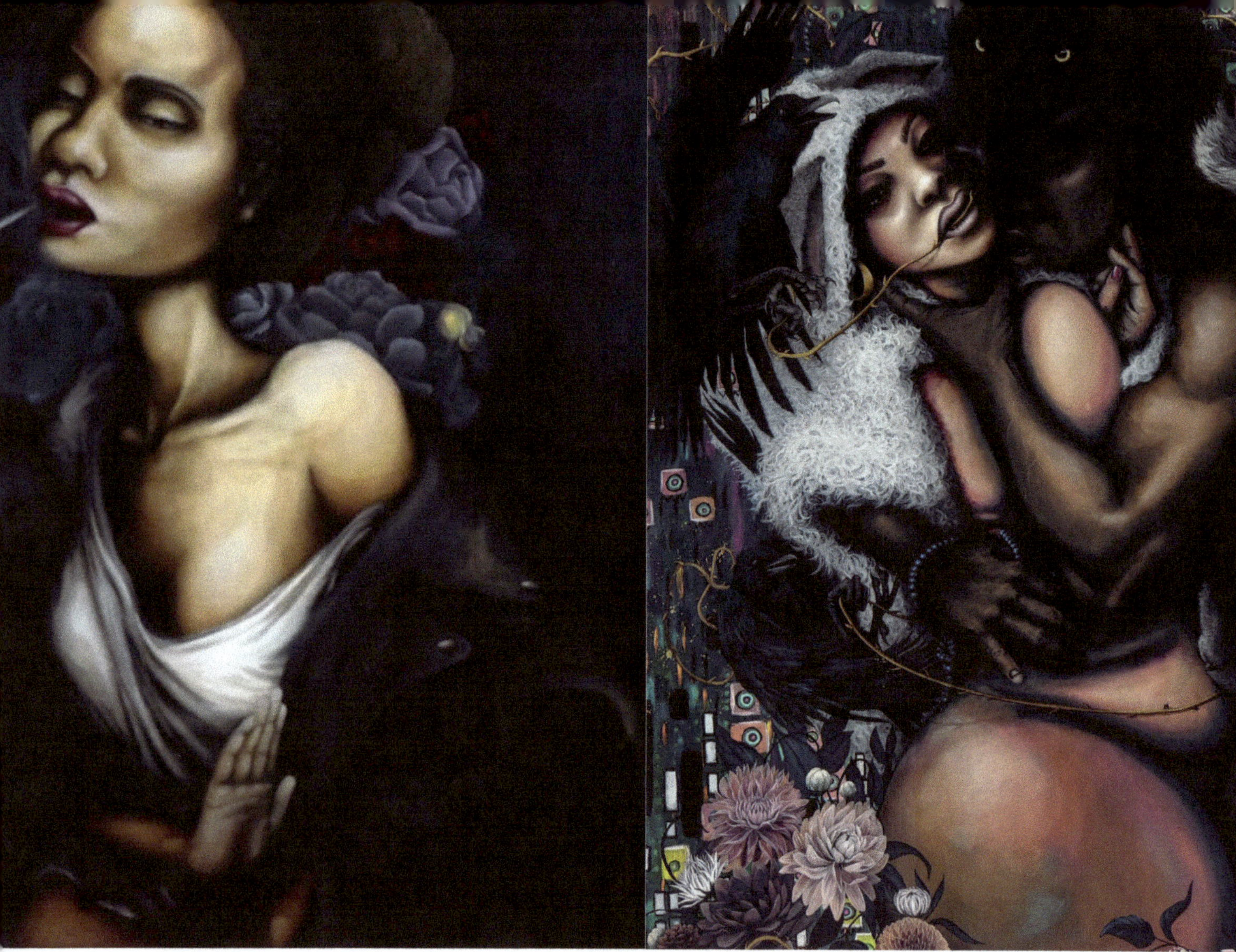

No New Friends, Acrylic on birch panel, 38" x 34"

An Embrace, Acrylic on wood panel, 36" x 48"

How do you cope with the vulnerability of sharing your art with the world?

Deep breaths and affirmations! (And maybe some whiskey, ha!) Dealing with the criticism of viewers is an art in itself. It has taken me years to have faith in myself and my craft. I am still not completely comfortable with certain levels of exposure, but taking baby steps and pushing myself to share more has been worthwhile in the end. I often remind myself of a chance encounter I had with a stranger. During our conversation, we discussed my art and I downplayed it as "nothing special." However, the stranger encouraged me to never sell myself short, that art is important, and to always believe in the value of my work. He reminded me that anything I am passionate about is ordained and that my art could be helping or inspiring others, even if I don't realize it. This conversation has stayed with me ever since.

How do you decide what to charge for your work?

I have a couple of formulas that I like to base prices on (varies based on size, materials, and time), and I divide those into tiers—under $100, $100-$1000, and $1000+. Occasionally, I get a little superstitious and adjust prices to be more auspicious numbers. Don't judge me!

How has your art helped you understand yourself better?

Painting has been therapeutic for me! I have worked through repressed emotions and traversed mountains by simply moving some wet paints around. It's truly amazing! Through the figures and symbolism in my artwork, I have learned to dream and stay encouraged, to see the beauty in the ugly, to love myself unflinchingly, and to believe in my craft and my voice.

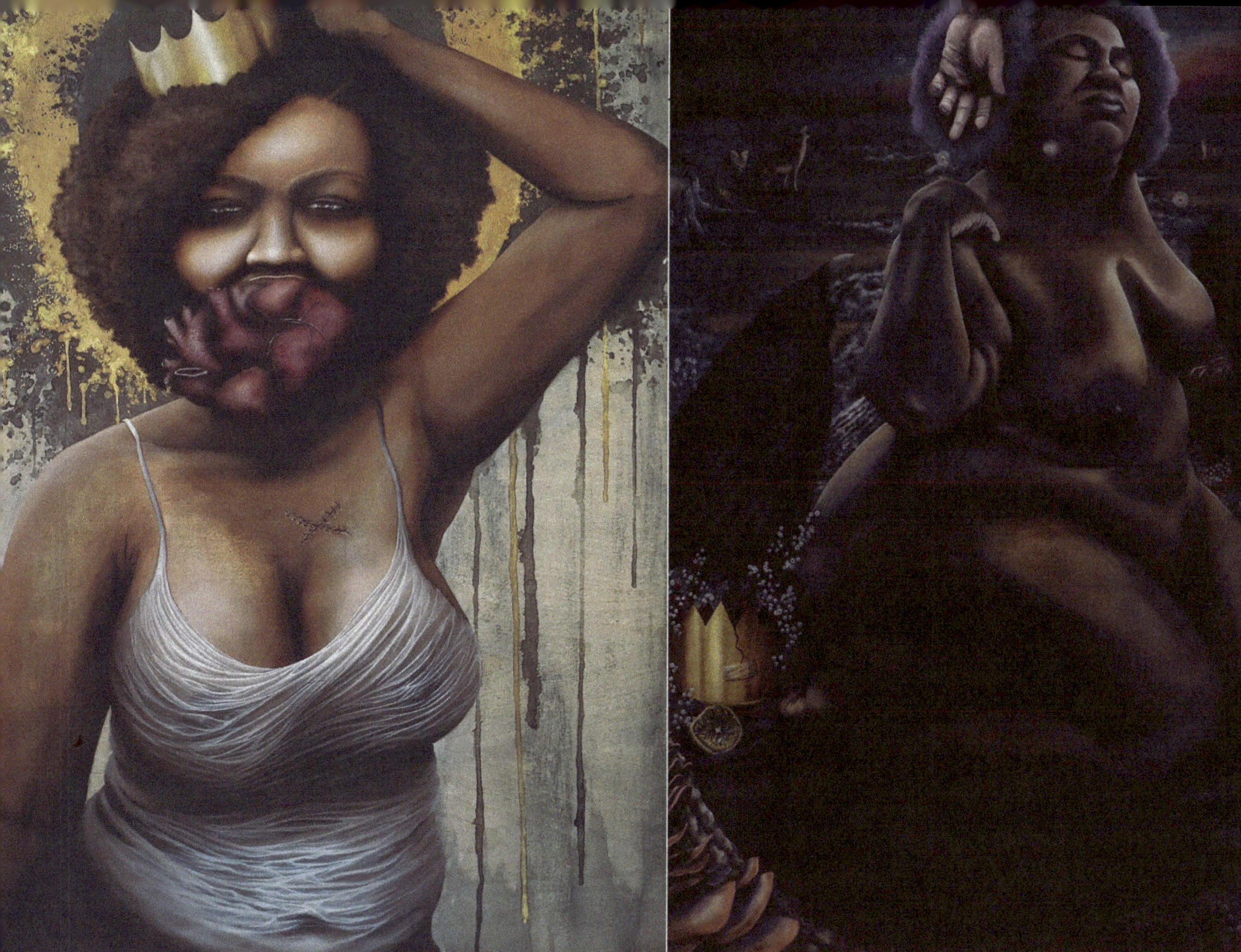

Pacifiher, Acrylic and pigment powders on birch panel, 40" x 30"

Evening Revelry, Acrylic on wood panel, 36" x 48"

Can you share a moment when you felt discouraged as an artist? How did you overcome it?

There have been many times when I faced failures or rejections in my artistic pursuits. However, I have learned to allow myself a few moments to feel the hurt because I am only human. Being an artist can make us feel vulnerable, but I don't let myself get stuck in self-pity mode. Once the initial feelings of disappointment start to fade, I begin to analyze and investigate what went wrong. This helps me reassess my audience and switch to a more objective perspective. Then, I revisit my work and try to apply any constructive feedback given, even if it's just mentally. At the end of the day, I understand that not everyone will love my work, and I'm okay with that. I still find joy in what I do.

What do you want people to take away from your work?

Frankly, if people take away something, anything at all, I am pleased. Art is subjective. So, I'd hope that what sticks in people's minds about my work is how they felt while viewing it, at the very least. I want that feeling or thought to linger a bit.

What's one piece of advice you'd give to aspiring artists?

Don't sweat the haters; there's something out there for everyone. Study the way-makers before you and your peers beside you to figure out what works, but don't try to become them—find your own style (even if it's inspired by someone else's at first), be brave, and make your own way. Most importantly, keep doing whatever it is that brings you joy!

Daniella Queirolo, born in Lima, Peru, Daniella relocated to the USA and achieved summa cum laude honors at The Tyler School of Art in Temple University, Philadelphia. Her subsequent travels across Europe, Asia, and America, coupled with residencies in Buenos Aires, Lisbon, New York, and London, profoundly shaped her artistry. This diverse exposure influenced her multifaceted style, reflecting her deep passion for various art forms, including performance, music, dance, and architecture. Daniella's work has graced numerous publications, and she claimed the "Best Overseas Painter Prize" at the United Kingdom's "Women in Arts Prize" in 2021 (formerly the "Holly Bush Painting Prize"). She has earned finalist positions in various international art contests, including "The British Art Prize." Her art has graced Solo shows, collective showcases, and art fairs in America and Europe. Artist Statement: In my art journey, I blend figurative and abstract elements, uniting the dynamic human form with its surroundings. This fusion combines various styles and materials, aiming to capture the synergy of energy and strength. My work portrays strong and modern women, inspiring and empowering others while celebrating human dignity.

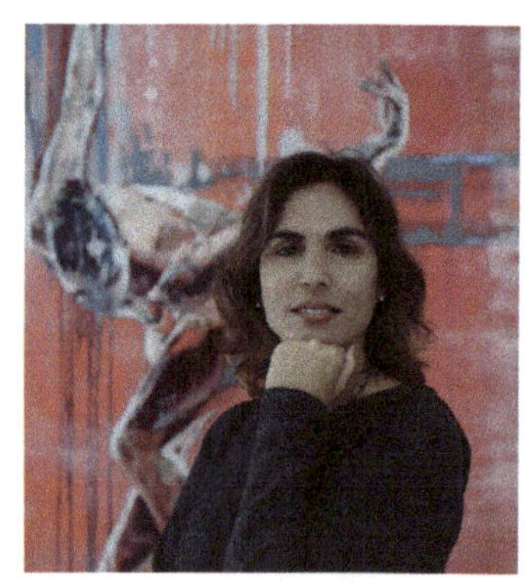

www.daniellaqueiroloart.com

daniellaqueiroloart@gmail.com

@daniella_queirolo_art_

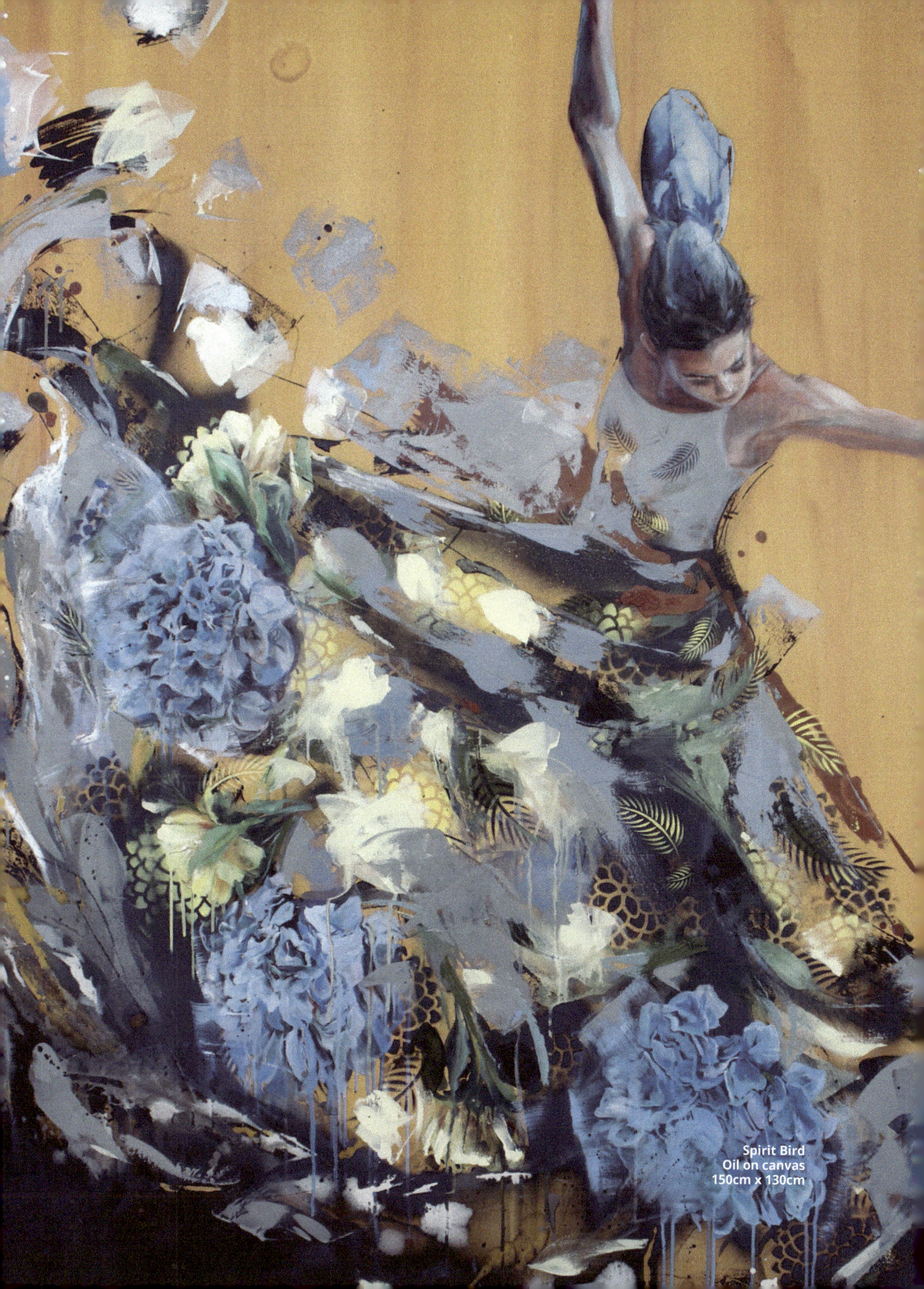
Spirit Bird
Oil on canvas
150cm x 130cm

Butterfly, Oil on canvas, 125cm x 95cm

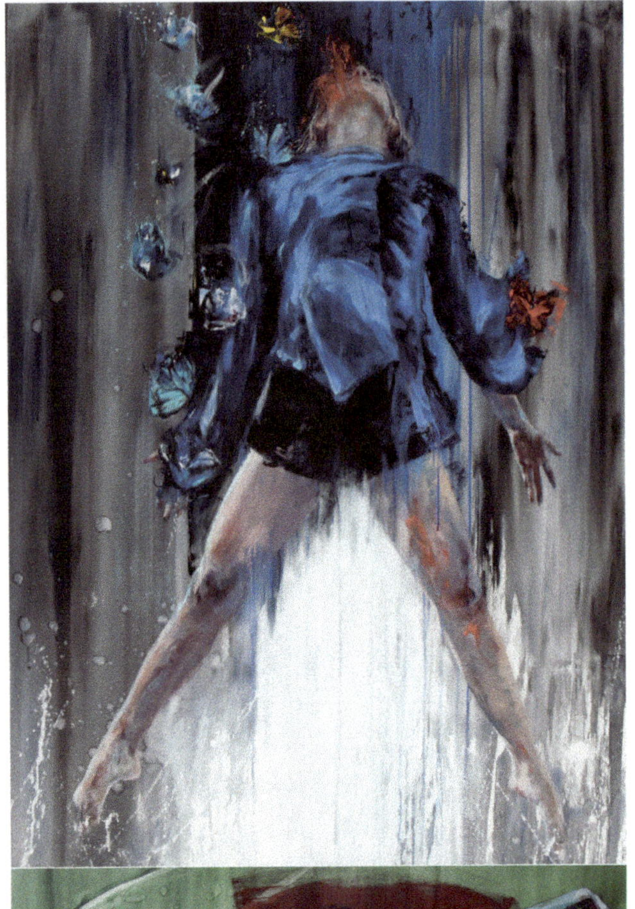

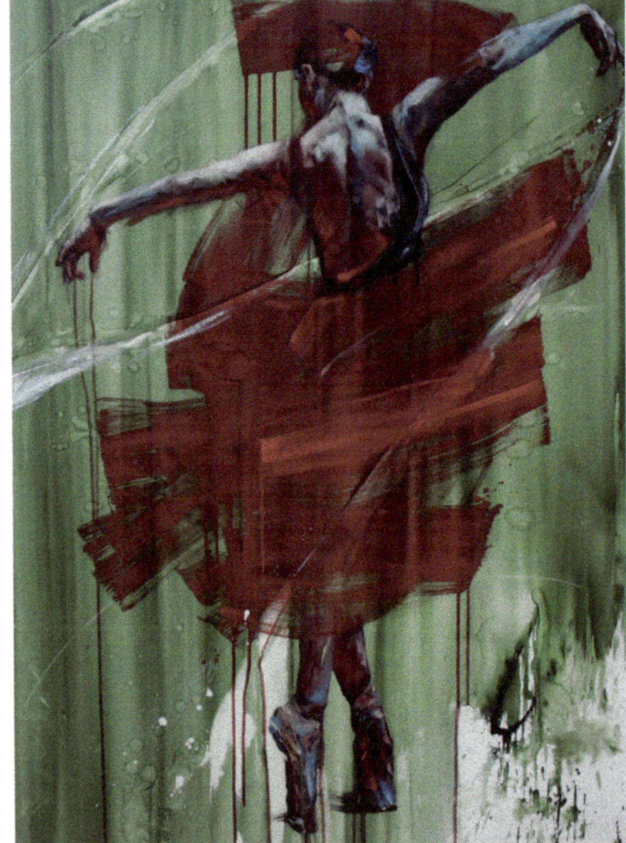

Dancing with Nature, Oil on canvas, 125cm x 95cm

How has your art helped you understand yourself better?

Each piece I create is a discovery. I let the experience of the moment flow spontaneously. It's like a journey into the depths of myself, unearthing things from my subconscious that continue to surprise me.

Can you share a moment when you felt discouraged as an artist? How did you overcome it?

There was a challenging personal moment that kept me away from the canvases, making it tough to start again. Eventually, I realized this event made me stronger, and that strength is now reflected in my paintings depicting brave women initially gathering courage and taking the plunge. That's how my latest collection began.

How do you cope with the vulnerability of sharing your art with the world?

From day one to today, I always feel a degree of vulnerability in sharing such intimate work. However, I believe it's necessary to convey and connect as it involves sharing profound and personal moments. Connecting with followers is crucial in this career, but I don't pressure myself to post too frequently. I prefer to let it flow naturally.

How do you decide what to charge for your work?

Determining my pricing is challenging, especially with diverse clients in Latin America, the USA, Canada, and even more distinct preferences in Europe. Ultimately, I believe it's a matter of responding to demand – when it's evident, that's when it's time to consider adjusting prices.

What do you want people to take away from your work?

I deeply cherish evoking positive emotions through my art, hoping it showcases the best of humanity, especially in challenging times.

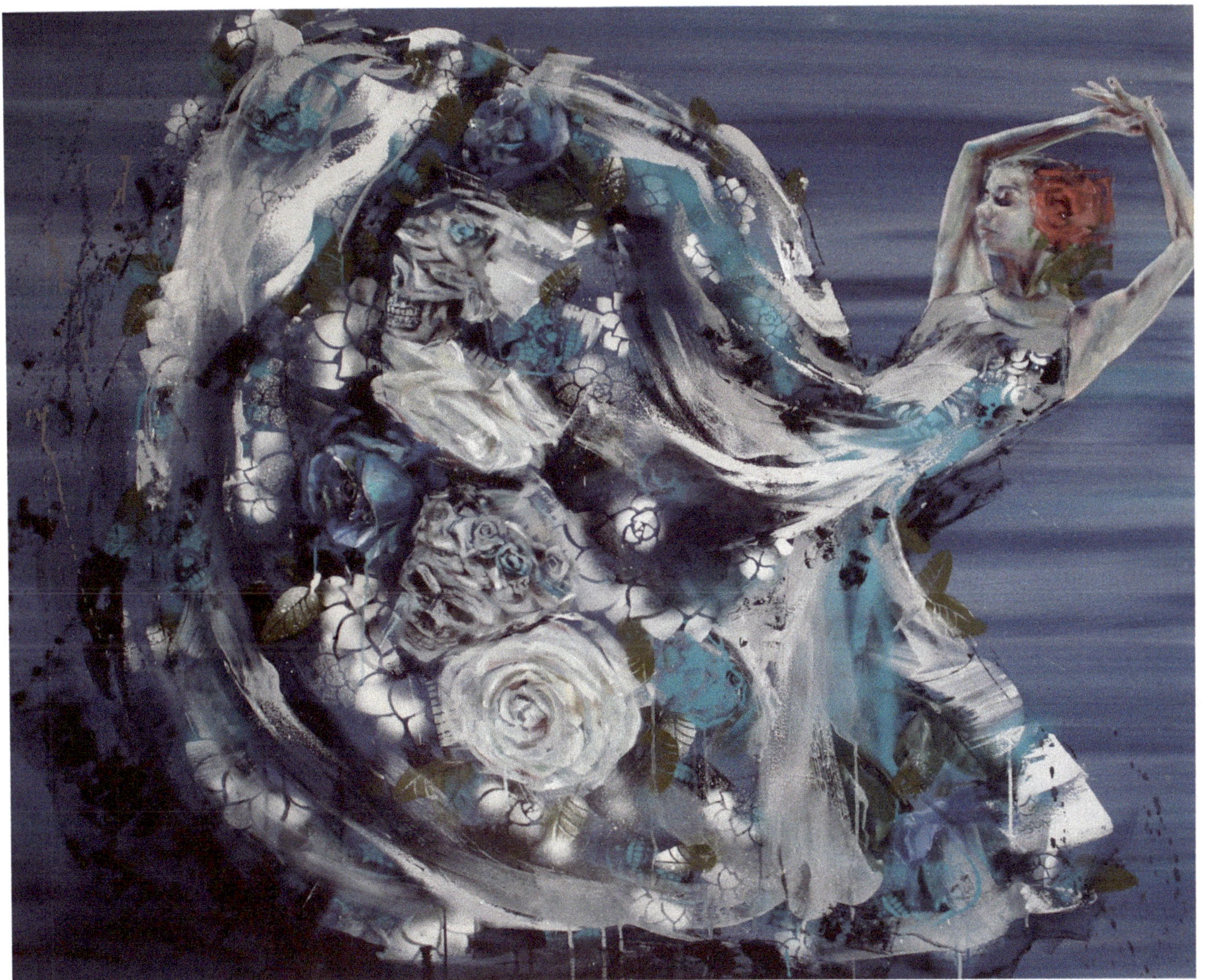

Cycle of Life, 2023, oil on canvas, 150cm x 130cm

What's one piece of advice you'd give to aspiring artists?

Paint as much as you can, concentrate on honing your skills, and discover your distinctive personal style. Opportunities will come your way through hard work.

Dimelza Broche is a Cuban-American artist residing in Jacksonville, Florida. She holds a bachelor's degree from the University of North Florida and a Master's degree from the University of Georgia. Broche has exhibited her work at Manifest Gallery, Marcia Wood Gallery, Era Contemporary Gallery, The Cummer Museum of Arts & Gardens, and at the S. Dillon Ripley Center, Washington, DC. The work of Dimelza Broche consists of drawings and paintings where she explores what the "Self" means to her. From inside her memory palace, she takes us on a journey to the uncharted land of the self and its relationship to the body. She describes and shows her inner feelings about the body as a vessel and that no matter how different it works or might look it is still beautiful in its own way. Artist Statement: In this new body of work, we can see experimentation not only on how the artist is portraying the subject matter but also on how she presents this with her collaged drawings and handmade frames. In this series, I examine the nature of change. The change that my disabled body has been going through as it ages. Even though my disability is not an evident theme in my work, it has definitely influenced the way I create these scenes inside my memory palace.

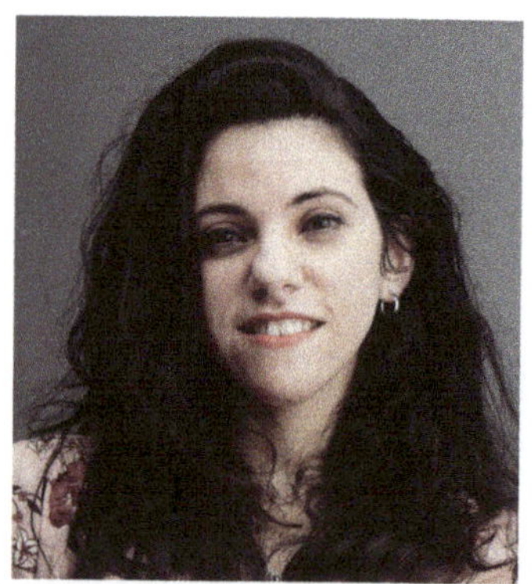

https://dimelzabroche.com
dimelzabroche@gmail.com
@dimelzabrocheart_

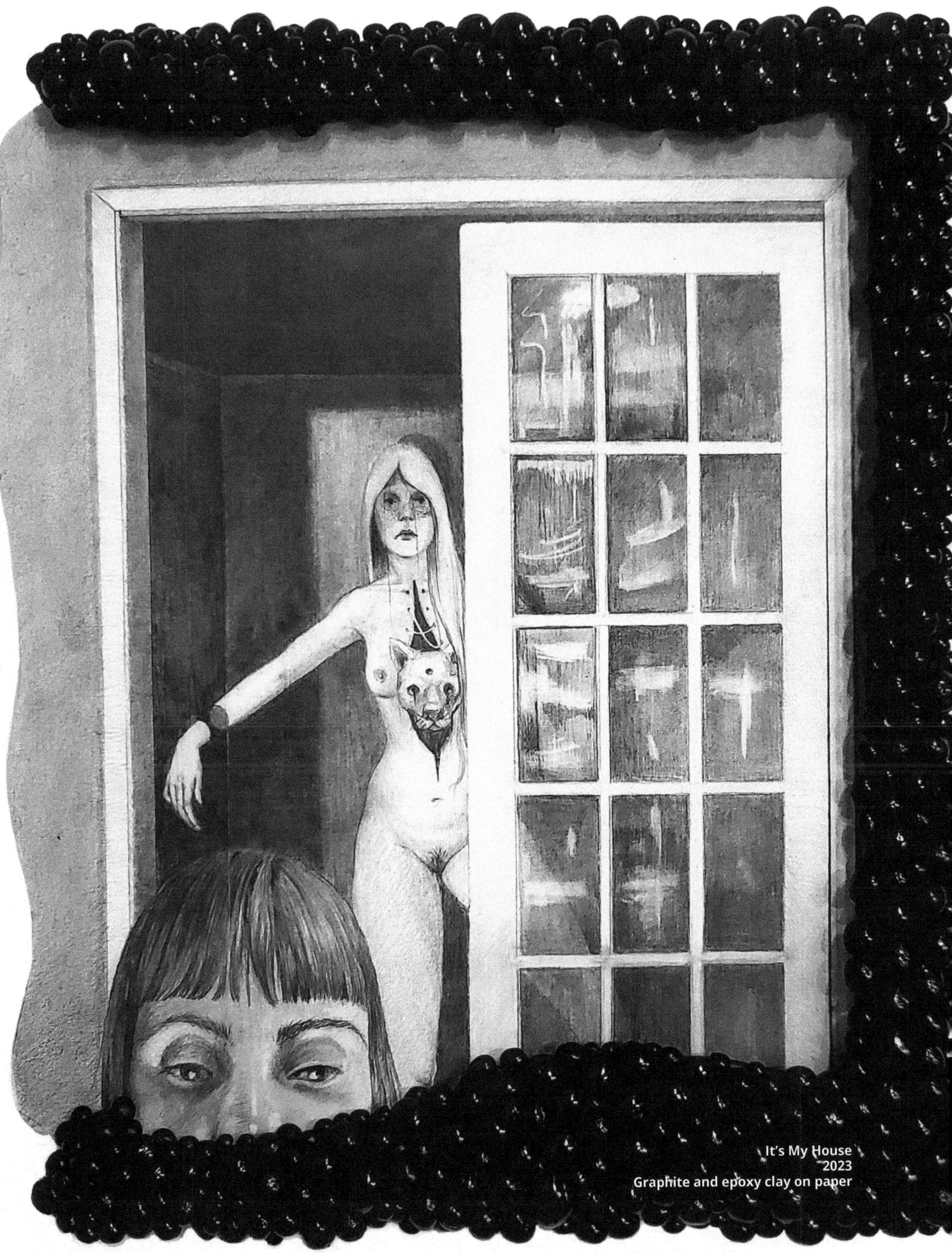

It's My House
2023
Graphite and epoxy clay on paper

How do you cope with the vulnerability of sharing your art with the world?

I think once I realized that there will always be someone out there who can relate on a personal level to my art, I was not afraid anymore to share part of myself through it. It is incredibly liberating to know that some viewers will see my work and connect to the scene unfolding in the same way I felt connected while making it. That helps so much when putting my art out there for everyone to appreciate, judge, love, or hate.

Can you share a moment when you felt discouraged as an artist? How did you overcome it?

When I have applied to different opportunities and most of them come back as rejections. I just continue making art. I am always trying to improve my art and learn as much as possible about whatever idea or theme I'm trying to paint or draw.

How do you decide what to charge for your work?

It depends on the materials, time spent creating the work, my years of experience as an artist, and the percentage the gallery will take for selling my work at their space.

The Uncharted Self, 2023, graphite and fiber on paper, 29"x 18"

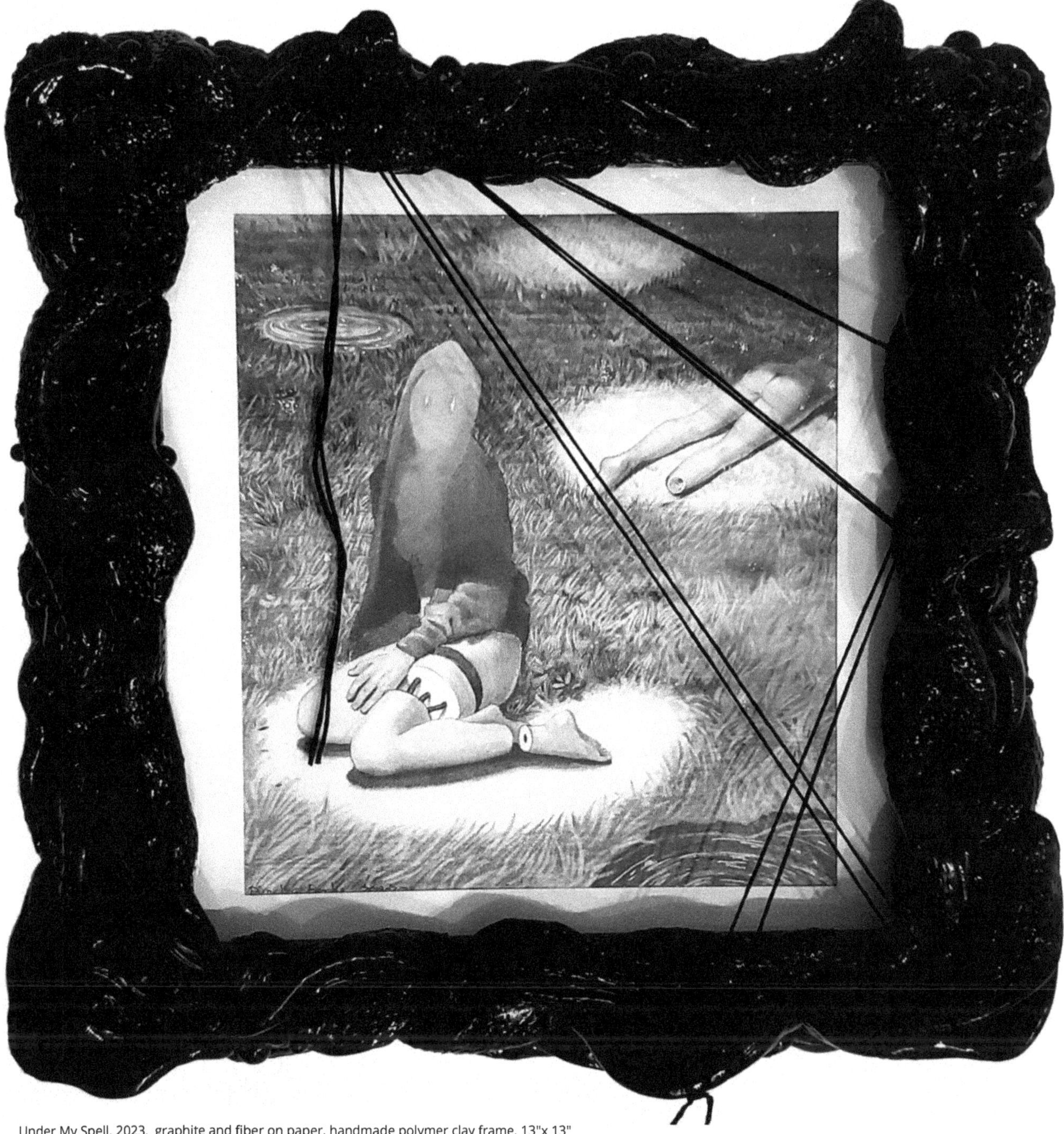

Under My Spell, 2023, graphite and fiber on paper, handmade polymer clay frame, 13"x 13"

How has your art helped you understand yourself better?

Since my art is deeply personal and I have painted my experiences through the years, it has helped me to accept myself and love who I am. I have learned to appreciate my disabled body and disabled experience while navigating a world that is not as accessible as it should be.

What's one piece of advice you'd give to aspiring artists?

Create as much as possible, and learn from each artwork you create.

What do you want people to take away from your work?

That we are in a constant state of change and that it is ok to feel all sorts of emotions while this happens. My art is about the embodiment of the experience represented in a surrealistic way. I do not paint or draw the experience as it happened but rather as it was felt.

Elisabeth Handelsby (b.1982) grew up on an island on the southeast coast of Norway. The closeness to nature and the ocean which she grew up with is something that is still reflected in her work. She is a graduate from the Norwegian School of Creative Studies, and Oslo and Akershus University College. Her work has been shown in several group and solo exhibitions, in Norway and abroad. She currently lives and works in Oslo. Artist Statement: I work with figurative paintings in oil and mixed media. My painting process starts with a photographic reference, but is very intuitive and brings the painting through several color phases. It is a constant back and forth of building up and breaking down, where all of the layers are important to create life for the finished result. Contrasts are important to me, and I often try to make the images balance between the beautiful and the unsettling, delicate and brutal at one time. The motifs circle around topics such as the human situation and our relationship with the world around us. Our relationship with nature has become a common thread in recent years. I look at my work as small glimpses of stories, where the viewer can form their own whole.

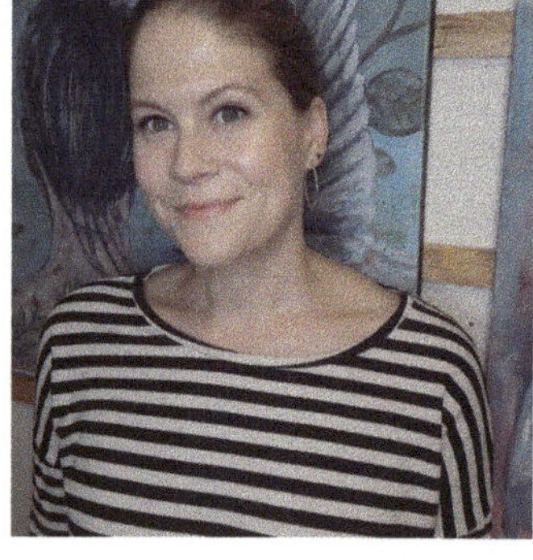

www.elisabethhandelsby.com

ehandelsby82@gmail.com

@elisabethhandelsby

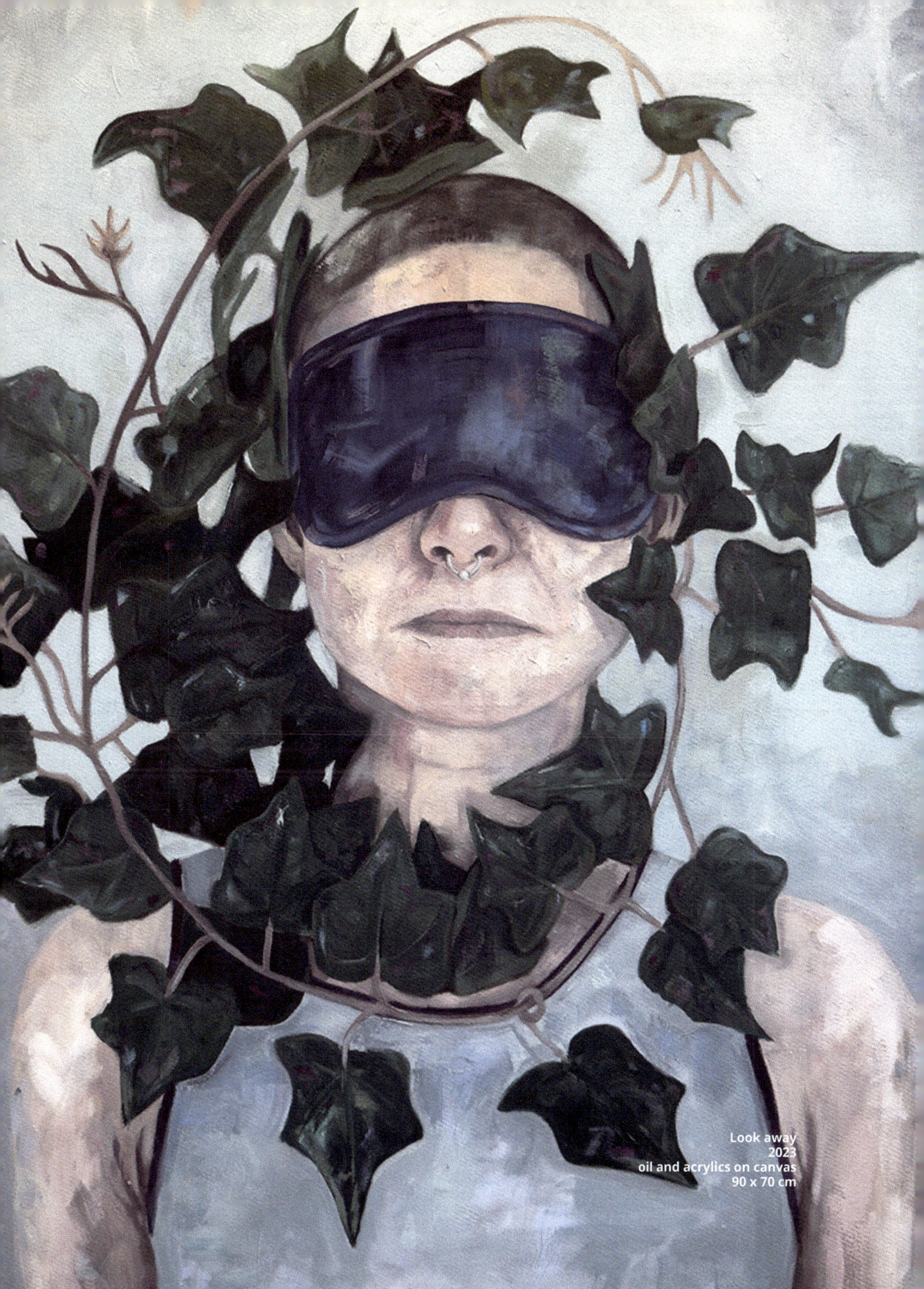
Look away
2023
oil and acrylics on canvas
90 x 70 cm

Can you share a moment when you felt discouraged as an artist? How did you overcome it?

From a young age I fell into the idea that being an artist is not a sustainable way of living, and as a result of that I spent many years trying not to be an artist. But I always knew that art and creativity needed to be a part of my life, so I sought education that was art related but that I thought would make my life easier than going the full artist route, first as an illustrator, then as an art teacher. I found out that I needed to express my own ideas more than what I could working with illustration. And after teaching almost full time in elementary school for a few years, I found that I needed to give my own art practice more space in my life. I did learn a lot from both of those experiences, and it has absolutely shaped me as an artist. But I needed to get over the starving artist myth for myself, and really give it a go.

How do you cope with the vulnerability of sharing your art with the world?

I think that is one of those things that comes with experience. When you keep making art, and putting it out there it gets less scary over time.

How has your art helped you understand yourself better?

I don't really see my art making as an inward journey. But I guess you can say that working with art always is somehow to work on yourself, even when you work on ideas and concepts that are rooted in something outside of you. Through painting I explore ideas that resonate with me, and ruminate on them throughout the process. You are always exploring ideas that are interesting to you, that somehow speak to you, and therefore you also learn about yourself, and how you see things. The process itself.

Last child in the woods, Acrylic and oil on canvas, 90 x 90 cm

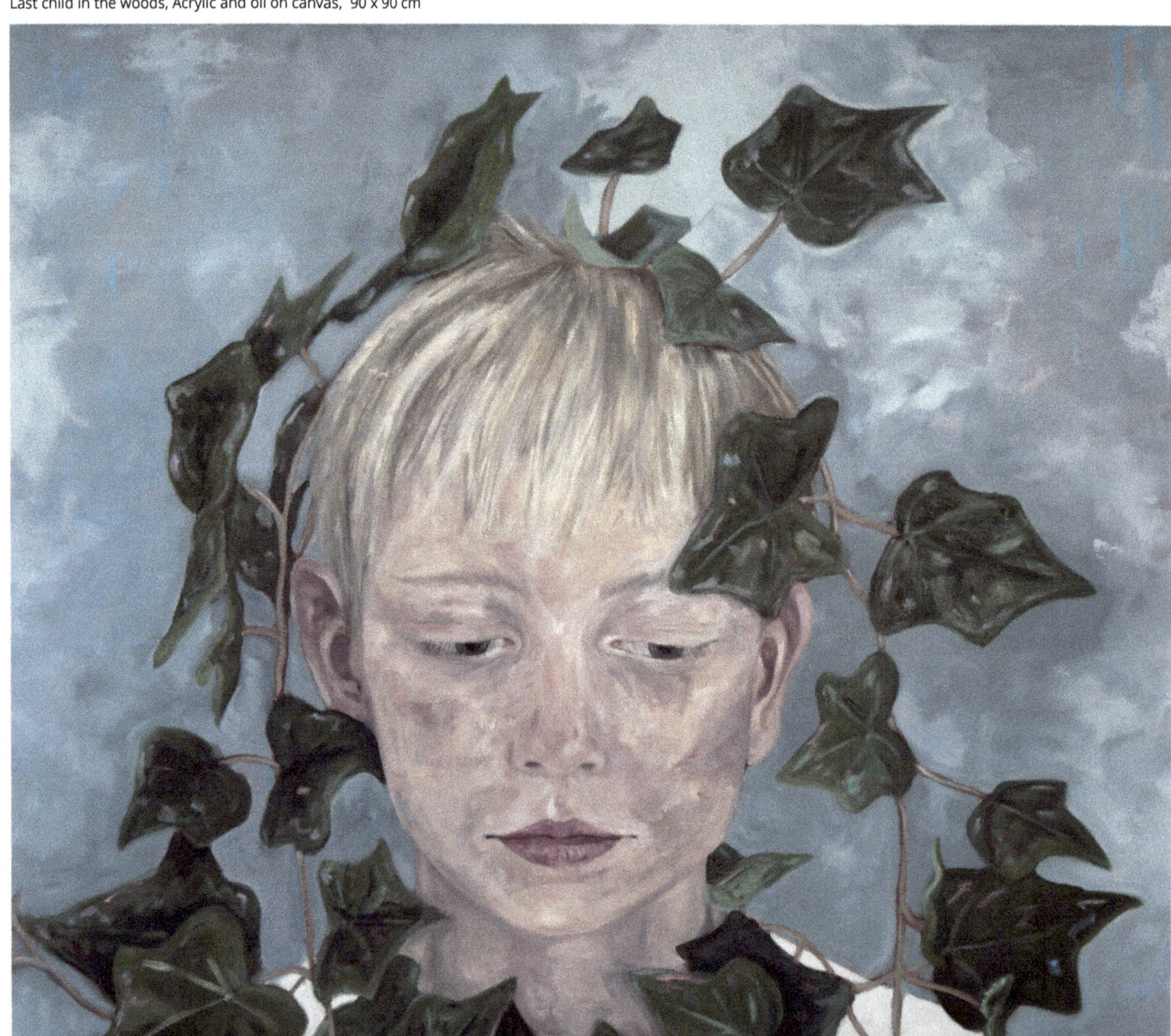

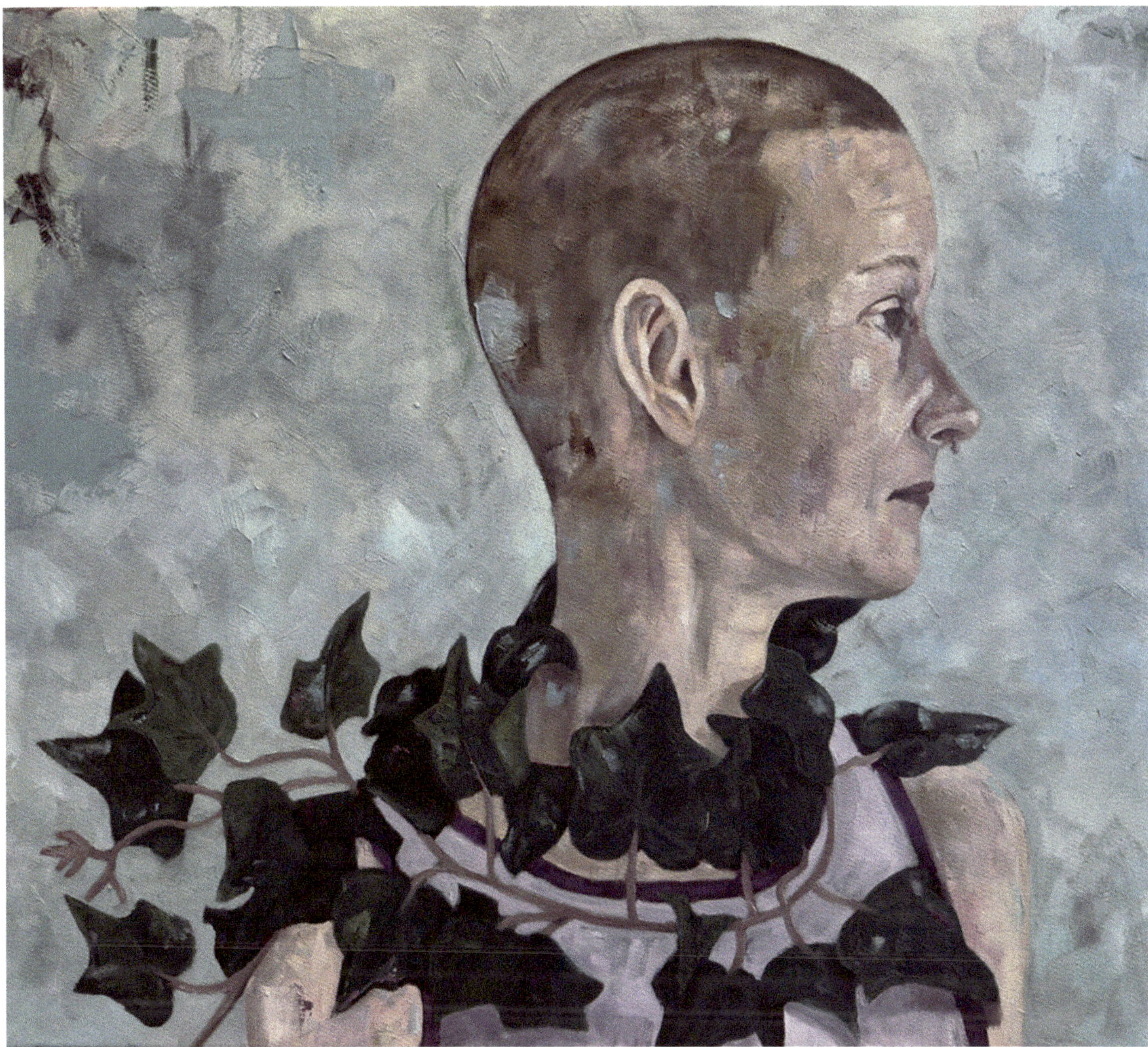

Untitled, 2023, oil and acrylics on canvas, 60 x 70 cm

requires flexibility and patience, so that is also something I am constantly learning about.

What do you want people to take away from your work?

I know from experience that people see very different things in my paintings. And I find that to be a good thing. I don't want to serve the viewer with an answer, but rather something that can make them think or wonder. I have my ideas and concepts when I make them, but people meet them with their own experiences and ideas and make their own narratives. I think whenever people have some reaction, and feel something when they see my art I feel like I have succeeded.

How do you decide what to charge for your work?

I price my work by size. It is the only way to keep it consistent as the time put in varies from piece to piece, and is also hard to measure as I always have many pieces going at once.

What's one piece of advice you'd give to aspiring artists?

It is important to find a community. Being an artist can sometimes be lonely, and finding people who can relate to the kinds of things you are going through and the challenges you meet is very helpful. And also, be sure you enjoy the process! Experiment, and work with subjects and material that really excite you!

Freeda Kingelin, an emerging artist of Scandinavian and Kashmiri heritage, paints under the pseudonym Spiraliens. She utilizes her mediums to convey the interplay of diverse cultures through color, contrasts, and the palpable energy she feels. This emotion is drawn from childhood memories and a multicultural upbringing, vividly brought to life on her canvas. Her paintings serve as a personal call to use art as a means to bridge opposing worlds and bring the energy of unity amid duality in our world. "Echoing an upbringing with parents from wildly opposite cultures, I paint to explore energy and connection through the interplay of culture and contrast – I paint to bridge the worlds of differing ideologies and to communicate joy and unity through shapes and color". What sets Freeda´s art apart is its universal resonance intertwined with cultural significance. Raised in a family where cultural and religious values collided, she grew up in a tapestry of Kashmiri and Scandinavian influences. The interplay of these two different worlds became the foundation of her artistic exploration. By embracing the richness in Kashmiri colors and simplicity in Scandinavian design, Freeda merges these seemingly opposing aesthetics to create art that resonates across boundaries. She believes a balance can be found by using color and shape to unite opposing forces, and she hopes her art evokes emotions and a connection in her viewers, independent of religion, culture or borders.

www.spiraliens.com

info@spiraliens.com

@spiraliens

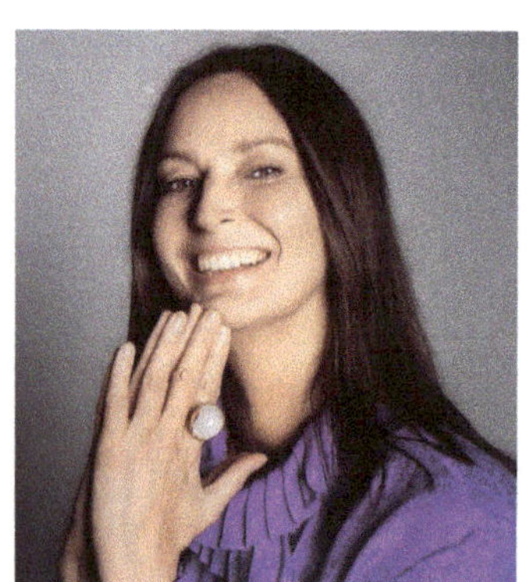

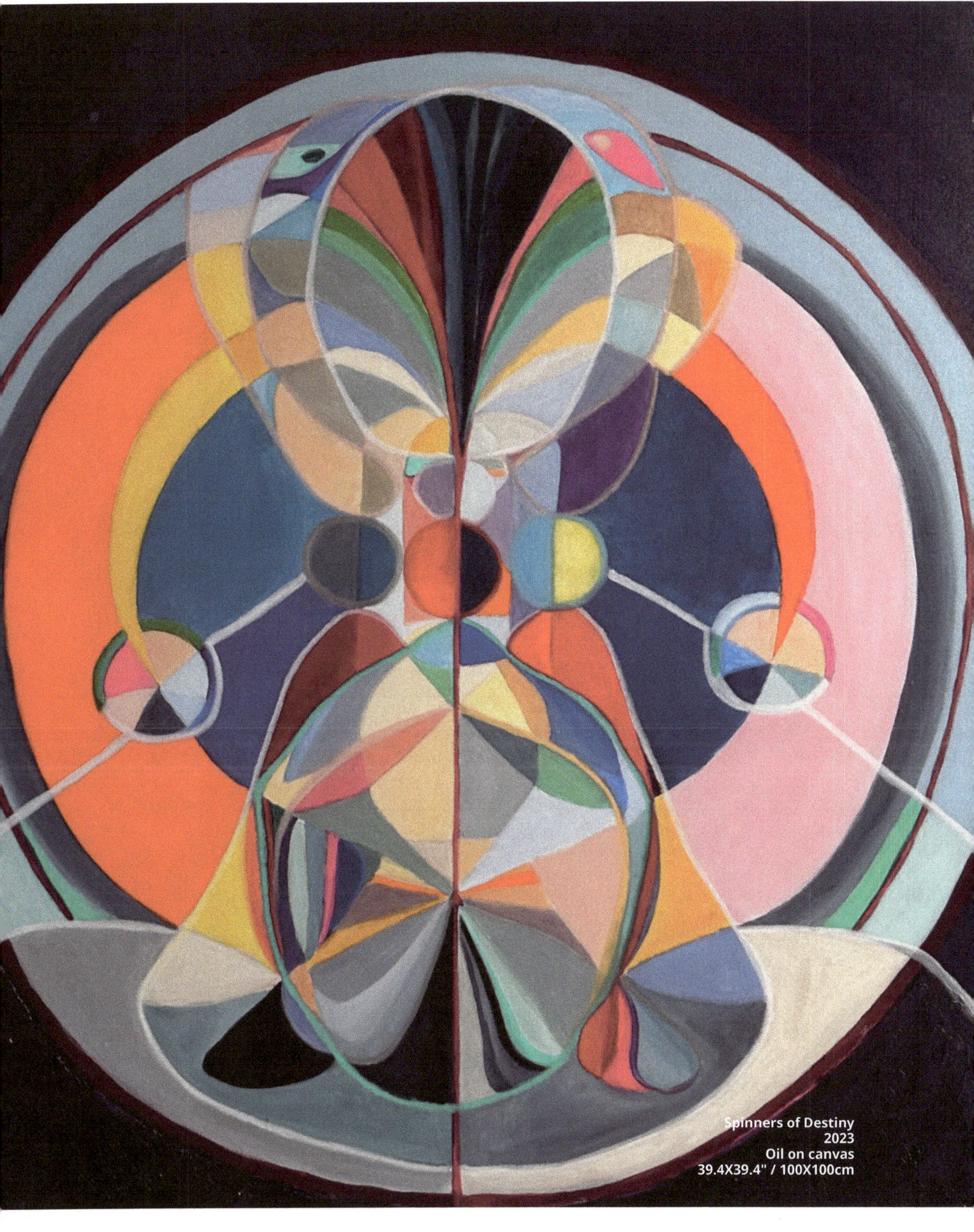
Spinners of Destiny
2023
Oil on canvas
39.4X39.4" / 100X100cm

C an you share a moment when you felt discouraged as an artist? How did you overcome it?

There have been moments where I feel disconnected from myself and my art and feel a total uselessness and dissatisfaction with my work. That annoying inner voice discourages me, labels me as a terrible painter lacking talent and skills. Having journeyed many dark tunnels in life, I know the dangers of unhealthy coping mechanisms. Fortunately, I've learned to cherish my body and health, and I steer to more positive outlets like exercising, being in nature, or booking a trip to observe people or culture. I get inspired by taking lots of photos. These help shift me into a better mental space and serve as a reset - I return to my studio reinvigorated, back in the flow with both myself and my art.

How do you cope with the vulnerability of sharing your art with the world?

'Vulnerability' is significant in my creative process; I pour my soul into my art for people to see the bridge between opposites - to feel the connection. If you feel alienated by my art, then it underlines a point I want to make, that art transcends surface comfort, there's more…to 'try to see with your heart'. I do grapple with insecurities. If someone dislikes my work, I can feel disliked personally. Wrestling with having my voice heard amidst the cacophony of others, I felt like an outsider ever since childhood, always looking for a way 'in'. For me, that way in is through my art. When faced with art criticism, I can feel alienated all over again. "Yes, it puts me in a vulnerable position, but it's one I consciously choose to share. Through vulnerability I create art, and for me art is freedom. I'm sharing the power of freedom."

How has your art helped you understand yourself better?

My art has been key to understanding my voice. I'm not a loud person, and when I speak, I often feel under-heard – a sentiment rooted in childhood. My life is marked by emotionally charged situations, spanning religious, cultural, socioeconomic, and

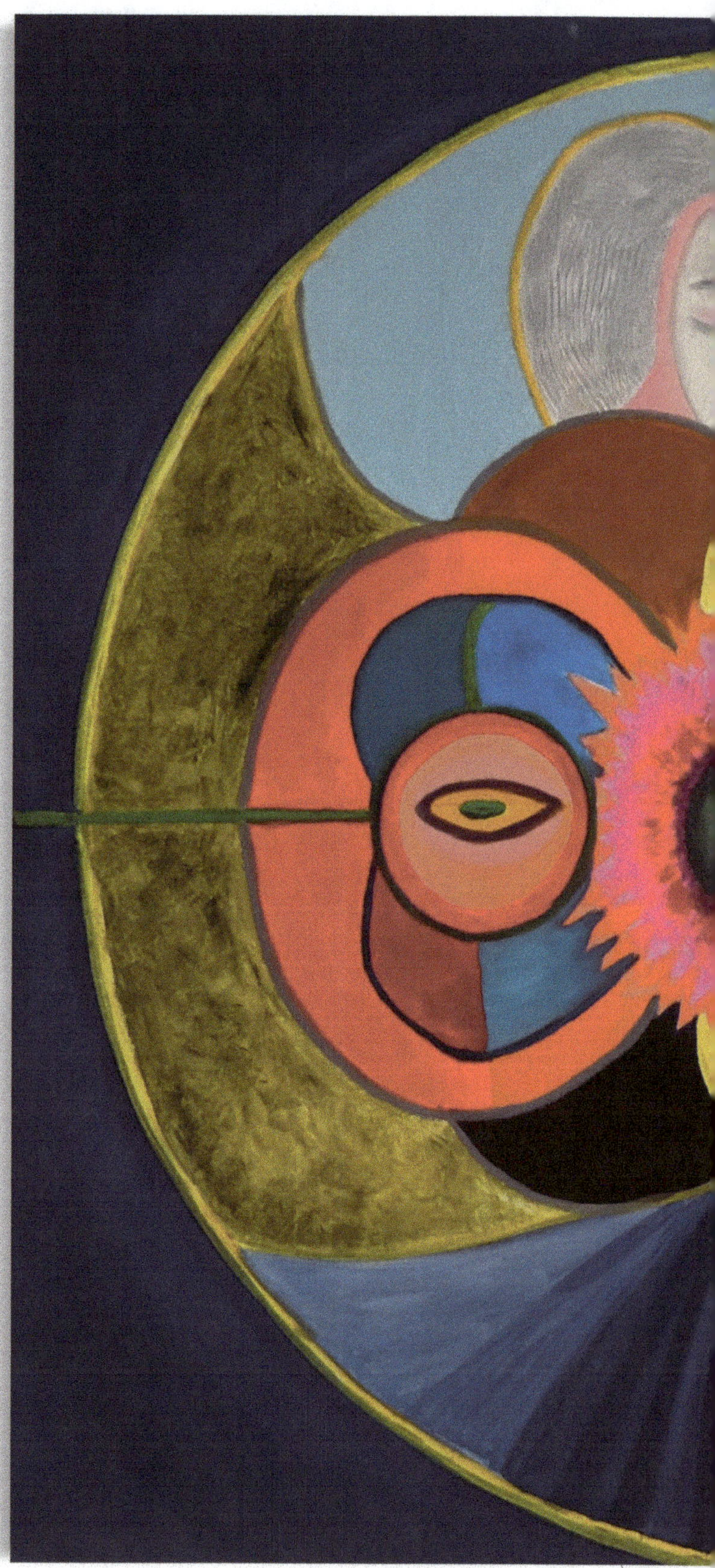

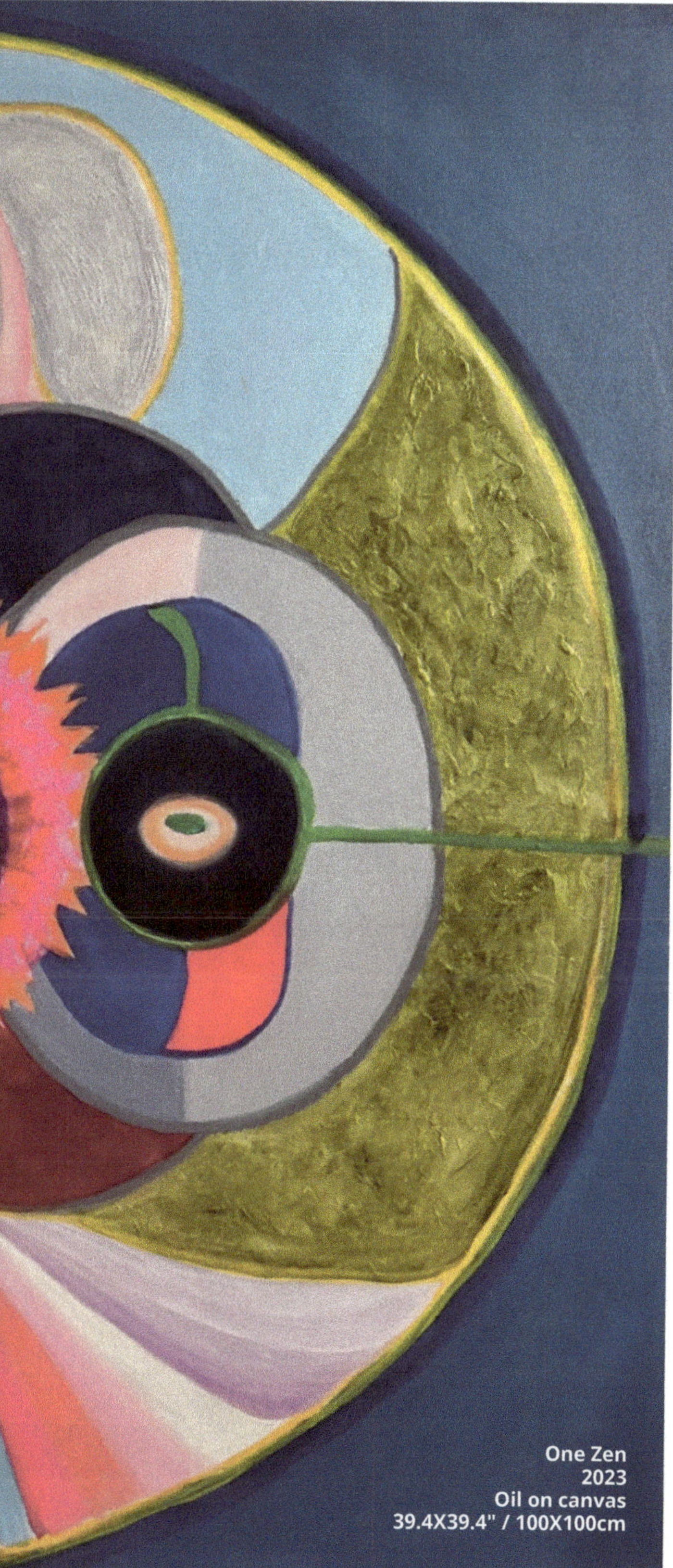

One Zen
2023
Oil on canvas
39.4X39.4" / 100X100cm

psychological conflicts. I have moved to many countries, experienced divorces, clinical depression, witnessed family kidnappings, torn myself down and built myself up again. These dramatic experiences have allowed me to live on both sides of the same coin. This 'both sides' dynamic serves as the force and voice in my art. When I paint, I relive the emotions and energy that are in that 'space between duality'.

How do you decide what to charge for your work?

Deciding what to charge for my work is a common struggle among artists, and I'm no exception. The challenge intensifies when a client deeply connects with one of my pieces, as it signals that my art has found its ideal home. Recognizing that the energy of my art resonates with the client's needs creates a serendipitous match. However, it's disheartening if they are unable to afford my work. In such cases, I'm often open to finding a solution, whether through a payment plan or another trustworthy agreement.

What do you want people to take away from your work?

I would love if my art can awaken people's hearts and remind them that we are all connected - also through the universal language of color and emotions that art can convey. The pseudonym 'Spiraliens', my art brand, reflects this intent: the 'spiral' in the word represents energy flow and its embodiment of balance and harmony, and the 'aliens' speaks of my desire to remind people not to 'ALIEN'ate themselves from each other because of differences, but to connect across cultures, borders and even across unseen realms. Isn't it funny how in actual an alien in the U.S is any individual who is not a U.S. citizen, and in other countries an alien is someone without a valid travel document? Now that's food for thought.

What's one piece of advice you'd give to aspiring artists?

One piece of advice I'd offer to aspiring artists is to embrace the journey of self-discovery through your art. The philosopher Nietzsche said, 'One must still have chaos in oneself to be able to give birth to a dancing star'.

Hana Sebelova works explore the human form as a source of profound emotional and psychological expression. Artist Statement: Through my art I aim to capture the complexities of the human experience, revealing the inner thoughts, feelings and stories that lie beneath the surface. Each piece is a réflexion of the unique and universal aspects of the human condition, inviting viewers to contemplate the narratives within each figure. My hope is that my art connects with the observer on a visceral level, evoking empathy, introspection, and a deeper understanding of our shared humanity.

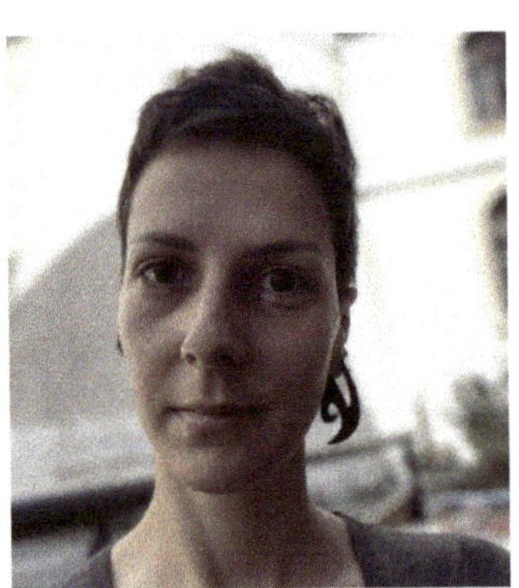

https://hanasebel.com

hanasebel@gmail.com

@hana_sebel_arty

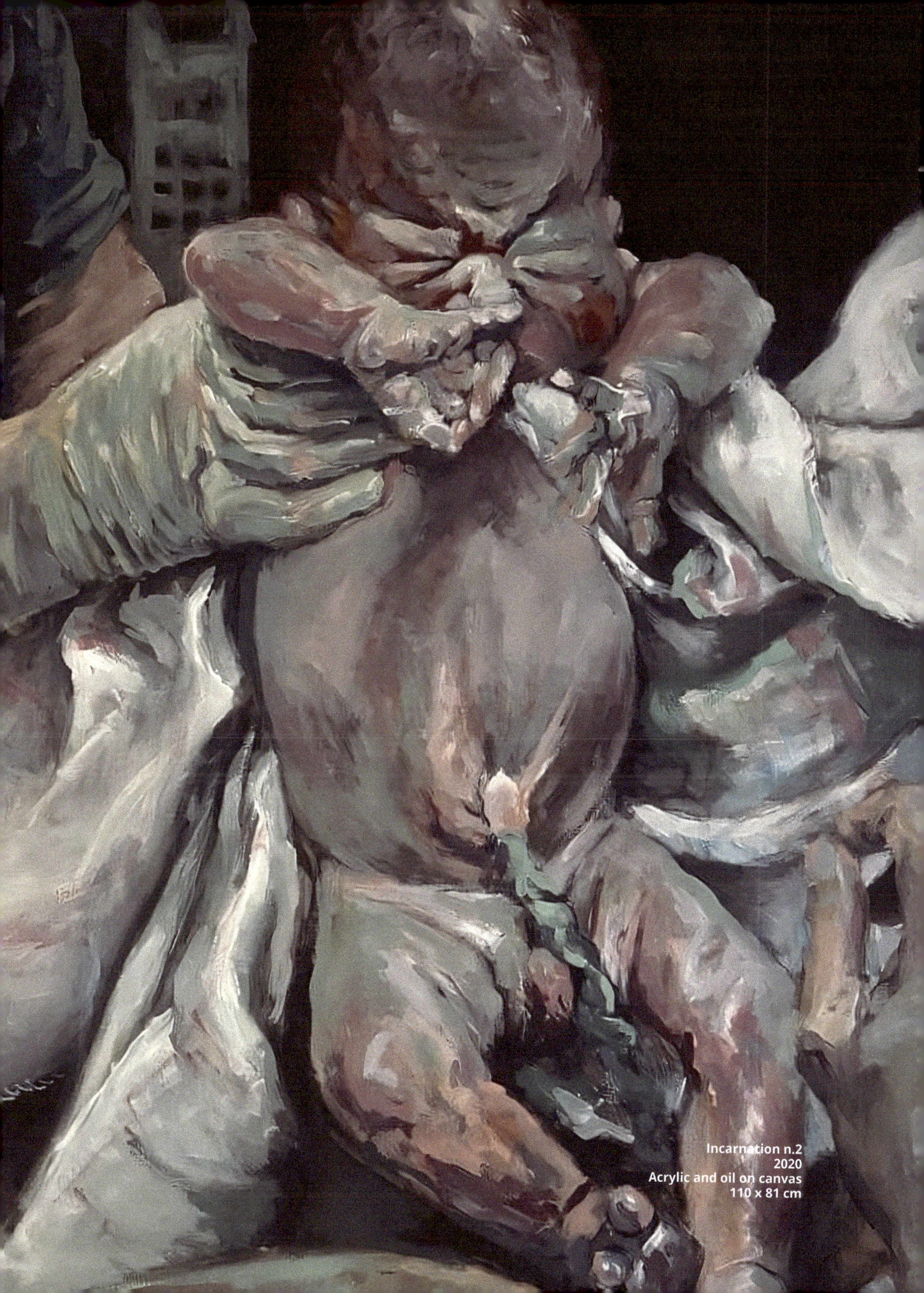

Incarnation n.2
2020
Acrylic and oil on canvas
110 x 81 cm

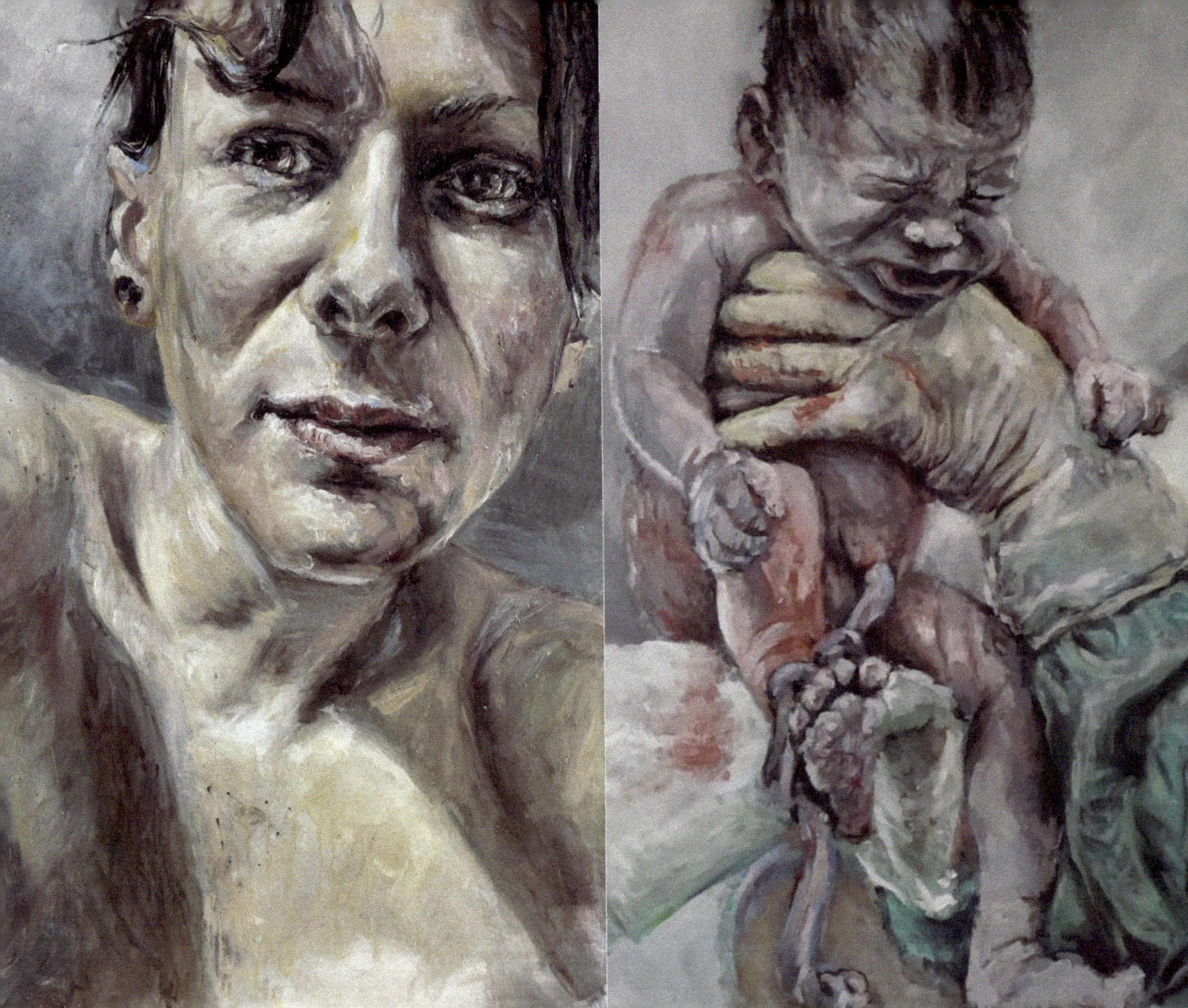

Self portrait after shower, Oil painting on cardboard, 74 x 52 cm

Incarnation n.3, 2019, Acrylic and oil on canvas, 110 x 81 cm

How do you cope with the vulnerability of sharing your art with the world?

I don't have any strategy in particular regarding this issue. By nature I'm very sharing person, and from my experience, it can be a great opener to others' hearts too.

What do you want people to take away from your work?

My hope is to make the observers connect with my art on very deep, almost visceral level, evoking empathy in them and possibly some introspection and deeper understanding of our shared humanity. Probably I want to make all the world kind of hypersensitive :) hahaha

How has your art helped you understand yourself better?

This is something that can be hardly described in words. Recently I've just learned about myself that I'm a hypersensitive person (that we are sure many among artists), and therefore my art helps me with the output of my emotions. It can be as simple as that. But there are also many subconscious processes which are running in my interior, particularly during portrait painting. I think it works like a mirror, we watch others, empathize and learn about the emotions in ourselves or in others.

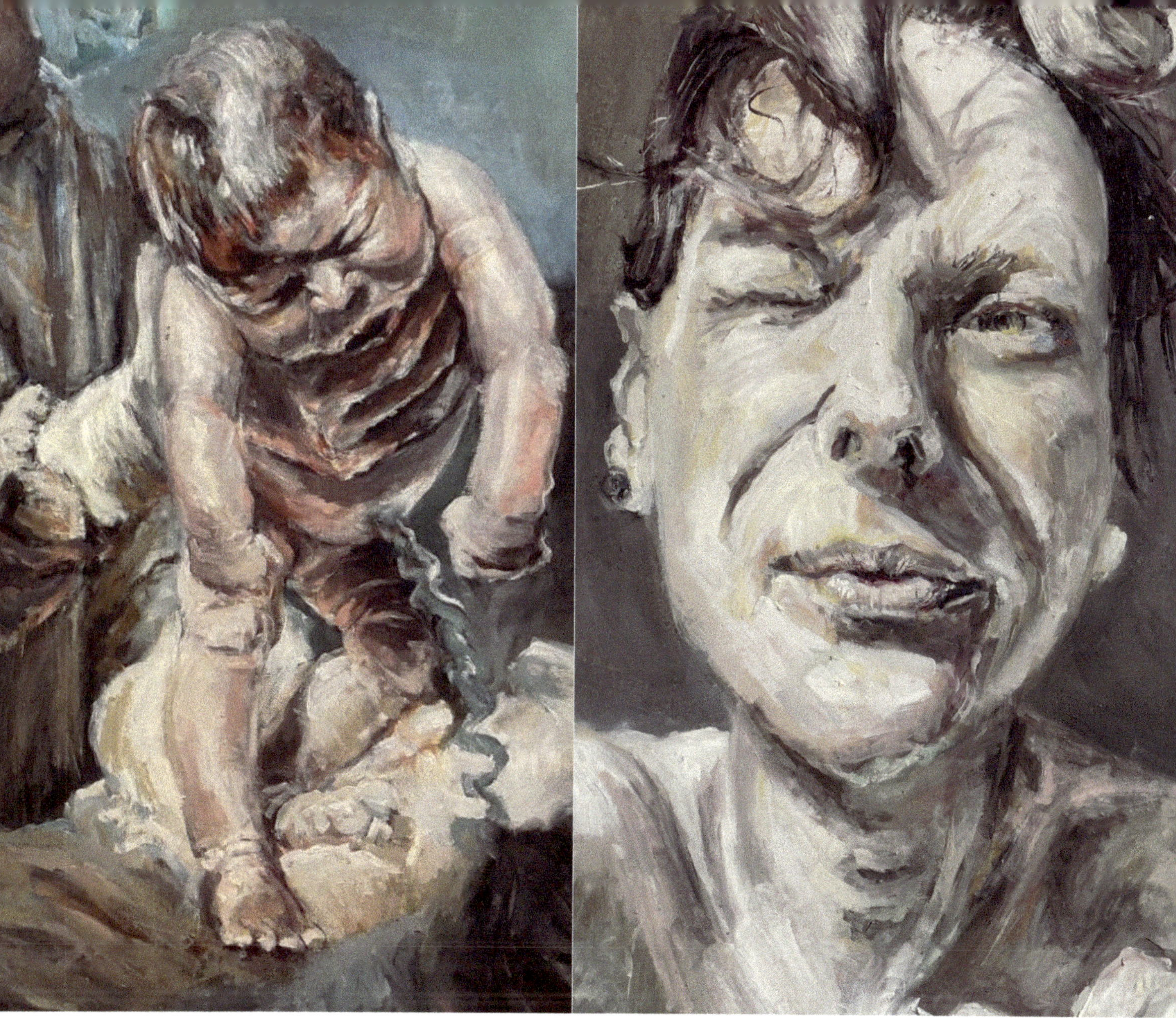

Incarnation n.3, 2020, Acrylic and oil on canvas, 110 x 81 cm

Self portrait on the sunlight ,Oil painting on cardboard, 7 4 x 52 cm,

Can you share a moment when you felt discouraged as an artist? How did you overcome it?

Honestly, I feel that way just right now. It's a difficult period of my life, when I try to build my artistic career while raising my very little children and all this in a country where I've been since four years. What is helping me a lot is my art itself and moments of diving into it, but sometimes there are so many obstacles that I don't even dare to start. I think what helped me since now is to appreciate really simple moments of beauty, nature, and existence. To deeply experience the efemerity of our lives and every being around us helps me to appreciate more every day.

How do you decide what to charge for your work?

It's a combination of methods. I use a method counting square centimeters of canvas. Plus, I use my intuition and compare with others creating a the similar artwork.

What's one piece of advice you'd give to aspiring artists?

I would tell them: Do some some spiritual work as well, it's important to keep you motivated, to find your WHY and it brings your art to the next level. It can be meditation, mindfulness, psycho-therapy, you name it.

Hannaleah Ledwell is a multidisciplinary artist born and based in Tiohtià:ke/Montreal. Her current work focuses on the relationship between visual and sensorial memory translated through the lens of oil painting. She studied at the University of Lapland and Concordia University, Montreal, from where she graduated with a Bachelor of Fine Arts. Recipient of the Canada Council for the Arts' Concept to Realization grant, Ledwell's work has been shown in Scandinavia and several galleries in Montreal. Focusing on intimacy with oneself and others, Ledwell seeks to convey tangible bodily sensations born of emotion. She examines the visceral nature of touch, the softness of a caress, the blossoming of pleasure, all through the perspective of autobiographical memory.Ledwell's main tool is an acute awareness of her own body, its physiognomy, its fluctuations and the sensations provoked by the smallest imbalances. This gives her the capacity to work from visual and muscular memory; it grants her the ability to transport herself to a precise instant and immerse herself completely in the sensations experienced at that particular point in time. Her medium is a vehicle for bringing these memories to life.

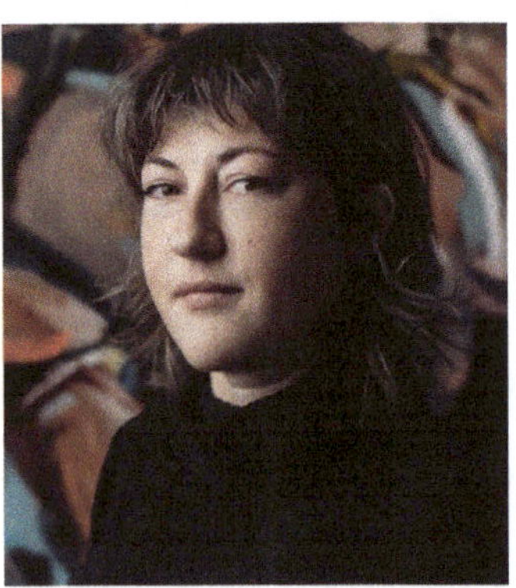

https://hannaleahledwell.com

hanna.ledwell@gmail.com

@hannaleah_ledwell

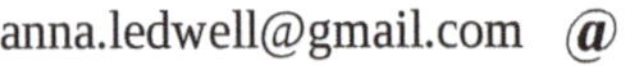

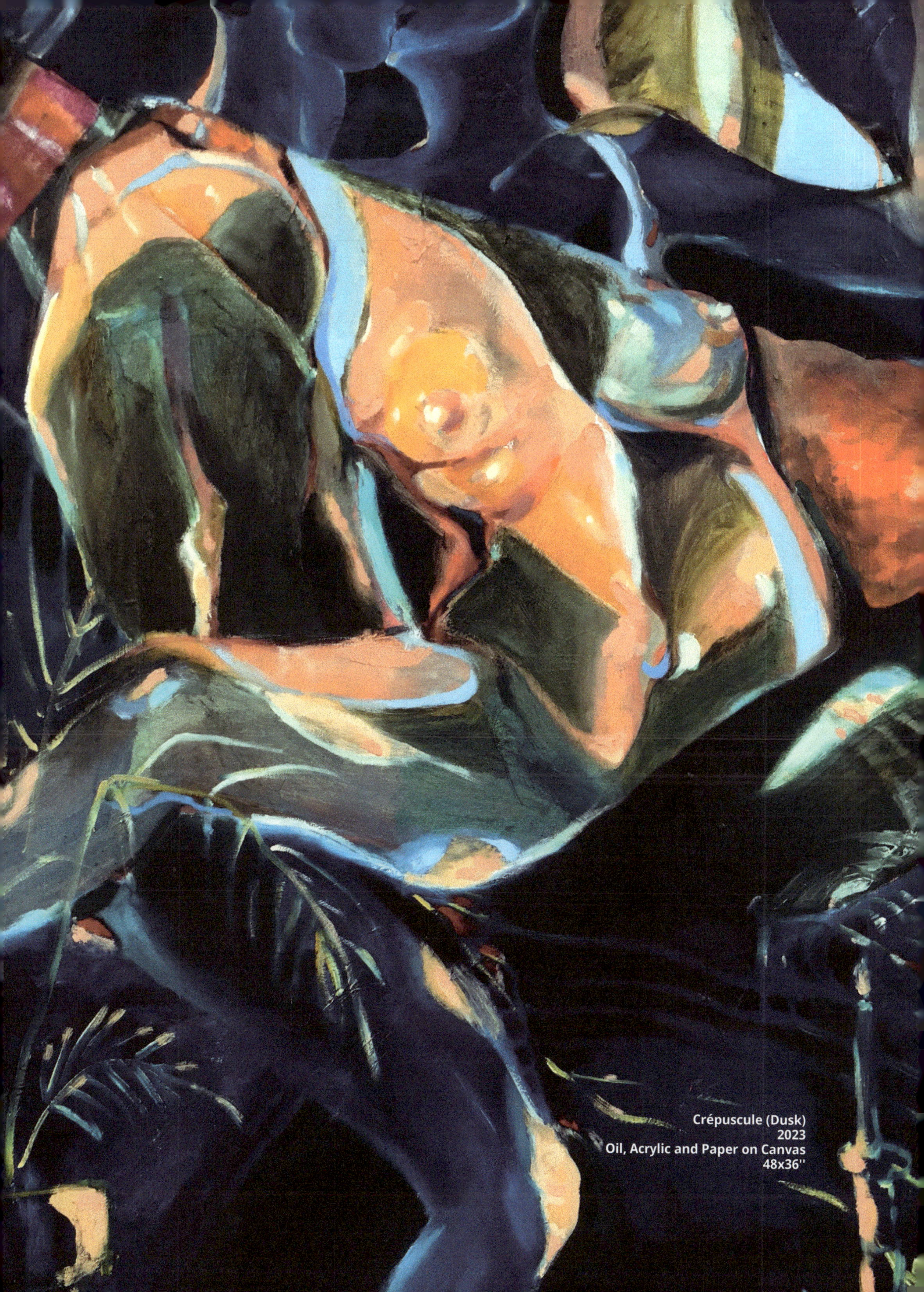

Crépuscule (Dusk)
2023
Oil, Acrylic and Paper on Canvas
48x36''

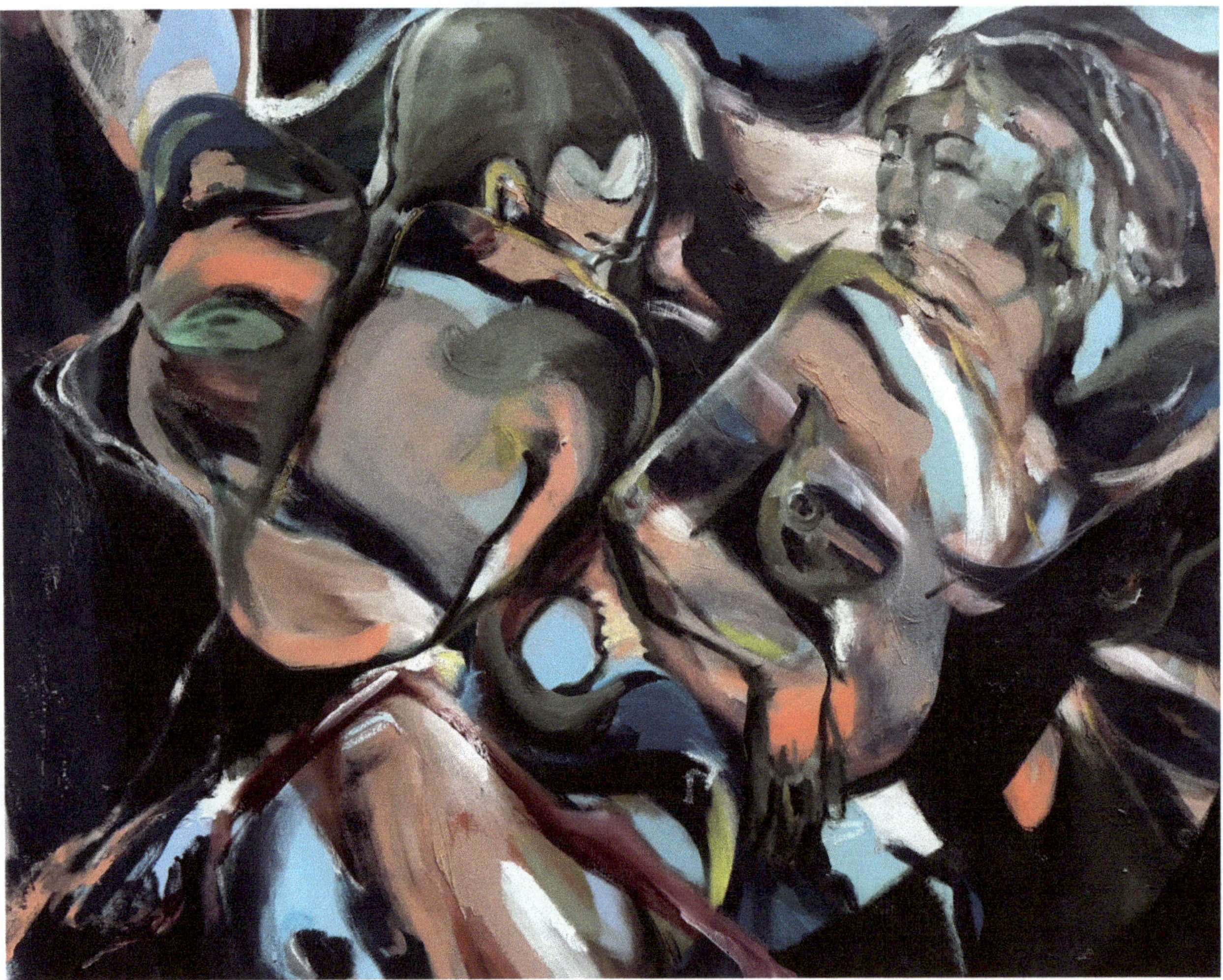

Love Languages, 2020, Oil on Canvas, 30x36"

Can you share a moment when you felt discouraged as an artist? How did you overcome it?

I have often felt discouraged. The art world can be quite difficult to navigate, it is very competitive, it involves a lot of bureaucratic work in order to get grants, residencies and shows. I deal with it all by producing for myself. As long as I get to keep making art that matters to me, when it's time for applications, I can power through knowing that this is just the less fun part of the job.

How do you cope with the vulnerability of sharing your art with the world?

When I feel nervous about sharing my deepest feelings with the world, I focus on the beautiful human interactions that sharing my work brings me. These interactions are worth it. When my work has an impact on someone, resonates with them and they want to open up and share something vulnerable about themselves with me, that's a moment I can hold on to. Sharing my vulnerabilities is much less daunting when I know there are others who can share those moments with me.

How has your art helped you understand yourself better?

As a visual person, art is the way I communicate, it is the way I understand the world, the way I connect with it. From a very young age I reverted to drawing and painting in order to express things that I didn't know how to put into words, and that outlet has remained a constant throughout my life. Art is the tool I use to process the world around me as well as the world of emotions within me.

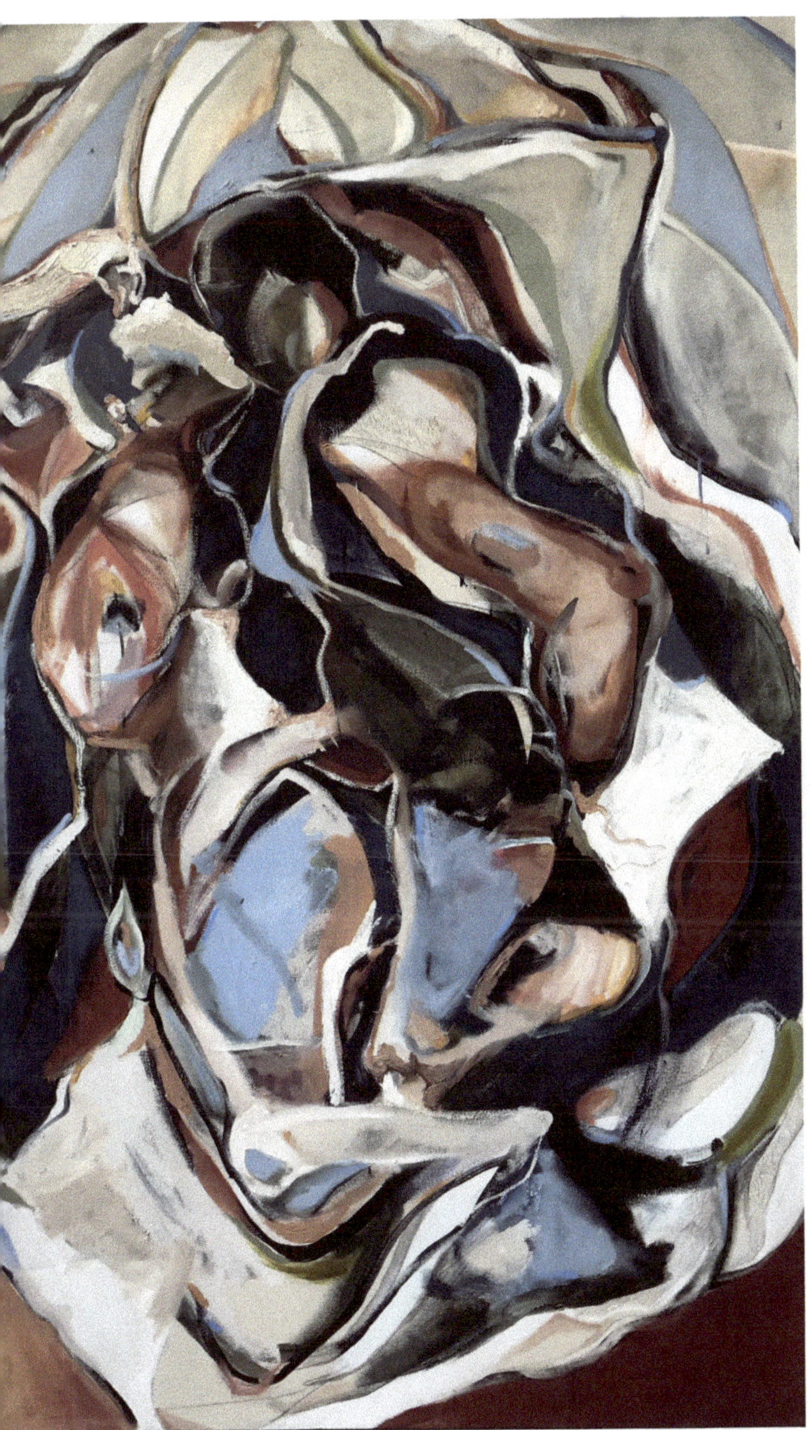

Portrait of Artist, Cacophonies, Oil and Graphite on Canvas, 72x48", 2022

How do you decide what to charge for your work?

It has been difficult! I feel like I am still learning this part!

What do you want people to take away from your work?

My practice stems from a need to communicate lived experiences, the ones that can only truly be felt or seen, the ones that hurt or overwhelm, the ones that feel warm and fuzzy, the ones beyond words. I willingly share these moments in all their vulnerability but I present them jumbled and fragmented so that the viewer can take away their own narrative. This intentional ambiguity aims at making the work accessible to people from every walk of life as there is no right or wrong answer, but rather, just a question for the viewer: How do you feel?

What's one piece of advice you'd give to aspiring artists?

It's OK to take breaks from producing. Sometimes you need to take time to absorb the world around you, to find inspiration and ideas, to recharge. The moment you feel the need to create though, seize it, create. Don't waste that energy on anything else.

Hari Lualhati, an accomplished full-time artist based in Cape Town, South Africa, deeply connects with her recent creations, referring to them as "SOULWORKS." Born on February 12, 1985, Hari's artistic journey started early, leading her to win the "Artist of the Year" title in high school and graduate with honors in Fine Arts from the University of the Philippines in 2006. Her career has spanned various roles, excelling as a graphic artist, product designer, illustrator, and painter across international settings. Her artistry has garnered acclaim in numerous

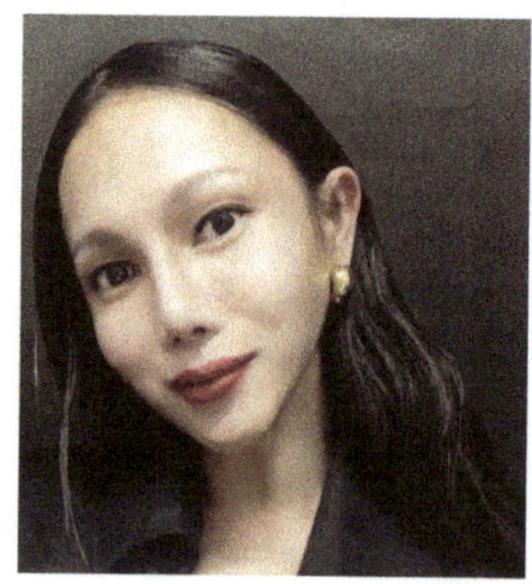

International Art Competitions, earning features in art publications and exhibitions globally. Hari's "SOULWORKS" encapsulate profound life lessons and personal realizations, aiming to communicate these shared experiences through interconnected themes in her art. Her artistic style harmoniously blends realism, expressionism, and symbolism, often intertwining human figures with elements of nature and animals to highlight our innate interconnectedness. Hari's ethos revolves around painting from the heart, intending to evoke emotions and convey clear messages that resonate with viewers worldwide.

http://harilualhati.yolasite.com

harilualhati_artist@hotmail.com

@harilualhati

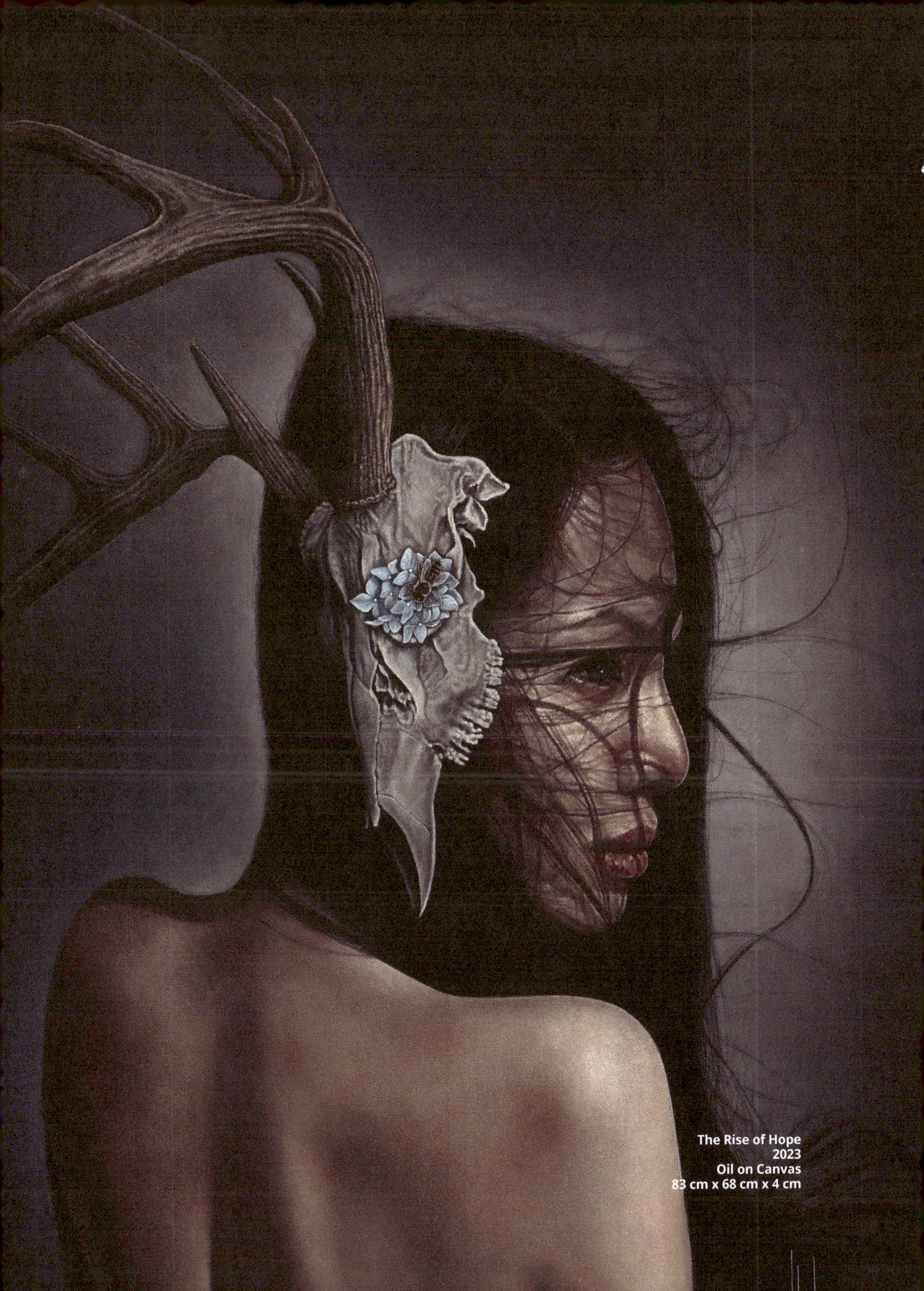

The Rise of Hope
2023
Oil on Canvas
83 cm x 68 cm x 4 cm

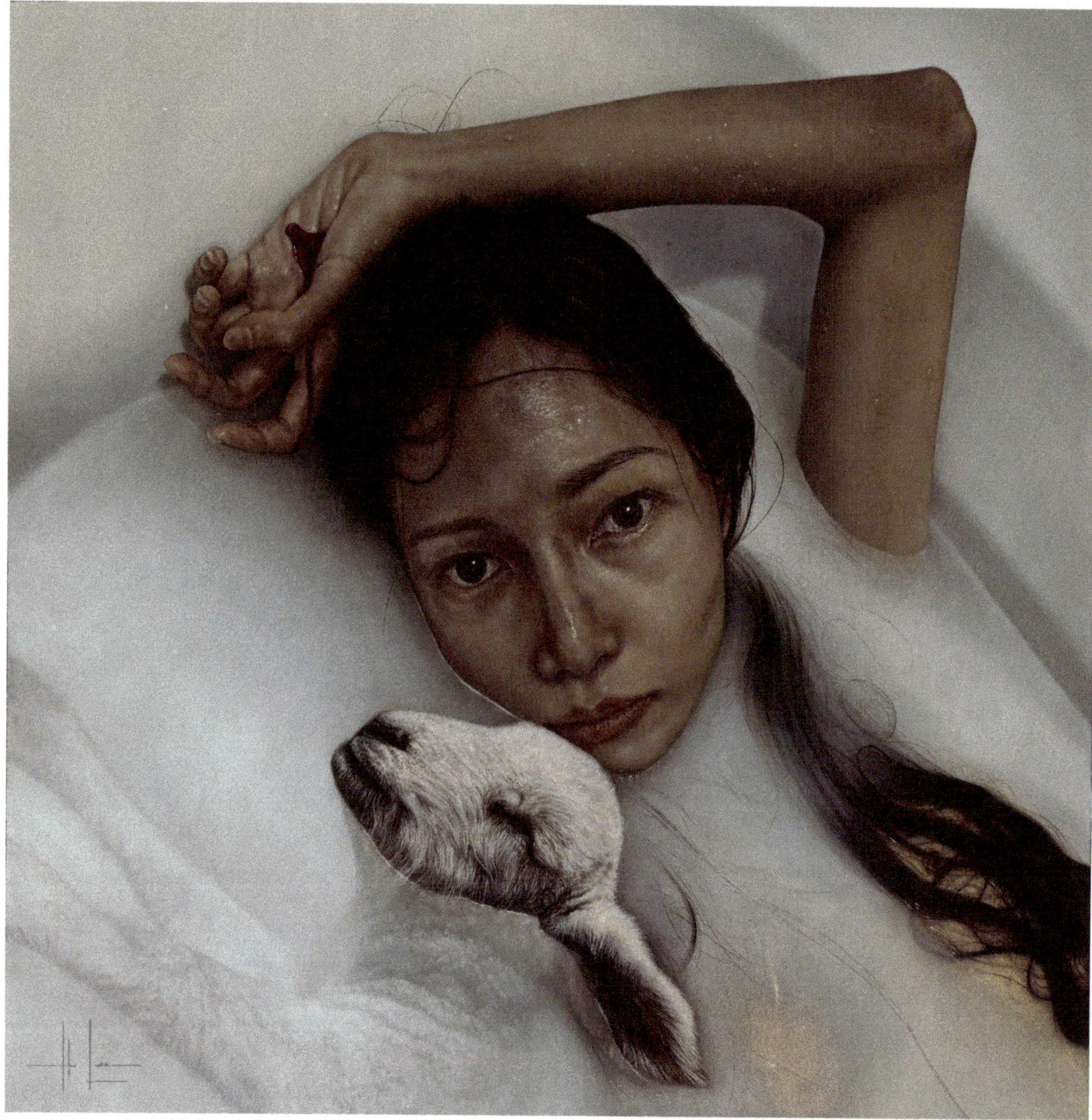

Washed in the Blood of the Lamb, 2023,Oil on Aluminium Panel, 71.5 cm x 71.5 cm x 6 cm

Can you share a moment when you felt discouraged as an artist? How did you overcome it?

One of the most impactful moments in my art career occurred when I was advised to alter my theme and painting style. Initially, it cast doubt on my artistic identity, prompting me to question the path I was on. However, this experience served as a profound reminder of the core reason why I paint. It reinforced that I paint because I possess ideas that hold immense personal value, and I aspire to share them authentically. Any deviation from my genuine themes and style would yield artwork devoid of the heartfelt connection I seek to convey. Consequently, I have chosen to paint only themes that resonate with me personally, employing a style that best expresses my true self.

How do you cope with the vulnerability of sharing your art with the world?

Navigating the vulnerability of sharing my art with the world is an intricate process that I approach with utmost care and commitment. To counter the inherent vulnerability, I ensure that I give my best in every artwork I create. By investing my sincere effort, I aim to create pieces that not only reflect my artistic vision but also evoke genuine emotions. This dedication acts as a shield, allowing me to share my creations confidently, knowing that each piece carries a piece of my heart and a commitment to excellence.

How has your art helped you understand yourself better?

My art has been a profound journey of self-discovery, allowing me to understand myself better. From a young age, I recognized that my creations serve as reflections of my inner self, extending from my soul—hence, I term them my Soulworks. Painting what holds personal significance effortlessly transforms the creative process. It's a realization that the final result mirrors the genuine emotions invested in each stroke. This connection between the subject matter and my soul translates into the art, revealing the authenticity and love embedded in the piece.

How do you decide what to charge for your work?

Deciding on the pricing for my soulwork is a meticulous process that intertwines my dedication to the craft with the value I place on each creation. I base my charges on the time invested in bringing a piece to life, ensuring that every moment spent contributes to its depth and essence. I adhere to a principle where I don't consider a piece complete until it resonates with me, signaling that I've devoted my utmost effort to it. This commitment to excellence becomes a cornerstone for determining the value of my work, allowing me to set prices that mirror both the labor invested and the heartfelt connection embedded within each piece.

What do you want people to take away from your work?

Through my soulwork, I aspire for people to glean the profound lessons life has imparted to me. Through my soulwork, I aim to offer more than mere visuals; they serve as tangible

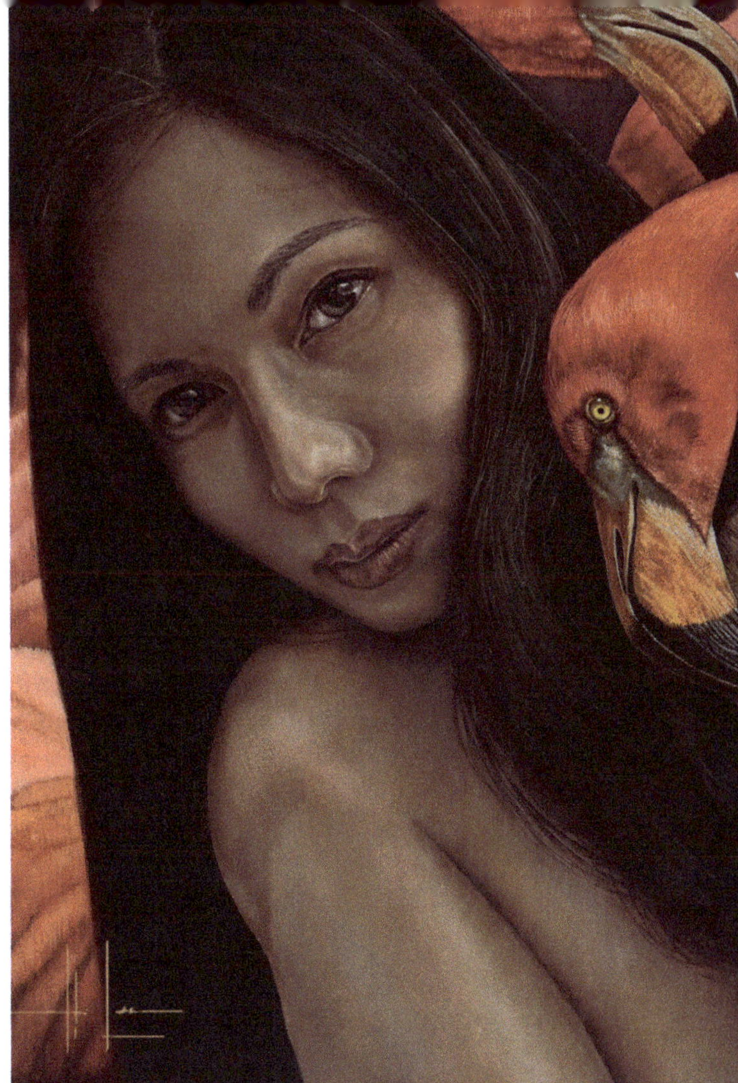

Lean On To Innocence, Oil on Canvas, 40.5 cm x 40.5 cm x 1.5cm

reminders of life's golden lessons. When my collectors wake up in the morning and are greeted by my paintings on their walls, it is my intention that they are reminded of these profound life lessons. This daily encounter serves as a wellspring of inspiration and positivity, providing a fortifying foundation as they navigate the challenges of each new day.

What's one piece of advice you'd give to aspiring artists?

One invaluable piece of advice I would offer to aspiring artists is to infuse every creation with their very best. Dedication to giving one's utmost effort in every artistic endeavor not only refines skills but also ensures that each piece becomes a true representation of the artist's capabilities. In everything you create, make sure you give your best, for it is this commitment to excellence that propels growth, fosters authenticity, and ultimately sets the stage for a fulfilling artistic journey.

Heather Heitzenrater was born in 1992 and grew up in Punxsutawney, PA. She now lives and works in Pittsburgh, PA. Heather received her BFA in Painting and Drawing from Edinboro University of Pennsylvania in 2015. Her work has been shown Nationally including Erie Art Museum, Westmoreland Museum of American Art, and Baton Rouge Gallery. She has been published in Poet Artist Magazine, and featured in Create! and Beautiful Bizarre blog. Heather has won awards, given artist talks, curated and juried local art shows. Along with showing her work, Heather instructs figurative workshops at Pittsburgh Center of the Arts and is a Scenic Artist for ScareHouse.

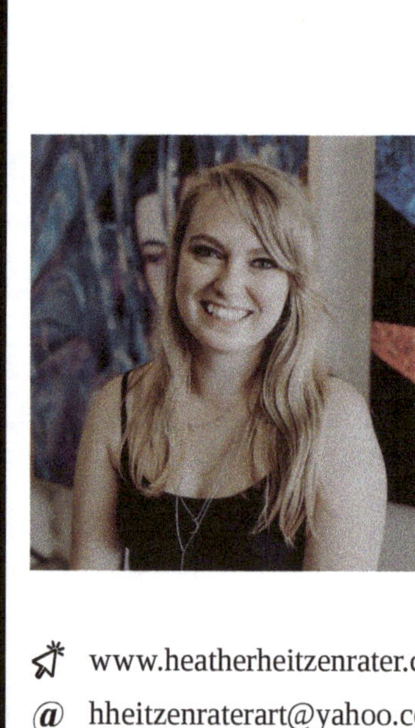

www.heatherheitzenrater.com

hheitzenraterart@yahoo.com

@heather_heitzenrater

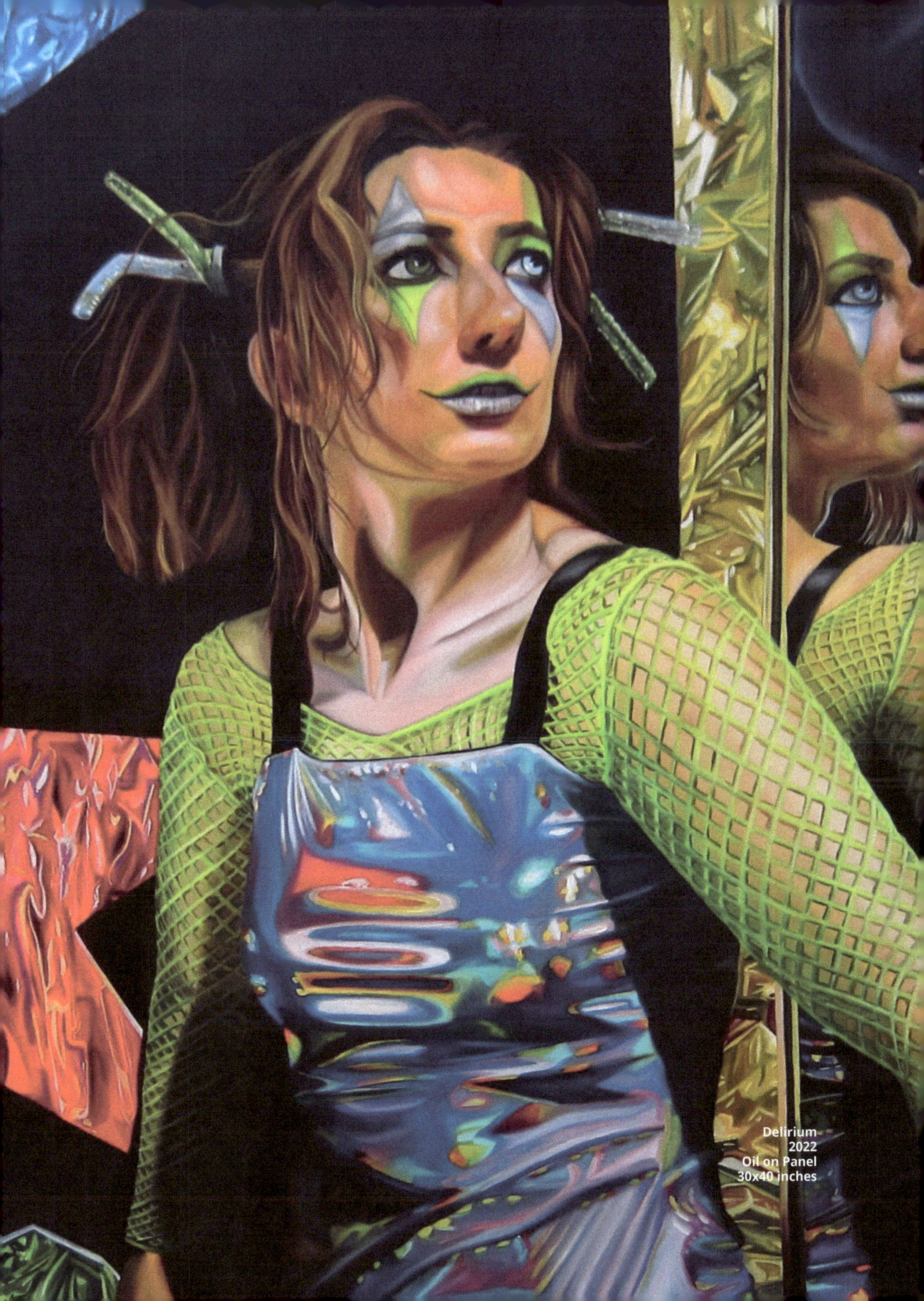
Delirium
2022
Oil on Panel
30x40 inches

Can you share a moment when you felt discouraged as an artist? How did you overcome it?

Last winter, I felt super discouraged. I wasn't getting into shows. I lost count of how many rejection letters I got. I usually handle rejection well, but after so many I started to take it personally. I wasn't selling any artwork. I felt like I was a failure that I couldn't support my family like I had been. I was comparing my self-worth with how many sales I had. I started to try and flip the script. Instead of pondering over how many rejections I got, I started to think about how many galleries looked at my work. I painted what I wanted, not just what I thought would sell. I kept applying to shows and eventually got into a big one in San Francisco. I talked with other artists and learned that it had been a slow year for most creatives. It made me feel like I wasn't alone and that I was doing the right thing.

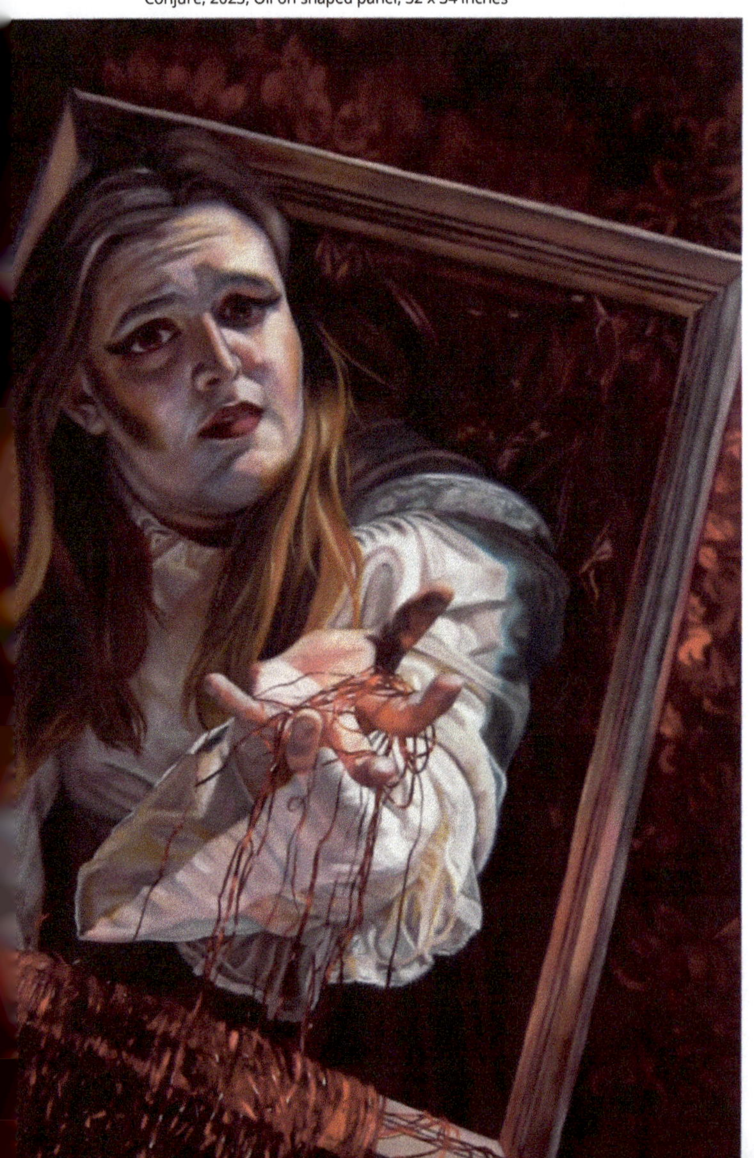

Conjure, 2023, Oil on shaped panel, 32 x 34 inches

How do you cope with the vulnerability of sharing your art with the world?

My work takes me a long time to create. When I spend 3 months on a painting, I am usually ready to share it with the world. I am proud of what I do, and I just want as many eyes on my work as I can get. I know my work is niche and not going to be for everyone. The right people will come along and enjoy it.

How has your art helped you understand yourself better?

I feel like my work has helped me find a crowd of people I really enjoy being around. I like mysterious, spooky things and my audience likes the same things! Some of my collectors have become good friends of mine. My work has also helped me understand some situations in my life. When I am working on a painting, most of the time I am not sure what it is about until I'm done with the painting or months after. Once the life lesson dawns on me, I will look back at my work and go, "Oh it all makes sense now".

How do you decide what to charge for your work?

I charge per square inch plus the cost of the supplies. I have a rate per inch, and I multiply that by the paintings square footage. I also want to make sure I am getting paid to support myself. For example, if a painting takes me a month to do, I want to make sure that the painting's price can support me for the time it took to make. If a gallery takes a commission, I factor that in as well.

What do you want people to take away from your work?

I really want people to leave their reality for a while and be immersed in my world. I want them to feel a sense of childlike wonder. Maybe forget their troubles for just a few minutes and enjoy being curious again.

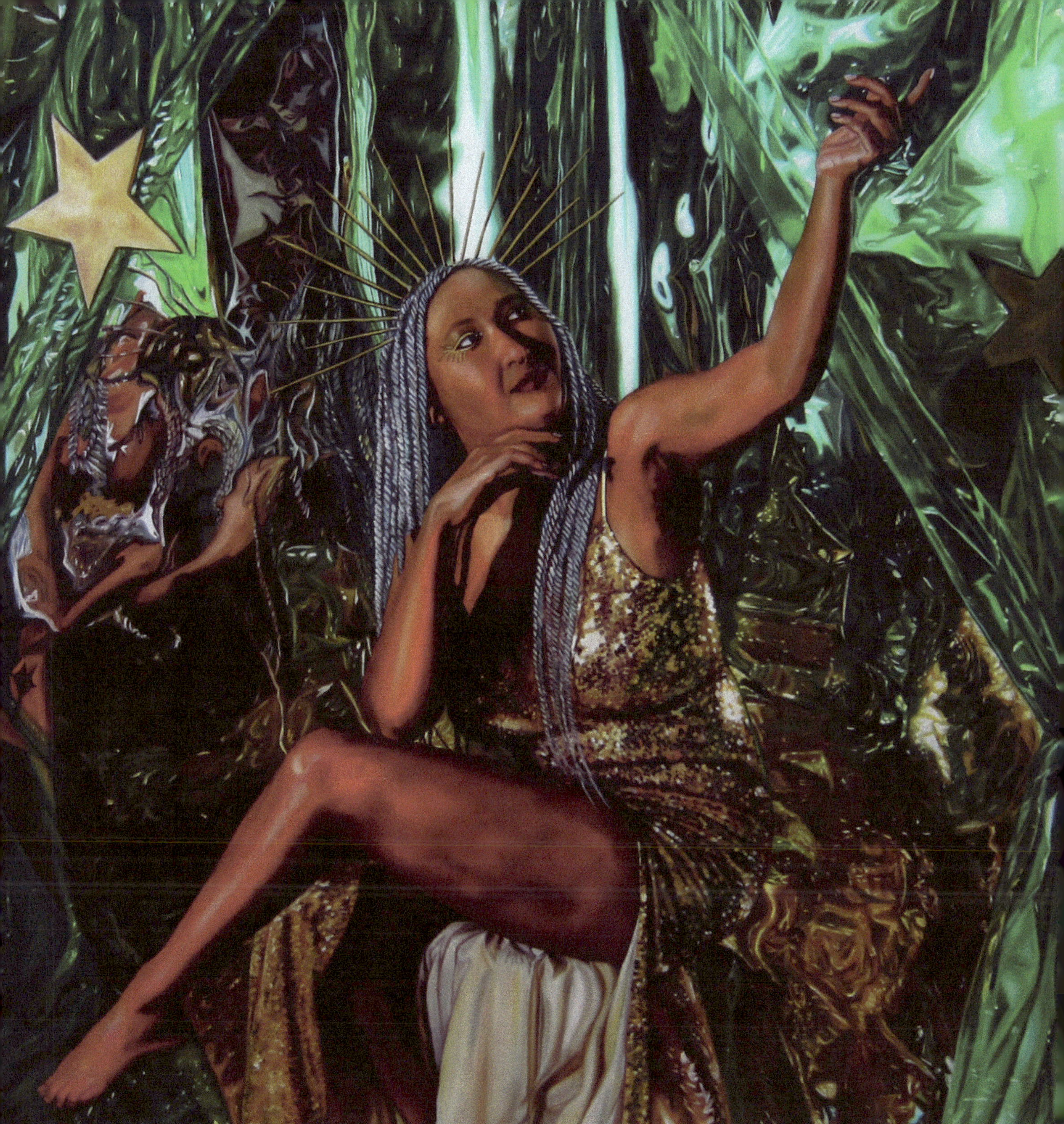

Absinthe, 2023, Oil on Panel, 36 x 33 inches

What's one piece of advice you'd give to aspiring artists?

Just keep going and make what makes you happy. You are going to get a lot of no results and not everyone is going to like your work. Keep going! Also, to never stop learning. Take some classes and learn from your peers to broaden your creative soul.

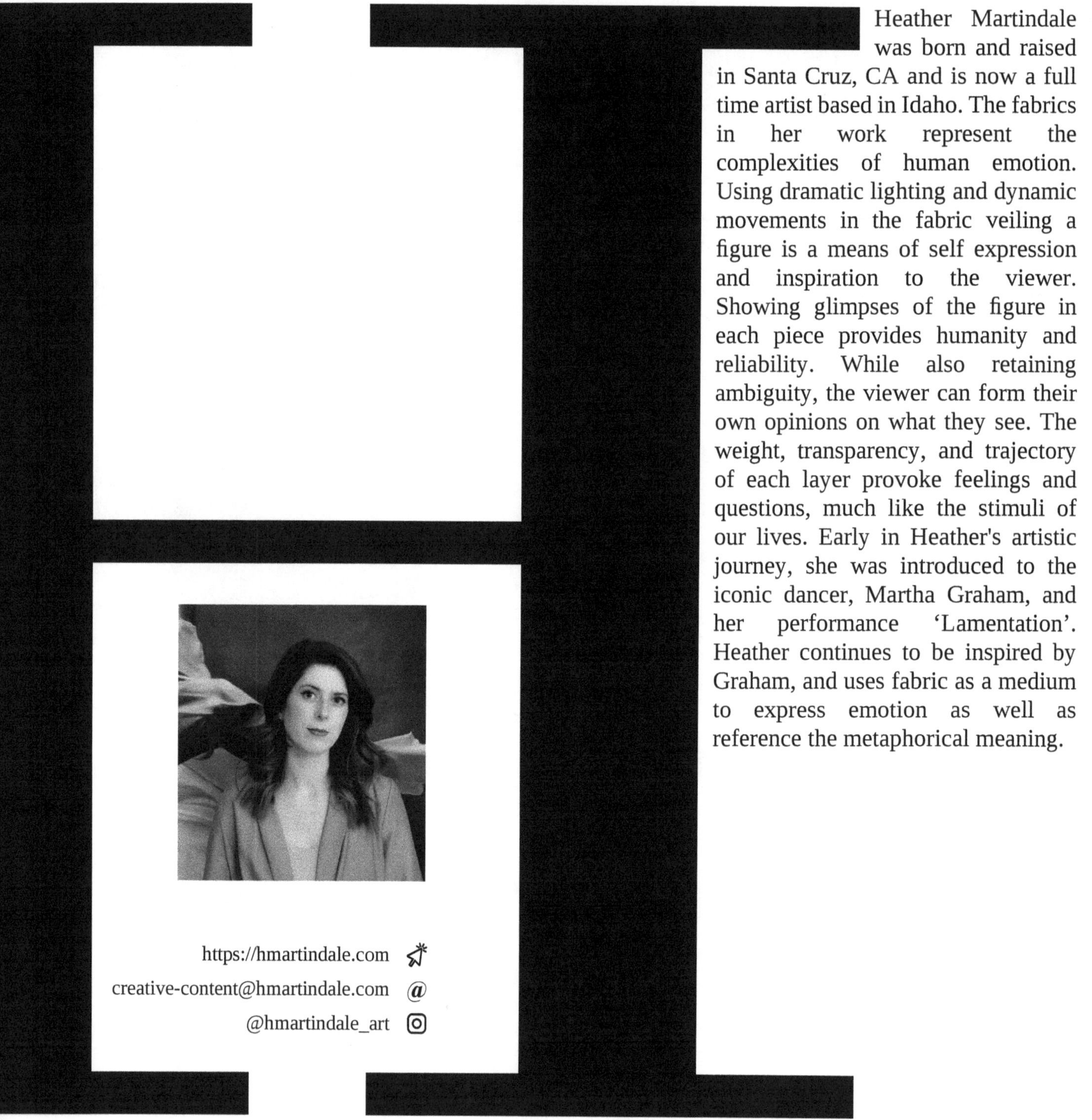

Heather Martindale was born and raised in Santa Cruz, CA and is now a full time artist based in Idaho. The fabrics in her work represent the complexities of human emotion. Using dramatic lighting and dynamic movements in the fabric veiling a figure is a means of self expression and inspiration to the viewer. Showing glimpses of the figure in each piece provides humanity and reliability. While also retaining ambiguity, the viewer can form their own opinions on what they see. The weight, transparency, and trajectory of each layer provoke feelings and questions, much like the stimuli of our lives. Early in Heather's artistic journey, she was introduced to the iconic dancer, Martha Graham, and her performance 'Lamentation'. Heather continues to be inspired by Graham, and uses fabric as a medium to express emotion as well as reference the metaphorical meaning.

https://hmartindale.com

creative-content@hmartindale.com

@hmartindale_art

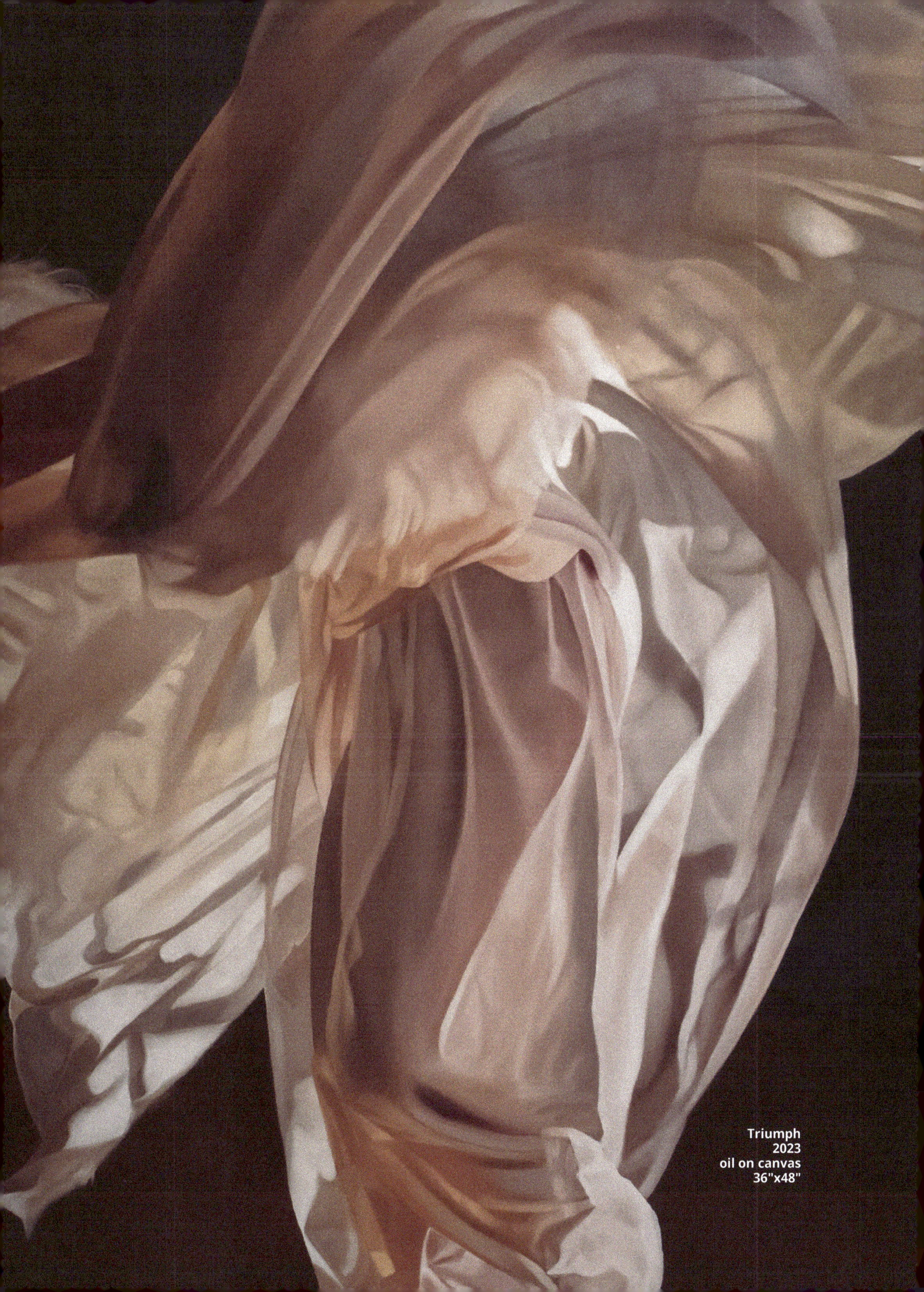
Triumph
2023
oil on canvas
36"x48"

How do you cope with the vulnerability of sharing your art with the world?

I have just recently started sharing more openly about the personal nature of my work as it relates to trauma and abuse. The very first post or share that was undoubtedly vulnerable, where I could not hide from people knowing such an intimate part of me, was scary! But the more courage I get and keep sharing through my work and writing, the more I realize that there are more people who connect with the vulnerability on some level than I could have imagined. There is strength in vulnerability.

What do you want people to take away from your work?

My main purpose in creating work is to inspire others. If they are not inspired or moved, I strive to at least cause them to think or question what they might be looking at or what they are feeling when they look at it.

Can you share a moment when you felt discouraged as an artist? How did you overcome it?

As a full time artist I have felt discouraged more times than I can count. Two themes that seem to show up are regarding sales being down and not turning a profit, and getting rejection emails when I was confident that the opportunity was a perfect fit. In both scenarios I have to remind myself that I did not become a professional artist for the money or fame. My mission is to make a difference and inspire others from my artwork. As long as I am making the work and sharing it with the world, I have done all.

How has your art helped you understand yourself better?

My art is the way I process the world and express the things that I can't find words for. Seeing an idea develop into a body of work and how it evolves along the way is very telling about how I see and experience life, and what I want to Inspire in those around me.

Surge, 2023, oil on canvas, 48"x36"

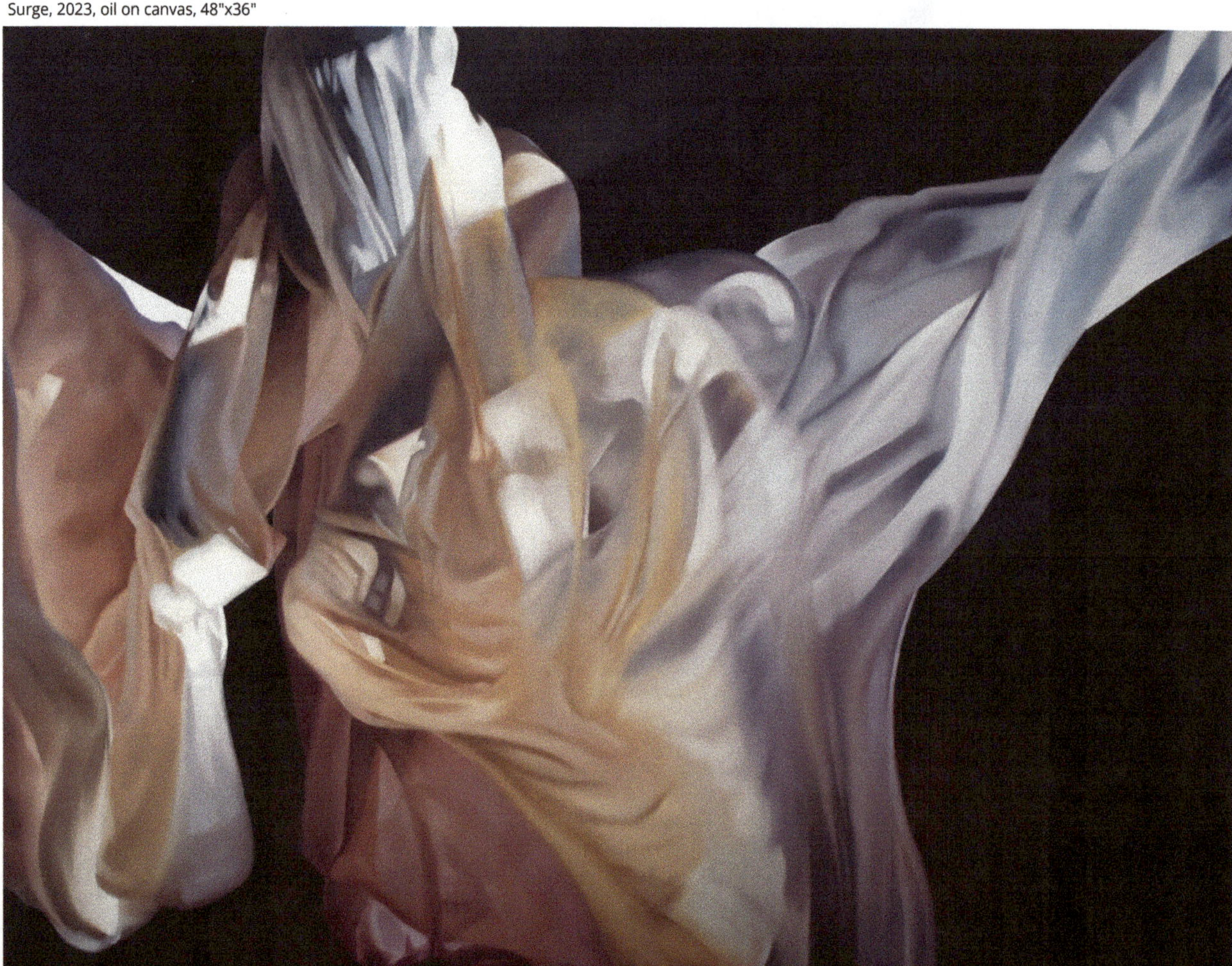

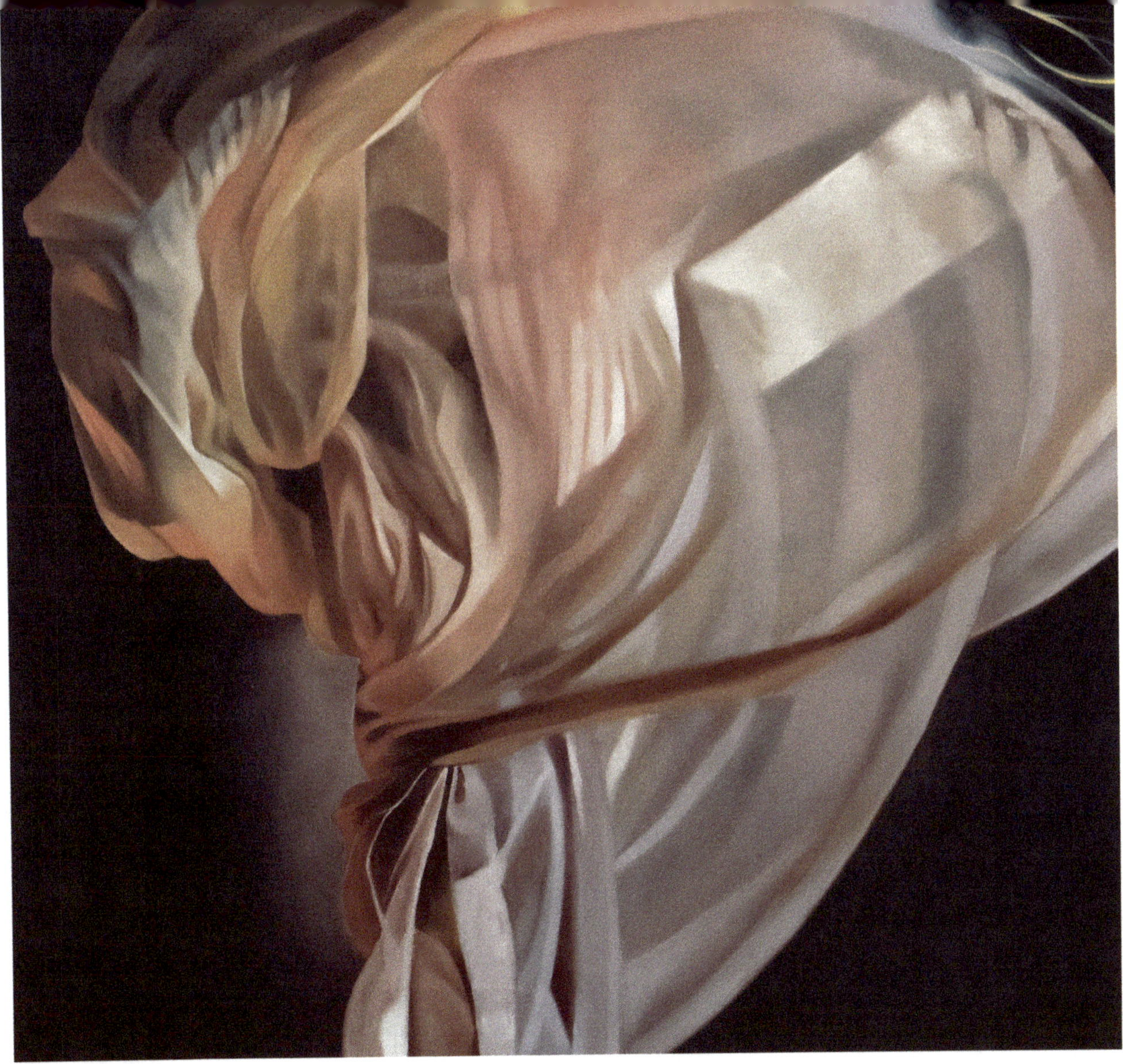

Wonder, 2023, oil on canvas, 24"x24"

What's one piece of advice you'd give to aspiring artists?

There is truly no "right" path or specific milestone that you have to meet in order to say "I have made it as an artist". When first starting out, it is easy to find another artist or two whom you aspire to be like and make it your goal to meet the same marks as them, show in the same galleries, etc. However, after experiencing this firsthand and actually meeting the same marks as some of my art idols, I quickly got pulled in another direction or felt like it didn't have the outcome that I expected. All of this to say, strive to carve your own path, don't be afraid to do it different, and don't be afraid of failing or succeeding.

How do you decide what to charge for your work?

Like most artists, I believe pricing my artwork is the hardest part of being an artist who wants to make money on my work. I had to start somewhere and get a baseline so I just set a price for a piece based on the size and what I thought was reasonable based on other artists on a similar level in their career and technique. Once I got a sale at that price, I use that as a formula to calculate the prize of other sizes based on price per square foot (I work large scale, but could be done based on square inch as well). I find that factoring in time spent does now work for me because there are so many variables in life that it each piece will take me varying amounts of time to complete, even though the imagery and technique are very similar.

Heidi Brueckner is a Professor of Art at West Valley College in Saratoga, CA where she has taught painting, drawing, and design for over 23 years. Brueckner holds a BA in Fine Art and a BA in Art History from University of California, Santa Cruz, and an MFA in Painting from University of Kansas. Professor Brueckner's work has been shown at museums, galleries, colleges, and in publications nationally and internationally. In recent years, Brueckner has had 16 solo exhibitions, participated in over 100 juried group shows, and won 13 first place awards. She currently lives and works in Oakland, California. Inherently, we are interested in observing others as a way of understanding ourselves. Her work is inspired by this curiosity and invites the viewer to participate. These works are individualistic narratives which explore personage through self-presentation, facial expressions, and gesture. They often inspect the under-revered, and appreciate the subject's presence and dignity, giving pause to honor the person.

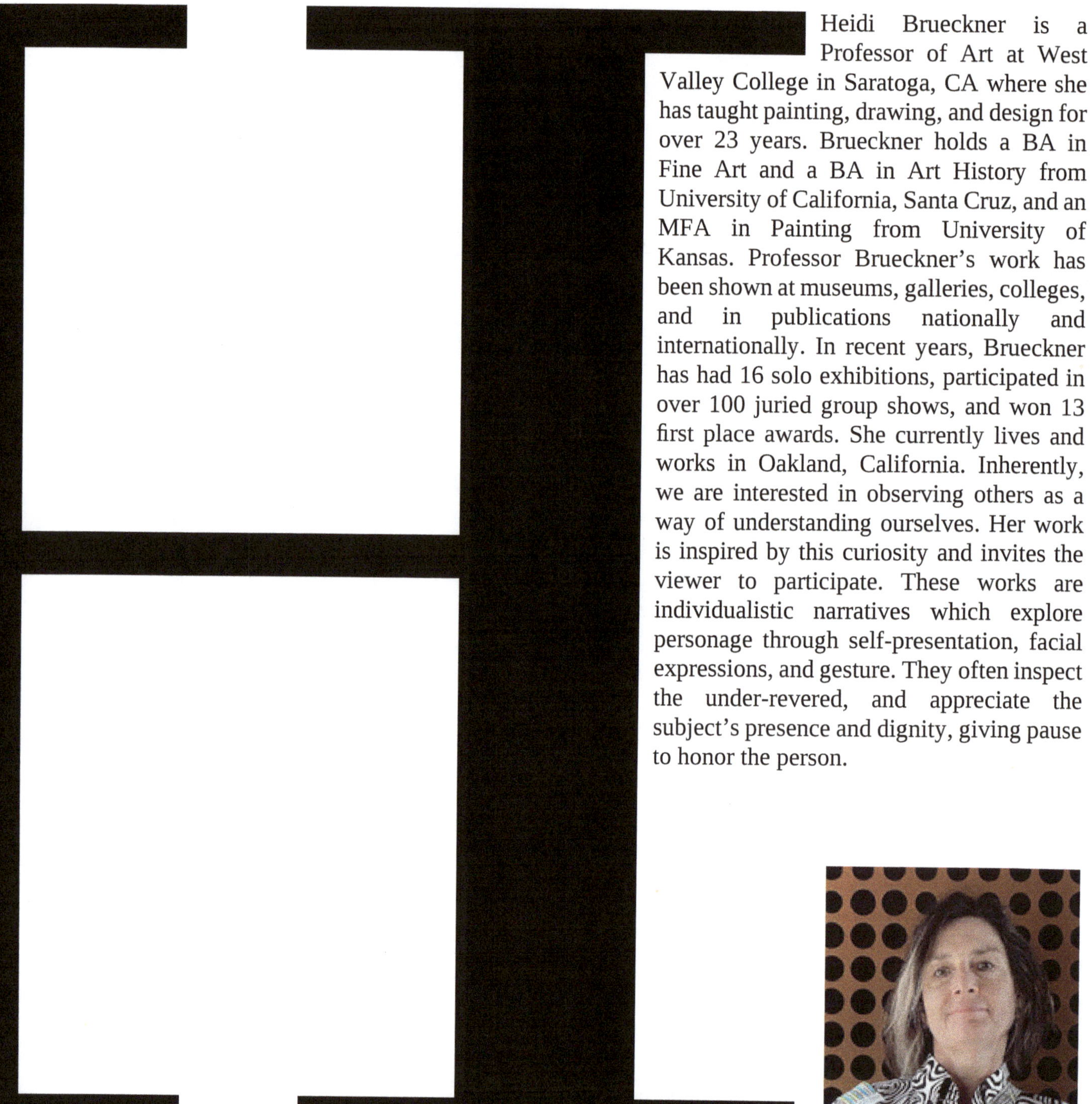

heidibrueckner.com

heidi.brueckner@wvm.edu

@heidi.brueckner

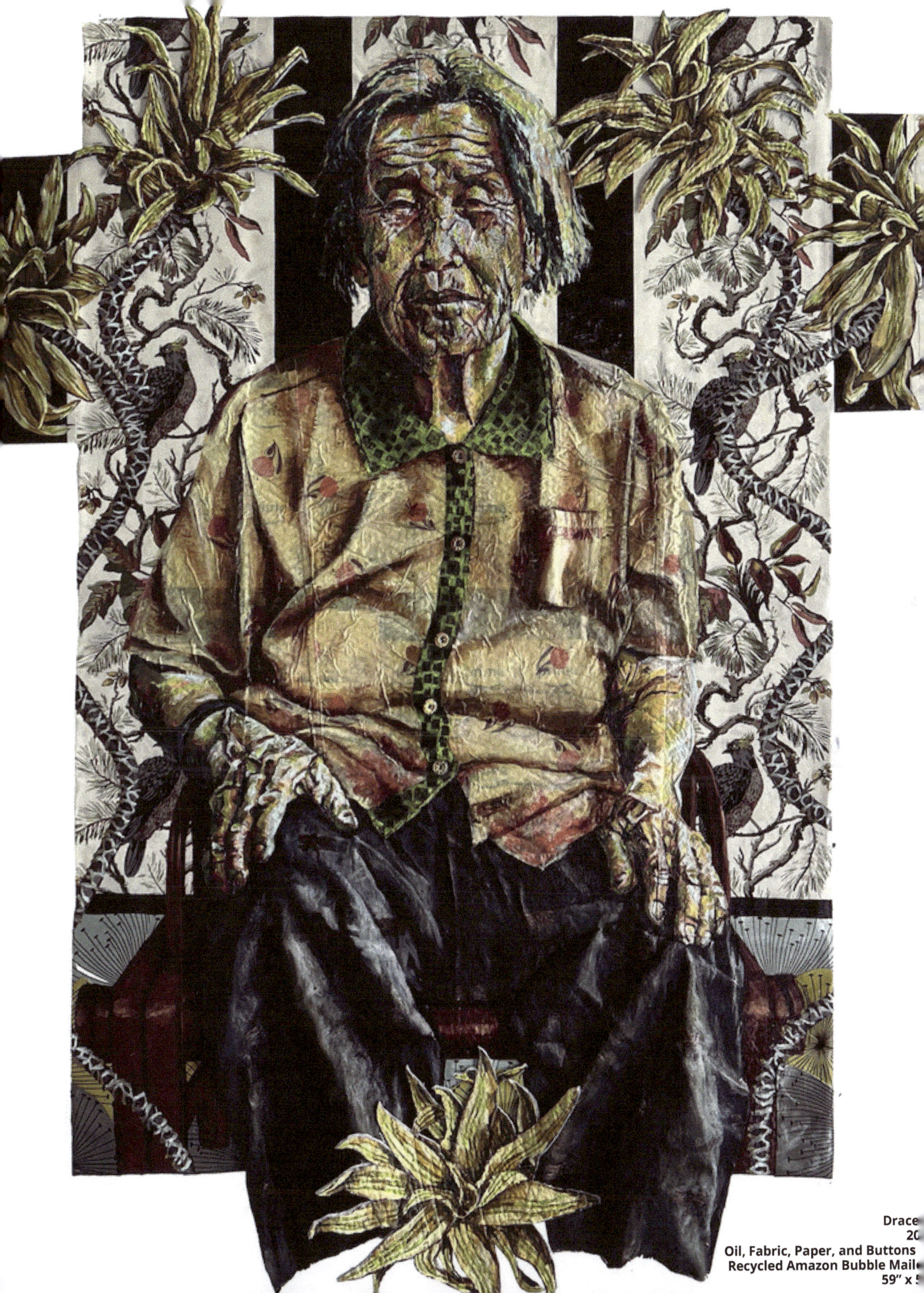

Drace
20
Oil, Fabric, Paper, and Buttons
Recycled Amazon Bubble Maile
59" x 5

Can you share a moment when you felt discouraged as an artist? How did you overcome it?

In graduate school I was ostracized for my strongly figurative-oriented work. Though I think of my work as being content-rich, it was not considered conceptual enough or abstract enough to satisfy the tastes of the people in charge. In order to survive, I eventually had to learn to trust my instincts, stay true to what interested me, be proud of my unique voice, and not care so much about what other people thought. Your work may or may not align with the trends of the current art world, and either is okay. Things are always changing. Art is a long game.

How do you cope with the vulnerability of sharing your art with the world?

The experience above was much worse than anything I experienced in the real world. I was able to break with those judgments and be true to what I thought was important and what inspired me. Doing art for yourself is the best route in my opinion.

How has your art helped you understand yourself better?

It has helped me to understand that people, relationships, and reverence for our natural world are all highly important for me. It has also helped me to know that I am much happier when I am creating.

What's one piece of advice you'd give to aspiring artists?

Stay true to yourself. Don't be influenced by trends if they do not speak to your authentic interests.

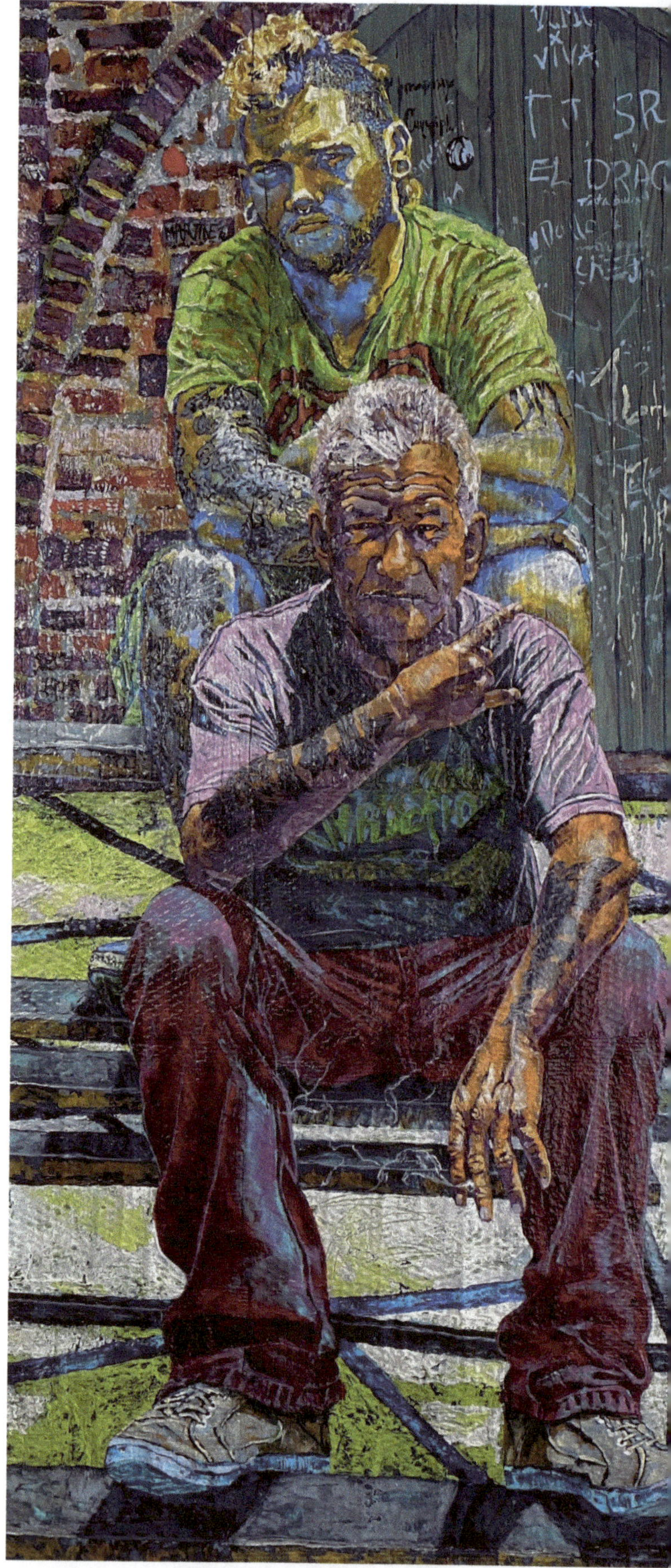

Squatters Club Cuba, 2021, Oil and Paper on Recycled Poly Bubble Mailers, 78.25" x 46.5"

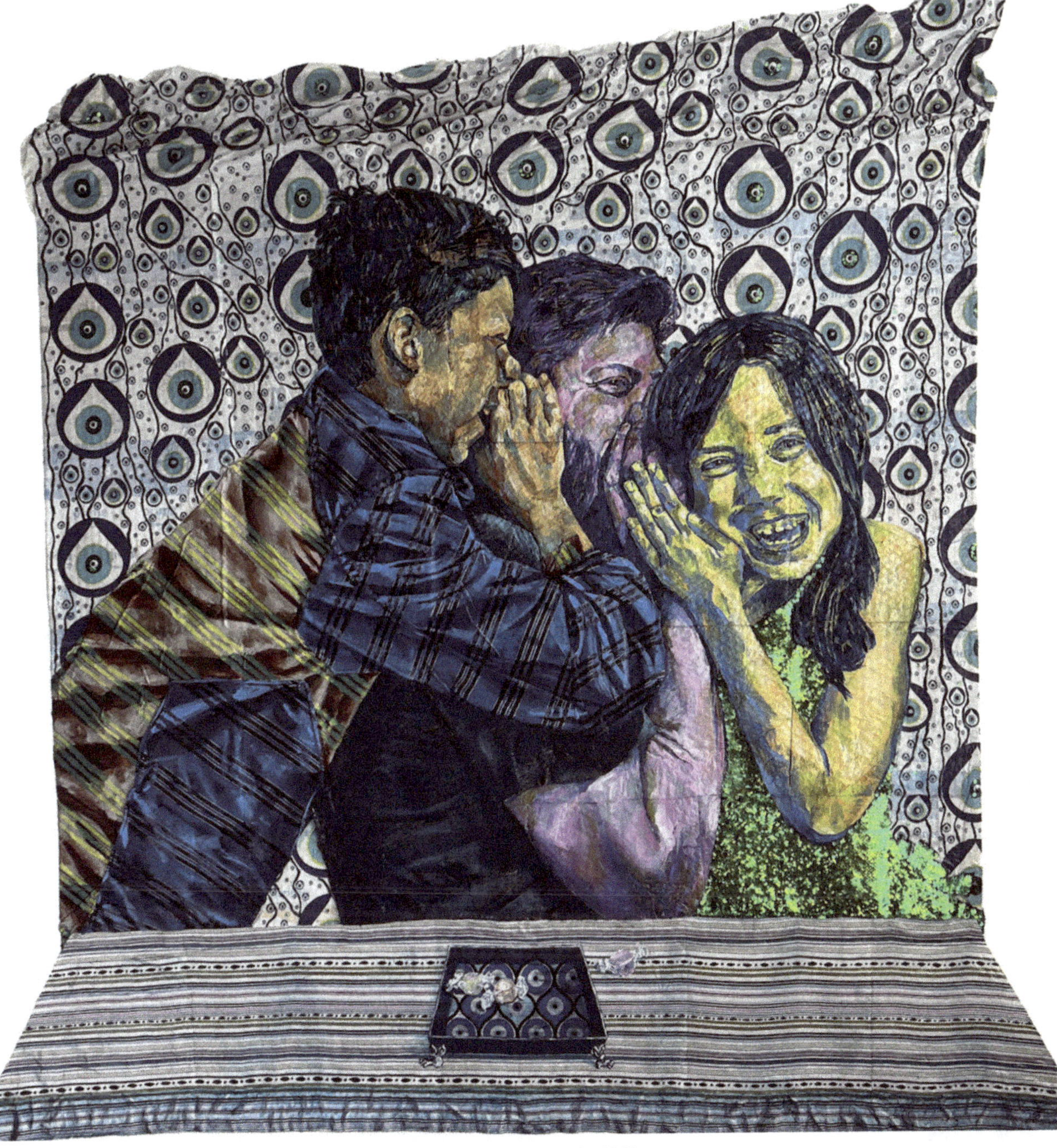

It's Raining Love, 2023, Oil, Fabric, Beads, and Sequins on Recycled Amazon Bubble Mailers, 56" x 57.5"

What do you want people to take away from your work?

I believe ultimately my work is about love, and the sentiment that we try to live in a more socially empathetic and environmentally just world. I want the work to encourage people to appreciate and love one another, and to in turn understand the importance of social justice and respect for our earth and all its creatures.

How do you decide what to charge for your work?

The size, the amount of time it takes to create, what similar artwork is selling for, and formulating a price that seems fair in exchange for "giving up" the piece.

Holly Cerna is an Austin, TX based artist and painter who holds a BFA in painting from Maryland Institute College of Art. Her oil and acrylic paintings explore how color relates to emotion and light as a representation of the soul or consciousness. She became a member of Contra/Common, an emerging artist nonprofit organization in November, 2021. Recent publications include Issue #150 of New American Paintings and Voyage ATX. Holly Cerna is a figure and landscape painter whose works explore the relationship between the temporary, tangible physical plane and the intangible, eternal metaphysical plane (spirit or energy) set in contemporary contexts. Her works depict the personal but universal experience of being alive. The subjects in her work emit a glowing inner light representing the soul, communicating how consciousness might appear if visible. Through color theory, contrast, saturation, and perspective, her work expresses her fascination with the human condition. Holly's paintings are characterized by the use of painting techniques of the Baroque Period while using alternative lighting and color to convey her subjects' normally invisible mental and emotional states.

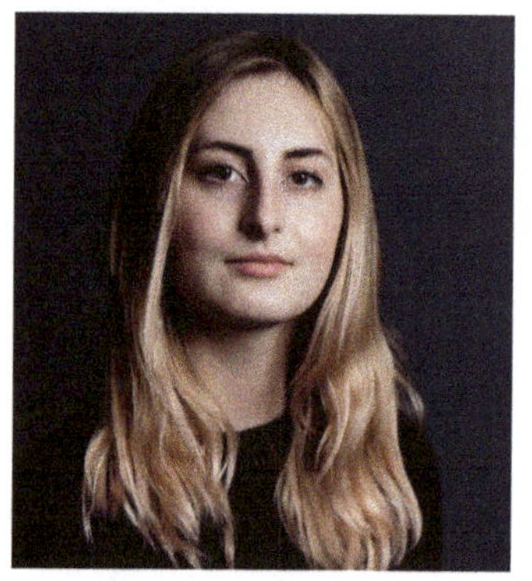

www.hollycerna.com

holly.cerna@gmail.com

@hollycerna_

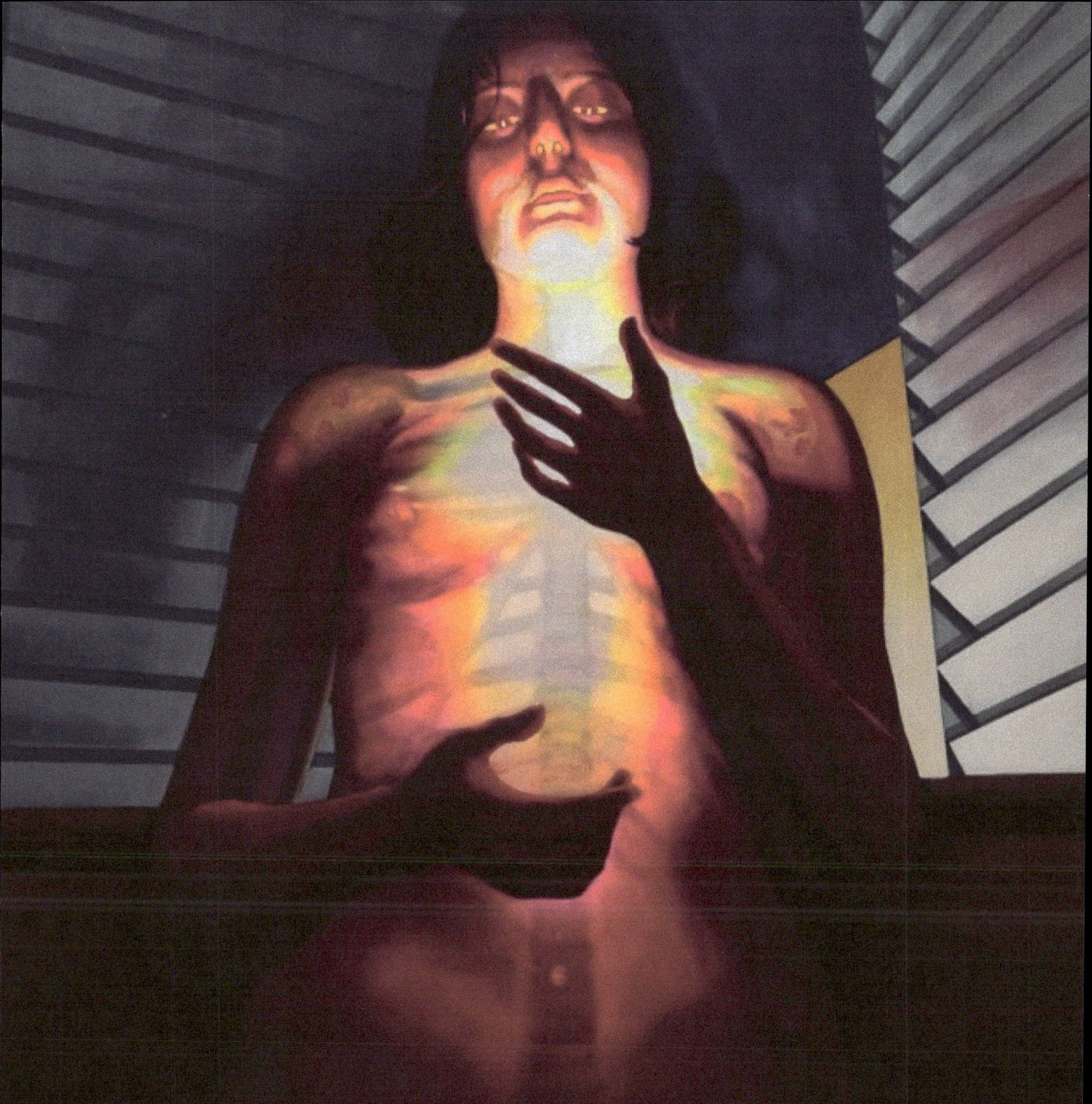

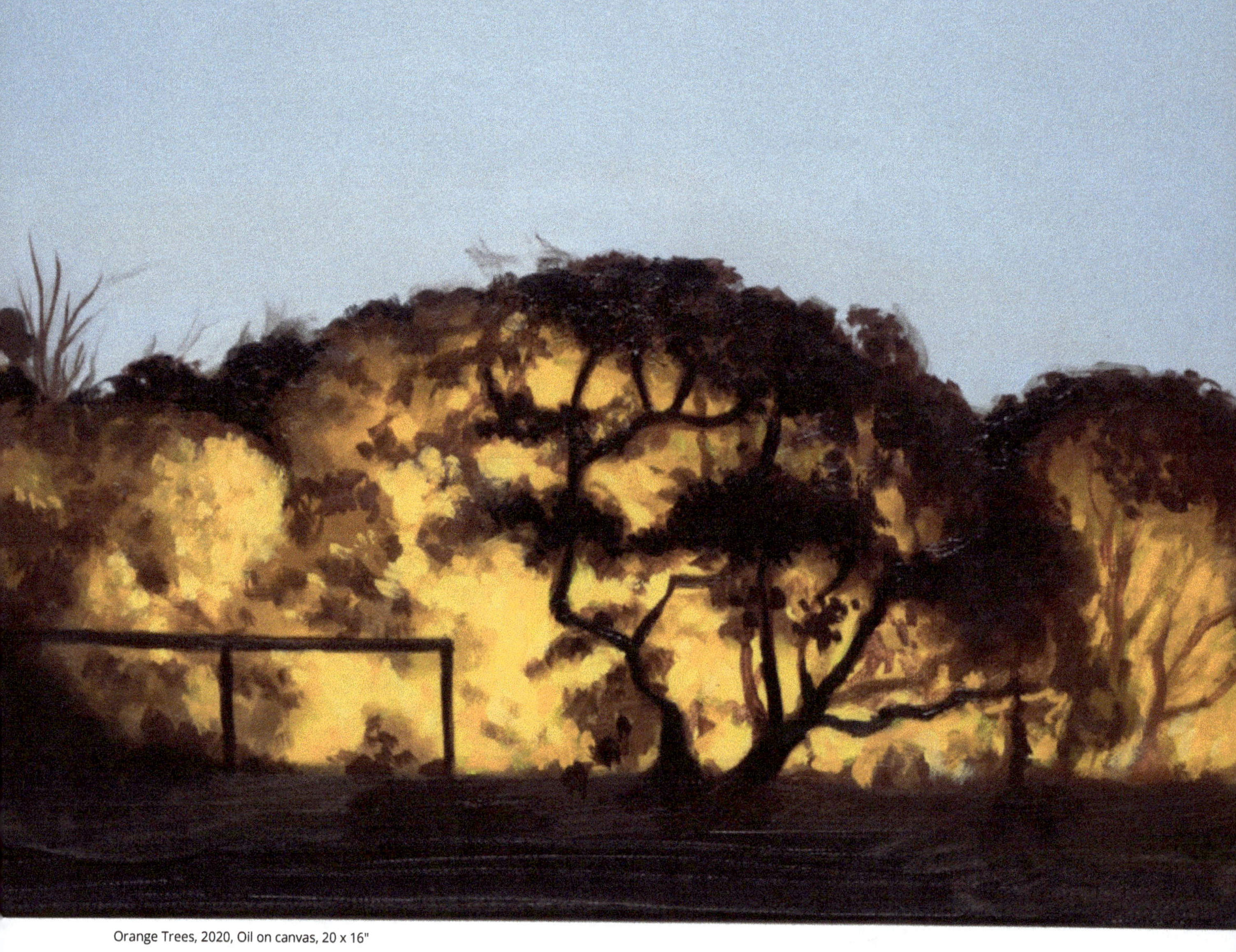

Orange Trees, 2020, Oil on canvas, 20 x 16"

How do you cope with the vulnerability of sharing your art with the world?

Honestly, it's an ongoing battle, and that's okay! Sharing your work with the world is a big part of being an artist. Virtual or in person, we put ourselves into our work and then into the public to be scrutinized and celebrated. This can be scary, but I have found that there is so much strength in vulnerability. To me, vulnerability is like honesty, it is what makes the art relateable. It's very important for artists to be aware of scams and to protect themselves and their work from exploitation. Talking to other artists about their experiences has helped me navigate my own path. We can learn from each other about what works and what doesn't.

Can you share a moment when you felt discouraged as an artist? How did you overcome it?

I remember being told by a classmate "it's stupid to want to be an artist as a career. No one will see or appreciate your work until after you're dead, and you're a girl so maybe not ever". This was said from one middle school-er to another so while it hurt to hear at the time, I took it with a grain of salt. There are many reasons to say discouraging things, but I try to take those perceptions and use it as fuel for my practice. It drives me to prove them wrong, to overcome stereotypes and statistics. It also helps reinforce why I want to create, for myself and to make others feel understood.

How do you decide what to charge for your work?

I factor in the scale of the piece, materials cost, and time cost. Every piece will have a different price because of this.

What do you want people to take away from your work?

When I look at art, I see so much human potential. We are capable of so much beauty as well as ugliness. I hope my work can inspire others the way others works have inspired me. I want people to see their inner conflicts, their positive and negative emotions, and their conscience, as their most valuable qualities. These are what make us human. Our time on Earth is limited. Let's allowourselves to feel deeply, to make mistakes, to uplift and connect with each other as much as we can.

How has your art helped you understand yourself better?

I have been using art as a form of therapy for years. I can freely express myself, experiment confidently through trial and error, and when people swant to connect with my work, that brings it full circle. As I mentioned in the previous tatement, vulnerability is like honesty, it is what makes the art relateable. Art makes us all feel less alone.

What's one piece of advice you'd give to aspiring artists?

Experience the world outside of the creation process to be reminded of why you create in the first place.

Compelled, 2023, Acrylic on canvas, 18 x 14"

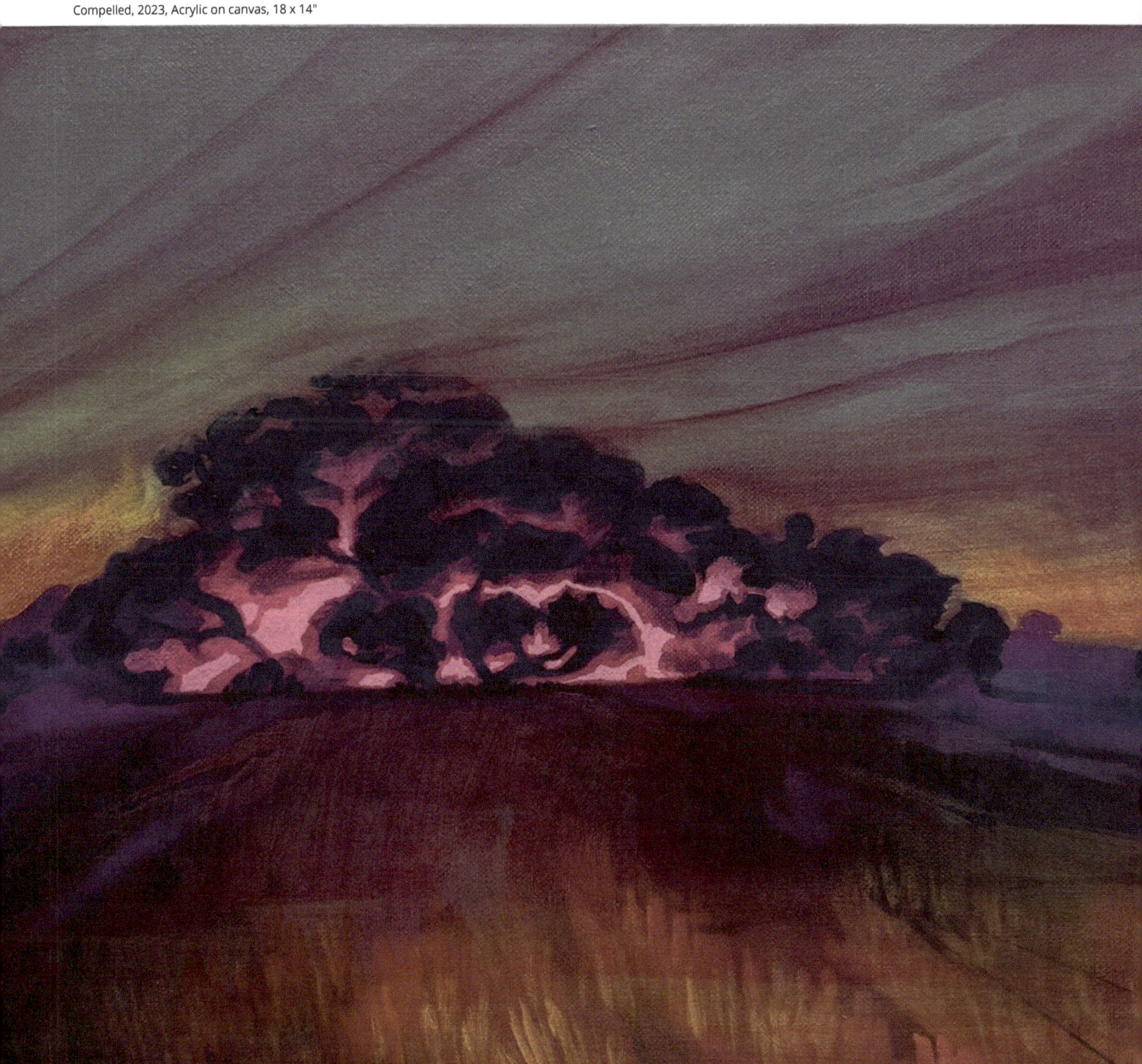

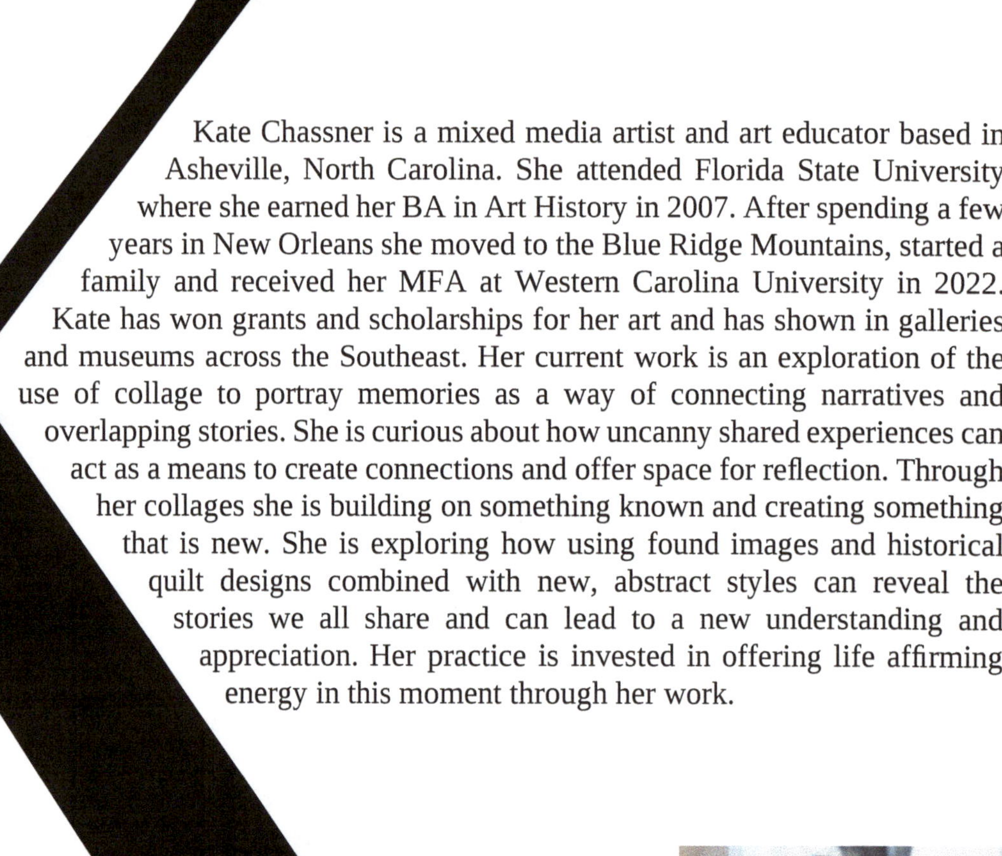

Kate Chassner is a mixed media artist and art educator based in Asheville, North Carolina. She attended Florida State University where she earned her BA in Art History in 2007. After spending a few years in New Orleans she moved to the Blue Ridge Mountains, started a family and received her MFA at Western Carolina University in 2022. Kate has won grants and scholarships for her art and has shown in galleries and museums across the Southeast. Her current work is an exploration of the use of collage to portray memories as a way of connecting narratives and overlapping stories. She is curious about how uncanny shared experiences can act as a means to create connections and offer space for reflection. Through her collages she is building on something known and creating something that is new. She is exploring how using found images and historical quilt designs combined with new, abstract styles can reveal the stories we all share and can lead to a new understanding and appreciation. Her practice is invested in offering life affirming energy in this moment through her work.

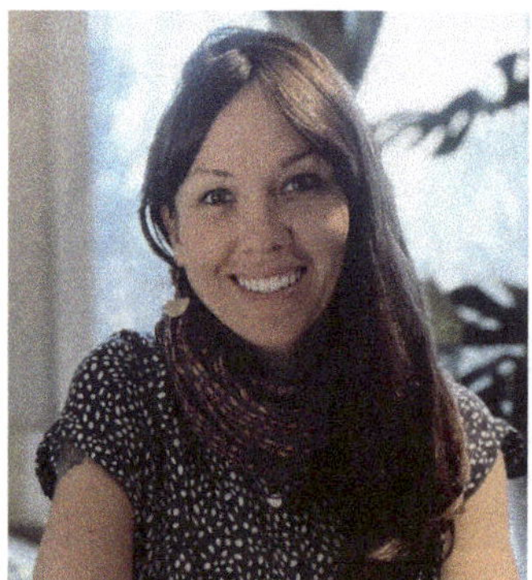

www.katechassnerart.com

kate.chassner@gmail.com

@kate_chassner

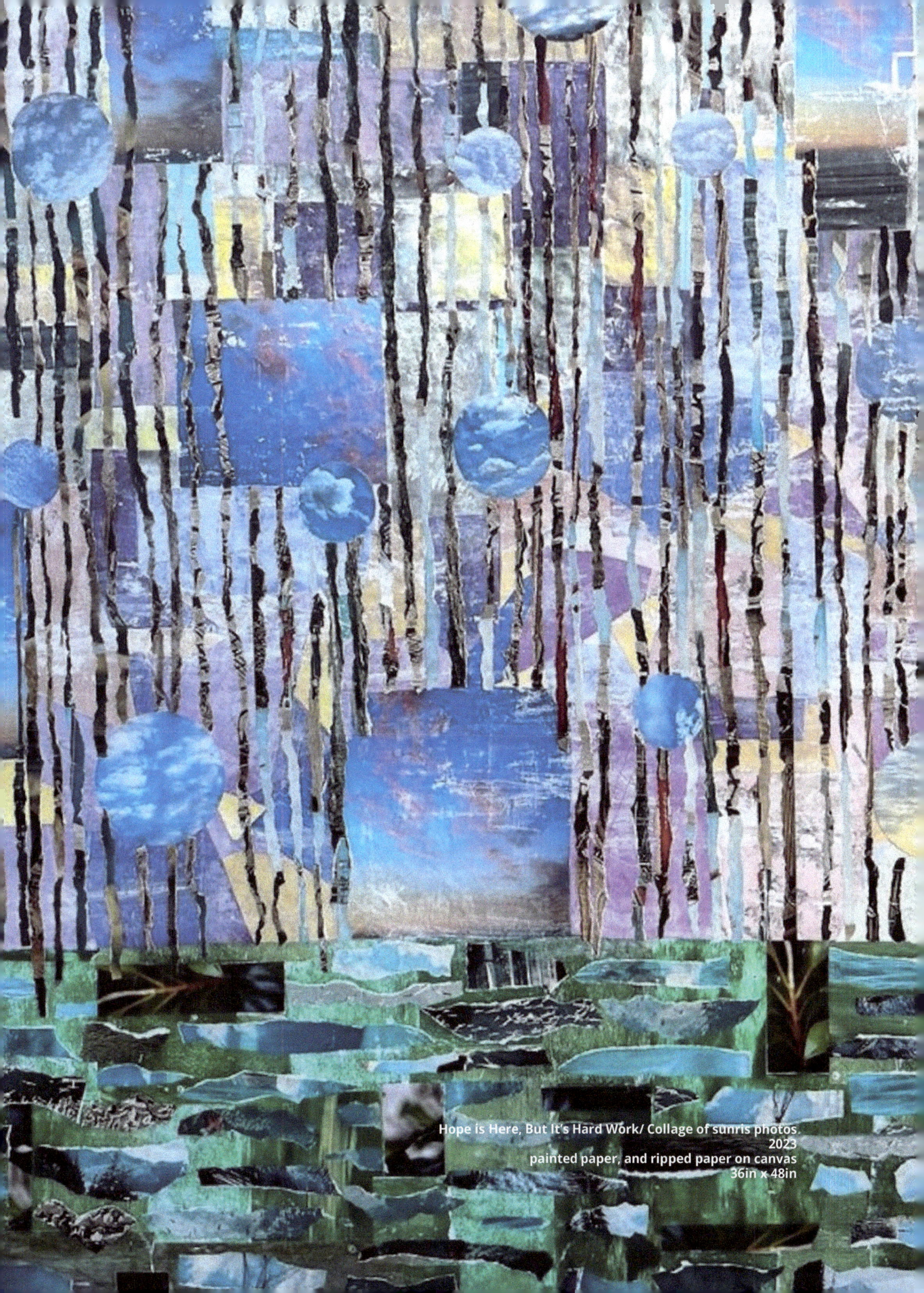

Hope is Here, But It's Hard Work/ Collage of sunris photos.
2023
painted paper, and ripped paper on canvas
36in x 48in

What do you want people to take away from your work?

I want people to look at my art and feel good about themselves and the moment they are in right now. My intention is to infuse each work with life-affirming energy. In the abstract composition and patterns of colors I hope the viewer can find a moment of peace, comfort, and most of all - hope.

How do you cope with the vulnerability of sharing your art with the world?

Vulnerability is good for us, as artists and as humans trying to improve everyday. Being vulnerable means we are putting ourselves out there and allowing room for the unknown and the unexpected to happen. If I am feeling vulnerable I try to see that as knowing I am taking risks and stepping out of my comfort zone.

Can you share a moment when you felt discouraged as an artist? How did you overcome it?

I feel encouraged, inspired, frustrated, and discouraged all in the course of making one art piece- pretty much every time I work on anything. Continuing to work through it and pushing myself to complete or start something new in my studio is the only way I have found to overcome the discouragement. I have Corita Kent's rules from the Immaculate Heart College Art Department up in my studio (and my classroom) and rule 7 says, "The only rule is work. If you work it will lead to something, it's the people who do all of the work all of the time who eventually catch on to things". I remind myself, and my students, that 'work' means making, to get over feeling down about my art or path I am creating as an artist, I try to just keep working and making.

Last Forever, 2023, Acrylic Painted paper on pape, 20in x 30in

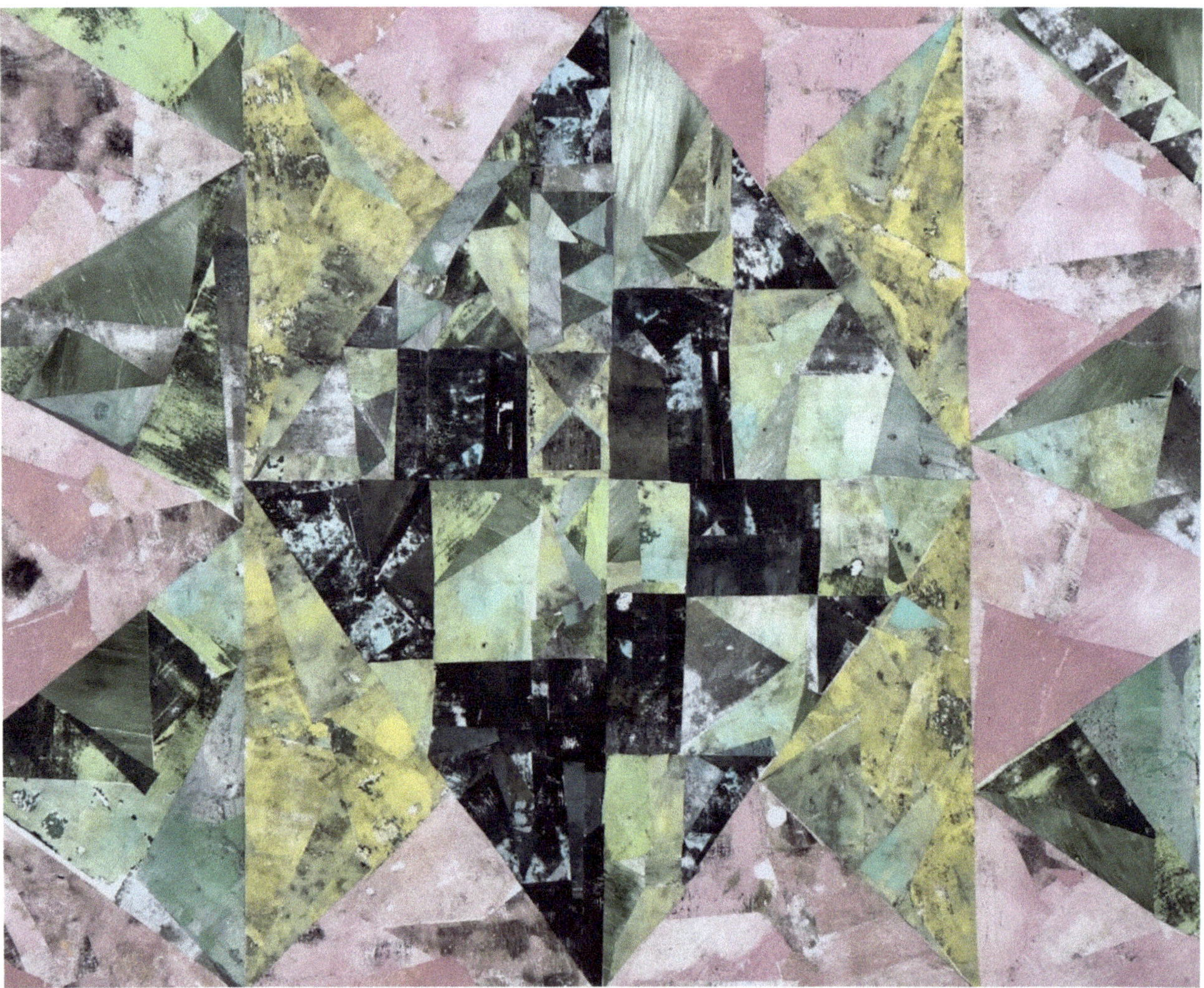

How do you decide what to charge for your work?

Deciding what to charge for artwork is challenging. I do not have a system for how I decide what to charge. I believe that people should be able to buy artwork that inspires them and they want to have for a long time and I believe artists should be paid fairly for their time and work. In a perfect world, there would be a balance of people who can pay more for art to cover the cost for those who appreciate art but cannot afford it.

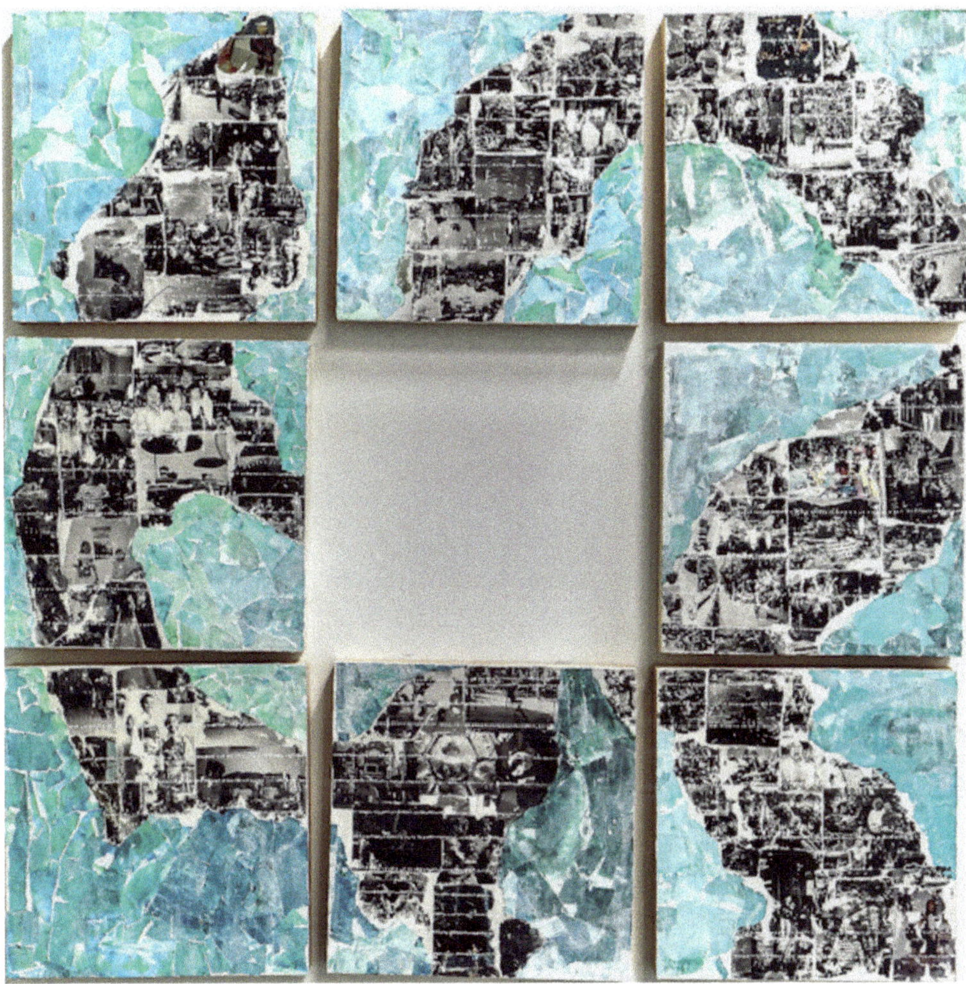

These Ghosts Don't Have Legs , 2022, 8 wood panels, Image transfers of home photos, Acrylic on rice paper and scraps, gesso on wood panels, 16in x 16in

How has your art helped you understand yourself better?

In the process of making art, I work through problems, have moments of success, and find inspiration in unexpected places. I grow and understand myself better the more I am open to these occurrences in each project. Taking time to reflect on past art pieces helps me understand themes and visual content that I return to and teaches me about myself and my journey.

What's one piece of advice you'd give to aspiring artists?

Embrace the journey of finding out who you are and how you can appreciate and uplift that energy within your artwork. Do not worry about how your art is received while you are making it, just make art that is true to you and acceptance will come later.

K

Kathrin Kolbow, born in 1987, lives and works in Bonn, Germany. She studied photography at the Fotoakademie Koeln. Since receiving her diploma, she has worked primarily in artistic photography. The photographer has published three photo books so far and has been part of various exhibitions, such as GUP Magazine's Fresh Eyes Exhibition in Amsterdam. Her work can also be seen in different art magazines. In Kathrin Kolbow's artistic works you often find yourself in the gray areas of human existence and the strange worlds of fantasy. The photographic focus here is on the subliminal conveyance of information and feeling. In this way, far from commercial influences, the photographer creates visual worlds whose themes often deal with things for which there are rarely the right words.

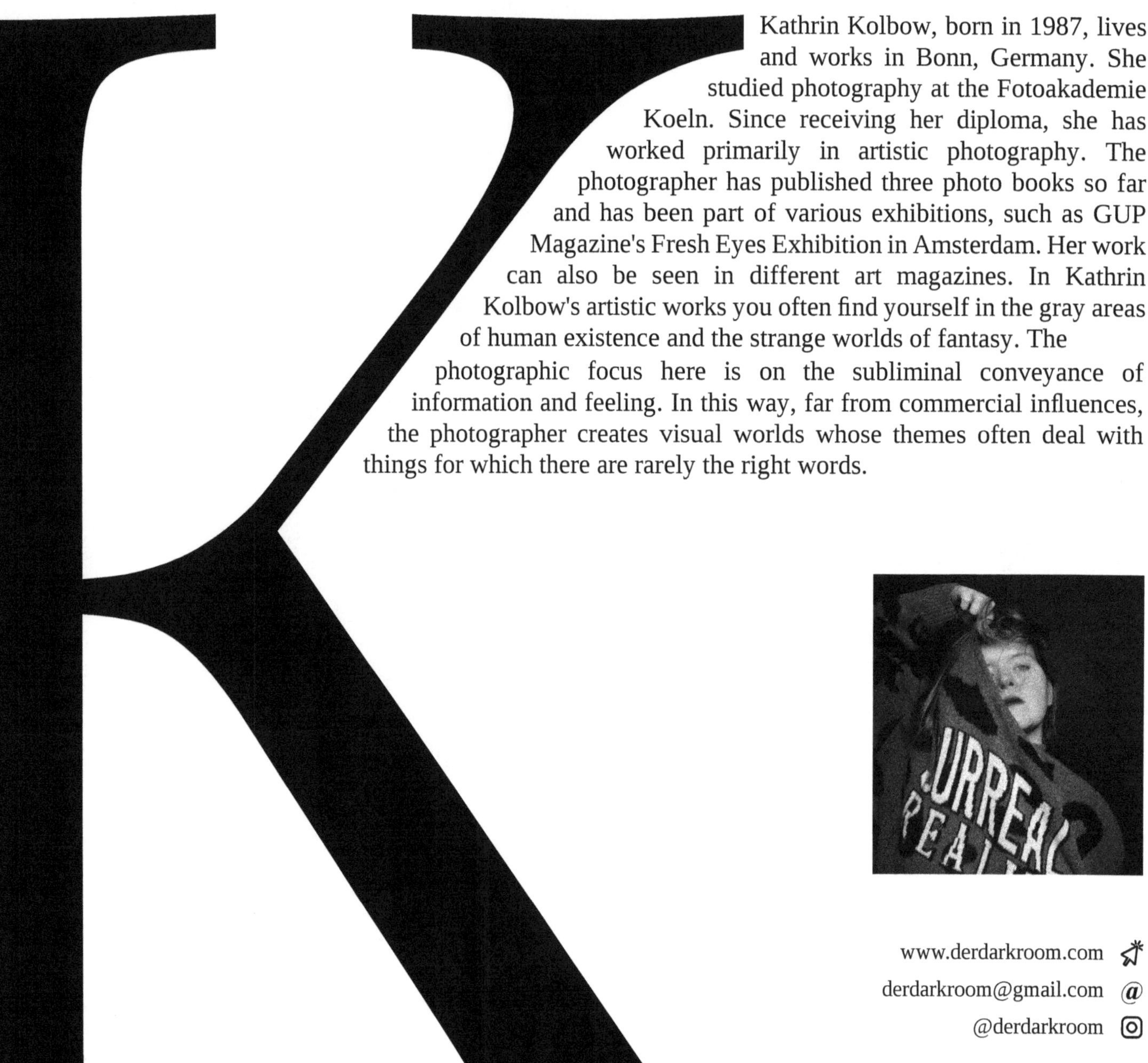

www.derdarkroom.com
derdarkroom@gmail.com
@derdarkroom

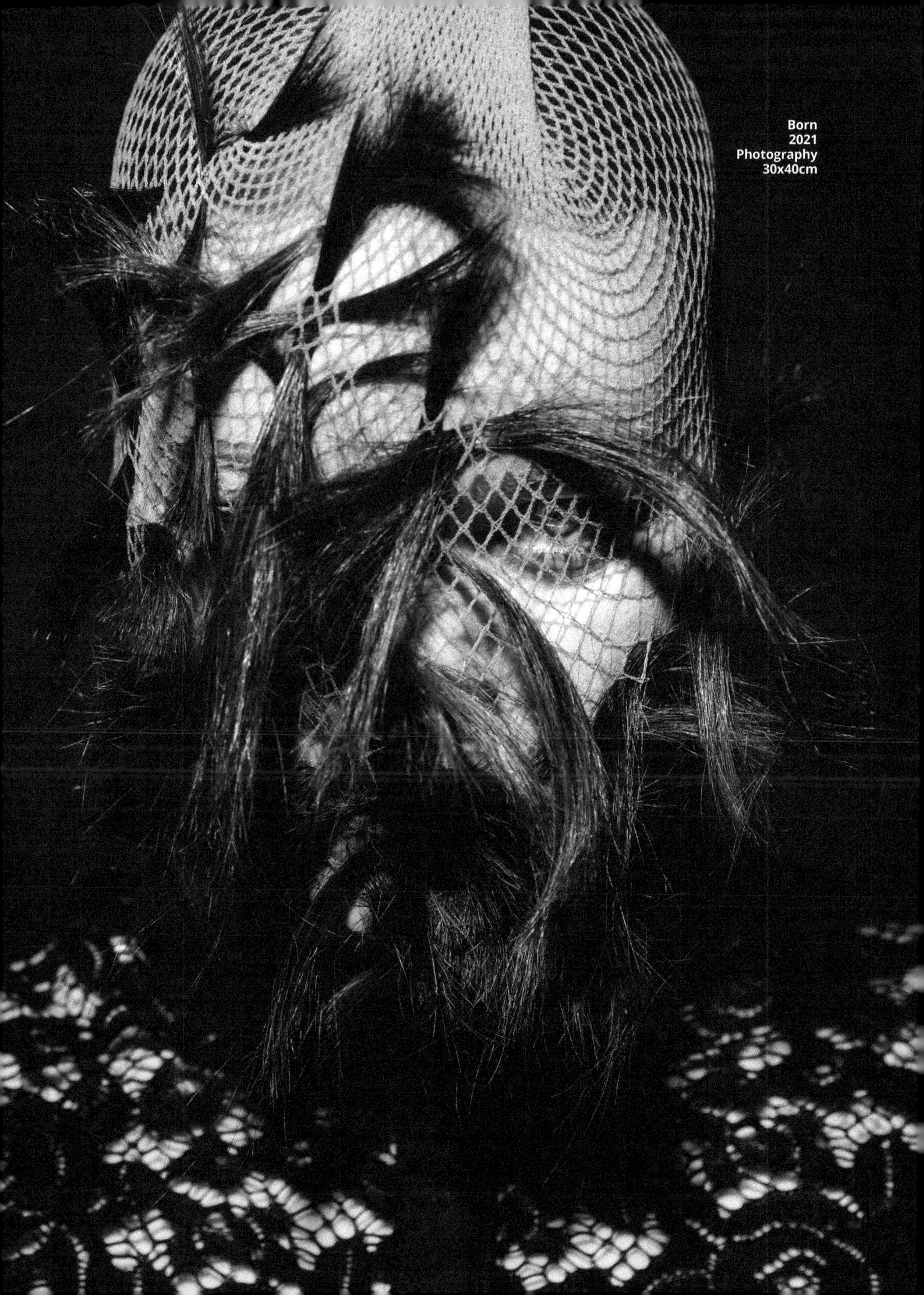
Born
2021
Photography
30x40cm

Can you share a moment when you felt discouraged as an artist? How did you overcome it?

After graduating, I searched for meaning. And as a result, everything gradually lost its importance. The photographic tasks I set myself became increasingly analytical. Most ideas didn't even make it past the pages of my sketchbook. I started to drift away and slowly drowned. Crisis of meaning. Depression. Call it what you will. For me it meant standing still. This standstill lasted for almost six years. I never lost my love for photography, but somehow access to it remained blocked. To the point where I decided to sell all of my equipment. But first I wanted to give it one last chance. One last little project. And it worked. Suddenly everything was there again. All of this felt right again. I can't say exactly how I found my way back. Maybe it was this, all or nothing situation that erased the doubt, that I felt in all this years.

How do you cope with the vulnerability of sharing your art with the world?

Honestly, I had to get used to it. To throw your soul in front of others is a scary feeling. You have to strip all your defense mechanisms down to zero without losing your bit of confidence. I learned that it's worth it. I am able to find so many kindred souls through sharing my work. The important thing is not to lose sight of yourself in the process. If something feels off, I don't do it. If a person feels weird, I don't let them into my life. Even if I bring my inner self to the public through my work, it doesn't mean that I'm selling my soul to them. This way, I am able to keep control over my work and how and where it is shared. That is really important to me.

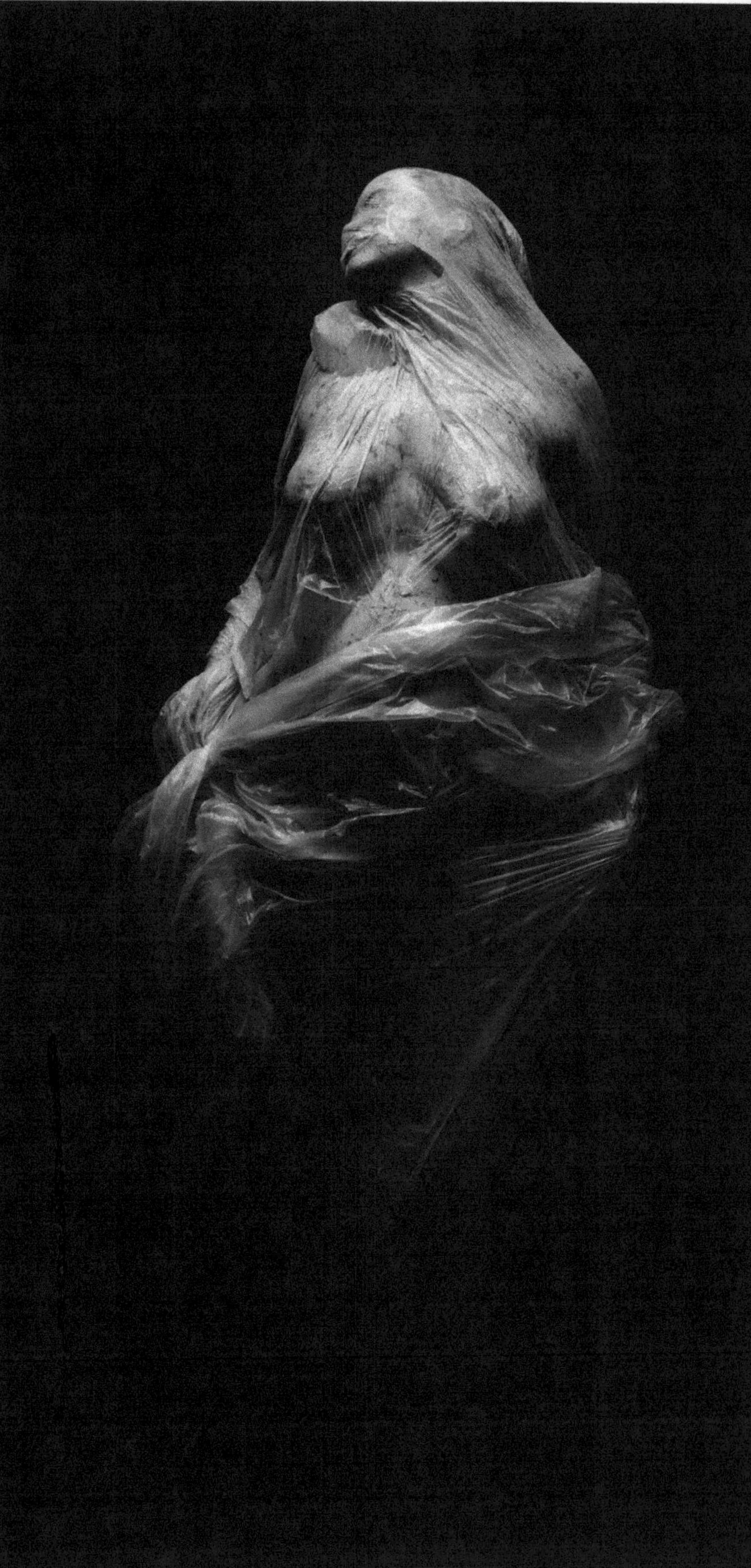

Liberation, 2021, photography

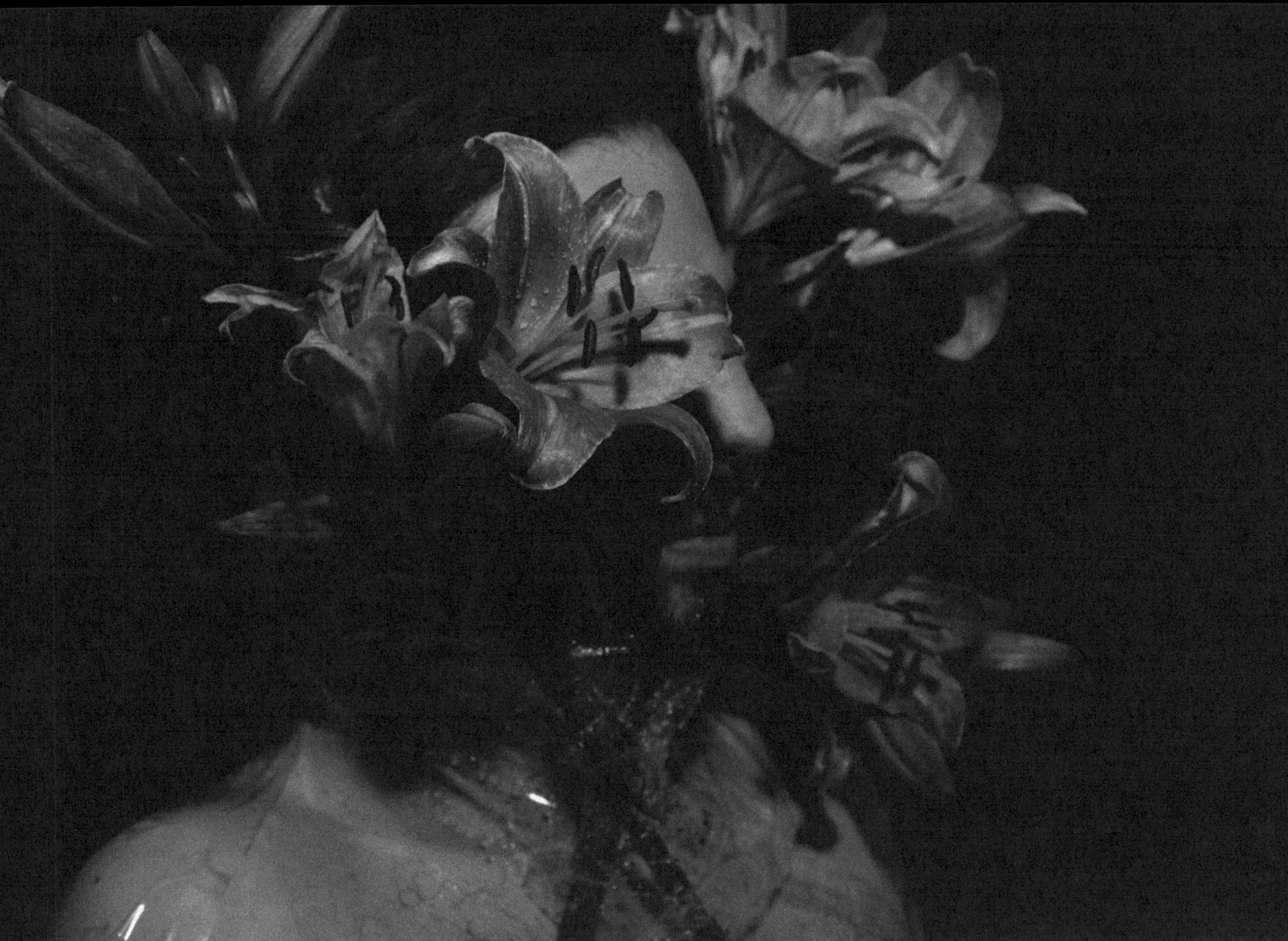

Lilies, 2021, photography

How has your art helped you understand yourself better?

When I'm working on a project, I think a lot. Before a single picture is created, I think about it a thousand times. My work is strongly autobiographical. That means every new series is always a part of me. This way I can process a lot of things that I wouldn't otherwise have access to. In a way, photography is my language for all the things I wouldn't otherwise find words for. And when I talk to others about my work, I become more aware of how the world affects me and how I affect it back.

How do you decide what to charge for your work?

I look around to see what others charge for their work. I don't want to be overly expensive. For me it is more important to be able to share my work than to make a lot of money out of it. I usually have a limited edition of the books or prints that I offer for sale. So this limitation makes everything a little more pricey.

What do you want people to take away from your work?

I want my works to open up spaces within the viewer in which they can wander and work with in order to understand themselves better. I want to create a safe space to talk about the heavy things, that society often marks as unspeakable of. My message would be, that it is okay, not to be okay, and that even the darkest places are able to teach us so much about ourselves that can help us, to fight on.

What's one piece of advice you'd give to aspiring artists?

Whatever art you do, do it for yourself. Not for money, not for fame. Create, because you feel the urge to create. This way, you will be happy and proud of what you did, even if no one else might understand it.

Katy Williamson (b. 1982) is an award winning collage artist (originally from New Zealand) based in the UK. She works primarily in analogue collage but also experiments with digital and animated collages. Her main subject is the human face and the exploration and distortion of it. Repetition, fragments of time and a sense of movement are recurring themes present in her works. She has exhibited in London, New York and New Zealand. Cutting images apart and then putting them back together is a puzzle of chaos and distortion. It allows different times and perspectives to come together to form a new narrative. It also highlights the complexities of the human experience and the many layers that make us up as people.

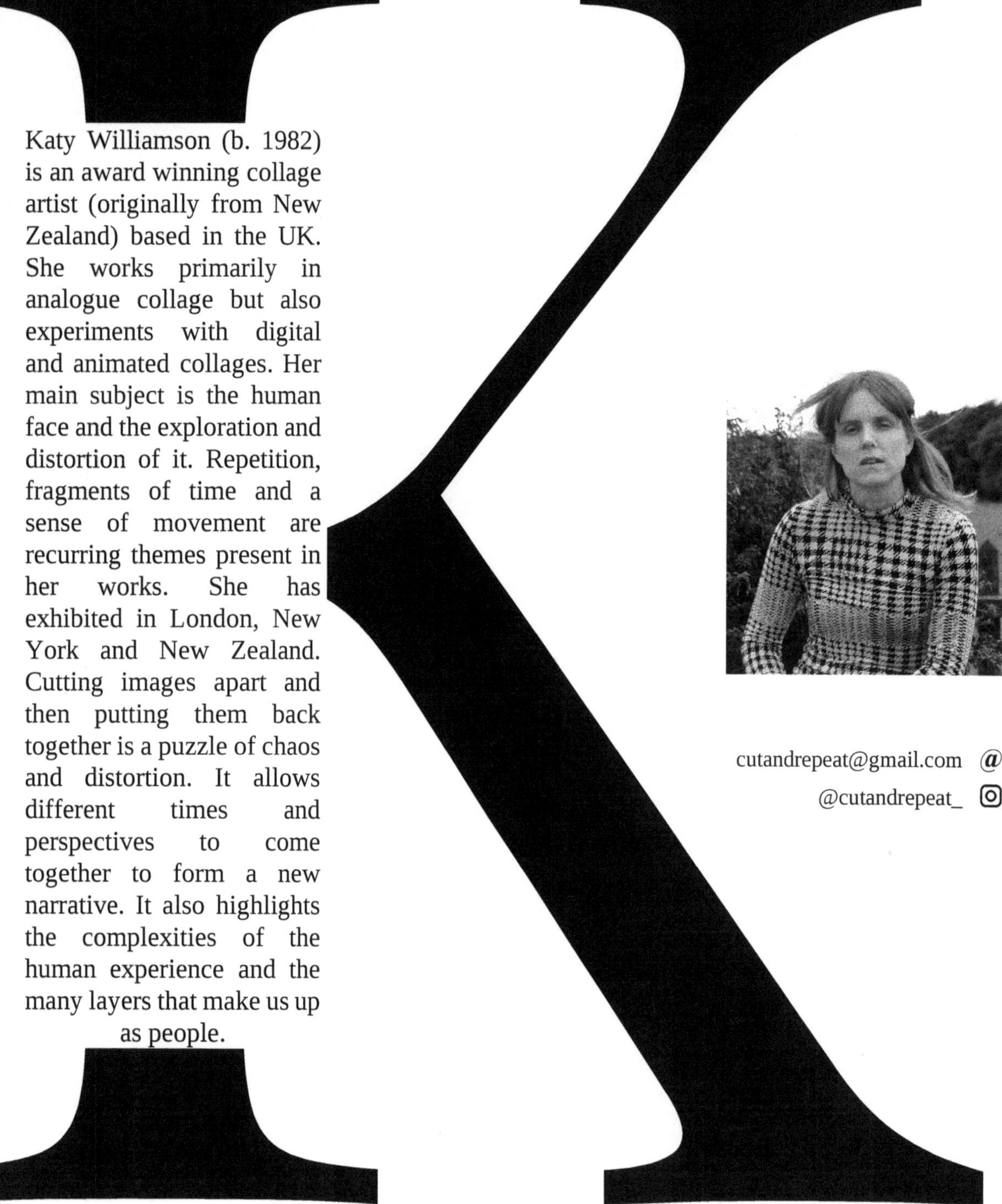

cutandrepeat@gmail.com @

@cutandrepeat_ ◉

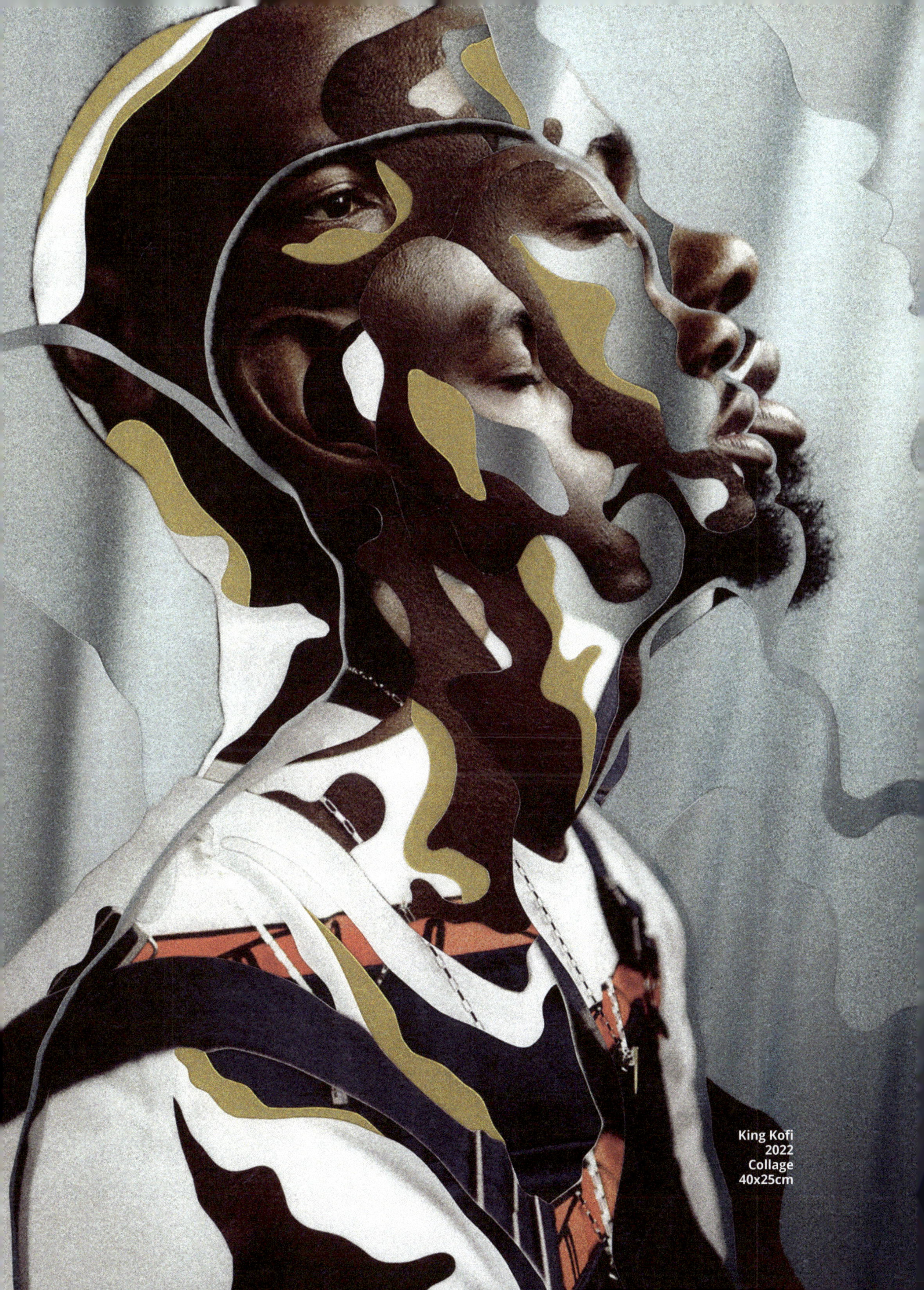

King Kofi
2022
Collage
40x25cm

Can you share a moment when you felt discouraged as an artist? How did you overcome it?

There have been times when I have posted work online and you get no response, or very little, which can be quite disheartening. But it is really important to remember that your work is of value and that is not dependent on likes and shares.

How do you cope with the vulnerability of sharing your art with the world?

As long as I like my own work I am quite happy to share my work with the public. I think it helps to understand that your work is not for everyone. That there is just a portion of people who it will resonate with and that's OK.

David, 2023, Collage, 30x30cm

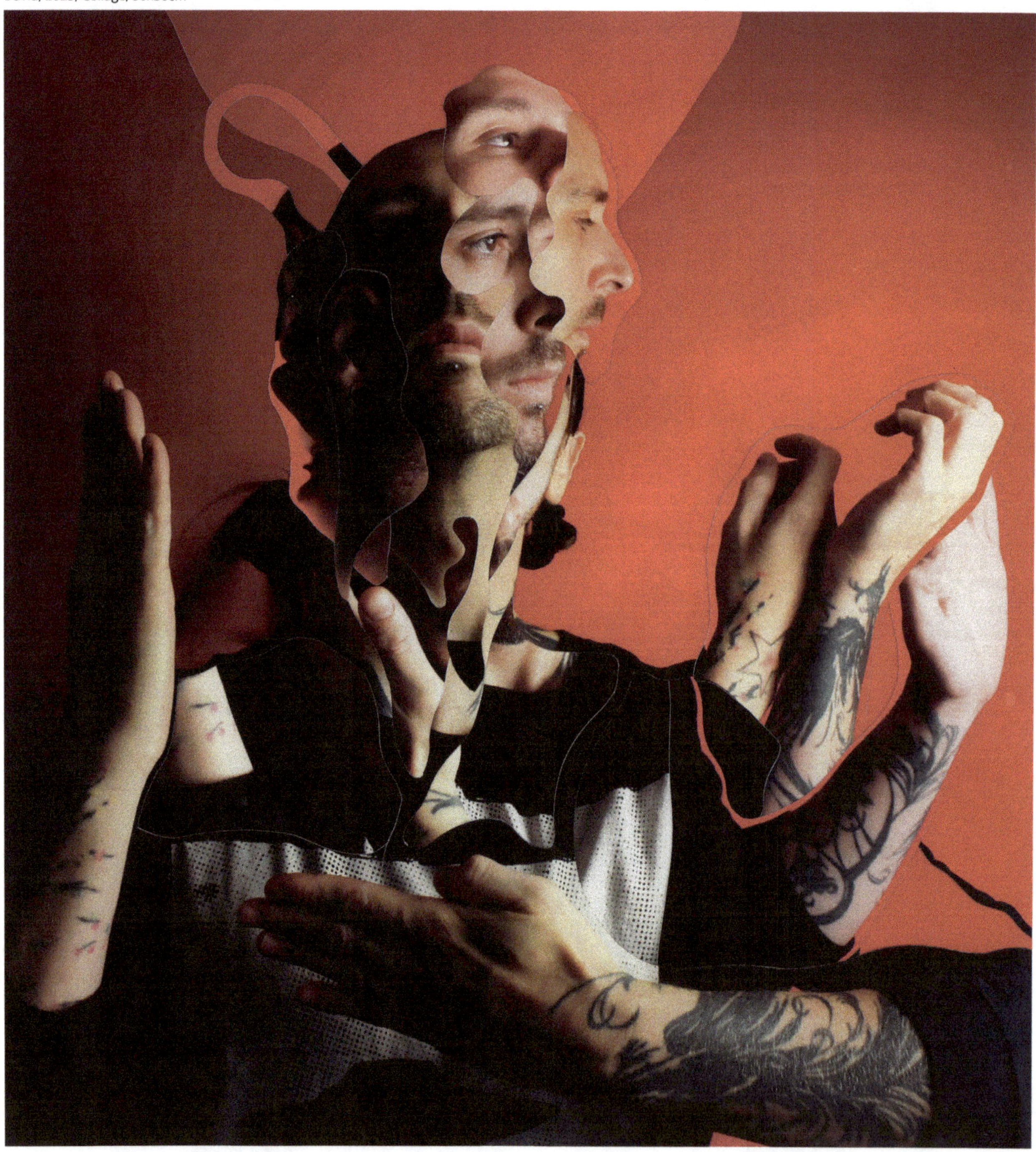

Unknowns, 2023, Paper/collage, 21x30cm

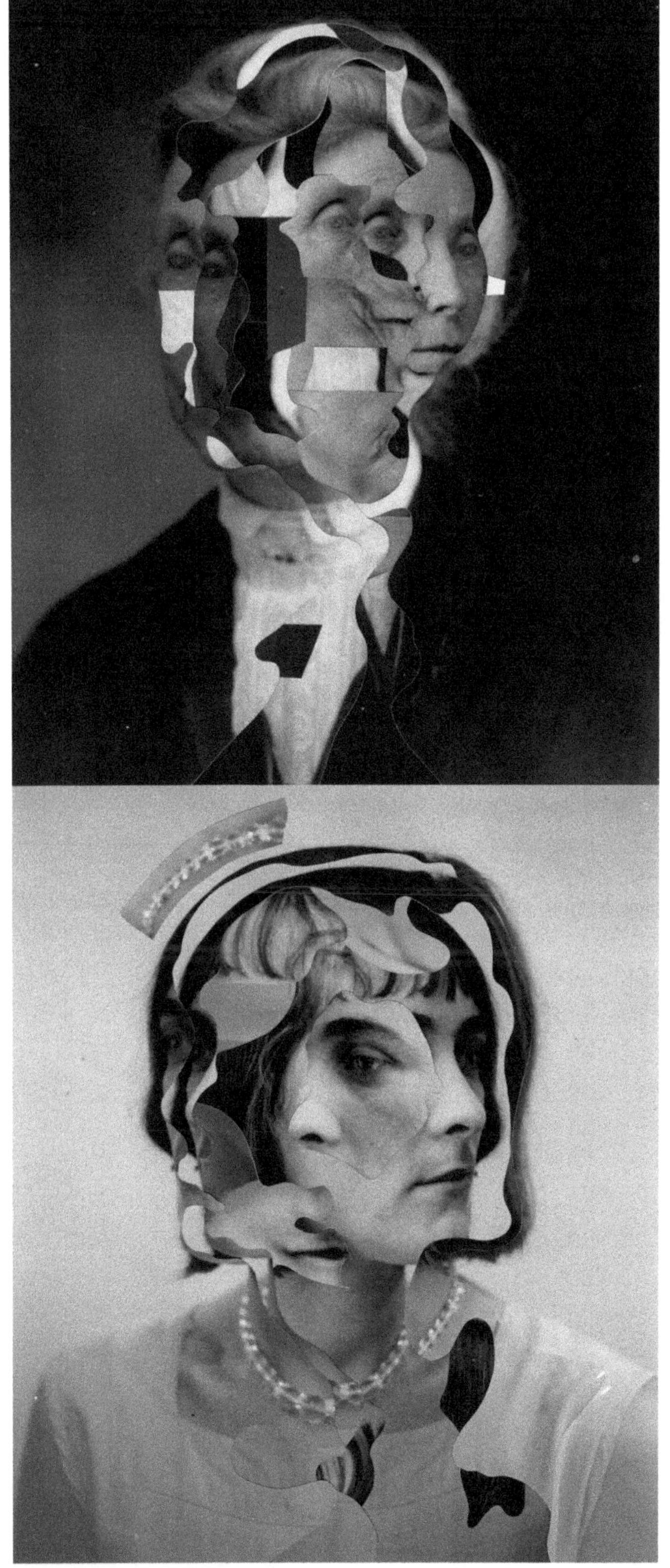

Unknowns, 2023, Collage, 21x30cm

What do you want people to take away from your work?

I want them to have a sense of wonder.

How has your art helped you understand yourself better?

I have been on a journey of discovery as to why I make the work I do and I'm still on it. I have realized that I like distortion. It helps me remember we are not just what we appear to be. That there is a lot more underneath the surface and what we consider 'normal' is really just a surface level of who we really are or what we are able to comprehend.

How do you decide what to charge for your work?

I guess that is made up of my own concept of money and what I think is a fair price. I try and sell my pieces at a price point that I feel comfortable with. I am sure as I progress in my journey the price points will increase.

What's one piece of advice you'd give to aspiring artists?

Keep making work and also it's OK to stop. We are not creatures that work like robots and sometimes you need to pause to see your work better, or to allow space for new ideas to come in. It's a fine balance because you don't want to slow your momentum. I also think its important to understand it's a long game, we are all on a journey and I think I'll continue with my art until I physically can't any more. How exciting is that!? I can't imagine what work I'll be producing in my 80's!

L

Latika Sridhar (b. 1993) is a painter based in Brooklyn, NY. After studying art in high school, she graduated from Dartmouth College with an engineering degree. After studying art in high school, she graduated from Dartmouth College with an engineering degree and worked for several years as a product design engineer. She took a course at Pratt Institute, which inspired her to pursue art professionally. Latika's work is predicated on the transformative power of curiosity about the self. In her paintings, she visually reconstructs her experiences with dissociation to clarify and understand them, exploring the nature of fragmentation, somatic memory, and transformation. Her portraits superimpose three iterations of a person's face to create a single strange humanoid head. Working in oil paint with an acrylic base, she uses an intuitive painting process to reveal her subconscious through texture, color, and form.

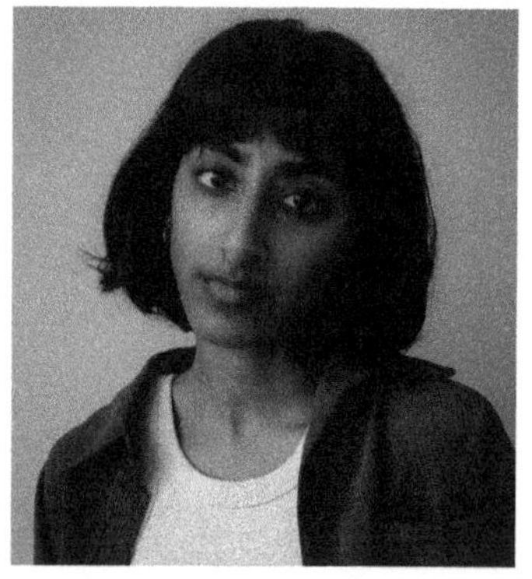

https://latika.art
latika@hey.com
@latika.tbd

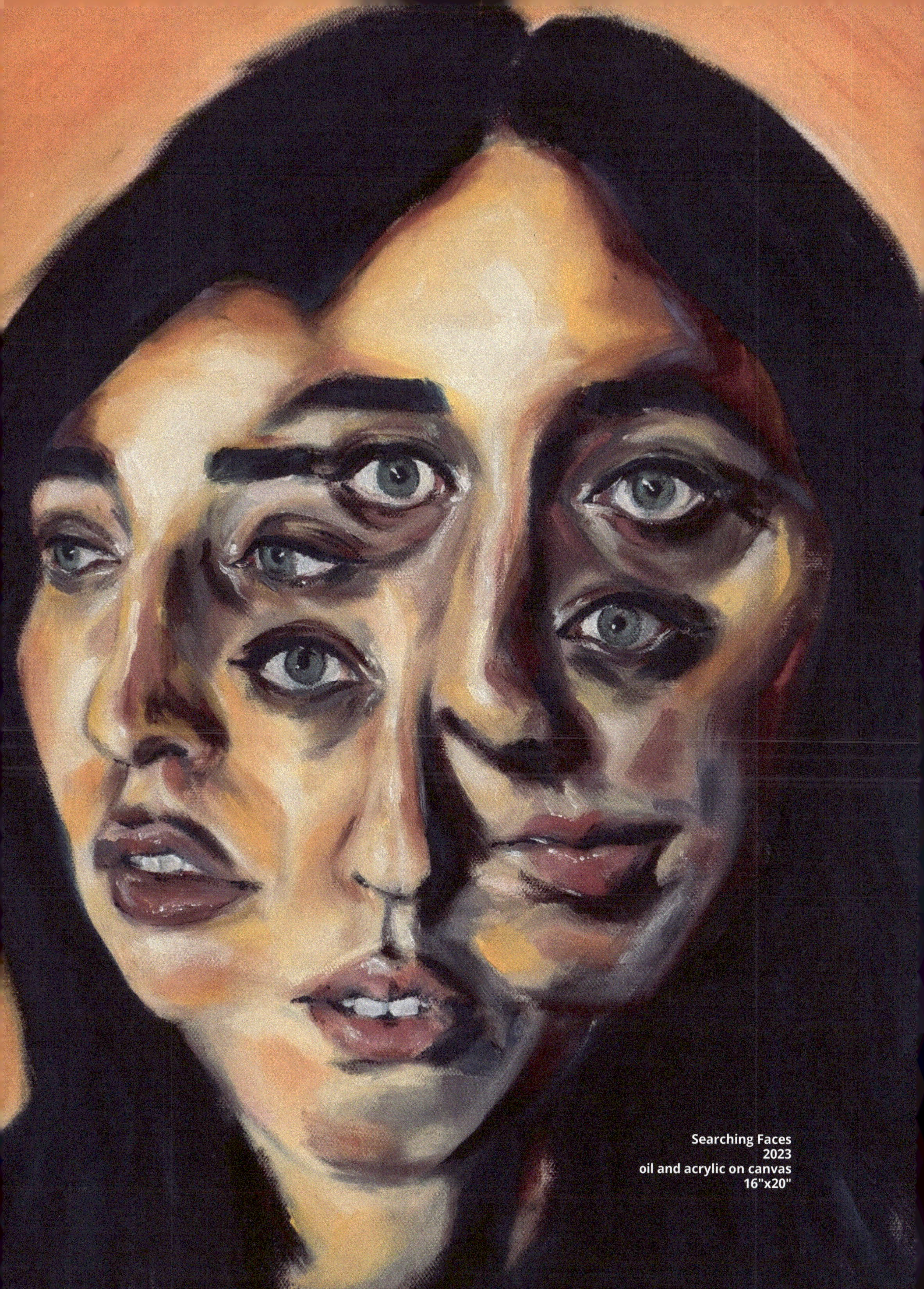

Searching Faces
2023
oil and acrylic on canvas
16"x20"

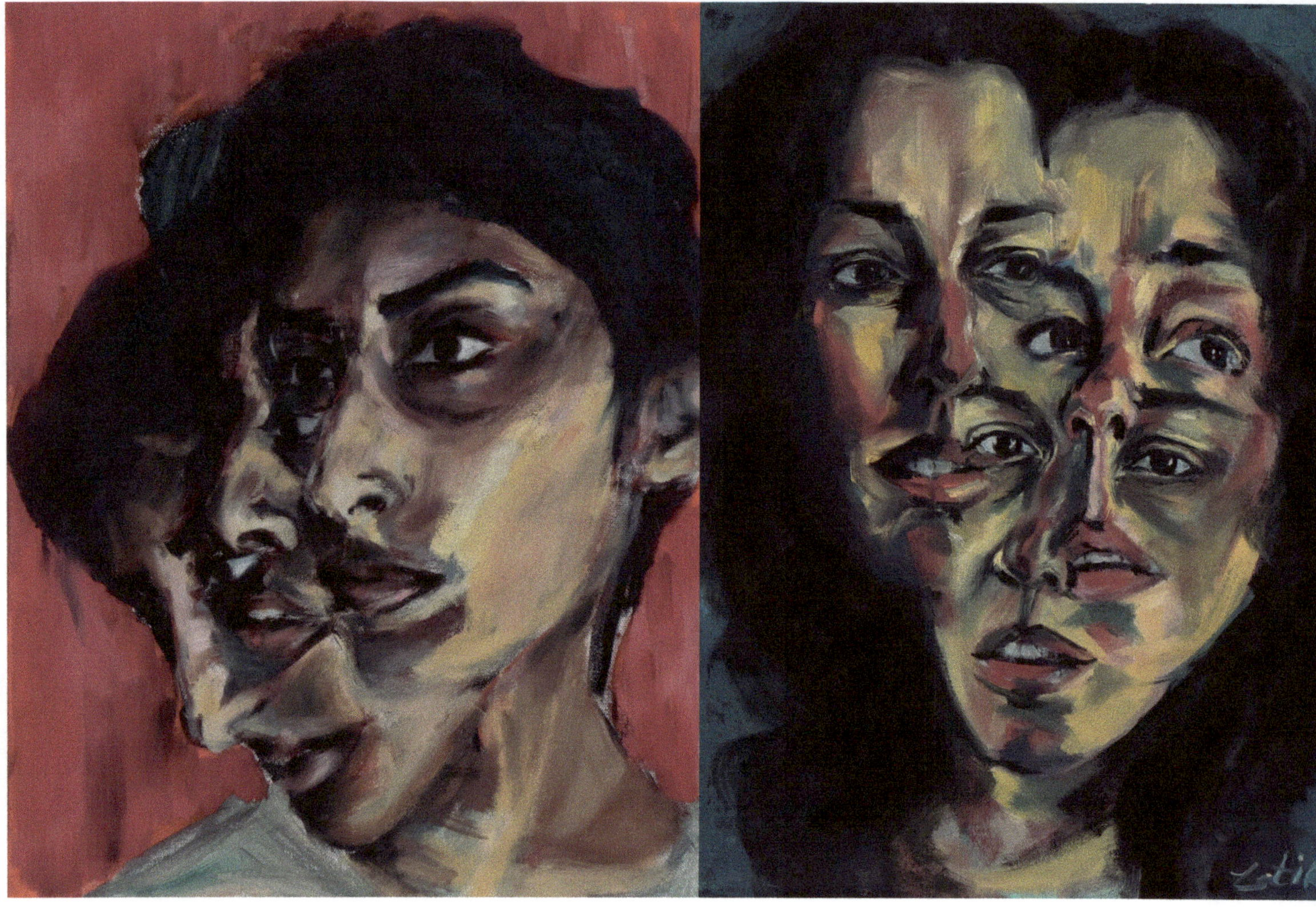

Morphing Faces, 2023, oil and acrylic on canvas, 16"x20"

Paper Faces, 2023, oil and acrylic on canvas, 12"x16"

What do you want people to take away from your work?

I'd love for viewers to simply notice what response they have, if any, to my work. I think art is most powerful when we allow it to reveal something within ourselves.

How has your art helped you understand yourself better?

My art is a practice and exploration of self-understanding so there's so much I could say about this. On a tangible level, it's helped me notice and validate myself more: my feelings, my senses, my pains, my growth. After years of clinging to rigid narratives about myself and consequently feeling blocked in my other creative pursuits, I'm finally honoring the parts of me that are less neat and more fluid. In some ways, it feels like I'm looking at myself with brand new eyes.

How do you cope with the vulnerability of sharing your art with the world?

The most vulnerable part of sharing my art has been exposing my deeply personal feelings and experiences to the world. There's always a fear of rejection of my innermost self. I have not so much coped with this as I have learned that where there is opportunity for rejection, there is also immense opportunity for affirmation and acceptance. When I presented my first two pieces of this series in a classroom crit, one classmate shared that my work was evocative of their own experiences with dissociation. Other friends and strangers have shared their stories with me. And what a beautiful thing — to reveal a part of myself that I was insecure of, even a little ashamed of, and find community in that. The more I have leaned into this vulnerability, the more strength I've gained from it.

How do you decide what to charge for your work?

For now, I'm keeping it simple. I use a formula based on the size of the canvas.

What's one piece of advice you'd give to aspiring artists?

Be intentional about when and how you want to receive feedback and don't be afraid to communicate those boundaries. I can't tell you how many people, artists and non-artists alike, have offered me unsolicited opinions or suggestions about my work. It's natural for people to want to help. But it was important for me to develop and build confidence in my own ideas, especially during the crucial early stages. Listening to lots of different voices often got in the way of that. It's okay to let people know you aren't looking for feedback right now. And when you do want feedback, it can be helpful to ask specific questions or request certain types of feedback that would be most helpful to you.

Can you share a moment when you felt discouraged as an artist? How did you overcome it?

I initially felt discouraged upon learning how important networking is in the art world. I felt totally unprepared to talk to strangers about my art and was worried that my social anxiety would get in the way. It's not easy, but I'm practicing putting myself out there anyway. I've met lots of artists and communities that are welcoming and supportive. And I've learned that viewing each interaction as an opportunity to learn rather than impress helps take the pressure off.

Chorus, 2023, acrylic on canvas, 12"x16"

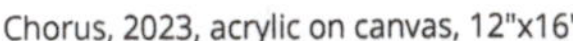

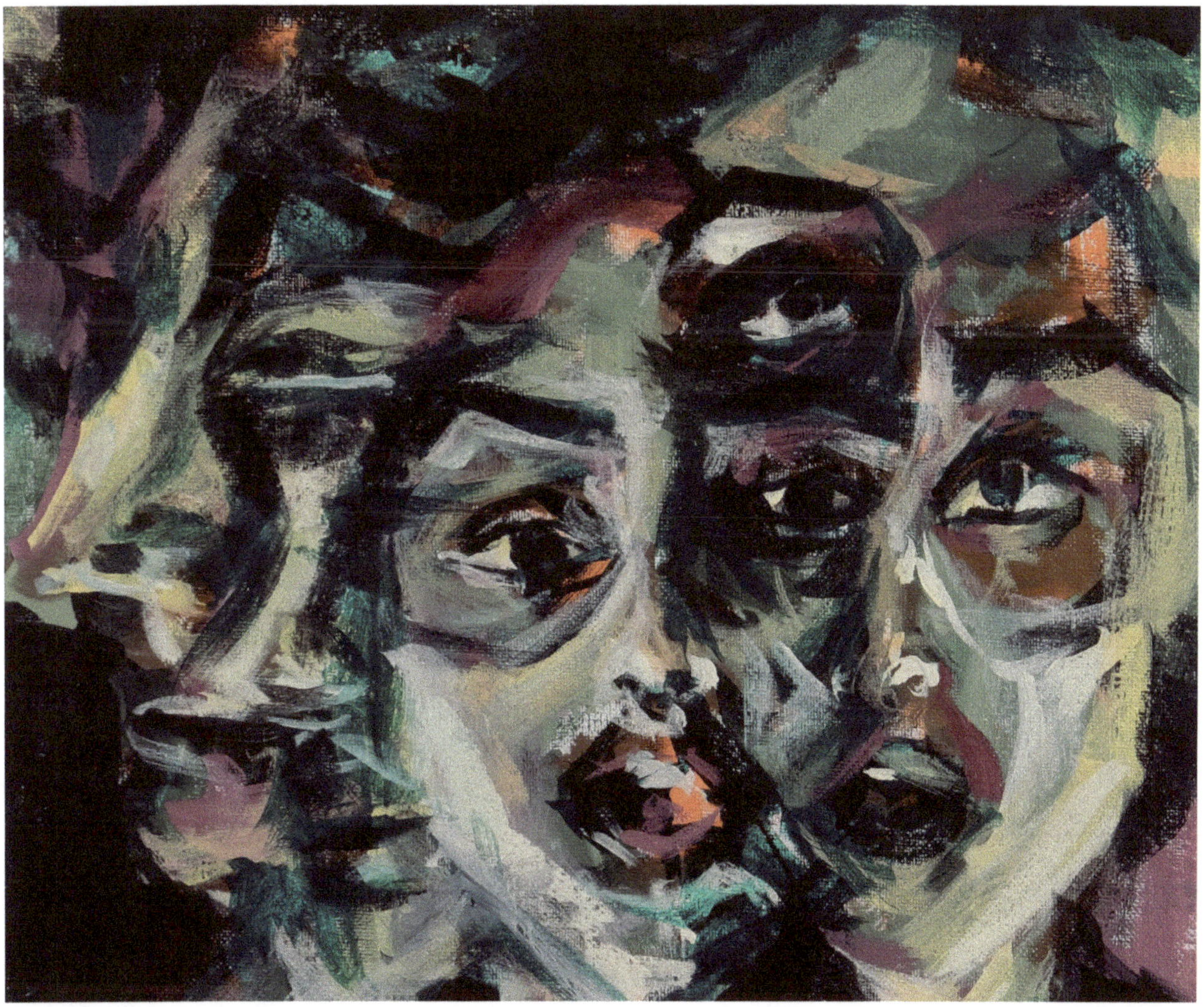

Luz Angela Medina is a textile artist born in Bogotá, Colombia, a diverse country in all its aspects, in nature and its culture, crossed by the Andes and that in the country become three very different mountain ranges.
Artist Statement:
4 years ago in my artist search I came across the language of textiles and between fabrics and stitches I am mending and weaving a story , a landscape that surrounds me that is part of me and I reflect on how each of our actions has a positive or negative effect in the place we inhabit, in this search about the impact of our transit on the planet, I have started a series of landscape faces where I want to Capture my Territory through a textile sculpture.

I was born in the midst of clouds, rain, moors and mountains of 3 mountains ranges, two oceans, plains, green valleys and tropical jungle, in one of the most bio diverse countries on Earth; this richness and fragility has always fascinated me, how it transforms by the impact of our contact. How it resists and adapts to survive. Through the textile I wanted to reflect that we are part of this planet and the universe, a very small and insignificant part, we are not the only ones nor the most important, with time.

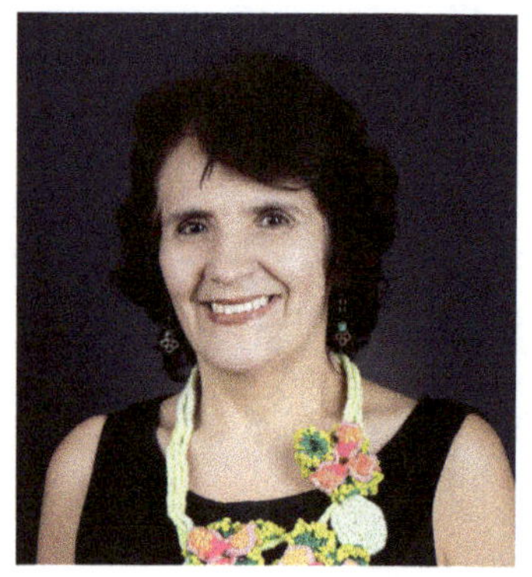

www.gangamedina.com
gangamedina@gmail.com
@ganagamedina

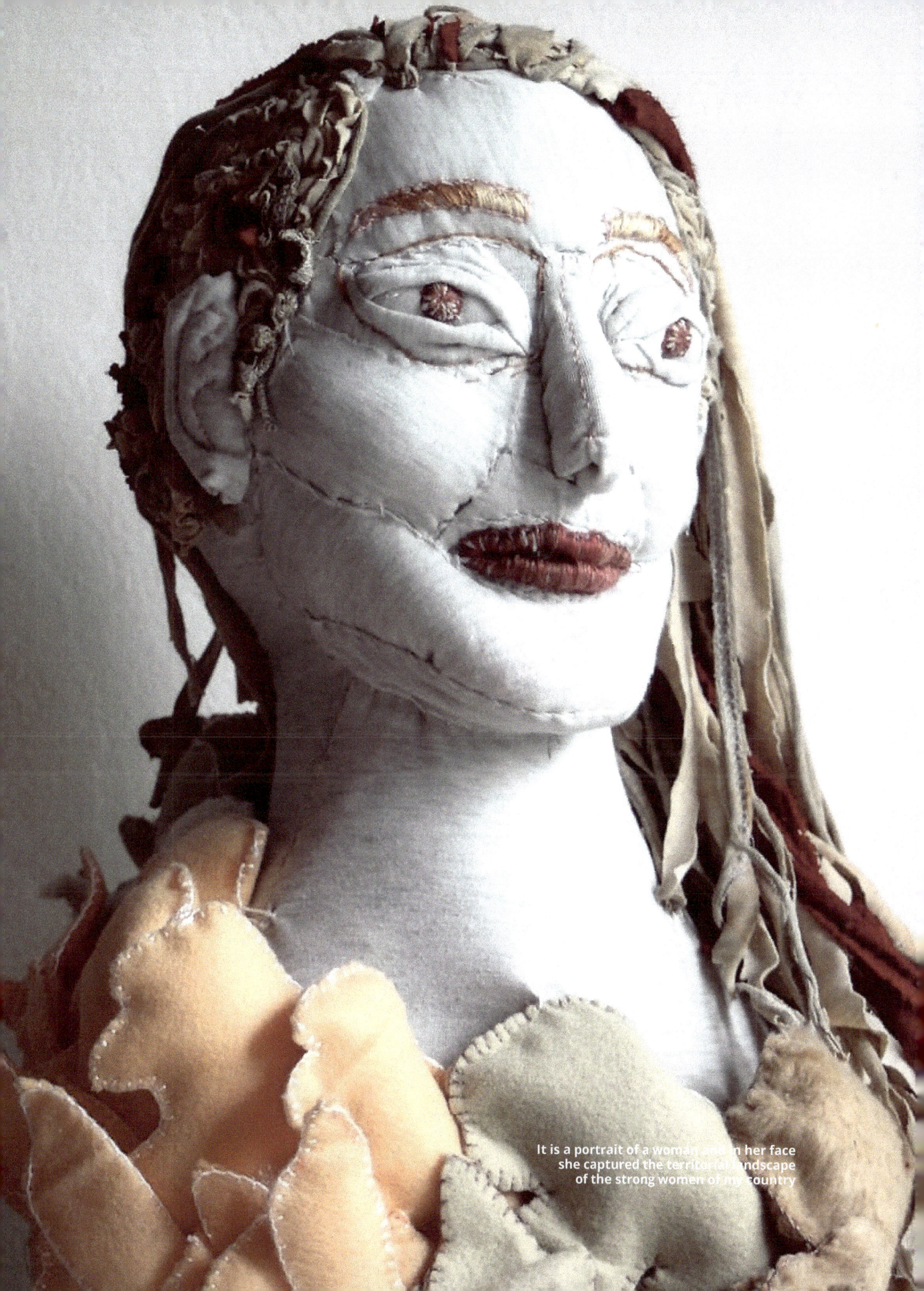

It is a portrait of a woman and in her face
she captured the territorial landscape
of the strong women of my country

What do you want people to take away from your work?

A work of art that they can display in some space where it beautifies the place and the same time can be admired and be a point of reflection.

How do you decide what to charge for your work?

It depends on the time you invest and the materials with which you carry out the artwork.

What's one piece of advice you'd give to aspiring artists?

Don't give up your dream of being an artist, persist, work hard, study and have discipline.

How do you cope with the vulnerability of sharing your art with the world?

What I make is vulnerable because it is made of recyclable materials, sharing it is a way to raise awareness about our own fragility and vulnerability.

How has your art helped you understand yourself better?

It has helped me understand myself to communicate with myself and others, my art form is a complaint so that we all reflect on our time on the planet, and the traces we leave behind, which makes you feel good.

Voices is a work in contemporary basket weaving born from the voice of the victims silenced by violence in my country

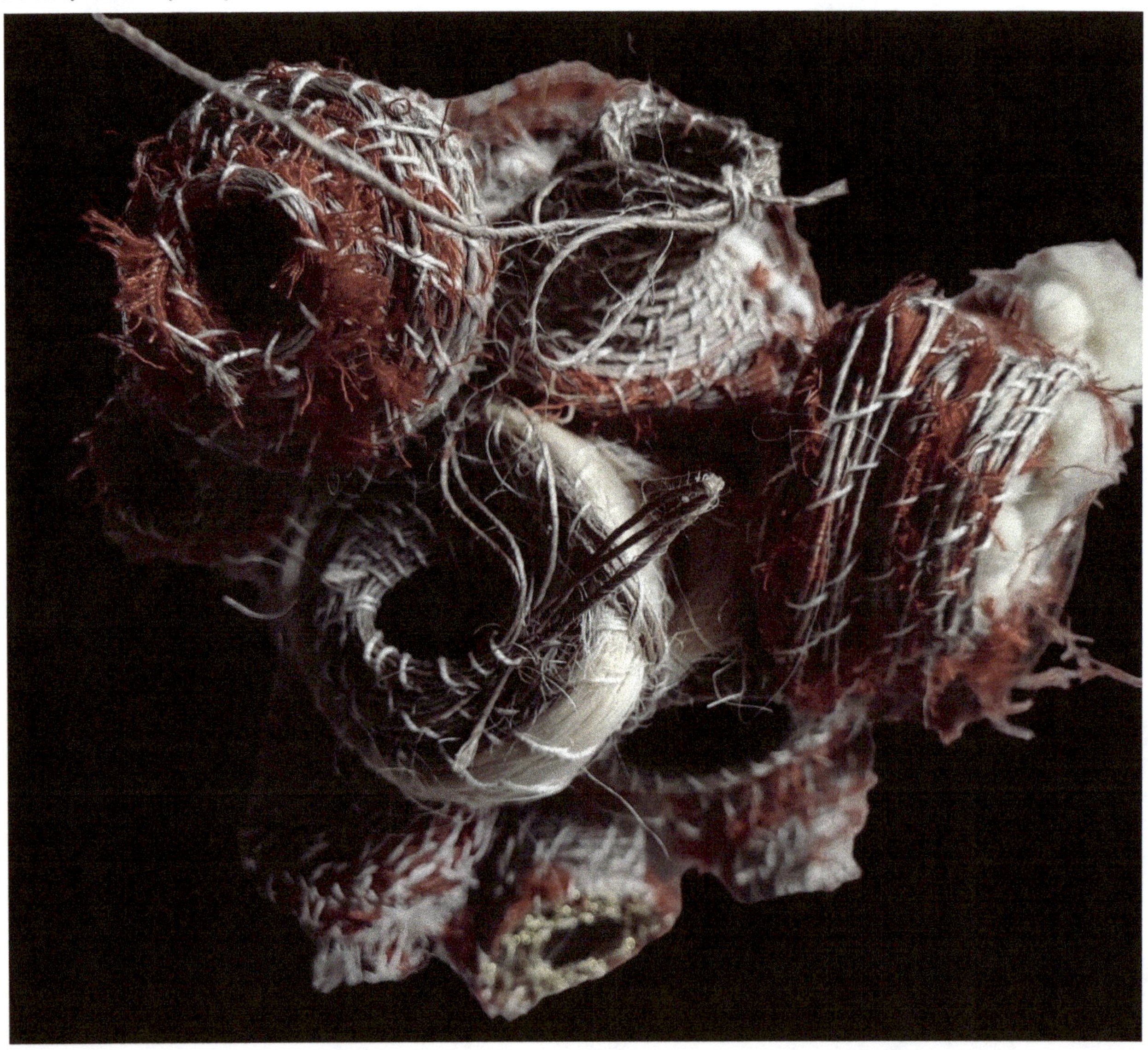

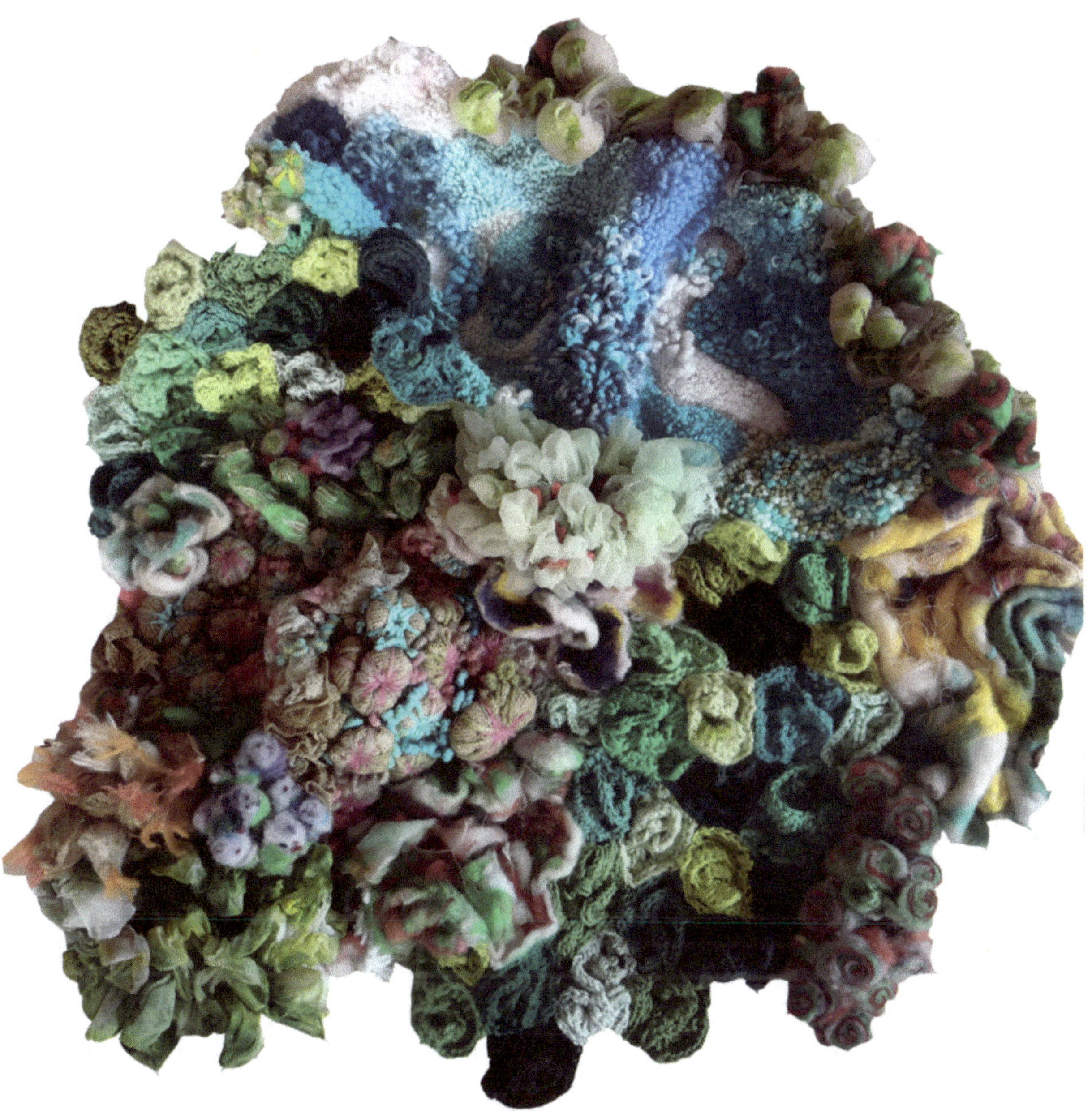

Play full Garden, 2023, Format Textile arte(felt, embroidery and thermoformer) 0.50cm X 0.46cm X 0.10cm

Can you share a moment when you felt discouraged as an artist? How did you overcome it?

I felt discouraged as an artist when I left university and did not know what to do how to continue. Many years later why I had decided to study art. When I me an adult, I asked myself. I was discouraged once I finished studying, I had my small children, I didn't know what to do and where to start, and life itself kept taking me away from artistic work. Many years later as an adult, I asked myself why I decided to study art. When I met my classmates again and saw what their lives had been like, I began to look for my paths, and 4 years ago I returned to art my only activity. I investigated. I studied and took classes with the young Argentine artist Morillos. She questioned me, opened the way, she led me to understand myself, to know why I did what I did and in that situation, sometimes of discomfort, I asked myself question.

M

Marina Schulze is a self-taught visual artist. She explores the freedom of this concept by working with stone, photography, paper collages, painting and drawing, from installations and stage sets to analogue 3D collages. She prefers to work with real colors and materials. Her works are figurative and move within the surreal. She explores and exposes the characteristical mutilation of the feminine principle in the global patriarchy with the utopia of the reversal of power relations. She is inspired not only by her studies in German language and history, Theater Studies, Art History, and Psychology but also by her special interests in Creation myths, matriarchal and gender research, as well as by the toxic effects of political decisions and the resistance of the female principle to them. Born in 1959 - A-levels 1977 - Birth of her son 1981, single parent. Since 2020 she has been a member of the bbk Berlin, 40 years of annual solo & group exhibitions, including the Berlin galleries Chrome-Art, Lite-Haus, Herzog, Villa Kult, Kunsthalle Deutsche Bank. Her project "Saturn/Shani" has been part of the curriculum of "Identity in Art and Feminist Art" by Dr. S. Parish at York University, Seneca College of Creative Arts and Animation, Toronto, since 2023.

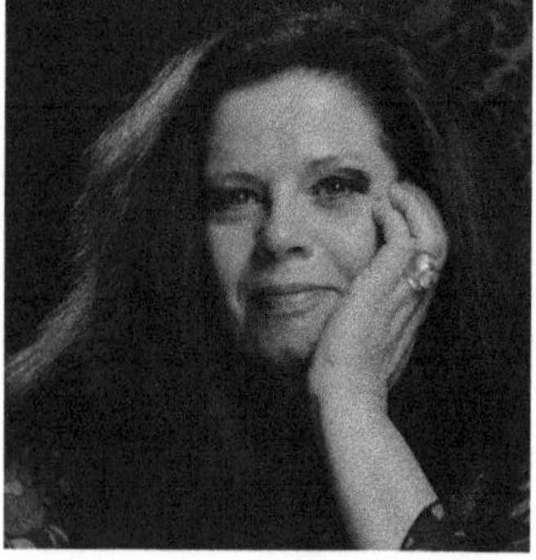

https://anasaea.com/artist/BsdQraxhYB55nTrZP

bluefish@bibest.de @

@marina.schulze.art

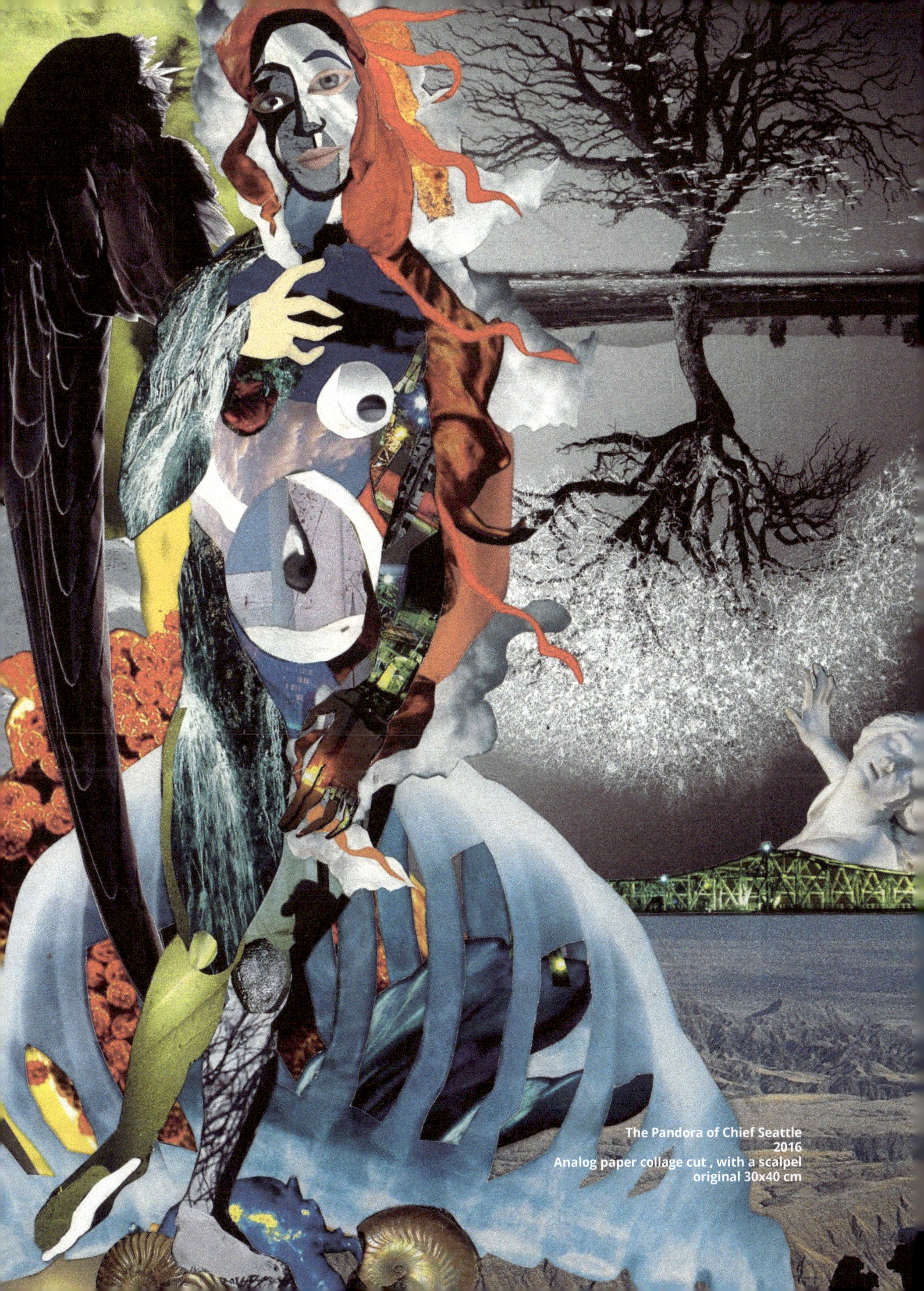

The Pandora of Chief Seattle
2016
Analog paper collage cut , with a scalpel
original 30x40 cm

C**an you share a moment when you felt discouraged as an artist? How did you overcome it?**

My journey to becoming an artist was disheartening. When I was 16, I expressed my desire to become an artist, but my parents replied, "You're no Picasso." I couldn't argue with that. I saw my talent as just a hobby and took lessons. I received particularly harsh criticism from my mentor and close friend. She looked at my first independent work, "Salome meets Leda", and said: " Storytelling is completely uninteresting." And then: "You're so talented, you won't amount to anything." These words paralyzed me for years. I put my creativity at the disposal of others and became seriously ill. In a clinic, I was encouraged to trust my talent and to experiment. I started sculpting and drawing. I rented a studio and worked non-stop. Discouragement and artistic blocks come and go, but when I can immerse myself in my work again and create something, it's all worth it.

How do you cope with the vulnerability of sharing your art with the world?

My vulnerability does not only arise through my work, which I expose to the gaze of others. Due to my high level of sensitivity, I always carry a very alert vulnerability within me. At different ages, I have tried to protect myself by withdrawing or by being provocative and extroverted and by sharpening my intellectual skills. No one notices how scared I am to enter a gallery full of people, for example, or to have to give a speech. My motto: "Where there's fear, there you go." I like to be courageous because sensitivity is also what enriches my life and makes my work possible. People who encounter themselves in my work and can read what I have to say take lifelong pleasure in deciphering its fullness of meaning.

How has your art helped you understand yourself better?

My work is created from my ability to perceive and reflect on the inner and outer world. It is like a river that is always in motion and can only be briefly analyzed before it changes. I learned to understand this process the hard way, realizing that I become sick if I don't nurture my talent and let it work. I have come to appreciate that I can live a meaningful life by staying in this flow. I have little control over it, but without full awareness, this life path is not feasible.

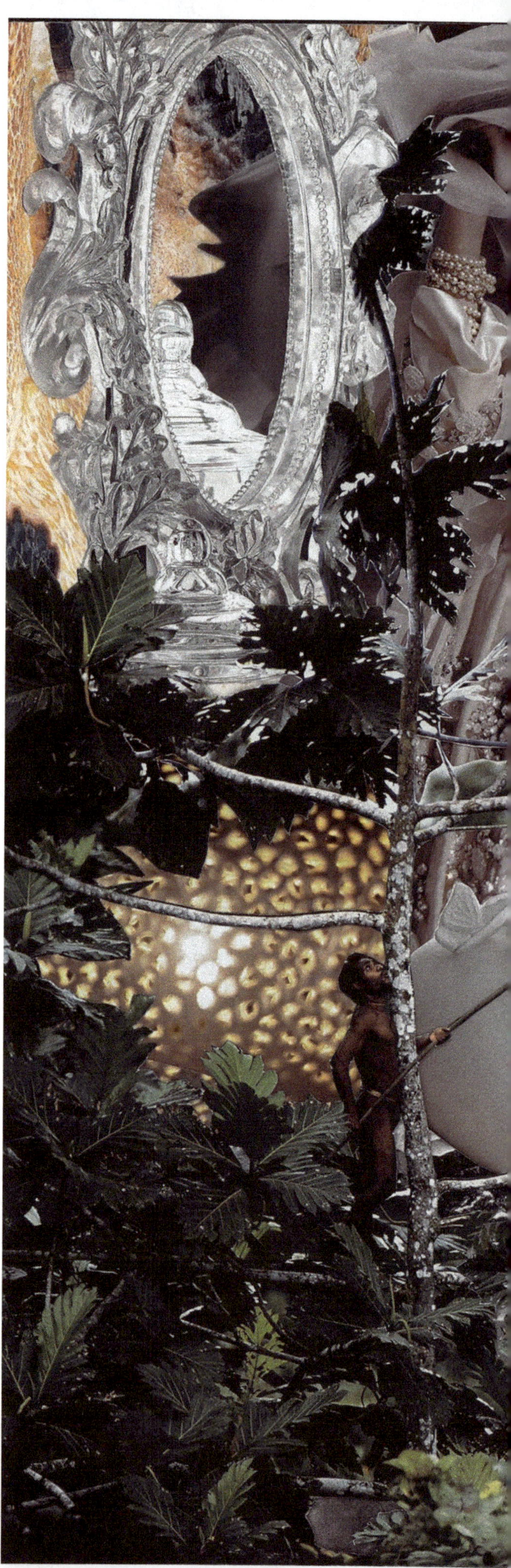

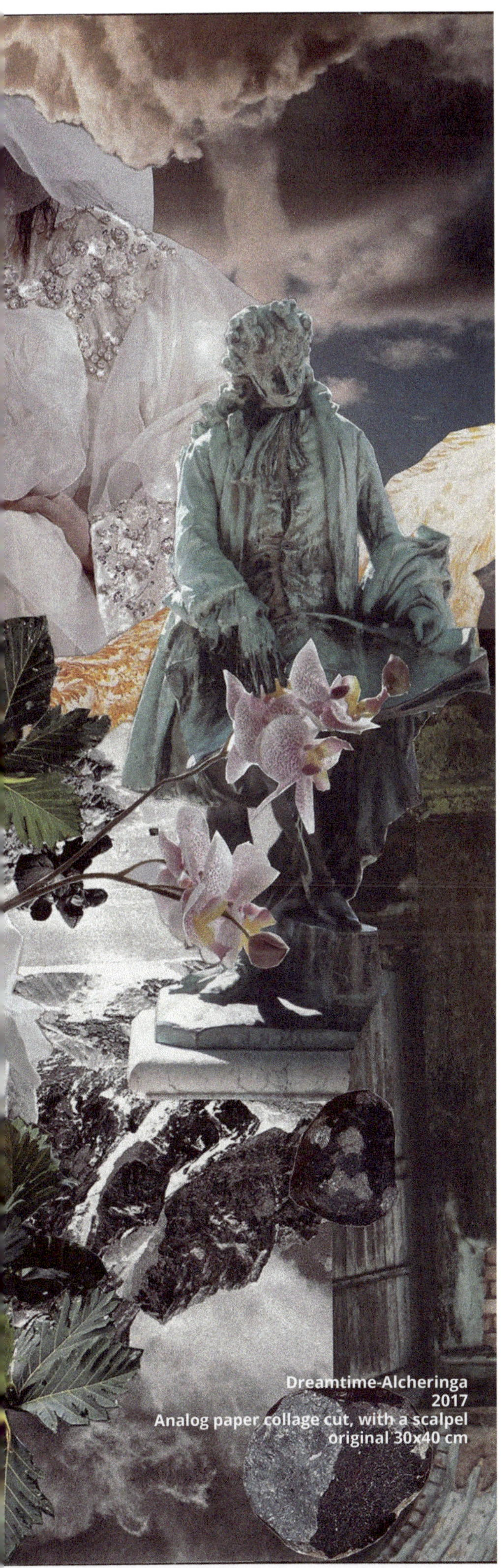

My journey as an artist in this society presents me with painful struggles, but also brings great happiness when I delve into the collective unconscious, experiencing the flow in my work as something under my hands finds its own voice and enters into a dialogue with me.

How do you decide what to charge for your work?

I use three factors for my original artworks: height plus width multiplied by a factor of 10 equals the basis of the price. For example, an original piece measuring 30x40 cm would actually cost 700 €. However, I worked on it for 3 months, so I would actually have to include my living costs. Without studio costs (which I can no longer afford) and without material costs, those would be 1500 € per month to survive. Therefore, I would have to ask for at least 5200 €. Unfortunately, yet nobody is willing to pay that much for one of my originals. So, I end up spending extra money again to have the originals scanned to a high standard in order to produce Fine Art prints in different sizes and in editions of 1/10 upon request. Sometimes I do ask the right price for an original because I really can't give it away.

What do you want people to take away from your work?

Serious female artists are not your entertainers. They fight for appreciation and sheer survival. They are underrepresented in art history and even in today's exhibition concepts. Appreciate the work and lifetime an artist invests. Don't bargain with artists for the price, that is undignified. Take an interest in the history of female art. Stop repeating 200-year-old arguments, e.g. what you can't recognize can't be art. Buy art because it touches you, not to match the couch. Women artists are indispensable, they preserve truths, culture and history.

What's one piece of advice you'd give to aspiring artists?

Dear female artists, have courage! There is no security. If you don't have a patron or were born rich, you only ever have yourself. Don't postpone your life as an artist. If you've been ignoring your inner voice, start now, it's never too late. I would like to recommend three books that have helped me: The Artist's Way, by Julia Cameron, - K - Kulturarbeit, by Michael Hirsch (Textem Verlag) - The Myth of the Normal, by Gabor Maté.

Megan King is a self-taught encaustic artist living and working in Washington, DC. Artist Statement: I work in encaustics because, like the artist, the work comes alive under fire. Encaustic painting and sculpture is, at once, an act of creation and destruction. Applying the medium builds the piece and torching it makes it something new and alive. My work often incorporates found and recycled materials. The use of unwanted materials reflects my concern for our resources and the idea that the objects we use carry meaning beyond their function. We can re-imagine our world through what already exists in it today. My work is largely abstract. I explore our relationships with the natural world and with each other. Mental illness, and in particular, my life with depression, is a major theme in my work. My work has been shown in various galleries and online, it is in the permanent collection of the Encaustic Art Institute(EAI) in Santa Fe, NM, as well as many private collections.

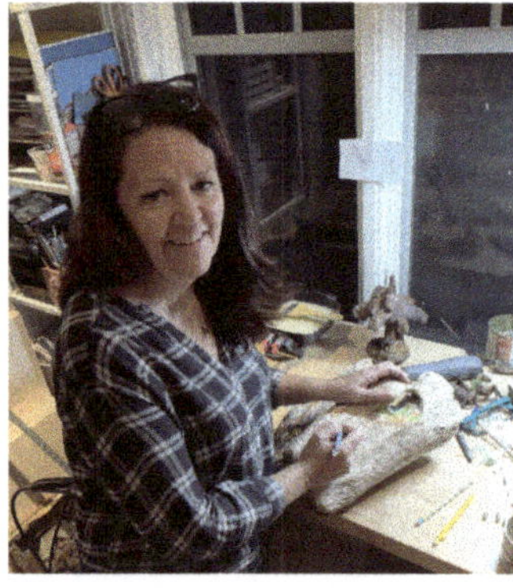

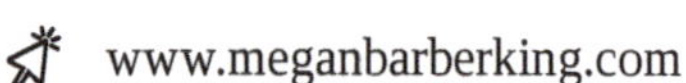

www.meganbarberking.com

@ meganbarberking@gmail.com

@meganbarberking

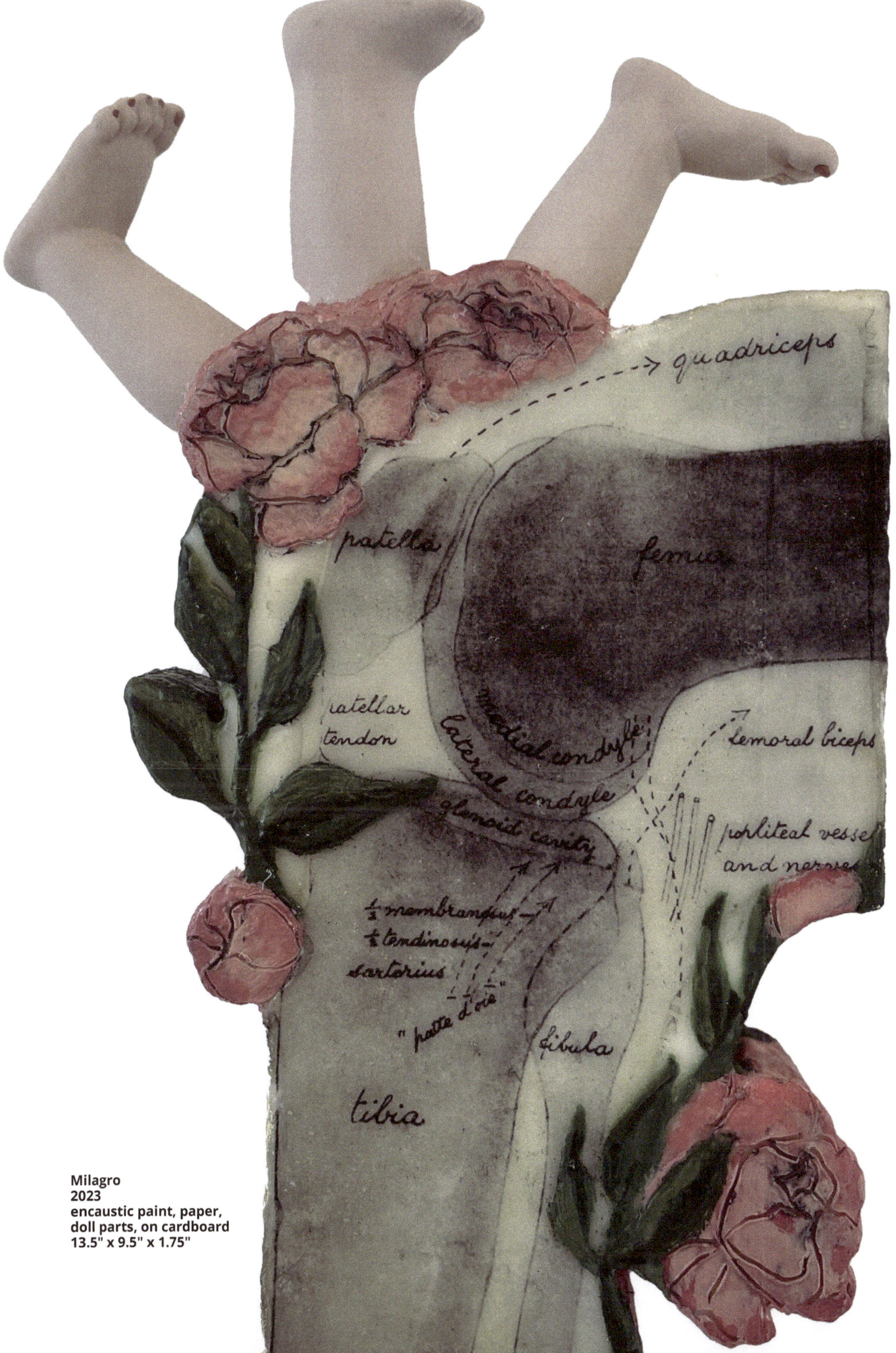

Milagro
2023
encaustic paint, paper,
doll parts, on cardboard
13.5" x 9.5" x 1.75"

Can you share a moment when you felt discouraged as an artist? How did you overcome it?

When I first began submitting work for shows I had no idea what I was doing. My work was worthy but submissions were being returned and I wasn't getting where I wanted to be. I realized pretty quickly that my shotgun approach was not working. So, I did a lot of research and reading about artists' statements, responding to calls, and the business of art. This helped me focus submissions and find success. I stopped worrying about the volume of submissions and instead looked for opportunities that fit what I was trying to say as an artist. I put in the work to take a critical look at my bio and statement to make it true to who I am as an artist, rather than what I thought the art world wanted to hear. The results were immediate. It was a time of growth for me and my work.

How has your art helped you understand yourself better?

Art has given me the tools to express emotions, thoughts, and ideas that I have difficulty putting into words. As someone who struggles with mental illness (major depression, anxiety, and ADHD), I have found great comfort in my focused studio time. I can explore who I am and how I am feeling without judgment. I can lose myself in the work and tune out the noise of the world for a brief time.

How do you decide what to charge for your work?

This was very hard for me. I have been creating my entire life and was mainly giving my work as gifts to friends and family. When I decided to make art a significant part of my life and work, it was difficult to imagine people spending more than a few dollars. Size, materials, and my time are a major part of the pricing formula. I also research pricing from other artists who are in similar stages of their careers. I spend time on art and gallery sites, looking at pricing at the shows that I attend or am part of, and browsing artists' websites and social media. I try to be consistent across my range of pieces. It is not easy.

What's one piece of advice you'd give to aspiring artists?

Be an explorer. Try lots of new things. Explore techniques, materials, and subjects. Do lots of work. Never stop learning and growing.

Resurrection, Mixed Media Encaustic Sculpture, 25x8x6

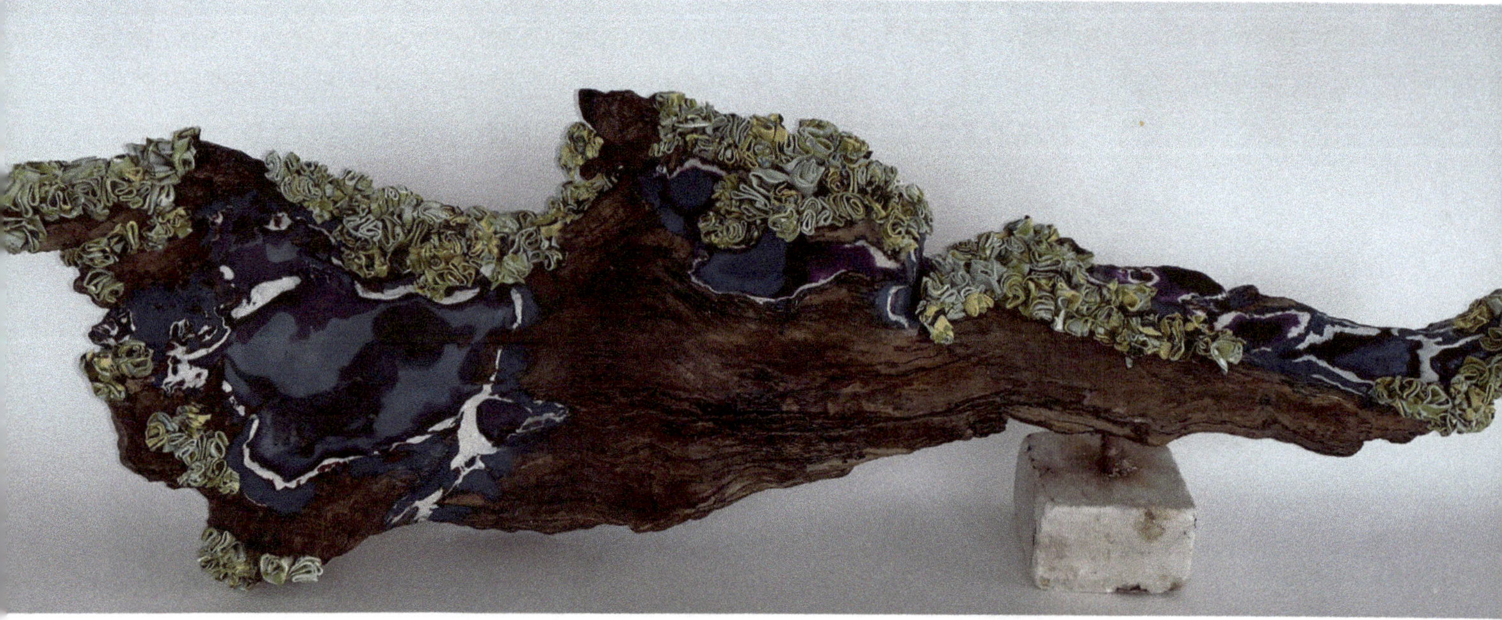

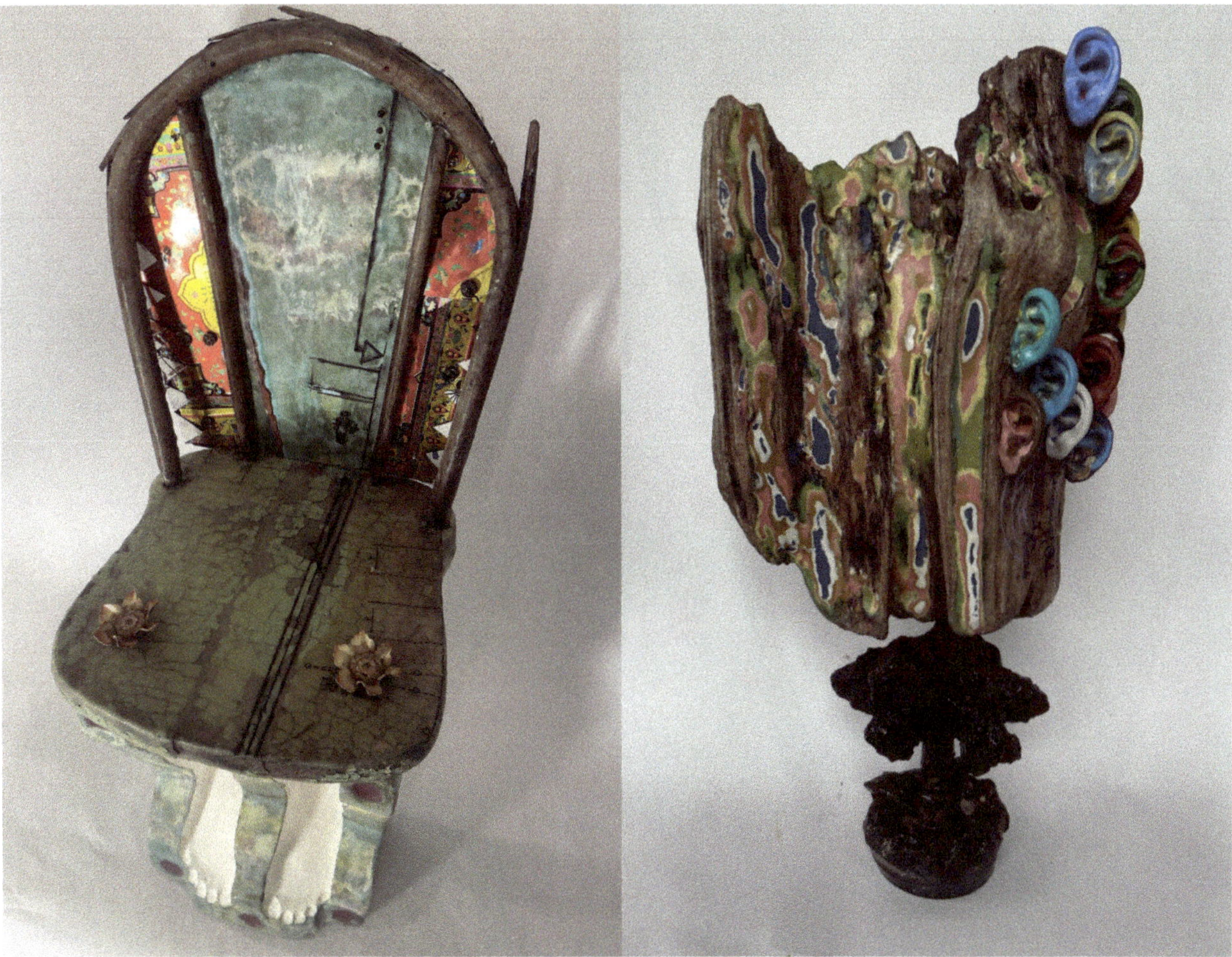

Gripping the Chair So I Don't Float Away, 2022, plaster doll mold, found child's chair, tin from food containers, paper, encaustic paint, oil paint, 12"x26"x12"

Listen to the Trees, 2022, Mixed Media Encaustic Sculpture, 21x12x8

How do you cope with the vulnerability of sharing your art with the world?

Vulnerability for me starts with creation. I am often dealing with my feelings in my pieces and need to allow myself to be honest and vulnerable to myself. I am my own worst critic. Yoga and meditation help me to lower the volume of my inner critic. As a Creative Director at a communications agency, I have a lot of practice sharing work with the world. I think that the more you share, the less scary it becomes. Just like a muscle, you need to stretch regularly to overcome the fear of sharing. The more you do it, the easier it becomes. You begin to realize that, while some will reject your work, you will always find more people who are supportive and encouraging.

What do you want people to take away from your work?

I hope that they take away the idea that beauty and expression are all around us—even in the things we take for granted, discard, and push aside. We often disregard ourselves and other people as irrelevant, useless, or unimportant when each of us is an integral part of our universe. By combining often discarded items with the transformative art of encaustic, I hope that people see that they are deeply loved and needed. Mostly I want them to discover something about themselves in my art. Art is very personal to both the artist and the viewer. Maybe they are coming to the work with a very different perspective than mine and take away something new. That is true success.

M

Molly Shivers is a visual artist from Denton, TX, living and working in Brooklyn, NY. Artist Statement: "I feel a strong understanding toward the people I paint, and try to inject as much of mine or my loved ones experiences into each image. Shared experiences, or at least the desperate desire to share them, are a driving force behind all of my paintings. The more contrived, the more delusional the better. There's something really beautiful about the desire to be wanted and loved, and the creepy thread of self awareness and desperation that can come with it. I hope that the tenderness that I feel for my subjects shows through, as well as a feeling of cautious optimism."

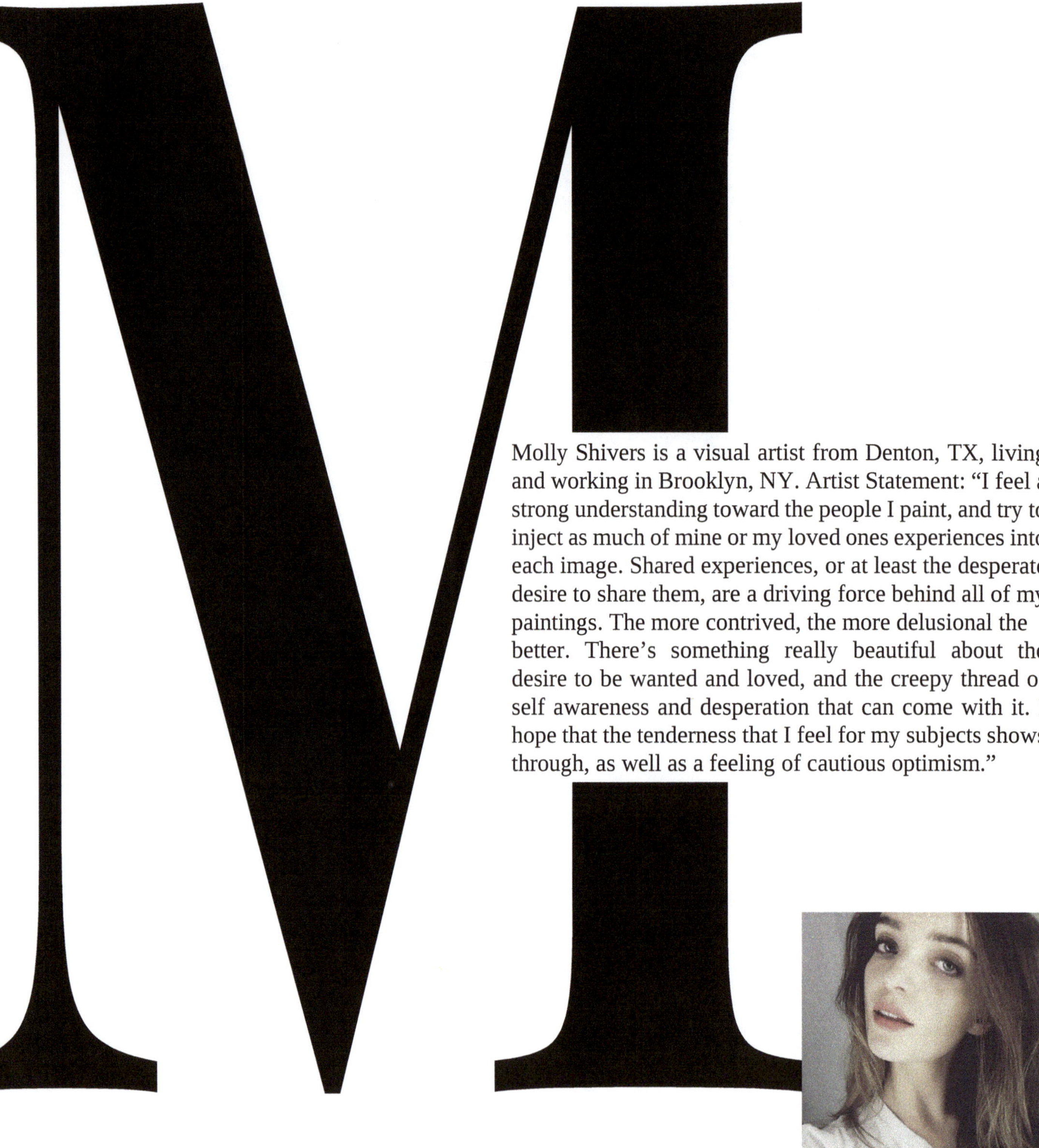

mollyshiversart.carbonmade.com

mollyashivers@gmail.com

@molly.shivers

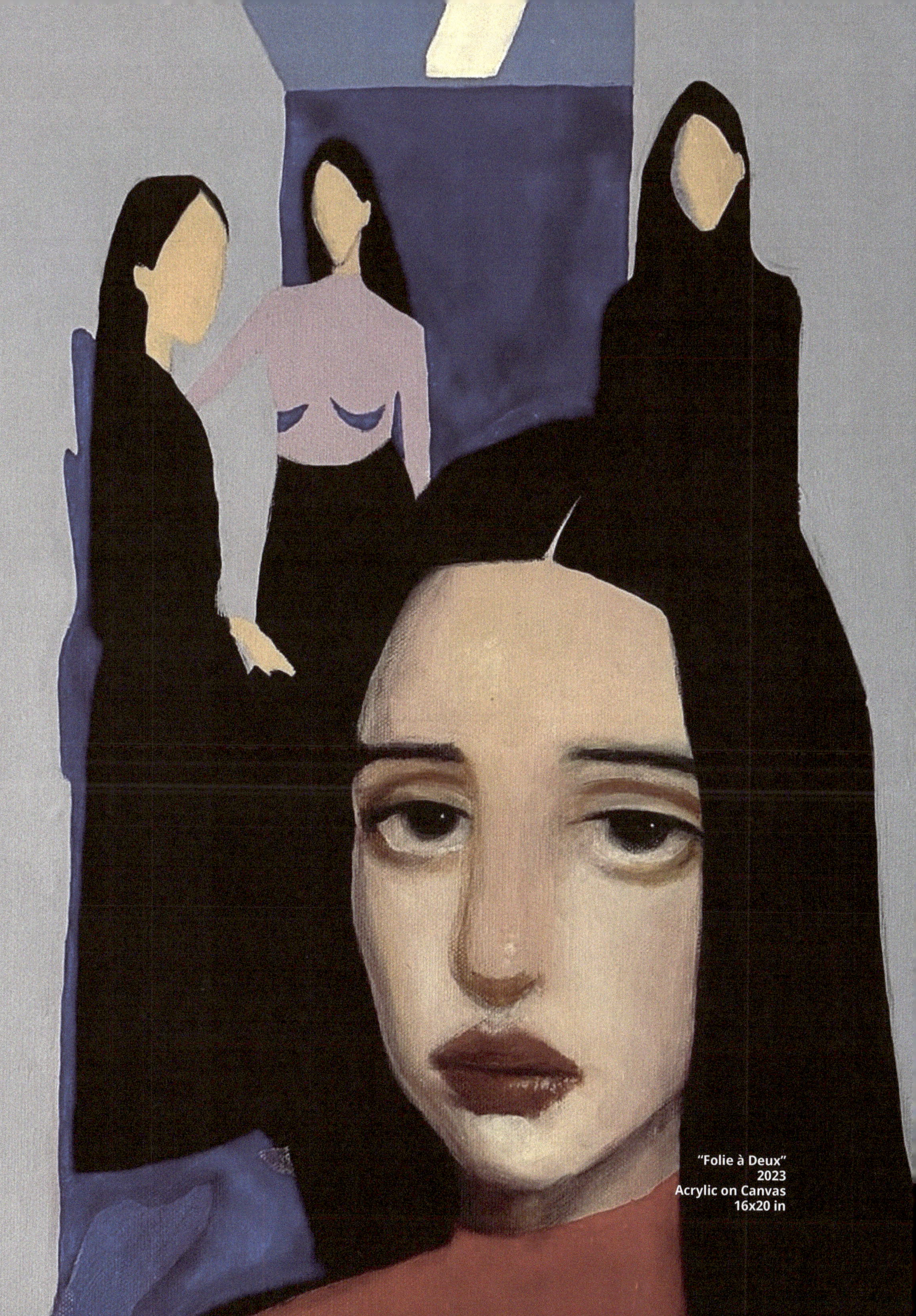

"Folie à Deux"
2023
Acrylic on Canvas
16x20 in

What do you want people to take away from your work?

Whatever they want! I like hearing people's interpretations of my paintings before they have any of my context. I usually have a little story or some personal reason why I painted something, and if people like to hear about it I'll tell them, but if someone feels inspired in a different way about something of mine I think that's so sweet and just as true as any meaning that I've assigned to it. Art is such a cool way to communicate and make connections.

How do you cope with the vulnerability of sharing your art with the world?

Lately I like thinking of everyone's perspectives as just what they're seeing from a window in a big building where everyone has their own view. That's what's so great about art and individual expression in general, it's a great way to translate your own view on the world and to learn from how others view it also. The more I see and learn about other people's perspectives, the more comfortable I feel sharing my own and allowing it to evolve over time.

"Edith", 2023, Acrylic on Canvas, 16x20 in

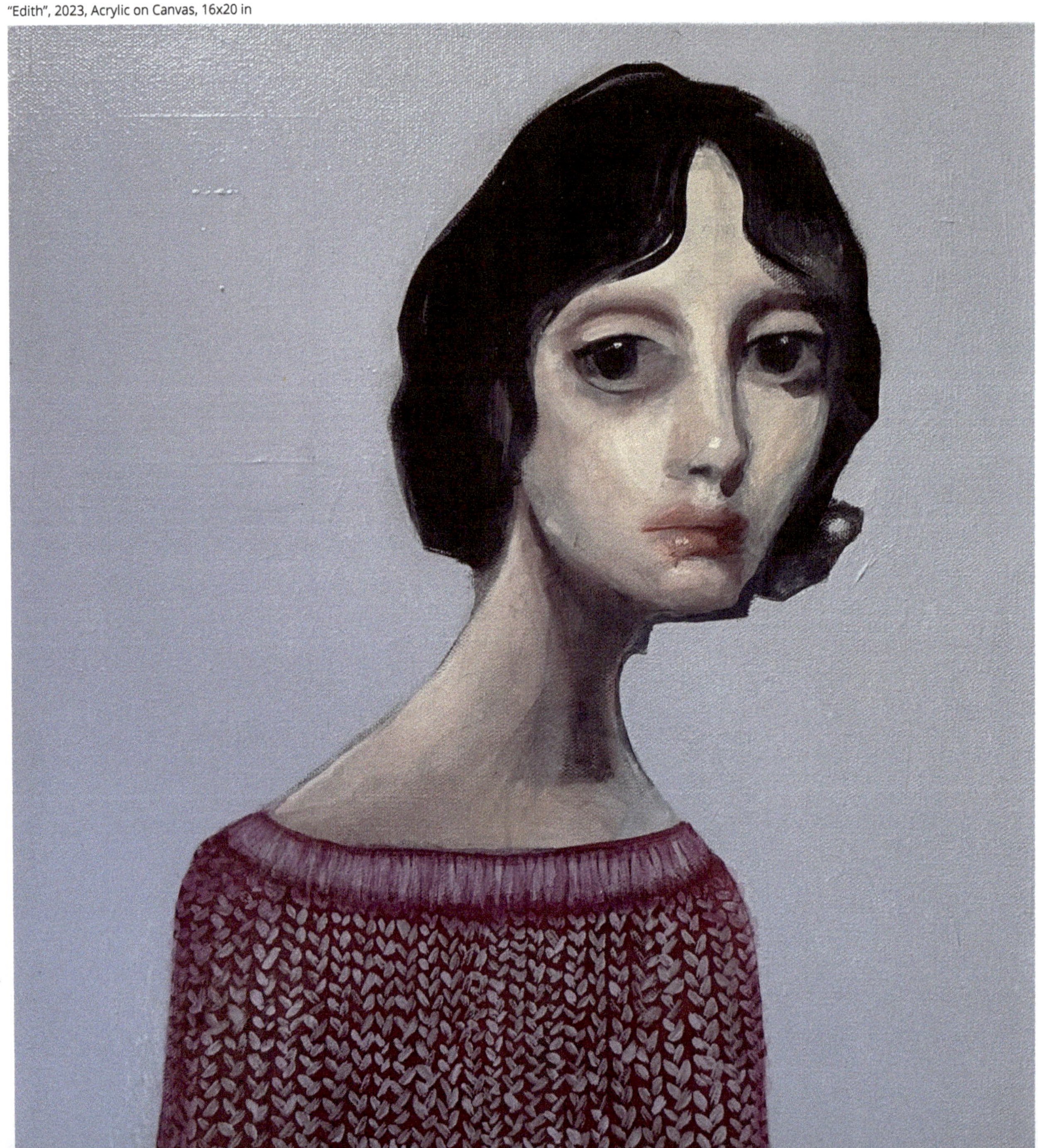

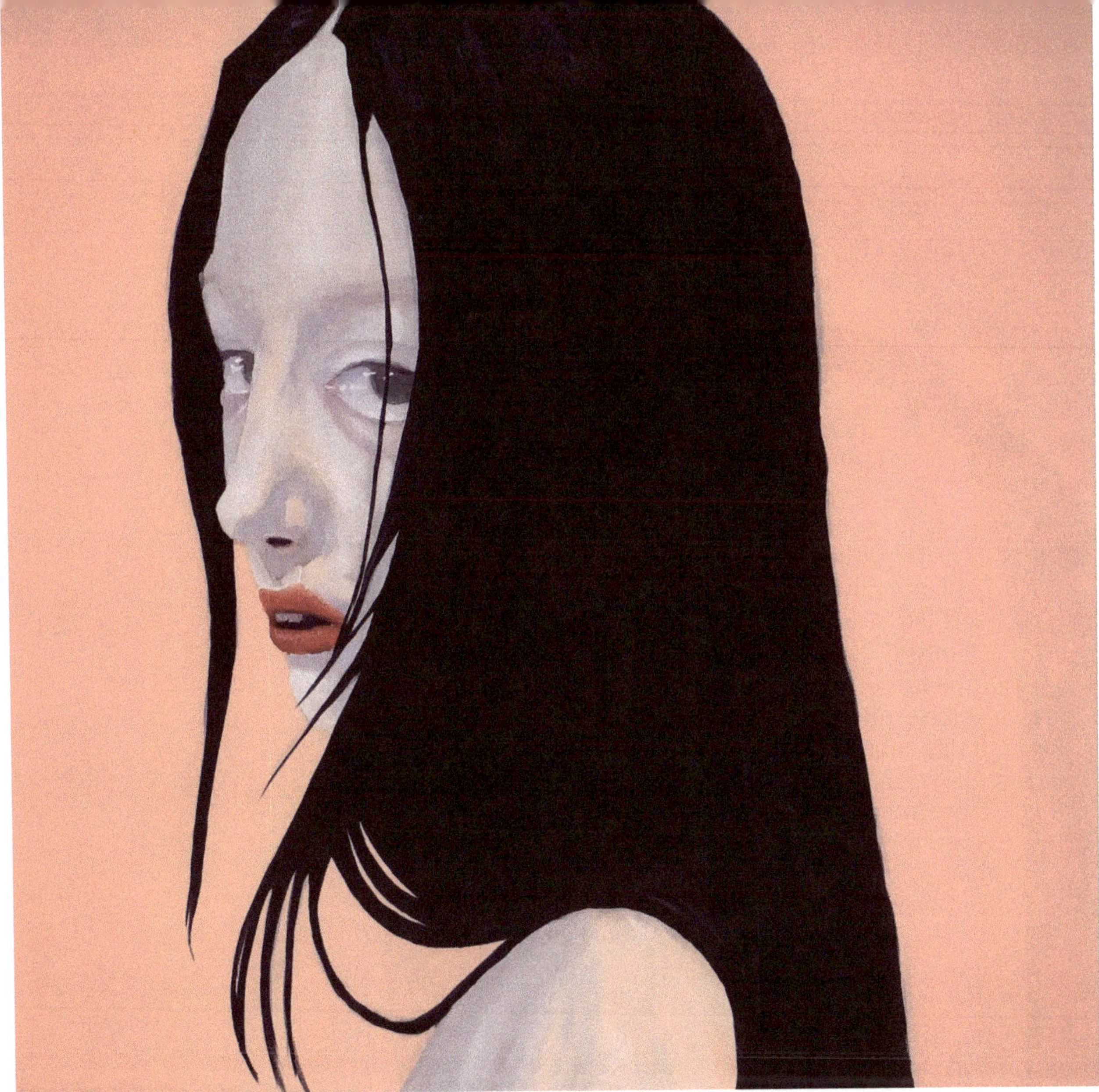

"Think I Am", 2022, Acrylic on Canvas, 36x36 in

How has your art helped you understand yourself better?

I'm definitely still working on understanding myself, but art has helped me a lot to express things that are hard to find words for. It's nice to be able to work through feelings like that, and interesting to look back at older work and be like, 'that's funny, I don't feel that way at all anymore.'

How do you decide what to charge for your work?

This is something I'm still working on. I've heard a lot of helpful tips and I think ultimately it's about accounting for the value of supplies and then basically giving yourself an hourly wage. Having said that, I rarely time myself when I'm painting so that's something I could improve at.

What's one piece of advice you'd give to aspiring artists?

Hang out with people who inspire you! I've had the opportunity lately to be able to spend a lot of time with some really talented artists, all at different stages in their careers, and just the time spent together learning about each others perspectives and process is so invaluable, and creates some really great friendships. I've definitely seen a difference in my life and work, and I think everyone should do it.

Omma Moon is a contemporary realist painter based in Östergötland, Sweden. Classically trained in the atelier school tradition, Omma Moon explores the meeting between figurative realist oil painting and bold, loose abstraction, using old materials and techniques in her timeless portraits. She is passionate about portraying diversity as well as the great and varied meaning of being a woman in today's world, sometimes through the lens of the past. The women in her paintings have a story to tell and often meet our eyes, inviting us into their worlds. Born in 1995, she grew up in Sweden, Ghana, and the United States, working in Australia and Ireland before returning to Sweden to begin her formal artistic training. Her artworks can be found in private collections.

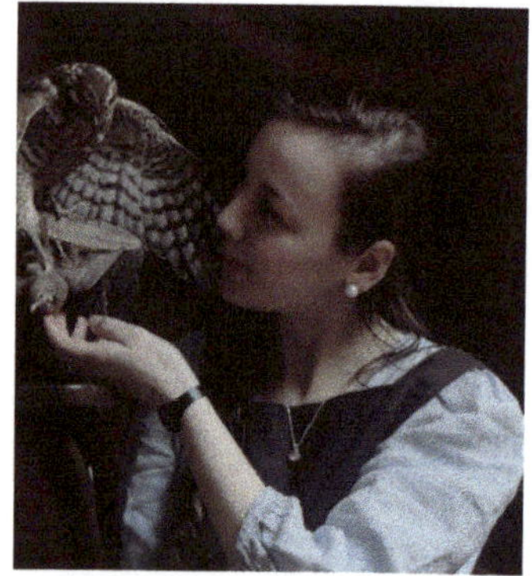

www.ommamoonart.com

contact@ommamoonart.com

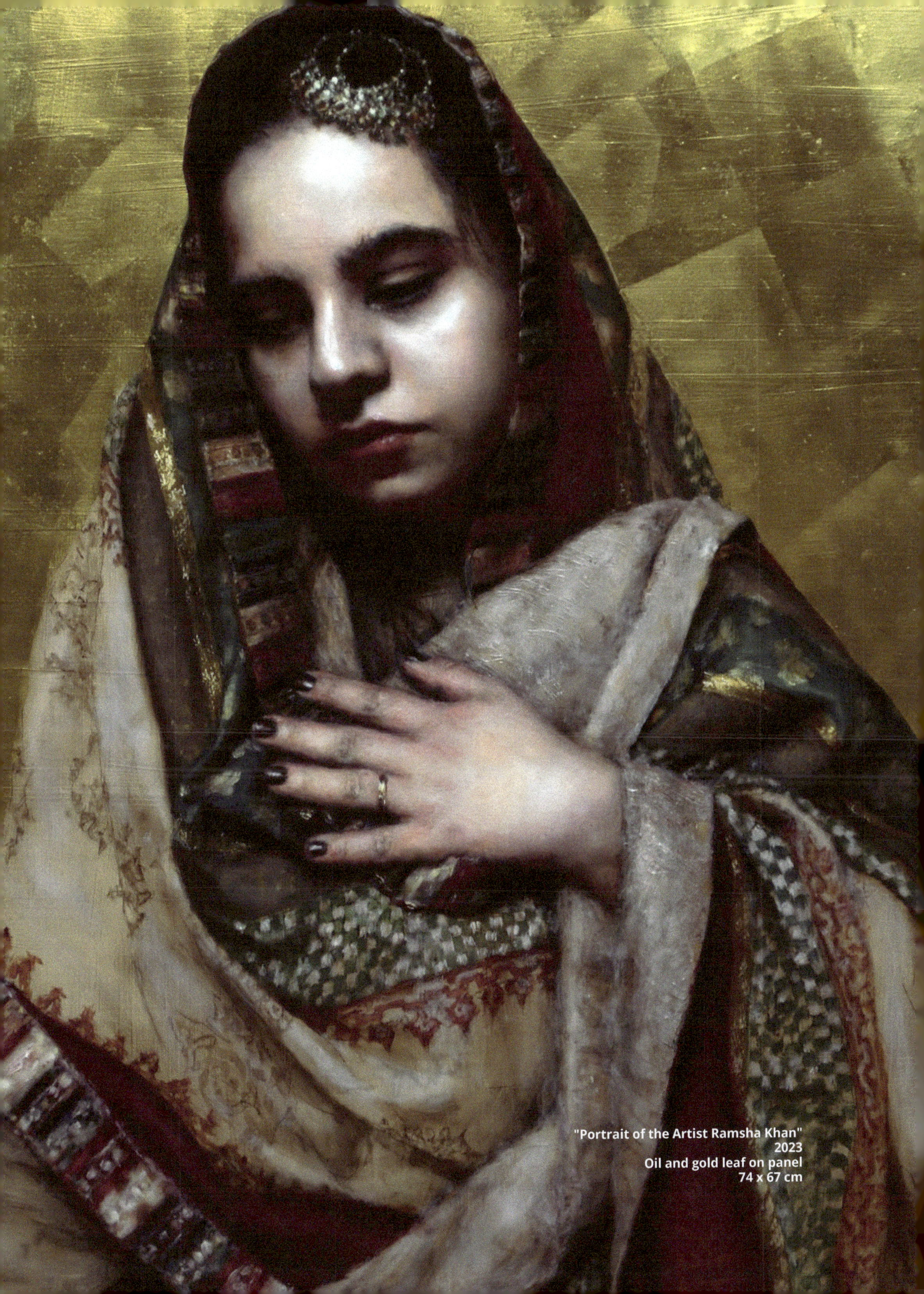

"Portrait of the Artist Ramsha Khan"
2023
Oil and gold leaf on panel
74 x 67 cm

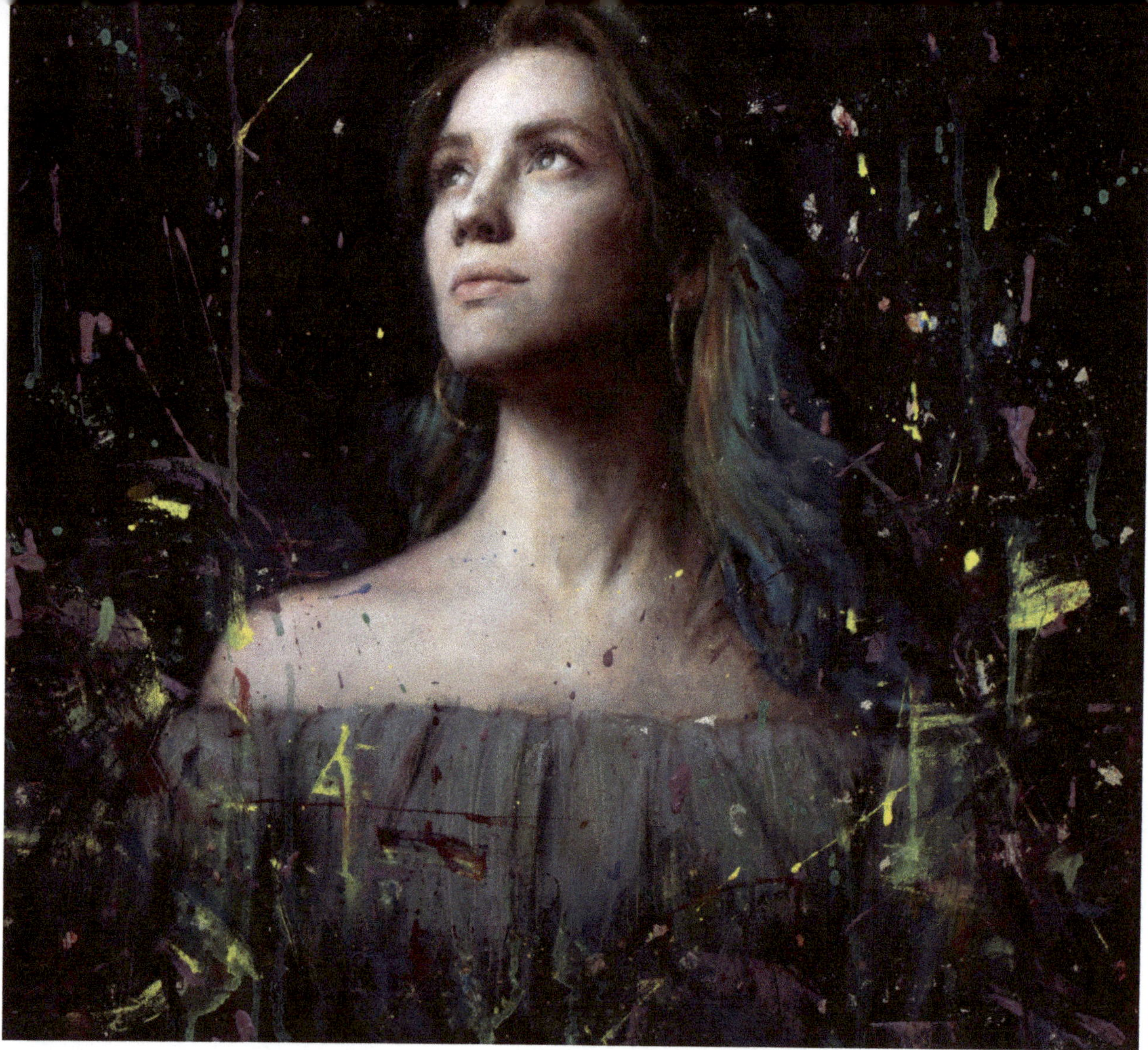

Stella, 2023, Oil and silver leaf on canvas; 70x60 cm

How do you decide what to charge for your work?

I'm a practical woman! I start with the cost of my materials. Then I count the hours it took me to make an artwork, multiply that with an hourly wage, and triple the total to account for taxes, gallery fees, social security fees that come with self-employment, and costs for storage and transport. Other than that, I charge the same for works of the same size made from similar materials and consult with my galleria about pricing before exhibitions, in order to stay consistent. That way I can always explain to collectors why the prices are set where they are.

How do you cope with the vulnerability of sharing your art with the world?

Sharing something so personal, so meaningful, can be nerve-racking. Personally, I always make it a choice. That way I get to decide – yes, today. Today I want to share. Making it a choice rather than a must helps me manage that vulnerability and take control. At the same time, regularly sharing my artworks normalizes the experience. So I try to set aside a little time each week. It gets easier every time I do it and the world doesn't end.

How has your art helped you understand yourself better?

Through my art, I discover myself and the world around me. Sometimes I feel as if I've never truly seen something until I have painted it. It is a deeper form of knowing, one based on connection. Much of my work is introspective, an exploration of myself through other women and their stories, our stories. Working directly with oil and brushes, I feel connected to my materials. And through my work, I learn what I

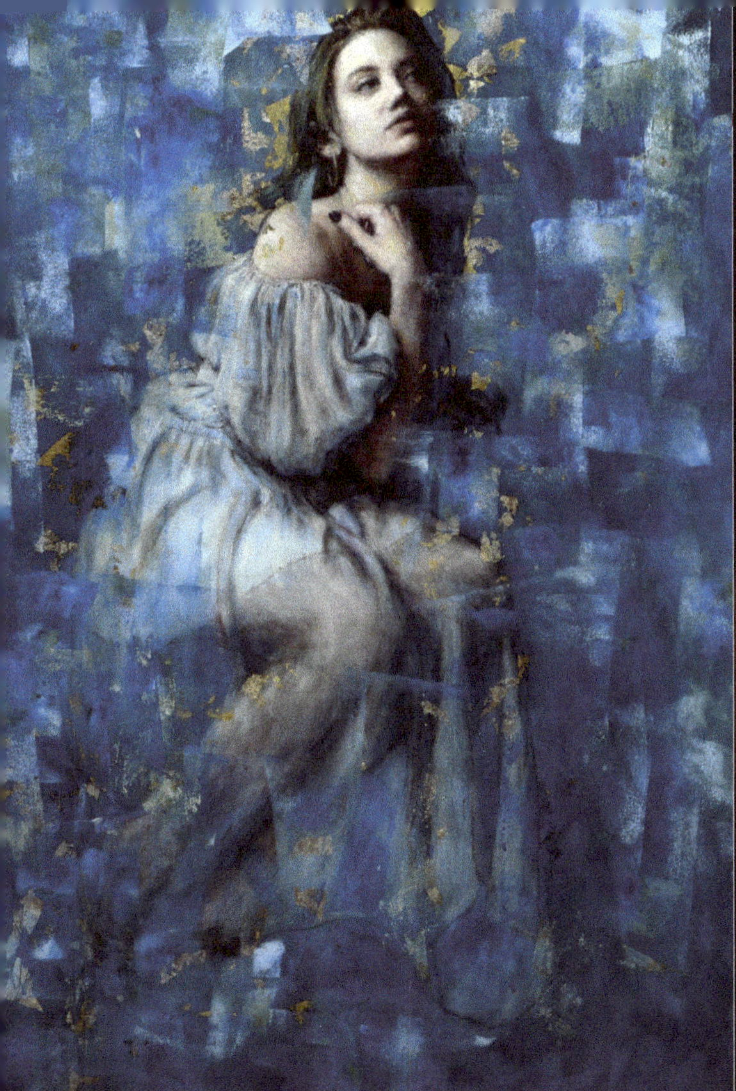

Arethusa Transformed into a Spring by the Goddess Artemis, 2023, Oil, gold leaf, silver leaf on canvas; 92x100 cm

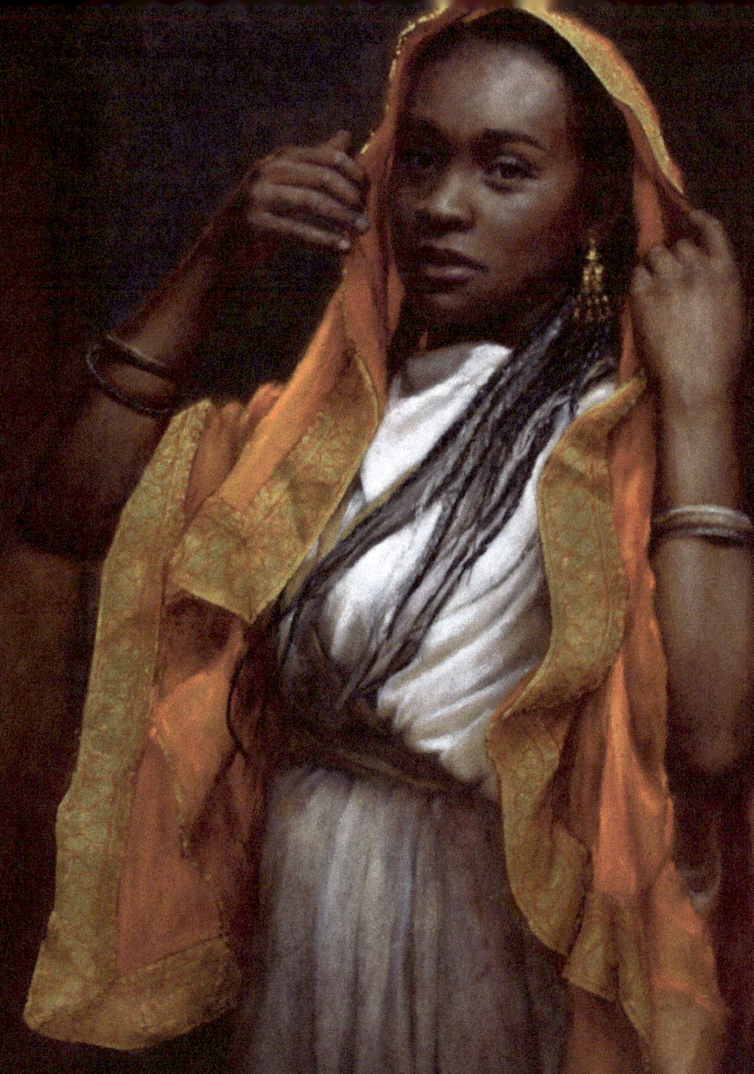

Princess Aida descending into the tomb of General Radamès, 2023, Oil and gold leaf on canvas,100x92 cm

am capable of, while at the same time it spurs me to continued growth.

Can you share a moment when you felt discouraged as an artist? How did you overcome it?

I dropped out of art school twice. There is a wealth of love to be found within the artist community but in that particular moment, what I really needed was to find the strength within myself. When I finally realized that I believed in myself – regardless of whether others did or not, regardless of accolades, regardless of likes – then I knew I had it in me to persevere. Some days you only have yourself. And those are the days that you learn...you are enough. Once you gain that conviction, no one can take it from you.

What's one piece of advice you'd give to aspiring artists?

I'm still an aspiring artist, and my best advice is

to engage with your local community of artists (online and in person). Support each other! Collaborations and emotional support will not only keep you going when you're feeling low, but also introduce you to gallerists, museums, competitions, publications, and open calls. Talk to people and help out where you can! You have more to offer than you think.

What do you want people to take away from your work?

Joy. Beauty. Wonder. I want them to see the sunlight sparkle in everyday things, and I want to share with them the soulful beauty of the many wonderful people I've had the privilege and pleasure to paint. I want to reveal a glimpse into their worlds, real or imaginary, to tell a story without words. Often, it is a story about women, about our lives and hopes. Paintings are mirrors and doorways.

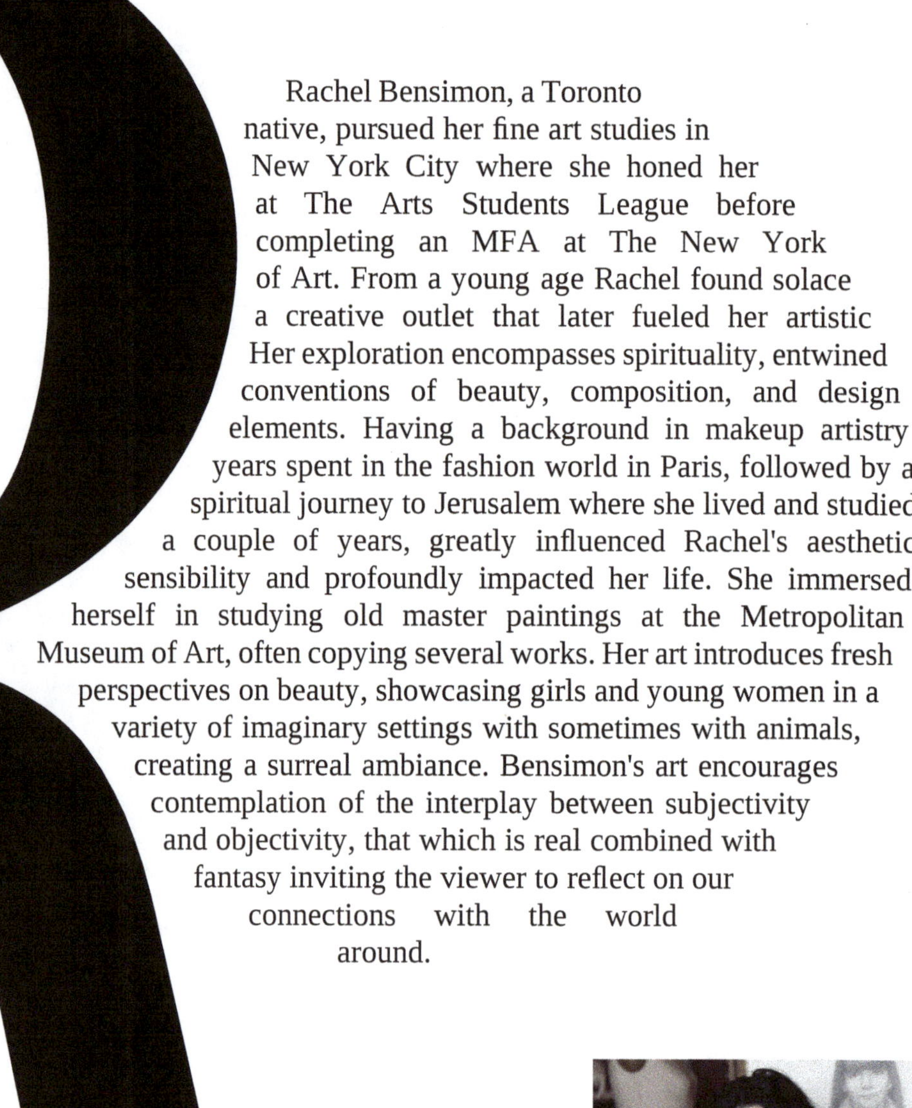

Rachel Bensimon, a Toronto native, pursued her fine art studies in New York City where she honed her at The Arts Students League before completing an MFA at The New York of Art. From a young age Rachel found solace a creative outlet that later fueled her artistic Her exploration encompasses spirituality, entwined conventions of beauty, composition, and design elements. Having a background in makeup artistry years spent in the fashion world in Paris, followed by a spiritual journey to Jerusalem where she lived and studied a couple of years, greatly influenced Rachel's aesthetic sensibility and profoundly impacted her life. She immersed herself in studying old master paintings at the Metropolitan Museum of Art, often copying several works. Her art introduces fresh perspectives on beauty, showcasing girls and young women in a variety of imaginary settings with sometimes with animals, creating a surreal ambiance. Bensimon's art encourages contemplation of the interplay between subjectivity and objectivity, that which is real combined with fantasy inviting the viewer to reflect on our connections with the world around.

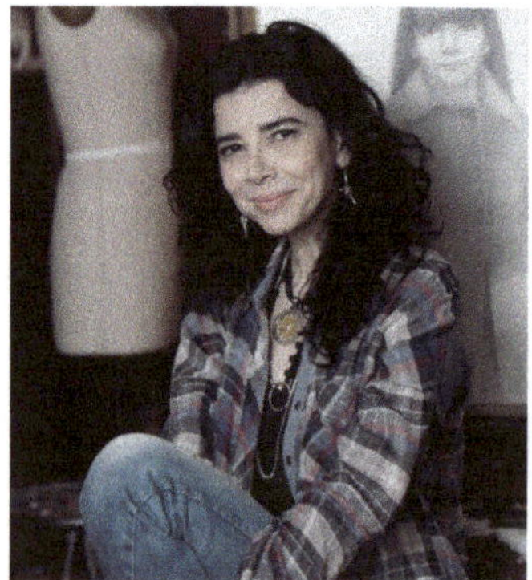

www.rachelbensimonfineart.com

rachelkben@gmail.com

@rachelbensimon_art

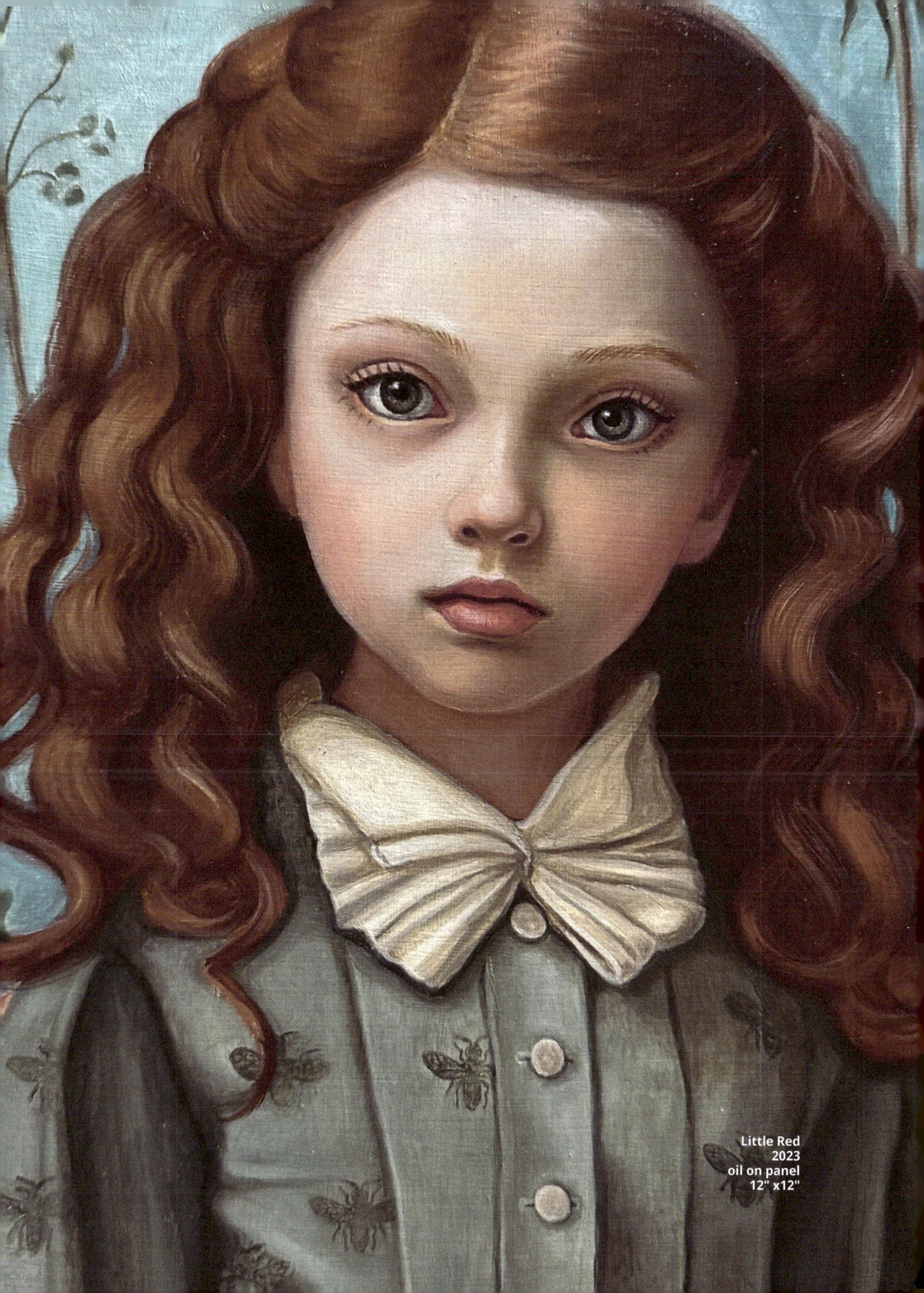

Little Red
2023
oil on panel
12" x12"

Can you share a moment when you felt discouraged as an artist? How did you overcome it?

I've faced creative blocks and discouragement as an artist multiple times. These periods of stagnation sometimes linger for months, leading me to believe that I may never paint again. It's a melancholic phase for me because my art is my gateway to inner joy, gratitude, and contentment. In the past, insecurities about my work haunted me, but life has been a profound teacher. Engaging in self-care practices, including affirmations, has been instrumental in cultivating belief in myself, even during moments of self-doubt. I've learned not to allow the voices of my ego mind to take control. A spiritual approach to my creative life has proven immensely helpful in overcoming perfectionism.

How do you cope with the vulnerability of sharing your art with the world?

Sharing the vulnerability expressed in my art with the world is not easy but is immensely rewarding and validating. As a sensitive artist, I've learned over the years to hold onto self-belief regardless of external opinions and to persevere in the face of challenges. The potency of art lies in its capacity to communicate a distinctive perspective and voice. I've learned over the

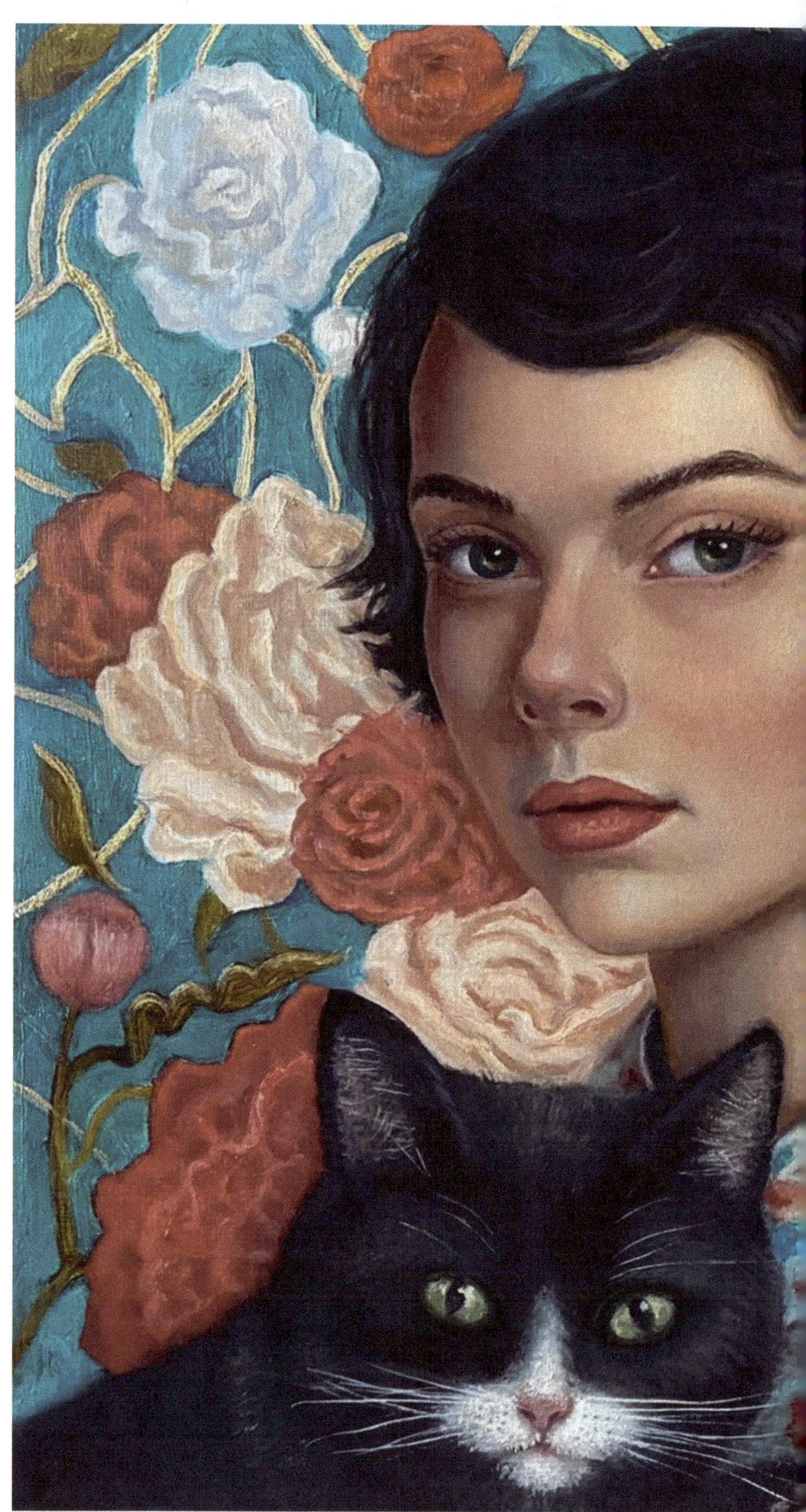

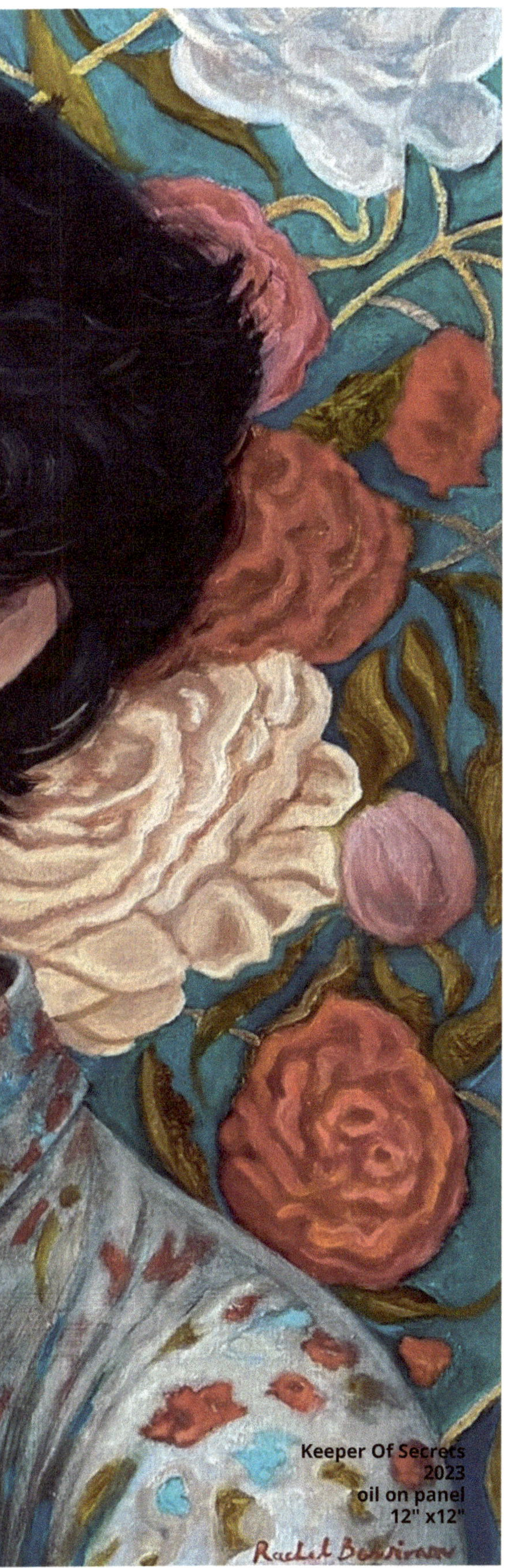

Keeper Of Secrets
2023
oil on panel
12" x12"

years to embrace my unique perspective without fear and channel it into my artwork.

How has your art helped you understand yourself better?

My art is not just a creative outlet; it's a profound tool for self-discovery and self-expression. It serves as an anchor for me emotionally, providing a therapeutic escape that unravels the complexity of my emotions. Amidst the chaos of my chatty mind, the creative process acts as a calming force, presenting inherent problem-solving opportunities. Within the realm of my artistic endeavors, I discover a space for quiet reflection and contemplation. Engaging in this creative practice initiates an internal dialogue, allowing different facets of myself to emerge. It becomes a journey into my subconscious, where past experiences are unearthed and processed on a conscious level, fostering a deeper understanding.

How do you decide what to charge for your work?

The decision to change aspects of my work is a dynamic and fluid process, shaped by my artistic vision, personal growth, and the evolving nature of my creative journey. It involves a delicate balance between adherence to the original concept and a willingness to adapt in response to the needs of the work. My art is constantly changing and evolving. If I feel something isn't working in my painting I try to "let go" of limiting beliefs and trust that I can find a way through.

What do you want people to take away from your work?

I would like people to feel inspired to feel whatever emotions my artwork brings out in them. My hope is that my work may resonate with viewers on a personal level, triggering memories, experiences, or aspects of their own identity. Ideally I would love to inspire creativity in others, encouraging them to express themselves creatively or see the world in a different light. To foster a sense of connection and communication, and hopefully a transcendent experience for the viewer. This can be characterized by a feeling of awe, wonder, or a shift in perception.

What's one piece of advice you'd give to aspiring artists?

One of the most powerful aspects of art is its ability to convey one's unique perspective and voice. Don't be afraid to embrace your individuality and express it through your work. Your unique experiences, thoughts, and emotions are what make your art special. Art is a journey, and growth and evolution are natural parts of that journey.

S

Sally Khoury is a renowned Lebanese-American artist currently residing and working in Doha, Qatar. She received her BA in Fine Arts from the Lebanese American University in 2004. Sally K's portraits capture the essence of empowered femininity, celebrating the strength and grace inherent in every woman. Her signature style features ethereal flower crowns that cascade across her canvas and obscure her subject's eyes. Unweighted by materialistic elements, their poise exudes a natural force depicting the powerful woman within. Each painting is imbued with layers of meaning. The deliberate selection of vibrant colors, imperfect petals, and unique arrangements evokes a sense of mystery and awe. But she is the woman within. A universal symbol of fierce feminine empowerment; unapologetic, unique, radiant and self-assured

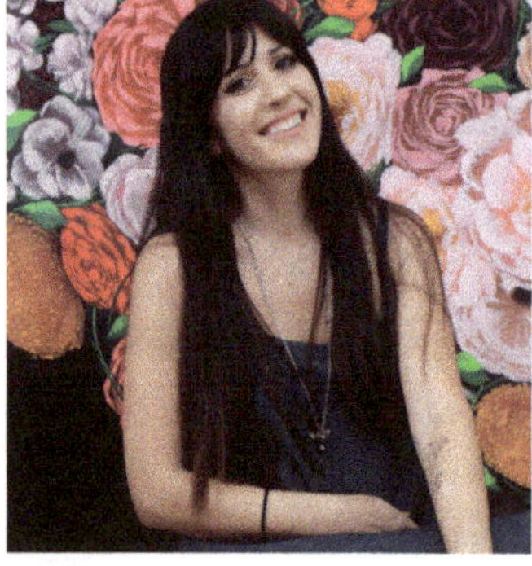

www.sallyk.com
sallykpaintings@gmail.com
@sallykpaintings

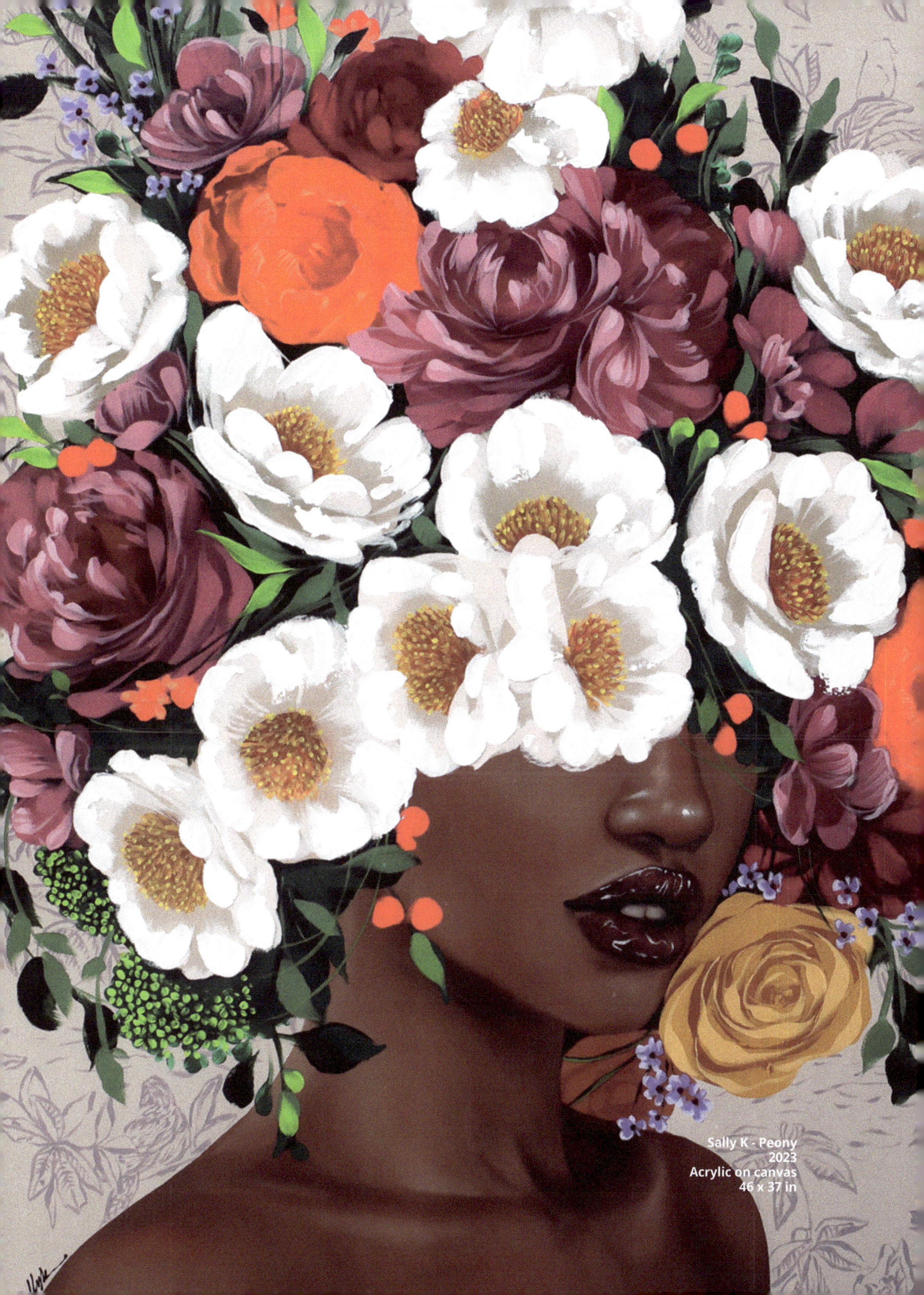

Sally K - Peony
2023
Acrylic on canvas
46 x 37 in

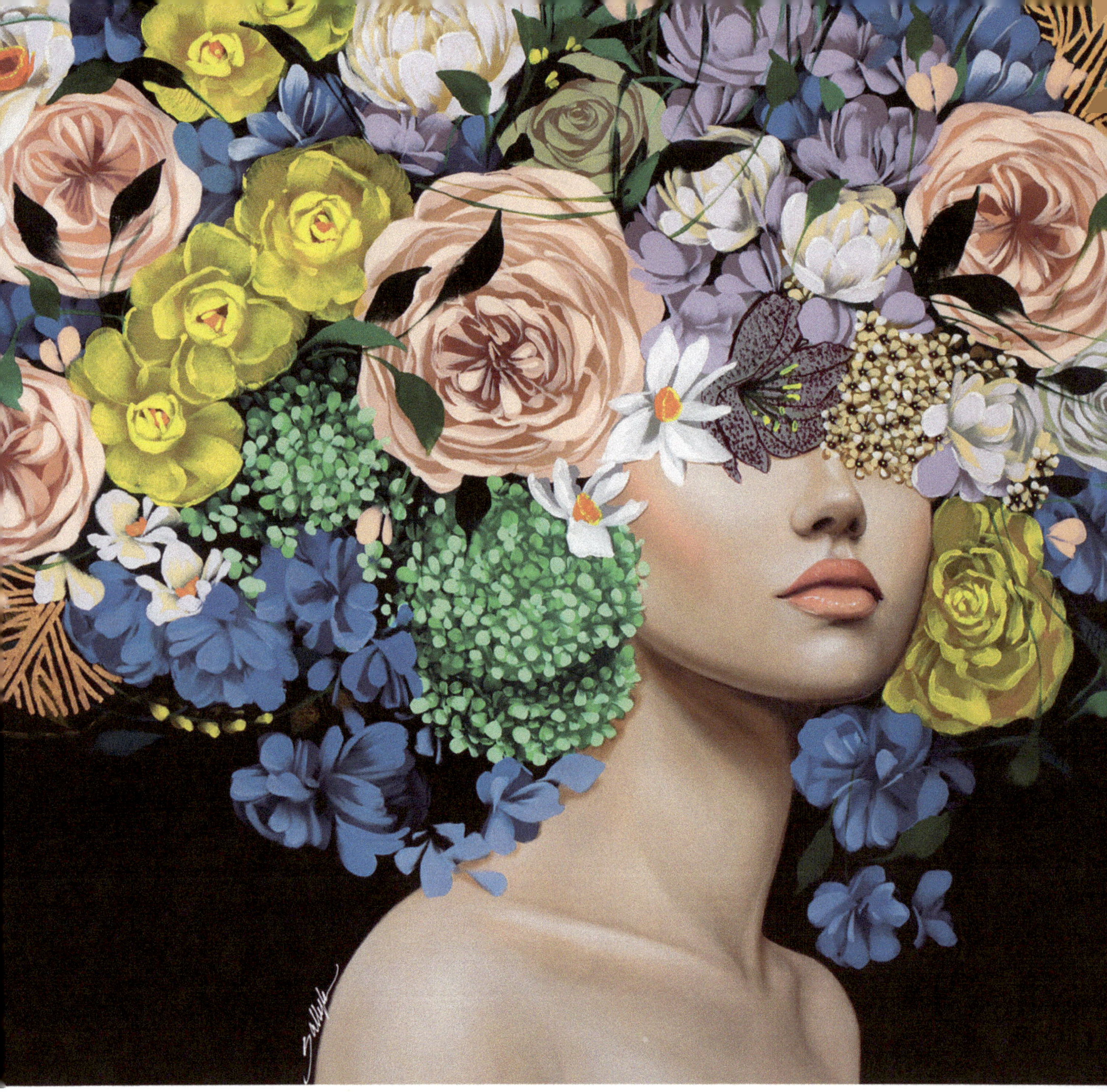

Midnight Bloom, 2023, Acrylic on canvas, 54x78 in

How do you decide what to charge for your work?

It was difficult when I was beginning my art career. Through years and years of working, you find a price point that works - the amount of work produced in terms of the sales. You have to compare your work to others at first as well. Once I started working with galleries, we priced the work together. I currently have a formula that I use to price my work in terms of size, and adjust if needed.

How do you cope with the vulnerability of sharing your art with the world?

I'm still coping with vulnerability of sharing my art with the world. It takes courage to begin, and the more you do it, the easier it gets - that's what I'm told. Having a support group is essential - for me, the support of my family, friends and coach is invaluable.

What do you want people to take away from your work?

I want people to feel empowered and uplifted.

How has your art helped you understand yourself better?

When you find a certain style or theme that interests you, it's interesting to know why. What led you to be interested in this topic, the way you paint, your influences - these are all questions that help you understand yourself better, and help you keep moving in the direction that is true to you.

What's one piece of advice you'd give to aspiring artists?

Your work will only get better if you continuously create - even when you don't want to. Find support financially, and get to work. It's going to be tough, but its also going to be great - get ready for a roller coaster ride.

Can you share a moment when you felt discouraged as an artist? How did you overcome it?

It's hard to choose just one moment, there are many. I realize that I am the only one holding myself back - discouragement comes from within. You need to have the courage to take those uncomfortable steps and ask the hard questions. It's not an easy process, and it's continuous work. Working with the artist and creative coach, Marc Scheff, enabled me to reflect on what is behind the discouragement, and gave me the ability change my perspective and move forward with actionable steps. Understanding and pushing through the discouragement, not letting it numb you and get you stuck, that is where growth happens.

Kelly, Acrylic and silver leaf on canvas, 48x36in

Helen, 2023, Acrylic on canvas , 53 x 71in

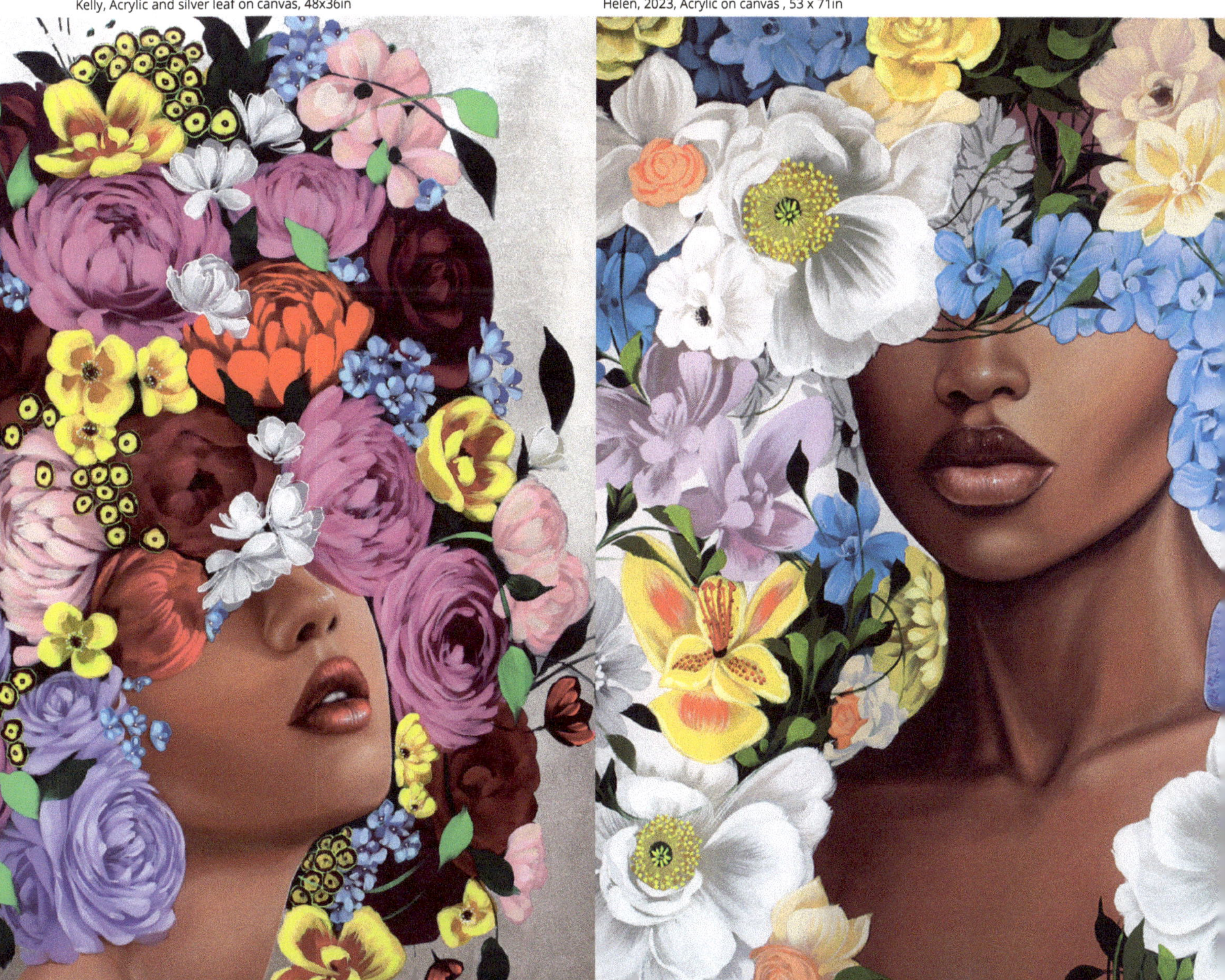

Sheri Rush (b. Fort Worth, Texas) is a Chicago-based painter whose work responds to the current world by considering the intersection of identity, landscape, and digital image. Rush's work is process-driven, emphasizing immersion and physical impact through scale and color while deconstructing a journey in nature. Rush holds a BFA from Texas Christian University and an MFA from the University of Chicago. Recent exhibitions include the Rockford Art Museum, Freeport Art Museum, Ralph Arnold Gallery, The Art Center Highland Park, Arc Gallery, Hofheimer Gallery, Mu Gallery, James Baird Gallery in Newfoundland, solo shows at Hyde Park Art Center, Evanston Art Center, and Epiphany Center for the Arts. Recent awards include a fully funded residency to the Pouch Cove Foundation in Newfoundland and a grant from the Illinois Art Council Agency.

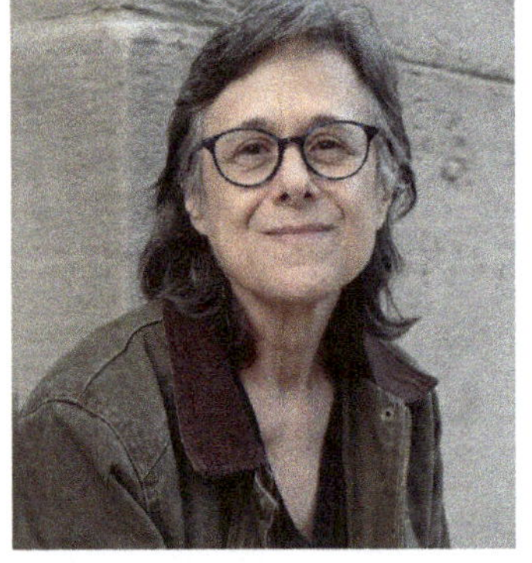

sherirush.com

sherirush2010@gmail.com

@sherilrush

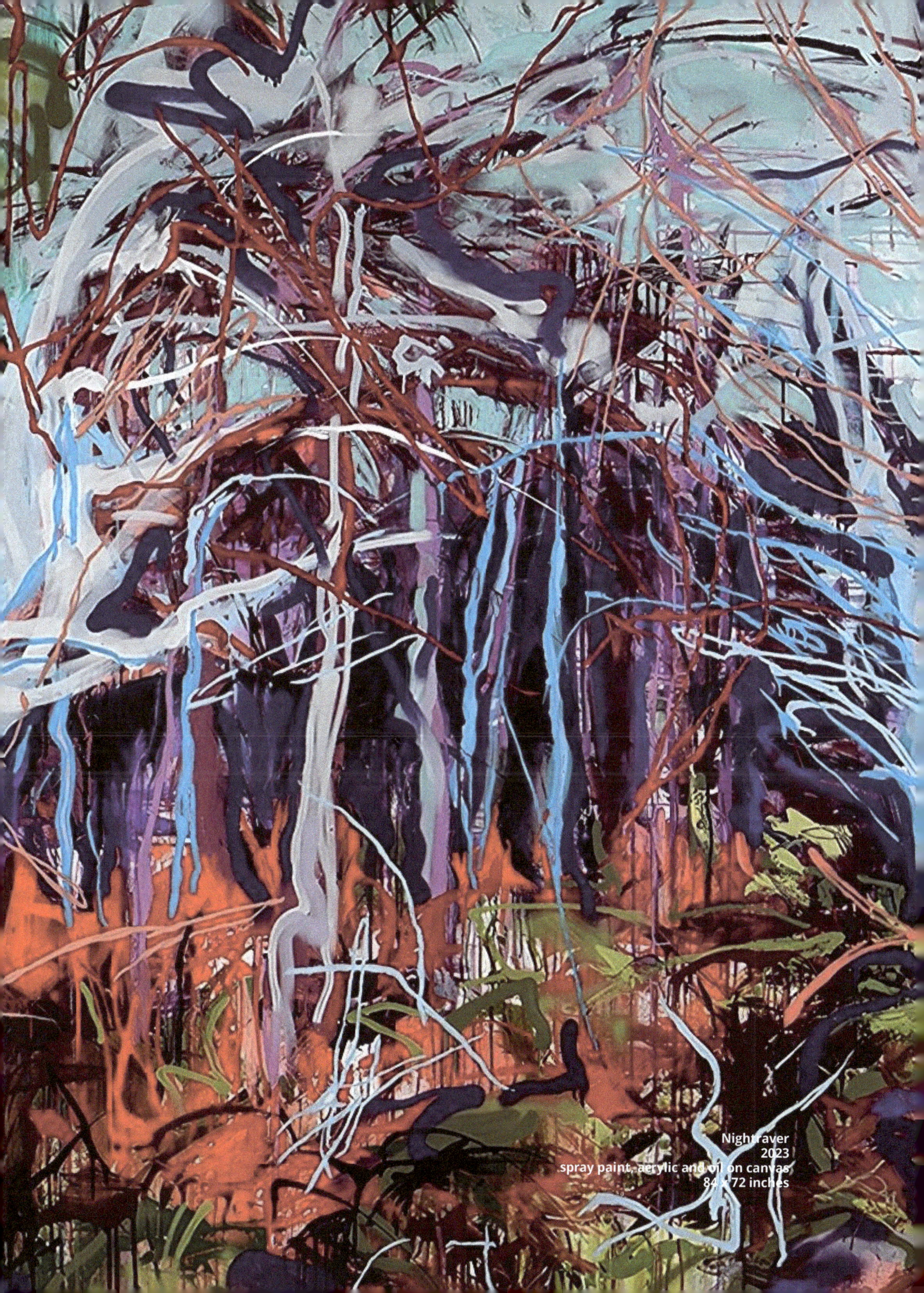

Nightraver
2023
spray paint, acrylic and oil on canvas
84 x 72 inches

What do you want people to take away from your work?

I want to give the viewer a space to reflect, process difficult emotions, and/or examine their relationship with nature. I have always looked to nature for inspiration, therapy, symbolism, solace, and refuge, so I hope people can take away any illumination for themselves.

How do you cope with the vulnerability of sharing your art with the world?

Age helps with that process, but along the way, I did make myself a few rules. First, if it's too raw and emotional and makes you flinch, don't show it – be kind to yourself. Second, give it space and time, then write about it. If you can't talk about it, don't share it. Wait. You know when it's right.

Can you share a moment when you felt discouraged as an artist? How did you overcome it?

The high rate of rejections received as an artist gives me many moments of feeling discouraged, and the best way to deal with that is to get in the studio and paint. I give myself the freedom to experiment with no expectations because it's that process that I'm passionate about. Strengthening that connection to my work after rejection puts me back in a positive head space to persevere and keep getting my work out there.

How do you decide what to charge for your work?

I take the advice of curators and art consultants I've worked with.

The Rules of the Universe Bend, 2023, spray paint, acrylic and oil paint, 72 x 96 inches

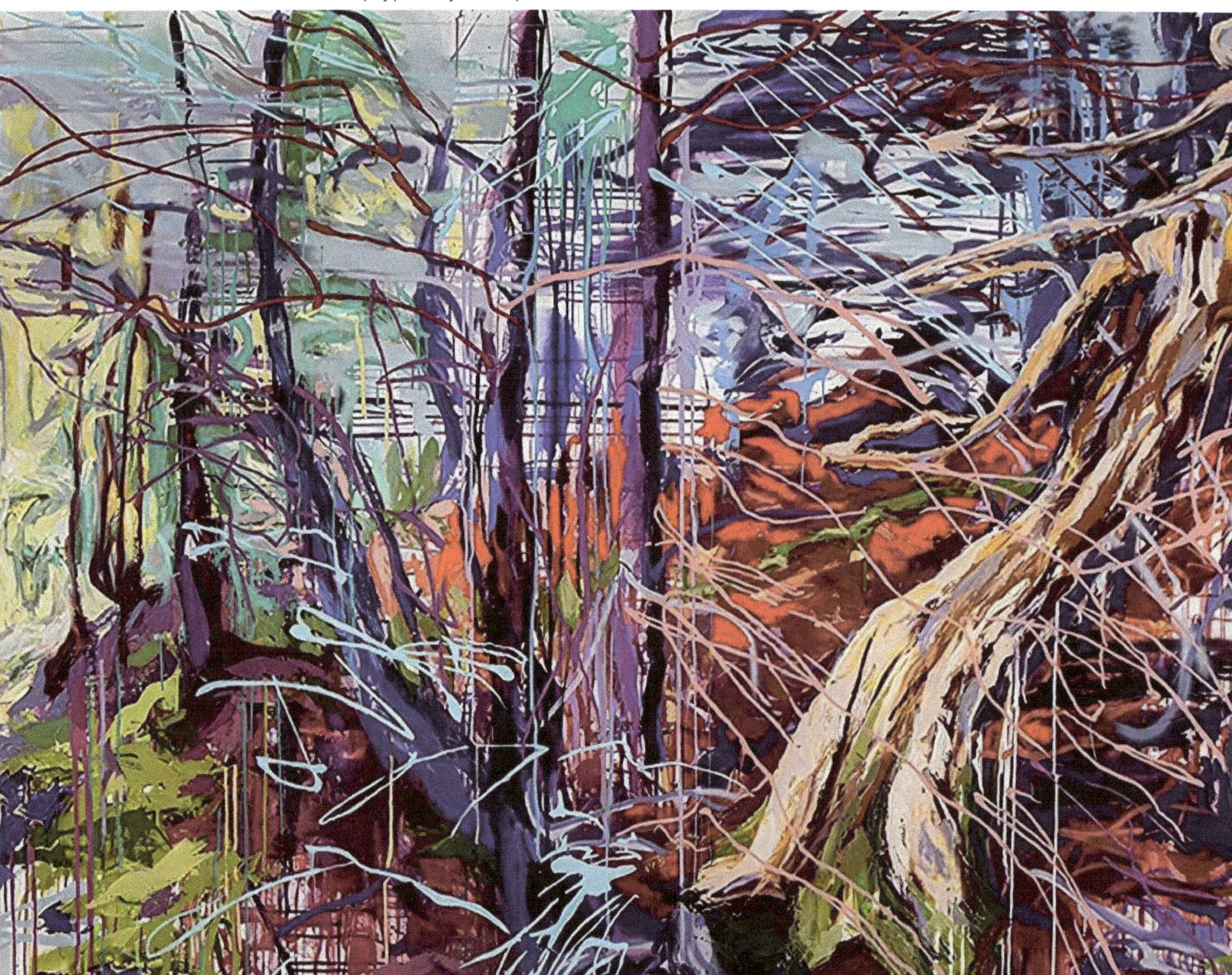

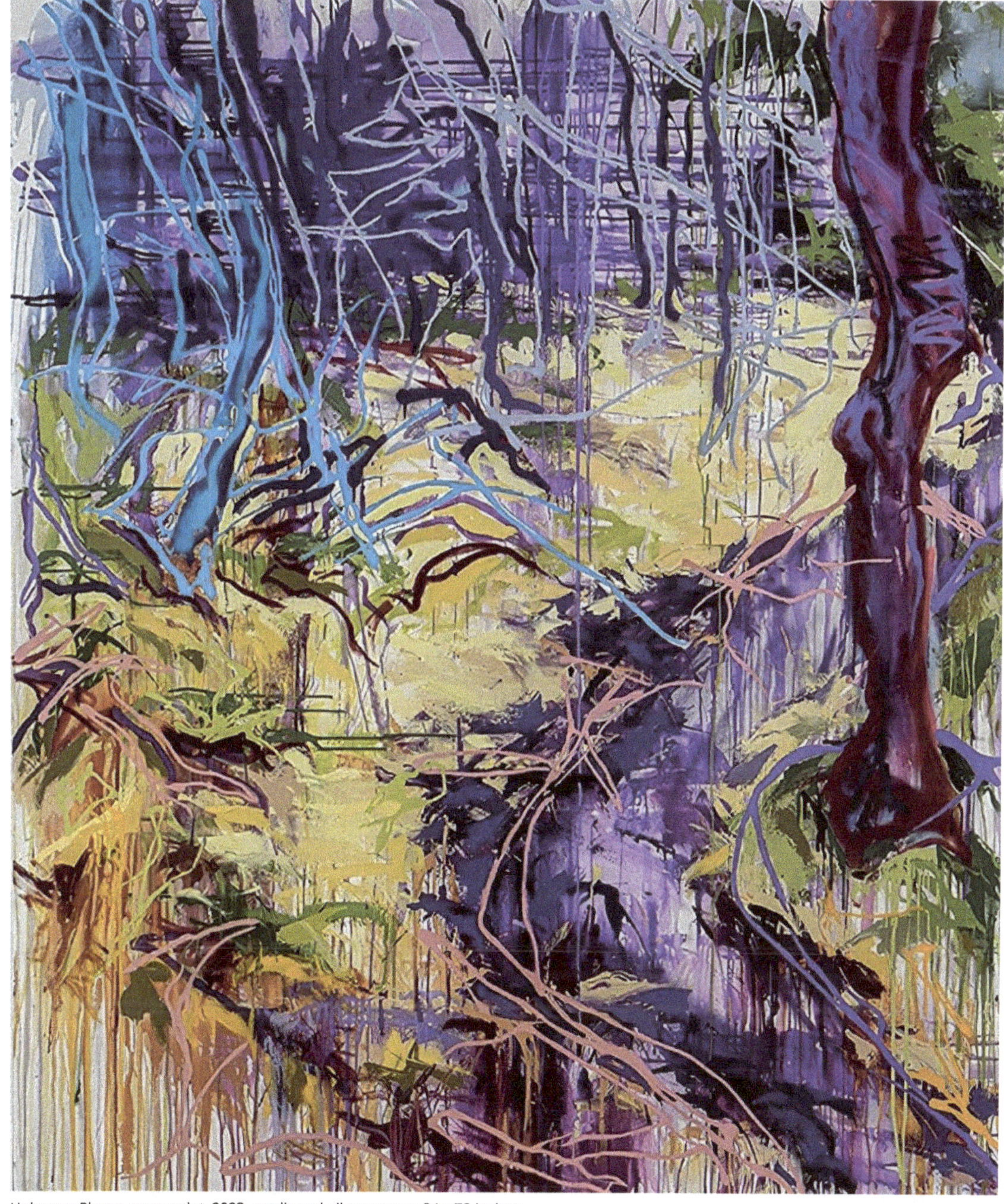

Unknown Places, spray paint, 2023, acrylic and oil on canvas, 84 x 72 inches

How has your art helped you understand yourself better?

I process everything in my life by making art. I've been painting since I was nine. I use my art for processing trauma, loss, anxiety, and locating my place in this world. My studio and work are a space for self-reflection, and yes, it helps me understand myself better.

What's one piece of advice you'd give to aspiring artists?

I heard Roberta Smith speak in Chicago ten years ago, and she said – if there is anything else you can do, then go do that. Lol. Don't overthink your art; act on every idea you have and see where it takes you. The work is the most important thing. Do work that you are passionate about and energizes you. As for the business side of being an artist, you can find help and support to do that part. Networking is crucial.

Sofia Ruiz is a Latin American artist born in San Jose, Costa Rica. At the age of 16, she initiates in art. In 2000, she decided to enter the School of Fine Arts in CR, majoring in Painting and Printmaking. She is also a Master in Education and has won several national and international art awards. She had participated in several international residencies from USA to South Korea and in more than 35 exhibitions in Galleries and museums. Her art work shows autobiographical elements from her childhood. As the child of a mother who suffered from amnesia and a grandmother with Alzheimer, she is acutely aware of the fragility of memory and the ways in which it shapes our sense of self. Her paintings often feature fragmented images from childhood and incomplete narratives, reflecting the ways in which memories can be distorted or lost over time.

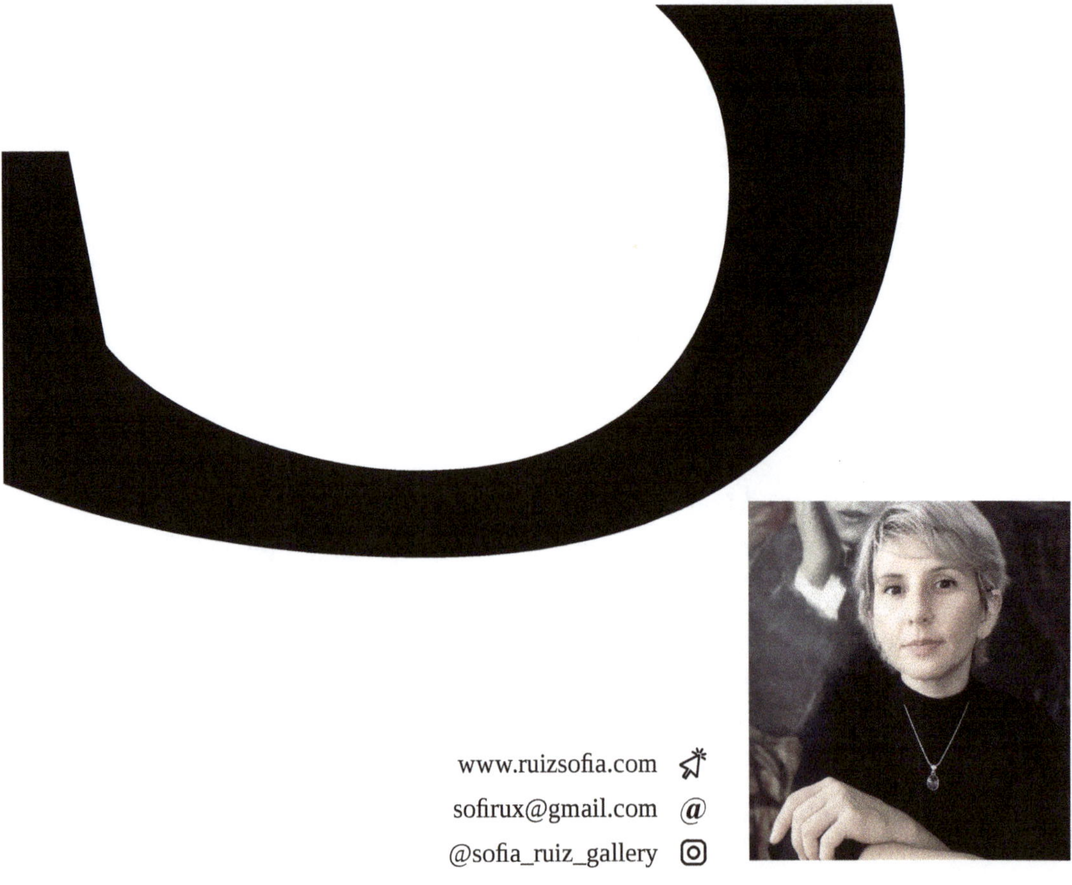

www.ruizsofia.com

sofirux@gmail.com

@sofia_ruiz_gallery

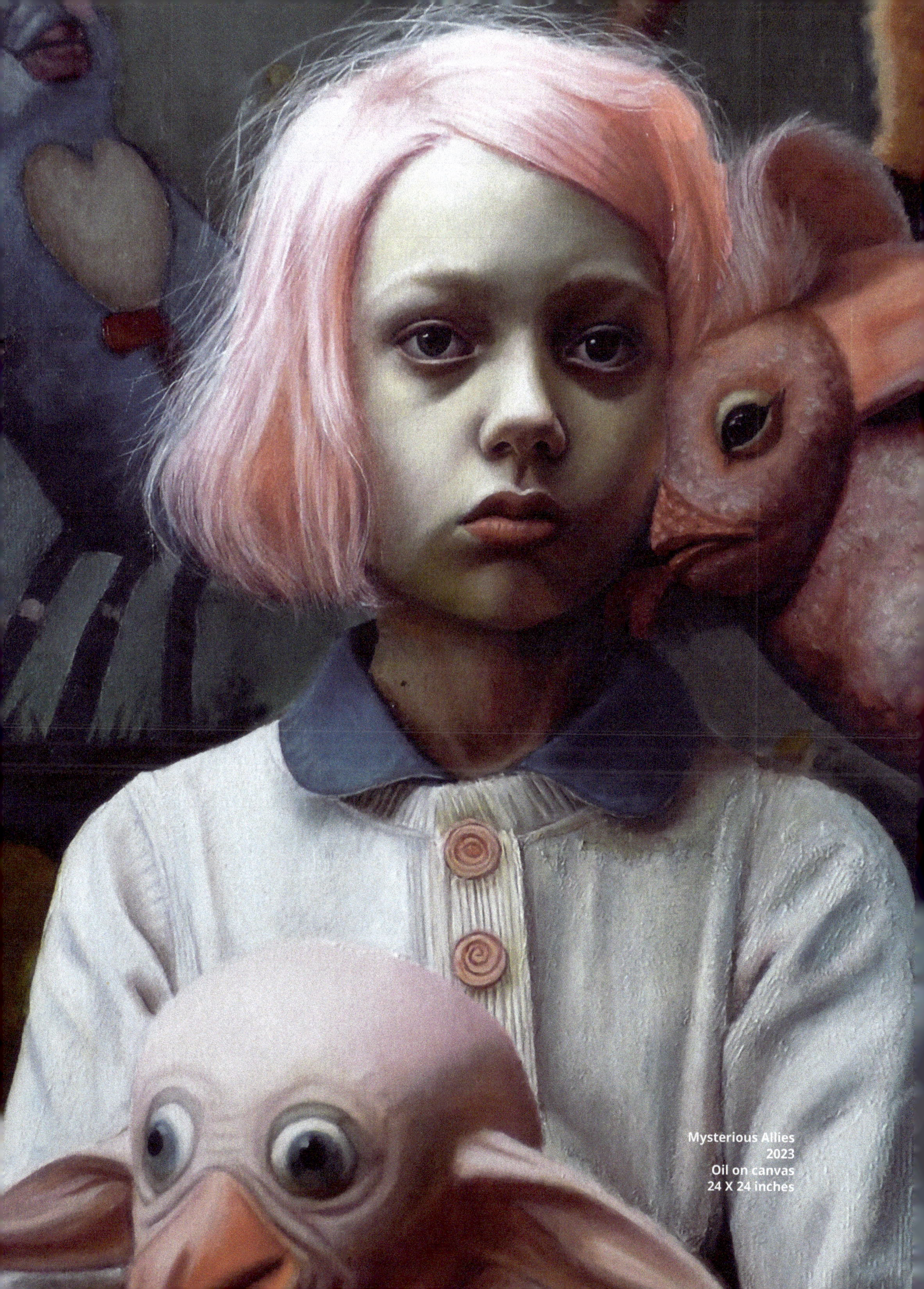
Mysterious Allies
2023
Oil on canvas
24 X 24 inches

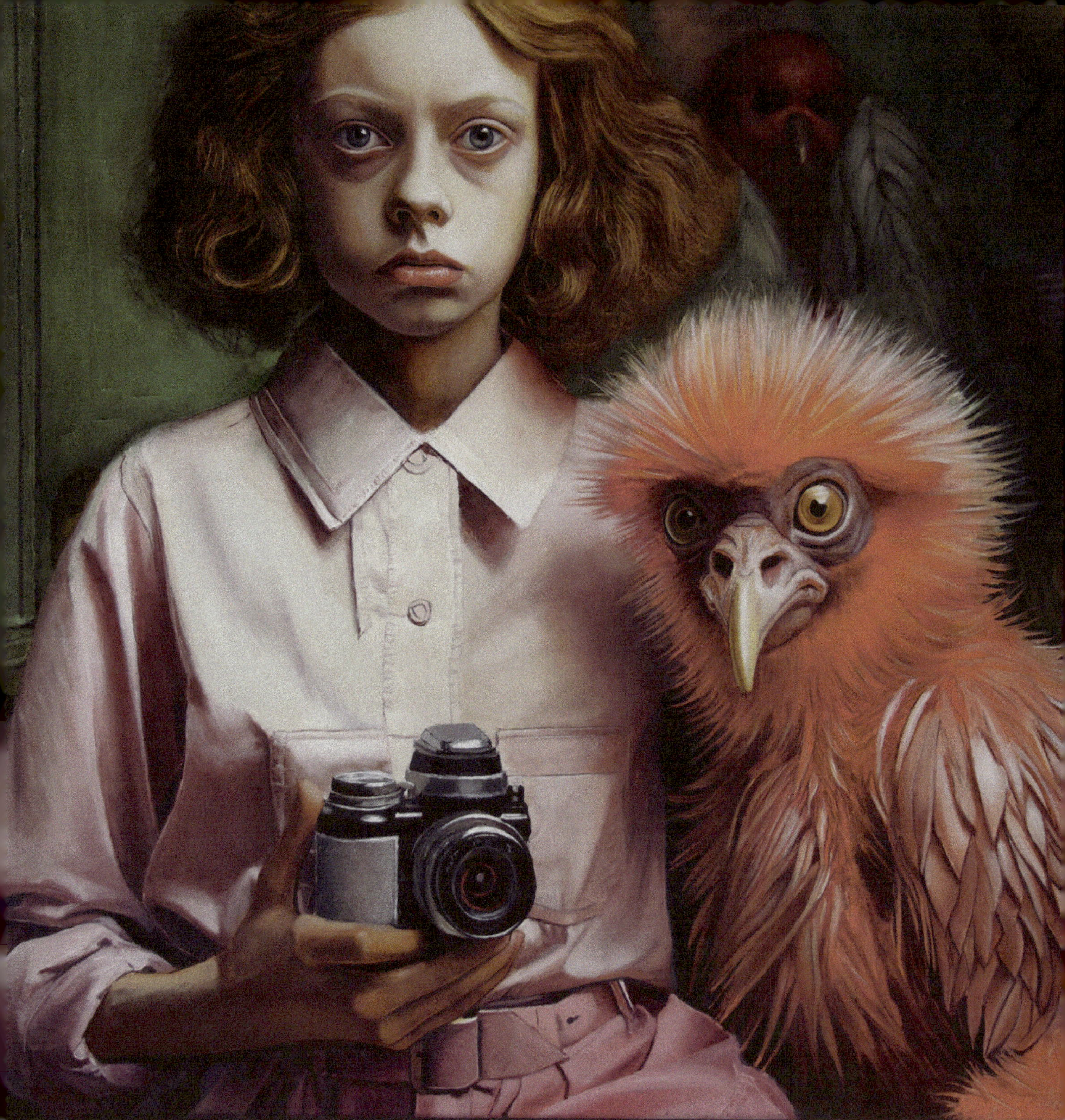

The Aloof Artist, 2023, Oil on Canvas, 24 x 24 inches

How do you cope with the vulnerability of sharing your art with the world?

For me, my paintings are like pages of a personal diary, so if I want to share it with people, I have to be able to expose or share some personal aspect of my life. I'm also aware that some of the viewers maybe won't like it, and that's ok.

What do you want people to take away from your work?

A glimpse of my world.

Can you share a moment when you felt discouraged as an artist? How did you overcome it?

I try not to take the rejection of my work as personal, I just keep working on things or projects that I want to do and make me happy.

How do you decide what to charge for your work?

I charge according to my experience, awards, exhibitions, and of course the work and detail of every piece.

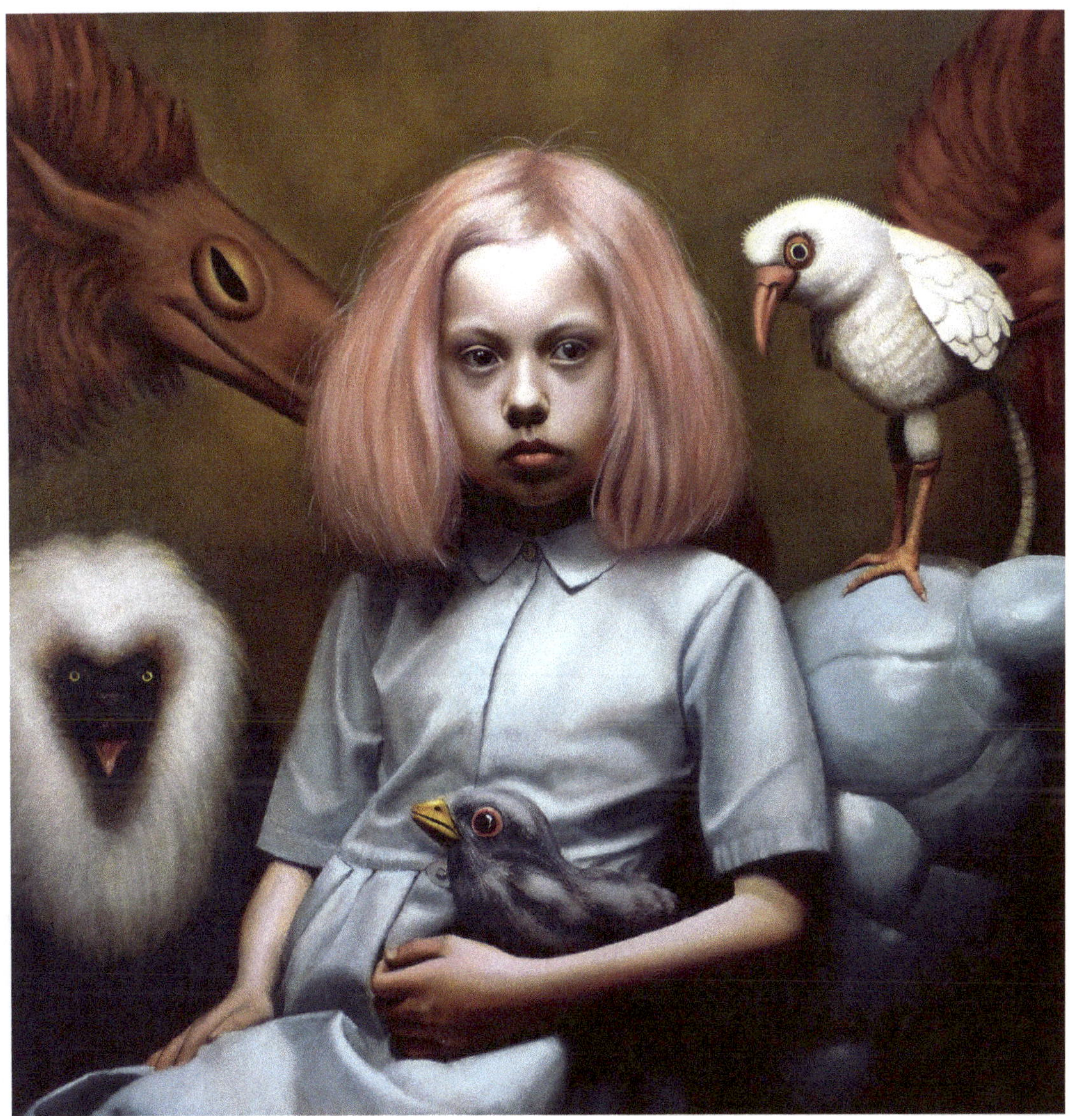

Lady Bird, 2023, Oil on canvas, 24 x 24 inches

How has your art helped you understand yourself better?

Art is the best therapy, and it has helped me to navigate in this world. Through art, I am able to recognize my limitations and find new skills at the same time.

What's one piece of advice you'd give to aspiring artists?

Be conscious that your work must mean something for you first, and then you can worry about the rest.

T eodora Stojanović was born in Belgrade on July 12, 1981, half Serbian and half Cypriot. She Graduated from the Academy of Fine Arts in Belgrade and Completed specialist studies in the class of academician Vladimir Veličković in Academy of Fine arts. In addition to painting, she has a master's degree in philosophy. She exhibited in the country and abroad and is winner of several international awards for painting at competitions in Italy, Spain, South Korea, Taiwan, America, Serbia. She held over 100 collective and 25 solo exhibitions. Artist Statement: I paint freely, extracting the form from the thrown colors on the canvas. It's as if my task is to extract from the canvas that mixture of colors of beings that are hidden and trapped in them, that try to free them and transfer them from another dimension of the visible world.

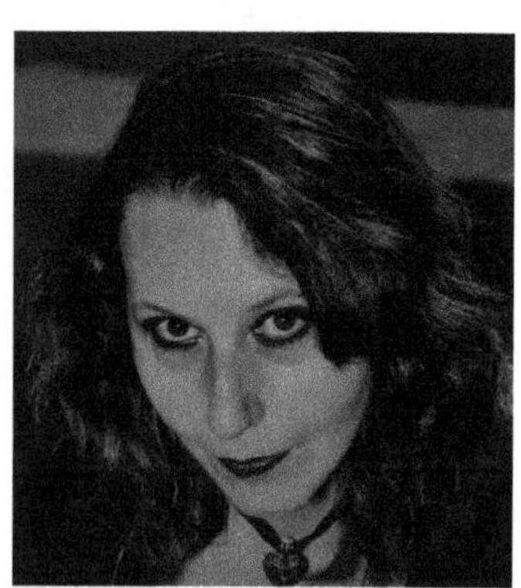

www.artpal.com

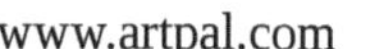 emailbusiness1231@gmail.com

 @teodoradarkart

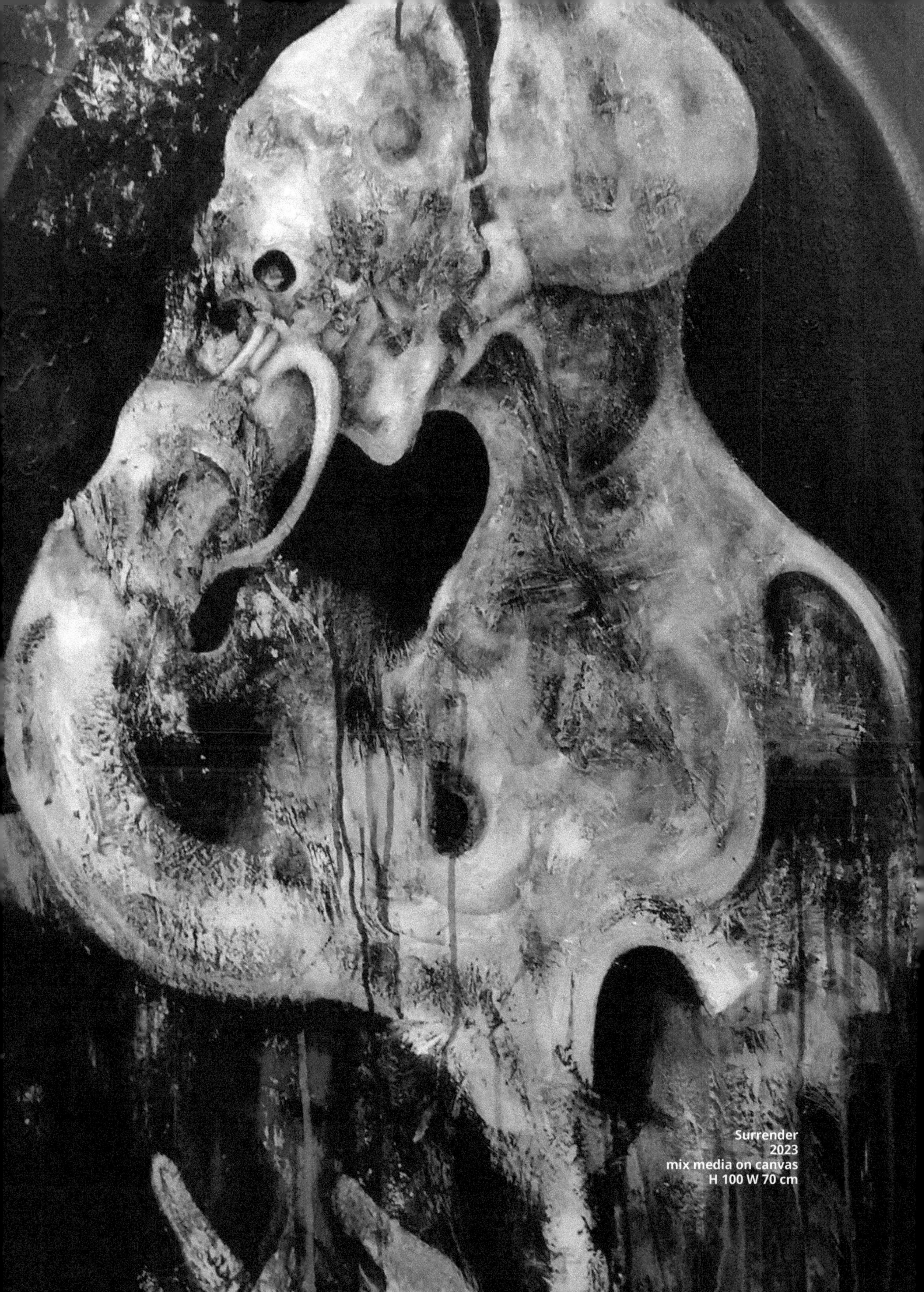
Surrender
2023
mix media on canvas
H 100 W 70 cm

Horus, 2024, mix media on canvas, H 100 W 80 cm

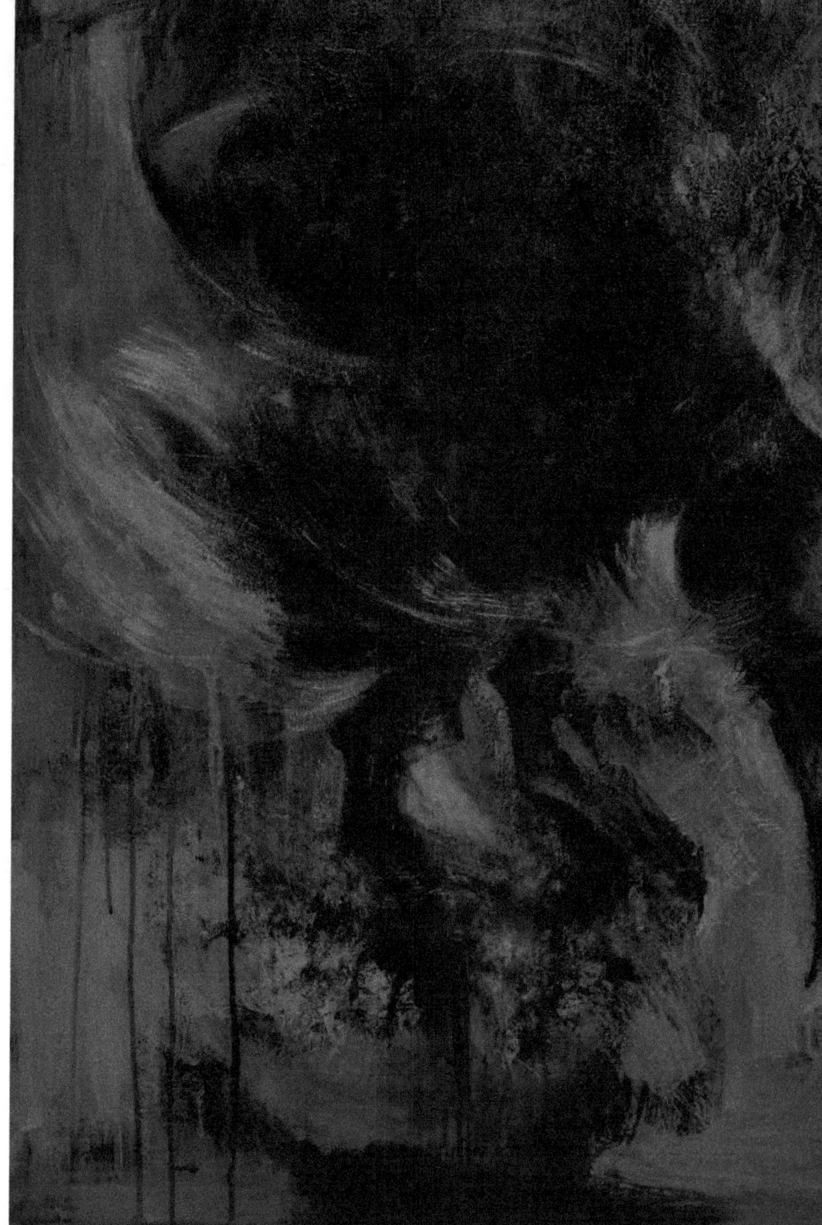

How do you decide what to charge for your work?

For a long time, I was sorry to sell my works, but at one point, when the flood destroyed almost all the works I had at the time, I realized that they should not be kept, but let them live on the wall, and allow someone to enjoy them, to be found in them. The price of the work depends on the effort I put into the work, the quality of the work, the time I spent on making it, the awards and exhibitions achieved both as a whole and for the specific work I am selling, and then the size of the canvas and the material used.

How do you cope with the vulnerability of sharing your art with the world?

I overcame that feeling with my first exhibition and a story about the theme of my works, which is related to my personal philosophy. I haven't had such a feeling of vulnerability for a long time. I believe that a work of art should go out into the world to live, and should influence the world and the observers. It should create a reaction, even if it is negative. Only through this contact with the sacred does the work have its meaning. While deciding that it is finished and can be exhibited, it is one of the best or almost the best version of the artist at that moment. When I say the best version, I mean the maximum that the artist gives of himself at that moment.

What do you want people to take away from your work?

My goal is for people to connect with my work, to find some parts of themselves that are hidden - to bring them out of the subconscious into consciousness by looking at my pictures. I want them to begin to take a deeper look at themselves, things and the world around them. To start thinking, to find what is holding them back in life, how far they have come, whether they have any goals, whether they are limited by norms or act in accordance with themselves, how they view death and life in itself. What are the values for them? So I want the impression that the work leaves on them to encourage them to think. To begin to see things from another dimension.

Can you share a moment when you felt discouraged as an artist? How did you overcome it?

Like every artist, I have phases when I'm not satisfied with my work, when I feel that I'm standing still and that my work needs to be better. This happens most often when I look at an exhibition of a world-famous old master whose paintings blow my mind. Then I think about what I could change and how to improve my work. Sometimes dissatisfaction occurs when I don't pass an art competition or when I don't sell my work. I overcome such situations by thinking and analyzing, and I also know that quality is often not the only and always decisive factor in tenders or sales, because there are many criteria on the basis of which the selection is made, and this does not necessarily mean that my work is not good. Regardless of the cause, without this dissatisfaction there would be no progress in the work.

How has your art helped you understand yourself better?

I think it's the other way around with me, but there are also moments when I understand myself through my paintings. I work according to the feeling that guides me. Through work I express myself, I express my understandings, feelings, thoughts. I would say that my works are a reflection of me. But there are also moments when I understand myself through paintings, as if I combine some parts of my deepest emotions and thoughts into wholes.

What's one piece of advice you'd give to aspiring artists?

First, that they draw and paint as much as possible so that their work is of high quality, so that they believe in themselves and their work, but also be realistic about it. To always strive for better no matter what they achieve. And of course, apply to as many competitions as possible and never give up, no matter how many obstacles there are.

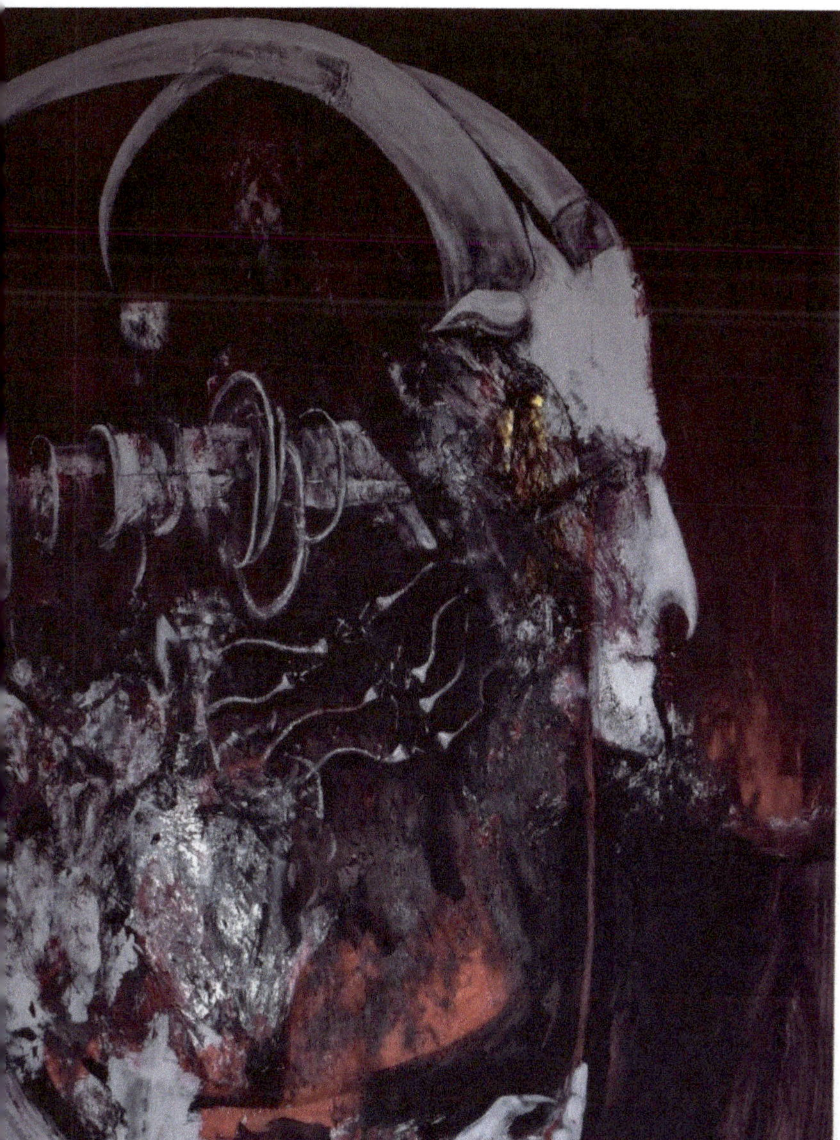

Interruption, 2023, mix media on canvas, H 100 cm W 120 cm

People's Choice

Feature Top 10

In this article, we spotlight the artists who emerged victorious by garnering the highest number of votes in ATH Magazine: People's Choice Feature.

Shweta Choudhari
1130 Votes

An Indian artist with a diverse background in animation and texture artistry. Worked for Crest on shows like Bratz and Jakers. Art is an integral part of her identity.

Memories are the essence of moments captured by your soul through your eyes

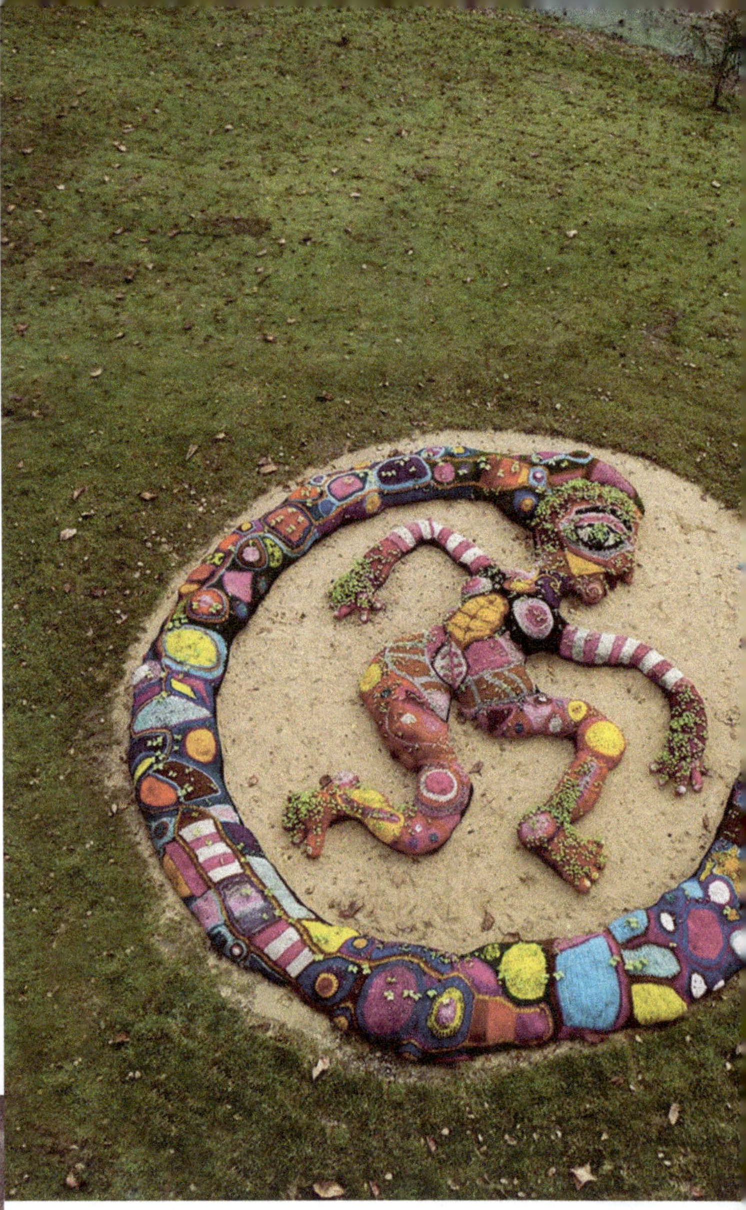

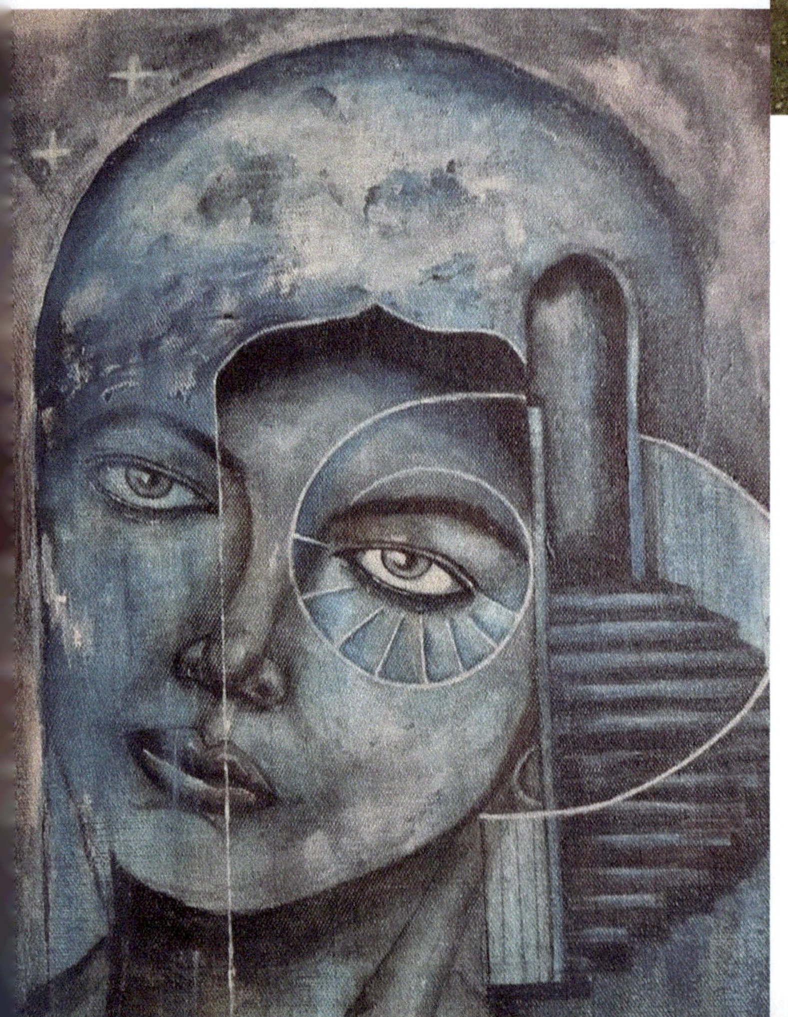

Cristina Salas
WINNER - 1259 Votes

Originally from Quito, Ecuador (b. 1985), I studied fine art in Italy and France, then earned a master's in Art Production from Spain. My artistic journey includes residencies in France, Puerto Rico, and Mexico. Also, I've worked as a teaching artist and hold a Master's in Architecture from the United States. Currently, I'm a full-time mixed media artist, exploring various mediums to create characters and stories that connect with people and nature. My work aims to bring joy and a sense of place, incorporating drawing, fibers, mosaics, ceramics, paint and found objects. I engage with public spaces, striving to give viewers a joyful experience.

Muñeca Viajera
Fibers, earth and Zinnia, Morning Glory and Moonflower seeds

Hari Lualhati

1011 Votes

A Cape Town artist, creates "SOULWORKS" that convey profound life lessons through interconnected themes. Her art blends realism, expressionism, and symbolism to evoke emotions and convey clear messages globally. Hari's artistic prowess has earned accolades globally, with features in Art Magazines, reflecting the resonance of her art.

Seed of Faith - Oil on Canvas

Una Gonzalez

569 Votes

I'm Una, a border woman from Tijuana and San Diego, exploring the laws that govern living entities through visual arts, writing, performance, and sculpture. I embrace the chaos of borders, reflecting the delicate balance of expansion and contraction. Nature Leaving Its Nature. Sphere and line echo in my work.

Toronjas - Oil and acrylic on linen

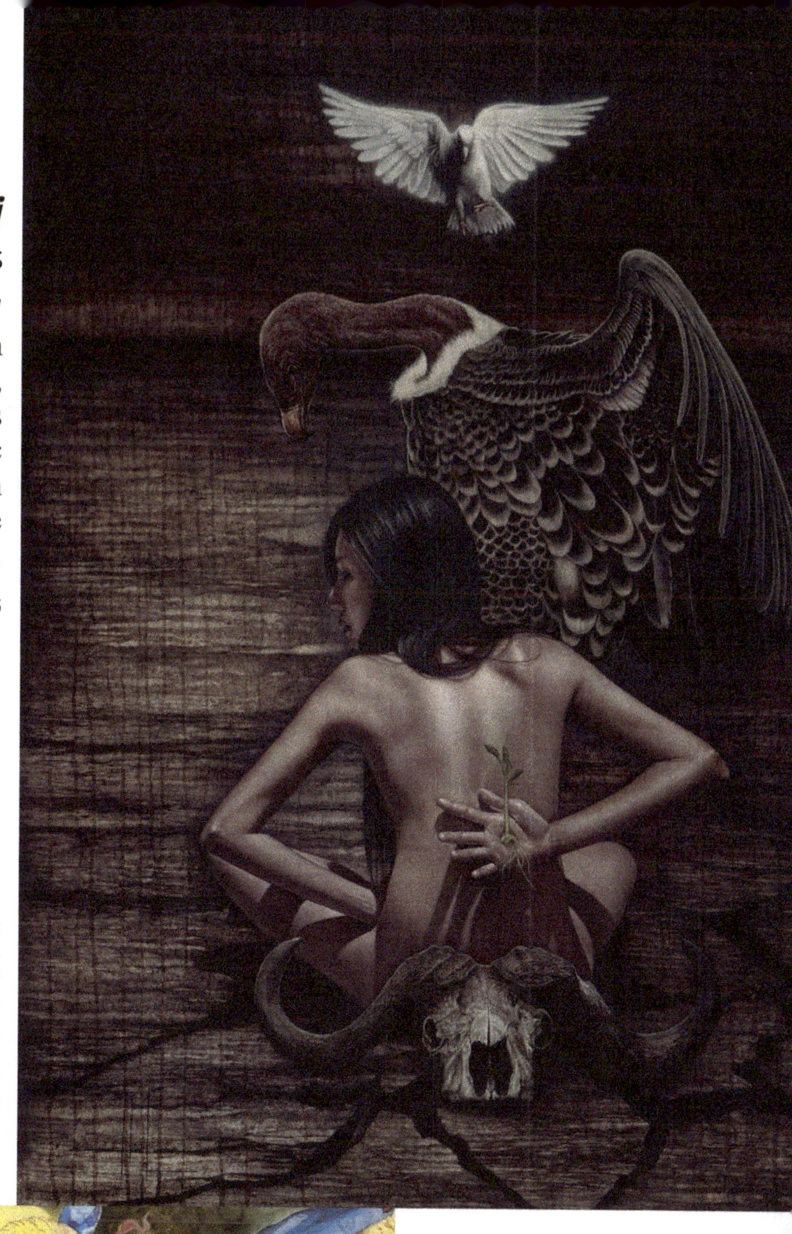

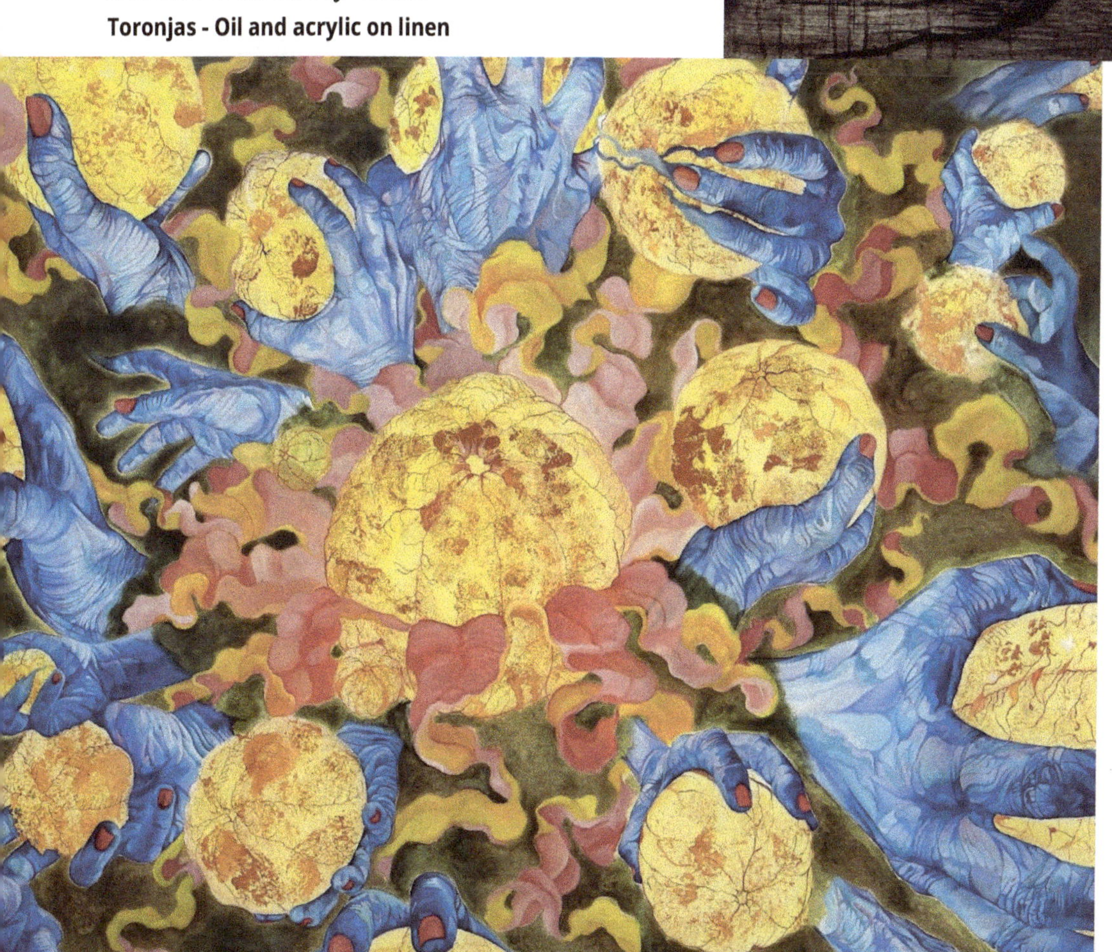

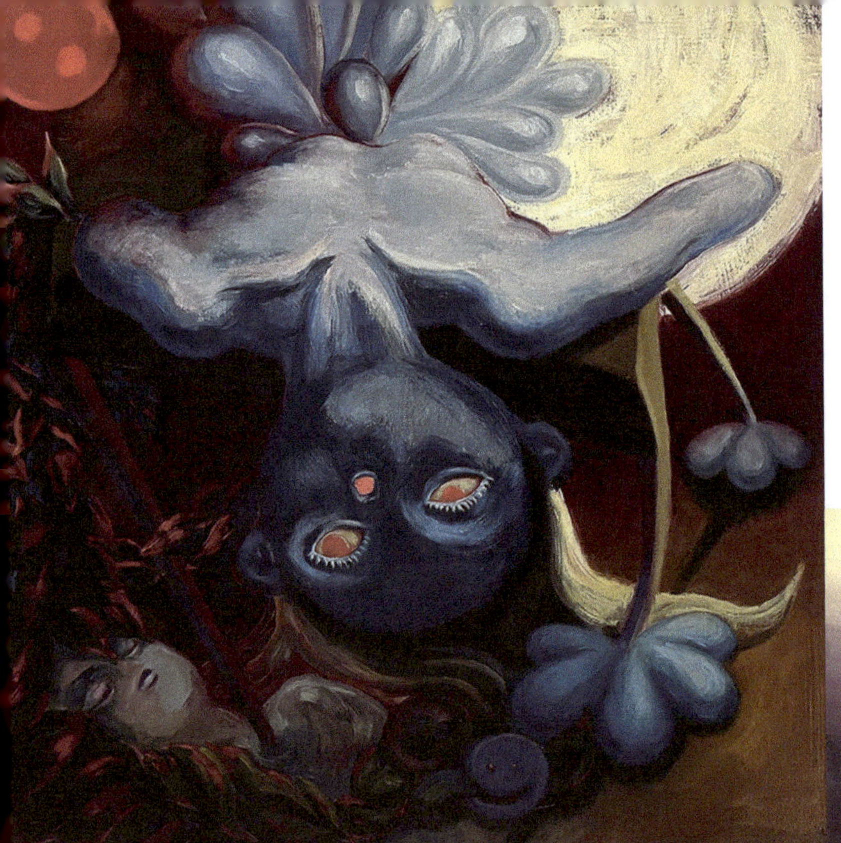

Yooyeon Nam
391 Votes

Yooyeon Nam, a colorist painter, explores the limited mutual understanding of human experience. Her unique perspective shines in solo exhibitions, while group exhibitions highlight her growing influence.

Night and I and Small Animals - Oil on Canvas

Lorena FrÃas
306 Votes

Lorena Frías, a Mexican artist and architect, creates captivating paintings that blend contemporary scenes with classical influences. Her work, featuring portraits and exploring color, is housed in private collections across New York City, Mexico City, and New Mexico.

Tattoo - Oil on canvas

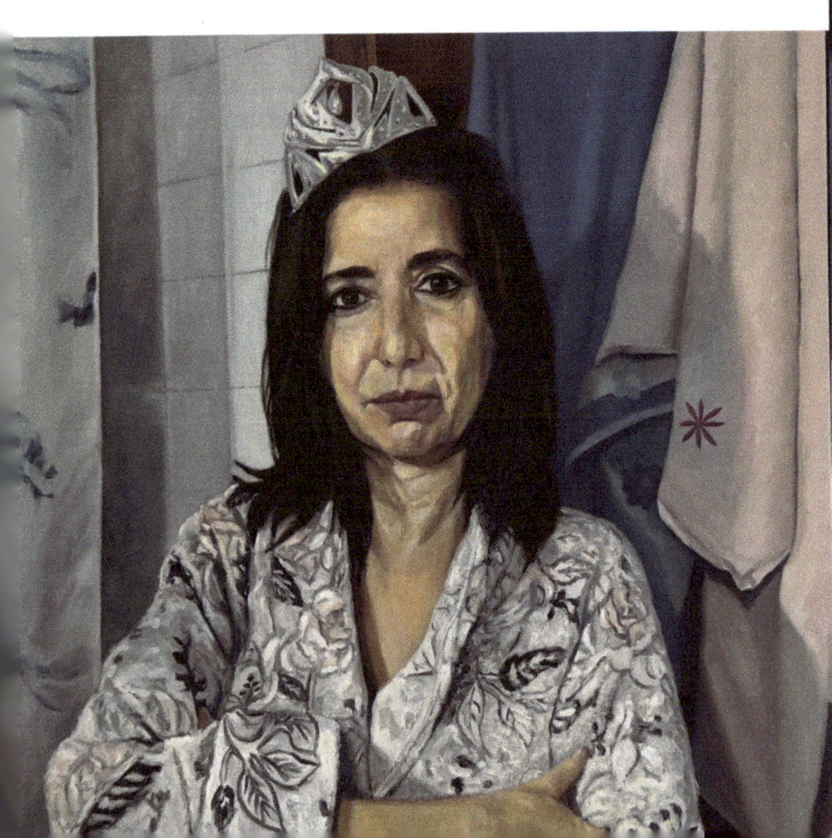

Maribel Martin
303 Votes

An artist from Spain, specializes in portraiture and capturing the essence of women. Her work explores the duality of emotions and everyday moments, reflecting passion and melancholy.

The queen of the golden koi fish pond - Oil on Canvas

Phuong Truong
216 Votes

From Vietnam, painting with oil on canvas, seeking balance, freedom, and meditation in landscapes. I explore questions about the world's beginning, randomness in life, and the boundaries between reality and dreams.

In the middle of somewhere - Oil on canvas

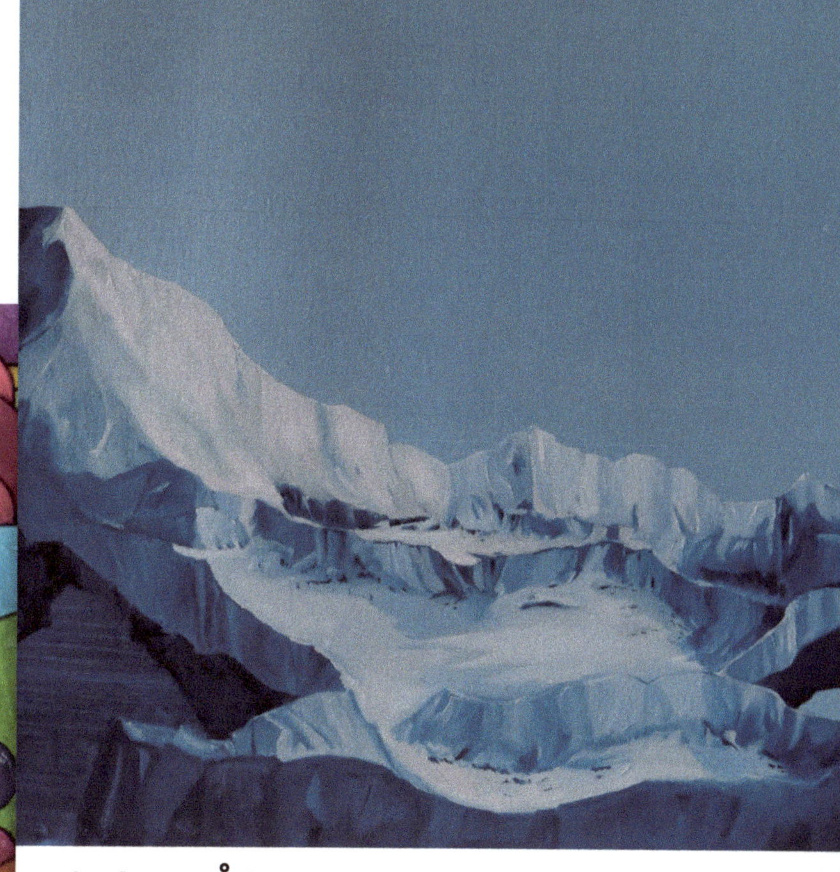

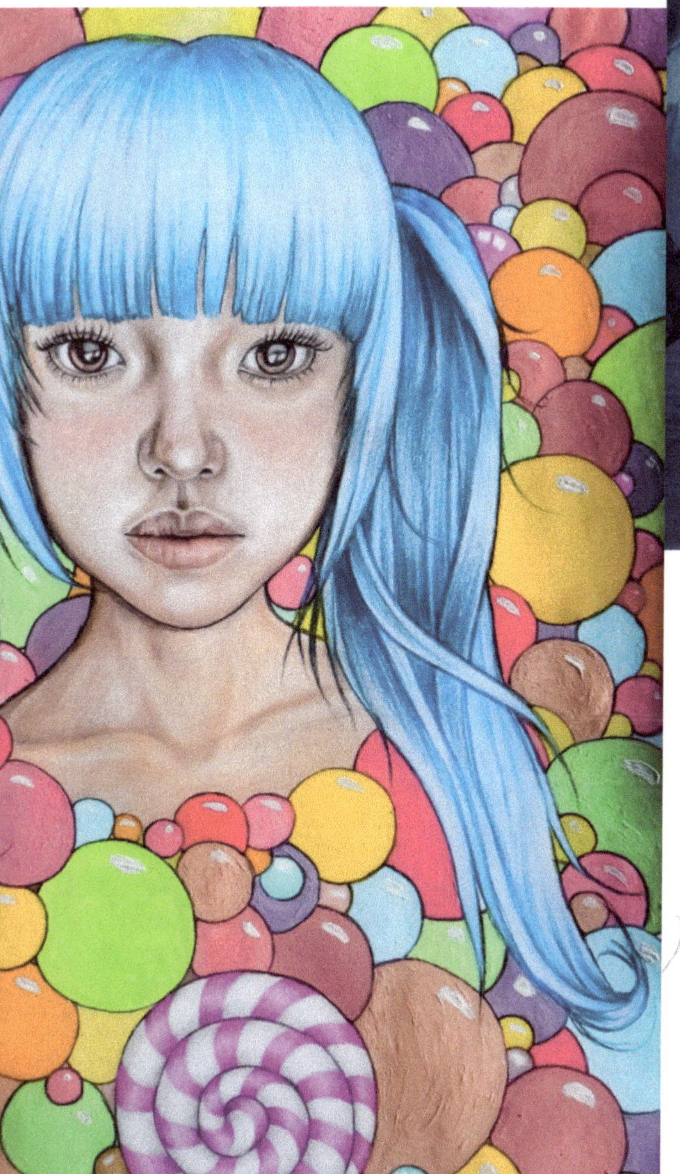

Marryam Moma
213 Votes

Tanzanian-Nigerian collage artist she tells vivid stories through multidimensional imagery. Her work illustrates Black joy and challenges perceptions of the Black body.

Hello, I Am Betty Davis - Mixed media

Timka SzÅ'ke
248 Votes

A visual artist from Budapest, creates figurative and realistic pop surrealist images. Using mixed media, she showcases the natural beauty and facial expressions of her characters.

Candy girl II. - Mixed media on wood pane

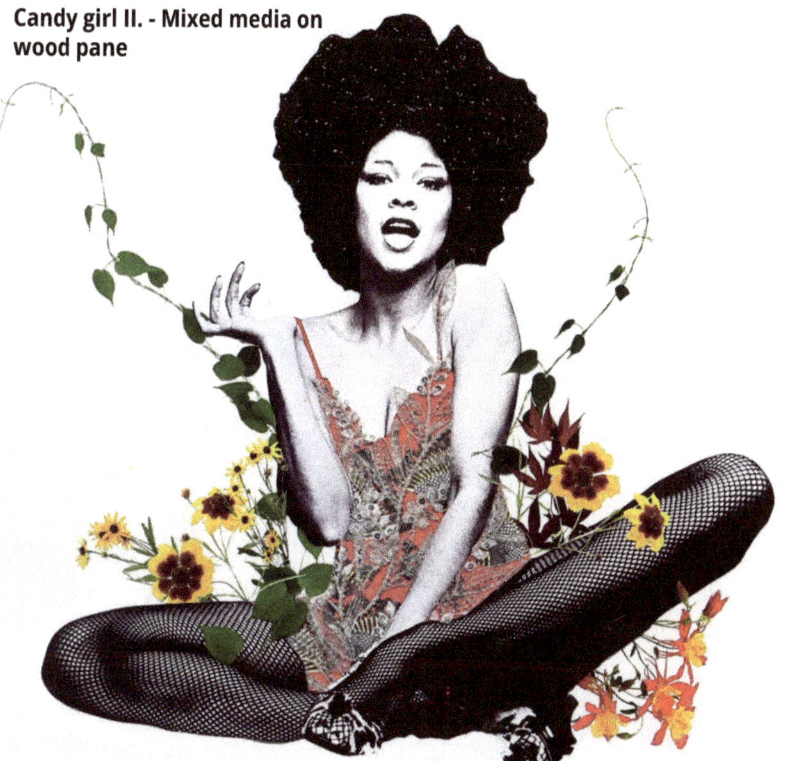

Artists talk about their

Personal and Creative

Growth

In the year 2023

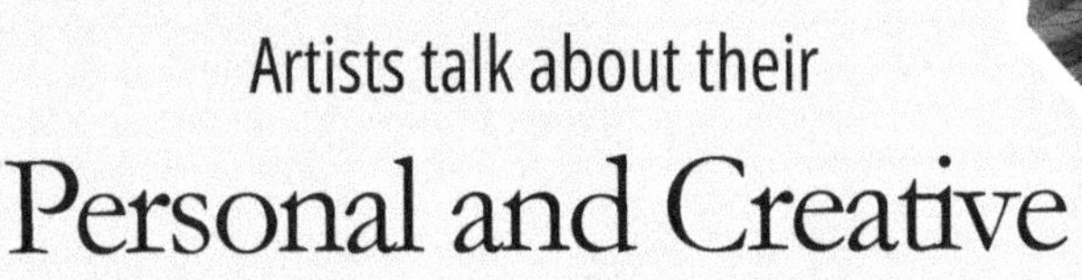

Written by Museerah Nisar

As we bid goodbye to the year 2023, we feel a sense of excitement for the year 2024. After all, a new year means a new start! As artists, we begin each year with some hopes and dreams and we can't help but look back at the year that went by. It's quite natural to ponder over your achievements of last year and to think back on all the things you were able to do. Here at Arts to Hearts Project, we value our community of artists. We appreciate their feedback, as not only is it a way for our followers to interact with us, but it also provides an opportunity for us to learn from them. So, each week on our Instagram page (@artstoheartsproject), we pose a question to get thoughtful responses that can be helpful to other artists who are in the same boat. For this particular piece, we asked our followers if there was a specific artwork or project from last year that holds particular significance to them, and if so, why? The response was overwhelming as always, and so we decided to share the feedback with you! As you go through these comments, we are positive that you'll also begin to reflect on each one of your projects from the year 2023, and come up with your own favorite one!

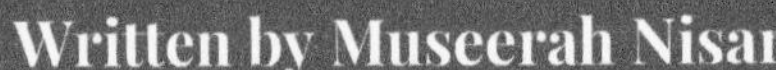

Artists:

Is there a specific piece or project from this year that holds particular significance to you, and if so, why?

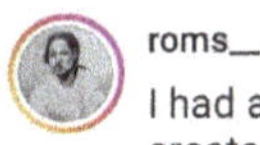
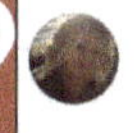
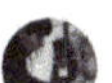
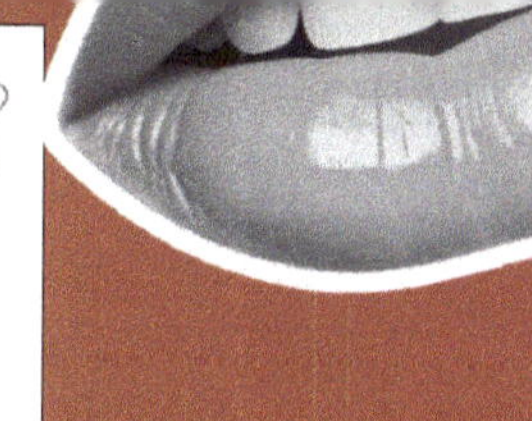

roms__art 2 w

I had a total hysterectomy in June and created in the lead up, on the day, and in recovery an automatic drawing (nearly) every day.

Reply

talitha_deetlefs_art 2 w

Yes, I completed a new sculpture this year that is very special to me. She represents the direction that my life journey has taken, as a woman. I walked away from what wasn't serving me and took on a new, unknown and truly transformational road. Thank for popping these questions on Insta @artstoheartsproject One very often overlooks one's achievements when you are faced with challenges 🧡

Reply

theeclecticcurator 7 h

There is a painting in my feed that took me 10 months to finish. I hated it at one point and almost set it on fire but I didn't quit and for that reason it holds the most significance for me this year. ❤️

Reply

Nevertheless, the artists on our Instagram page posted heartwarming comments on our post, where they shared their projects, highlighting their hopes and dreams. We want to share some of those responses here so they can also be a source of inspiration for others!

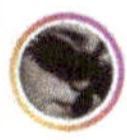

imagesbyblairecatherine 2 w

Yes. Being a part of the @eyemamaproject and their book. As a mother who also is an artist this project was immensely important for my mental health as an artist (being able to create at home with my kids) as well as my journey as a mom. A true honor.

Reply

Art is a reflection of your soul

@talitha_deetlefts_art has a very uplifting response to our question, where she talks about completing a sculpture in the year 2023 that represents the direction her life has taken as a woman. A very important message that she gives through her response, and something that we should all note down, is that it's always a good idea to walk away from what is not serving us in any way. This is a great affirmation to take into the year 2024 as well; to let go of things that are not helping us, and to embrace new things, no matter how scary or challenging it might feel. We never know when an unknown road can transform our creative journey for the better!

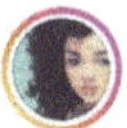

kabria.art 9 h

This year I made the least amount of work I've probably created in my whole life. I'm still trying to practice allowing myself some grace, as it's been a very difficult year/ few years. BUT at the beginning of 2023, I made a surrealist self portrait where my head is open and inside is my younger self. I think I am most proud of that piece this year as it symbolizes the inner, generational and trauma healing work I have put in the past few years.

Reply

Embracing change

Reading inspiring comments by artists, such as those of @imagesbyblairecatherine and @roms_art, can always be a morale booster. They remind us that apart from being an artist, each one of us has a role to play in our lives and that we have our own individual challenges. There are female artists out there with children, and being a mom and an artist can be extra challenging as juggling the two lives and creating a balance can be tough. But artists like @imagesbyblairecatherine reaffirm our faith, that no matter how hard it feels at the moment, with conviction, we can definitely achieve our dreams.

@roms_art's response is a clear indication of how sometimes even the most challenging of situations in life can lead to something unexpected. From her surgery in 2023, she was able to find the strength to continue creating, which led her to paint her heart out nearly every day.

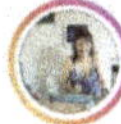

vinedesigns83 1 w

My mixed media mosaic that won me my first honorable mention. Also, my online portfolio of surface pattern designs.

Reply

mrsalyelliott 2 w

An image I created is representing my country in the World Photographic Cup- I am so thrilled!!!

Reply

guylenesolon 2 w

Sound healing project, playing my African harp in a organic greenhouse I designed inspired by sacred geometry. Seedlings grew super fast as I played music and sang words encouraging my plants to grow after irrigation. This project stems from the work of Masaru Emoto from Japan who claimed that human consciousness could affect the molecular structure of water. @artstoheartsproject

studiobotanicalsbhag 1 w

This year , I created a custom artwork for a client who wanted to combine several aspect of their lives and wanted me to create an abstract version of it. I combined their love for cycling in nature , their countries of origin, their plans to have another baby and life in general. ✨💛

Reply

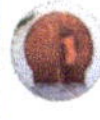
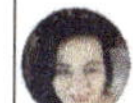
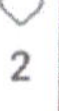

azzalajii 2 w

Yes I have it is a personal project called(a step, a window and a mirror) I inspired it this summer in Napoli I hope it will be the door for my future life as an artist

Reply

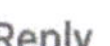

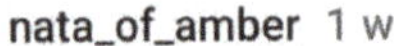

amandasilkceramics 1 w

I sculpted and created a ceramic portrait that discusses the Windrush generation, inspired by a local charity to voice recognition of its historical event and its impact. @amandasilkceramics

Re

nata_of_amber 1 w

I've traveled to Ukraine to document the war. As a person born in Russia, the aggressor country, and actively working and advocating for Ukraine this documentary trip holds an enormous significance to me.

Reply

@theeclecticcurator's comment is a reminder to us that no matter how you feel, it's always a good idea to keep going. As artists, we are often faced with skepticism and feel like giving up because we can't see its true potential at the time. But sometimes, it is one of those things that give us the hardest time that can end up holding the most value. And therefore, we must always trust the process!

As @kabria.art talks about her favorite self-portrait from the past year, she also reminds us that in a world that pushes us to be productive constantly, it's okay to listen to your body and take it slow every now and then. If you are someone who has been struggling for some time, this is a reminder that it's okay to allow yourself some grace and focus on your inner healing, even if that means not working as much as you would like to.

Manifesting dreams through art

Never give up on your dreams! Artists like @studiobotanicalsbhag, @vinedesigns83, and @mrsalyelliott are reminding us that if we keep following our dreams, and work hard for them, we will get there. No matter the challenges, we must always remember that there is light at the end of the tunnel, and we too can accomplish our goals. Getting our dream clients or having our artwork represent our country in the World Photographic Cup are just some of the things that are truly possible if we set our mind to it. So, keep working towards your dreams!

Nurturing your inner artist

Most of the responses that we received from artists had one thing in common: the best course of action is to be ourselves and listen to our inner voice! What do we feel about the world? What kind of artworks do we want to make? What brings us joy? These are some of the questions that can change the trajectory of our creative journey if we can answer them honestly. In the end, art is what we want to make. It doesn't matter what people expect from us, the world needs our talents, and it needs us to be true and authentic to our craft.

Artists can sometimes overlook their creative journey and successes. Whether it is imposter syndrome or self-doubt, artists can end up not giving themselves enough credit. This article is meant to shed light on all these amazing artists' accomplishments, and to act as a reminder that as long as we keep creating, we are on the right track. So, let's take this moment to look back and see how far we have come. Let's look back on our creative evolution and the art we were able to make so that we can celebrate ourselves and begin the new year with a positive note and new resolutions!

If you found this article insightful, share it with your friends and don't forget to tag us on Instagram (@artstoheartsproject)! Do check out our weekly question stickers and participate in the comment section to gain more insights into how artists are dealing with the art world!

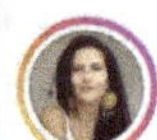

christina.georgieva.art 2 w

I love my high vibrational Ethereal Sacred Geometry Collection that I created this past year and how it has been uplifting people! 💗🙏🏻💗

Reply

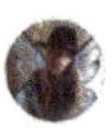

artims57 1 w

Yes! I've incorporated many of my mixed media techniques to make mini museums, to honour anniversaries, artists and people.

Reply

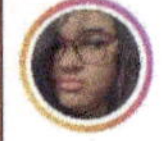

isunmirakhorli 1 w

Yes ! I create collages and my 2023 pieces are getting ready to go to next step to present and paint them in a bigger size and move on to an incredible level. And the main title is not chosen yet but the subject and thought behind these collages are about the protests and my memories and life included in Iran (my country) so its social and political and with some touch of expressionism . My collage notebooks are called "the resting place for Isun"

Reply

In CONVERSATION *With* POOJA SHINDE

Arts to Hearts Project Sponsorship Feature

Interview By Sonam Bindra

An artist from Mumbai and one of the finalists of the Manorama Young Printmakers Award by India Printmaker House, which was sponsored by the Arts to Hearts Project, Pooja creates artwork inspired by the Japanese concept of Wabi Sabi. The city's hustle and bustle has inspired her to give a very interesting perspective in her artwork. The artwork etched on metal has interesting linear perspectives which give the illusion of vastness in small compositions. She brights out the details from familiar images that often go unnoticed. Read the full interview to learn about her journey as an artist, the challenges she faced, and her vision for the years to come.

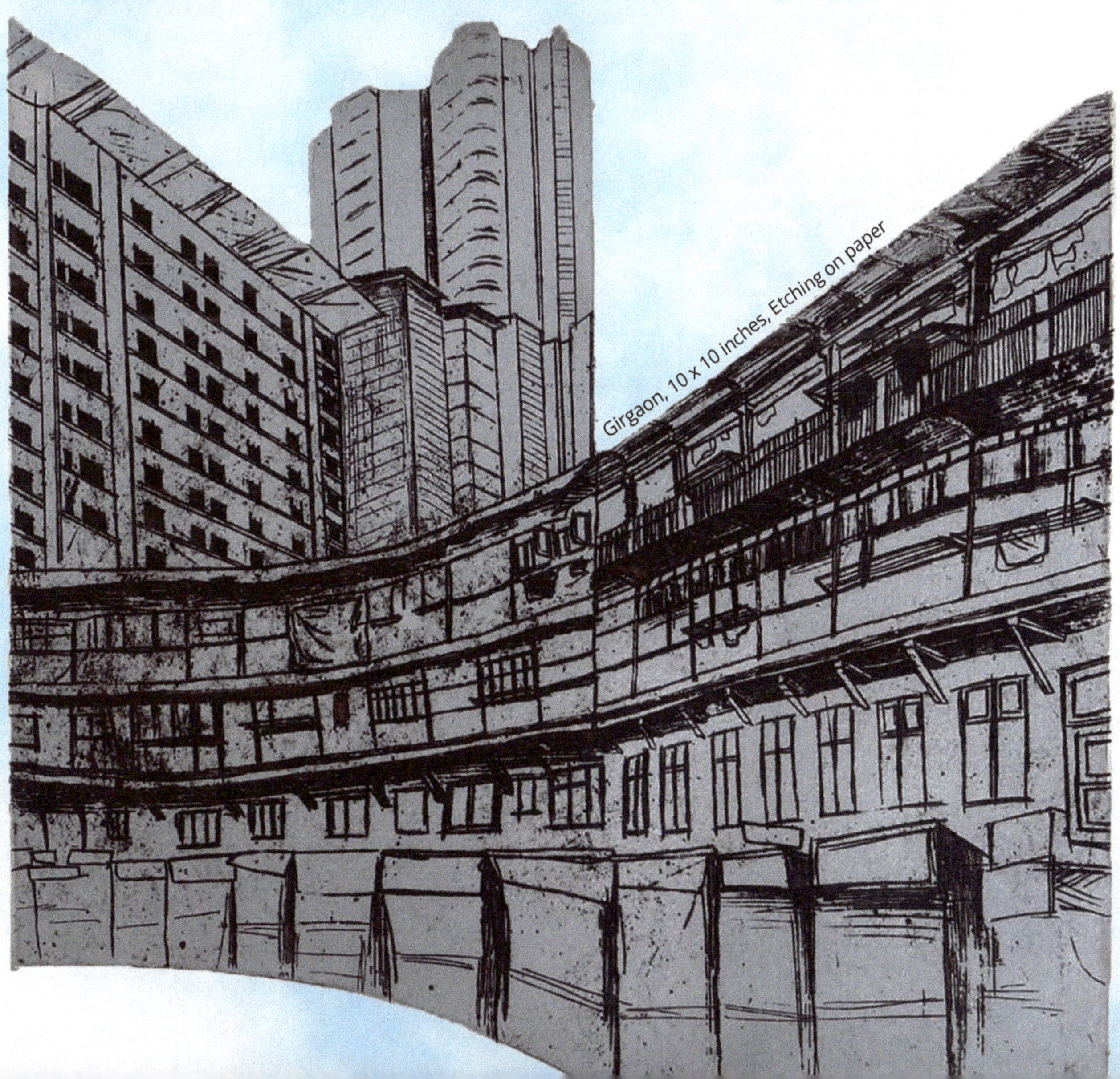

WINNER
India Printmaking House Award

A very interesting work with linear perspectives and illusions. I am curious to know how you started on this path?

Growing up in Mumbai, the city's hustle and bustle always influenced me. My inspiration primarily stemmed from architecture, especially during my time at an art school located in the heart of Mumbai CST. The diverse structures, including the chawls in Girgaon and Parsi colonies, fascinated me. These places, with generations living in them, held a wealth of memories and stories. They weren't just structures; they embodied history. I would quickly sketch them on the spot with a dry brush and ink, returning to the studio to transform those sketches into artwork. That's how it all began.

Working with metal plates could be quite a challenge. Pooja, What has been the most challenging part of working with this medium?

Engaging in the etching medium has consistently been an exciting endeavor for me. When planning my work sketches, the spontaneous drawing on the plate stands out as the most thrilling aspect of my creative process. I find a deeper connection and absorption in etching compared to any other print-making medium. Once the drawing phase concludes, I immerse myself in the technical aspect of printmaking, particularly the acid etching process. Expressing my thoughts spontaneously on the plate poses a challenge due to the required techniques and skills, making it the most interesting and challenging aspect as I embark on a new piece

Can you tell us about the ideas behind your artwork? What interested you in this subject matter?

My artworks stem from my daily observations of the spaces that surround me. The compositions feature linear perspectives, creating the illusion of vastness within small settings. I find fascination in the Cycles of life, including decay, and have drawn inspiration from the Japanese aesthetic concept of wabi-sabi. Exploring the beauty in the transience of objects, the process of aging, and the cycles of growth and decay, I often evoke emotional experiences from the imperfections and diversities present. This approach highlights details in familiar images that are often overlooked.

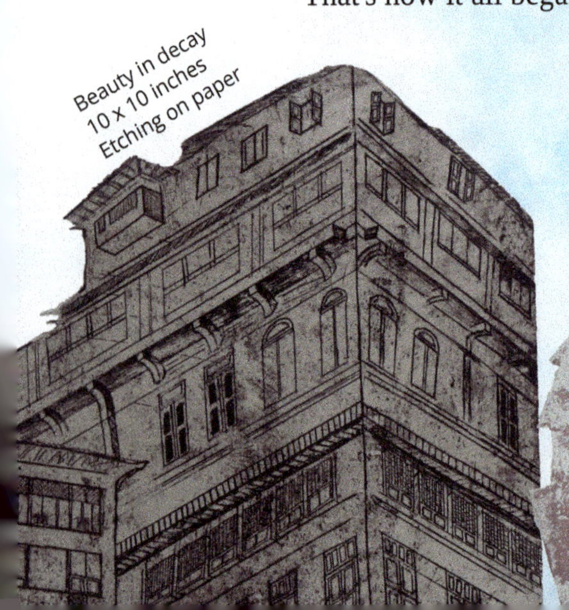

Beauty in decay
10 x 10 inches
Etching on paper

Pink wall
10 x 10 inches
Etching on paper

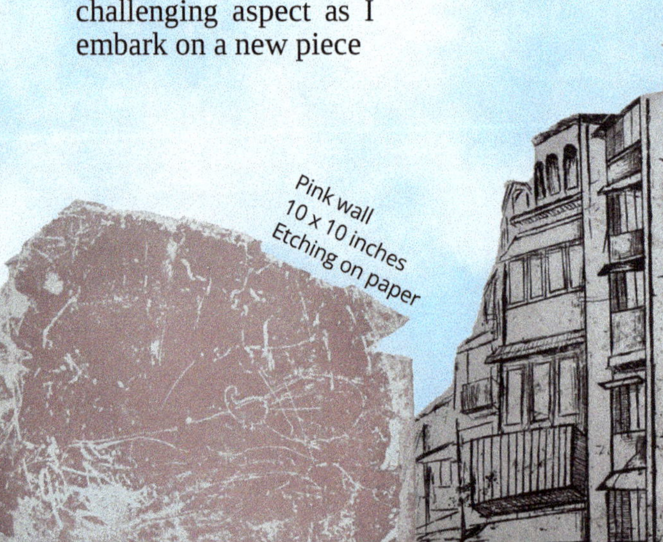

Structure 1
10 x 10 inches
Etching on paper

How has it been exploring different mediums for your artwork?

My journey in the printmaking, dating back to my college days, encompasses various mediums such as woodcut, etching, lithography, and cyanotype. Presently, my focus lies predominantly on the etching medium. The challenge and excitement of working with a metal plate have consistently pushed me to discover something new within myself. This particular medium holds a special place for me, as I derive the most enjoyment from working with it.

Pooja, can you talk about your journey as an artist? What were some hiccups you faced during the time?

My artistic journey commenced in childhood. As a young toddler, I would draw on walls and use tools like a rounder to scrape those drawings. Surprisingly, my mother never scolded me or discouraged this creative expression. This early experience shaped my understanding of freedom in self-expression, a theme that still resonates in my work today. Upon entering the art school, Sir J.J. School of Art, I explored new drawing techniques and refined my skills. My focus has always extended beyond creating visually pleasing works; I aim to enjoy and express myself spontaneously, whether on paper or canvas. Despite these obstacles, I am determined to keep my passion alive and persist in my commitment to the print medium.

Congratulations on being selected as one of the finalists for the Manorama Young Printmakers Award. What are your hopes for 2024? Where do you see yourself as an artist?

I express my gratitude to the jury members and India Printmaker House for this opportunity. Being a part of this community is truly fulfilling. I look forward to unveiling creative experimental works in 2024. My plan involves pushing the boundaries of my process, combining digital media and etchings to conceptualize new pieces. I aim to step out of my comfort zone, challenging myself to explore diverse approaches that will enhance and enrich my artistic practice.

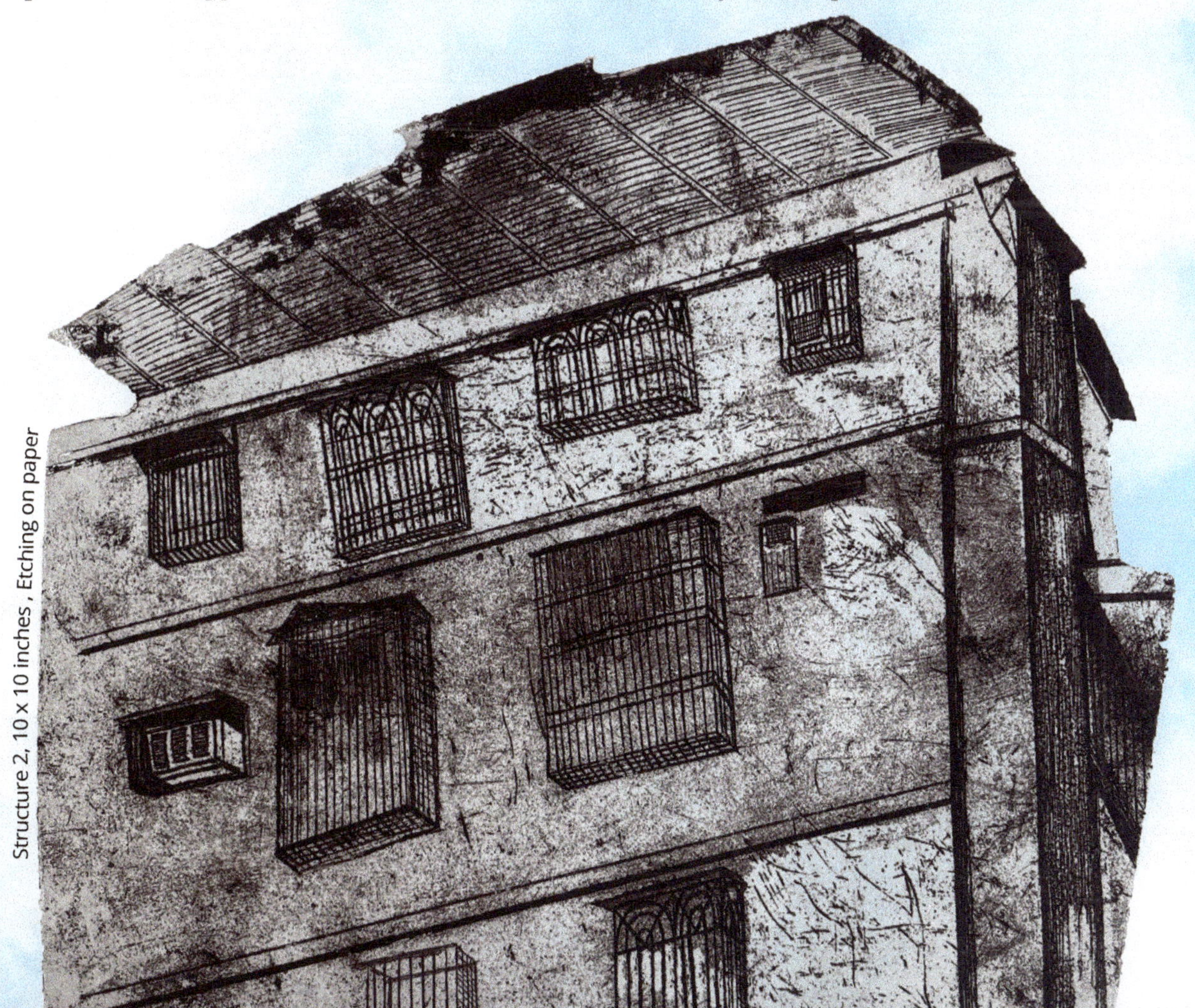

Structure 2, 10 x 10 inches, Etching on paper

WOMEN IN ARTS
NETWORK

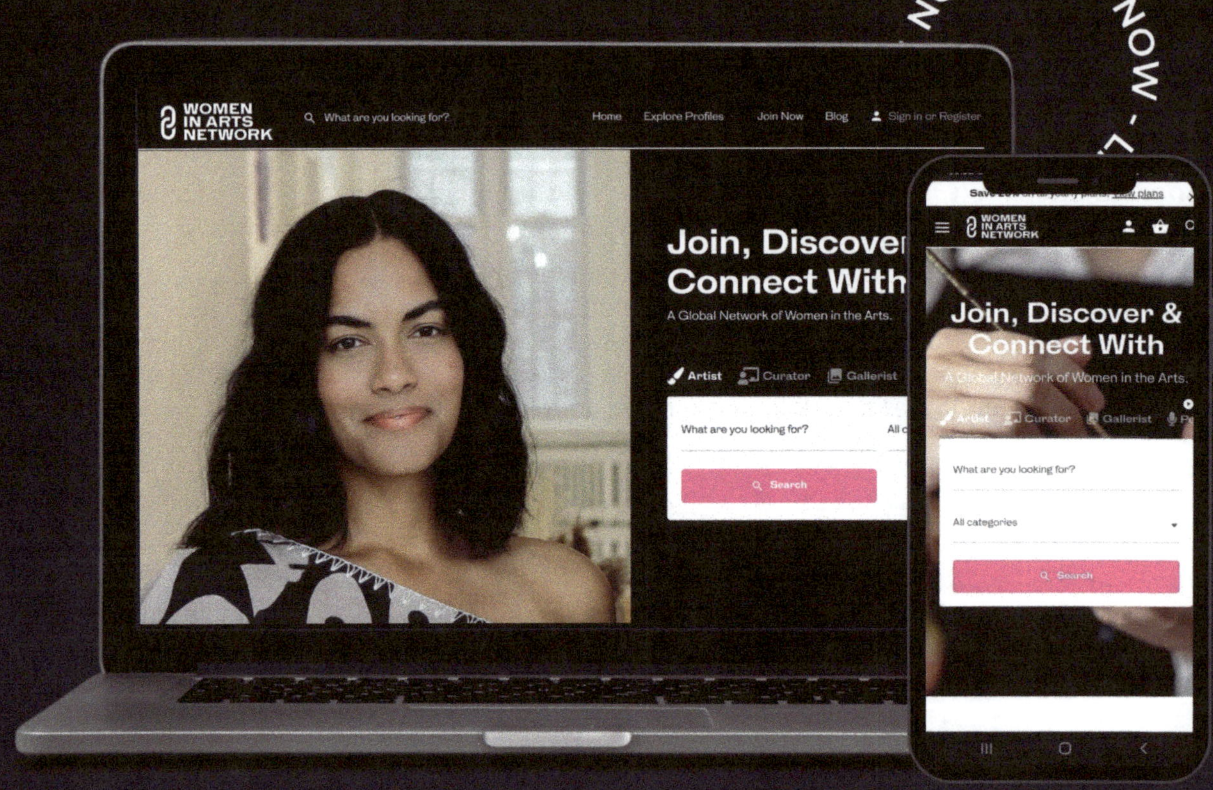

**A one-of-a-kind Global Directory
connecting women in arts.**

What's Included in your Directory Page?

**Personalized Profile | Portfolio Showcase | Contact Information
Location Details | Direct Links to Your Website & Social Media**

WOMEN
IN ARTS
NETWORK.

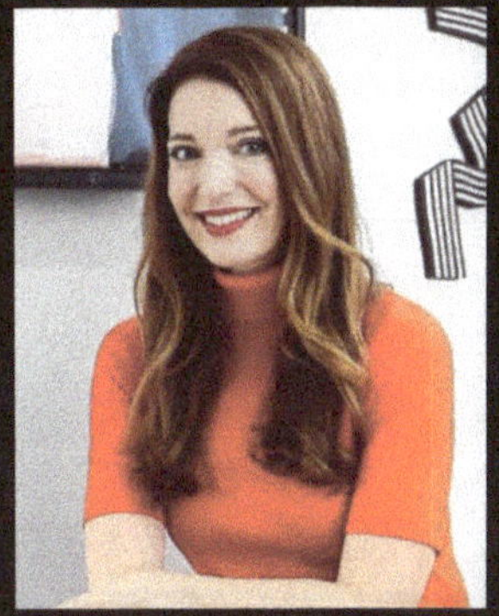

GALLERIST 

LIZ LIDGETT
United States

Liz Lidgett is an art advisor, curator, and gallery owner based in Des Moines. With expertise in corporate art advisory, online art advisory, and art curation, Liz is dedicated to promoting art and culture in her community.

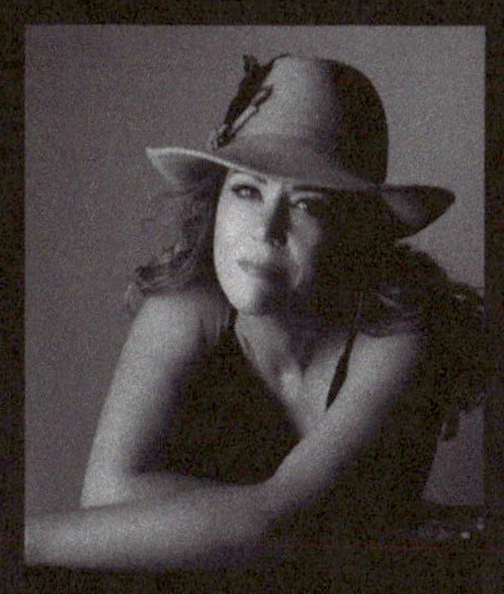

ARTIST 

JEN HAEFELI
United States

InterArtist Jen Haefeli: a versatile creator with a diverse portfolio, blending media and storytelling. Dedicated educator, advocate, and member of various art organizations. Believes in the power of creativity and encourages everyone to start somewhere.

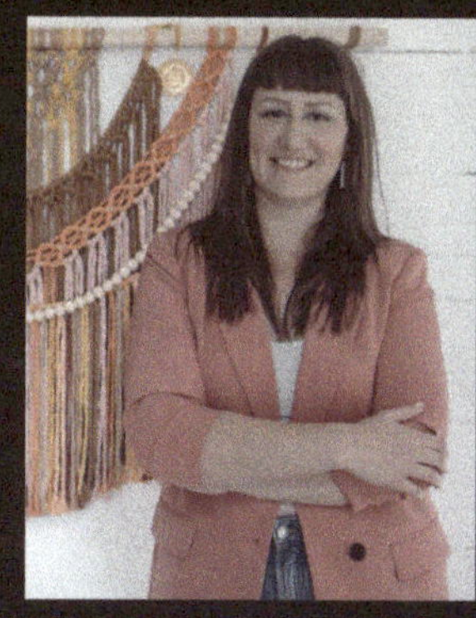

ARTIST 

KELSY SCHUMACHER
Scotland

Kelsy Schumacher, a fibre artist from Abbotsford, creates macrame wallhangings with passion. Each piece tells a story of delight, resilience, and introspection, inviting viewers to reflect on their own journey.

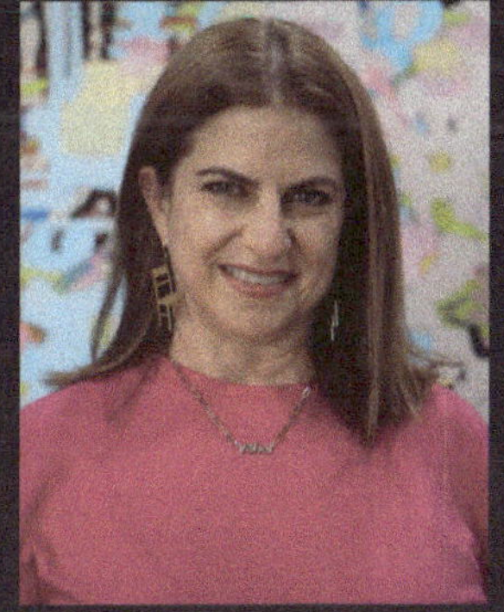

PAINTER 

YAHEL YAN
Maxico

Yahel Yan is a painter exploring the relationship between color and emotion. Yan was exposed to art from an early age and always knew that she wanted to become a visual artist. In her work, she explores the relationship between color, imagination, emotion, and memory.

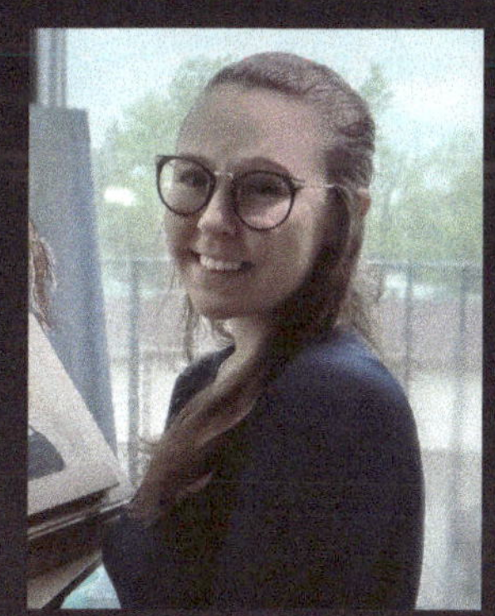

ARTIST 

HALEY BARCLAY
United States

Haley Barclay: a self-taught watercolor artist, creates vibrant illustrative portraits with a touch of surrealism. Her work is showcased globally, blending digital and physical gallery experiences. Passionate about nature, Haley brings joy and connection through her art.

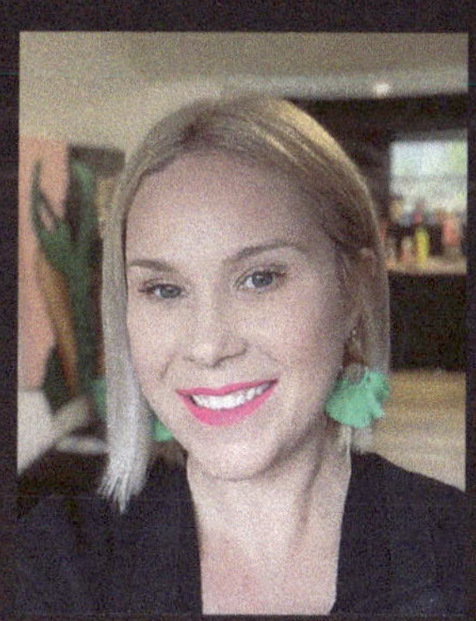

ARTIST 

CELINE GABRIELLE
Canada

I create art inspired by bold colors, fashion, and pop culture, telling stories through layers of acrylic and oil. Slow and meticulous, I refine each section to capture the essence of my inspirations. From the '20s to today, my work connects past and present in a vibrant and engaging way.

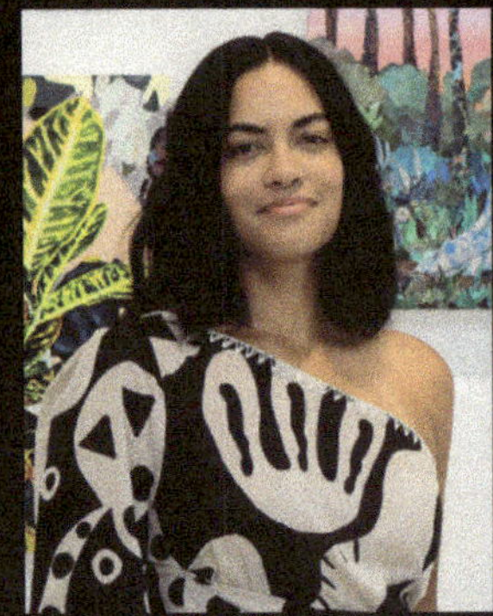

CURATOR 

ALICIA PUIG
Costa Rica

Alicia Puig is the curator & co-founder of PxP Contemporary, director at Create! Magazine, an arts writer, and co-author of The Complete Smartist Guide and The Creative Business Handbook. She has worked in the arts for over a decade in many facets of the industry.

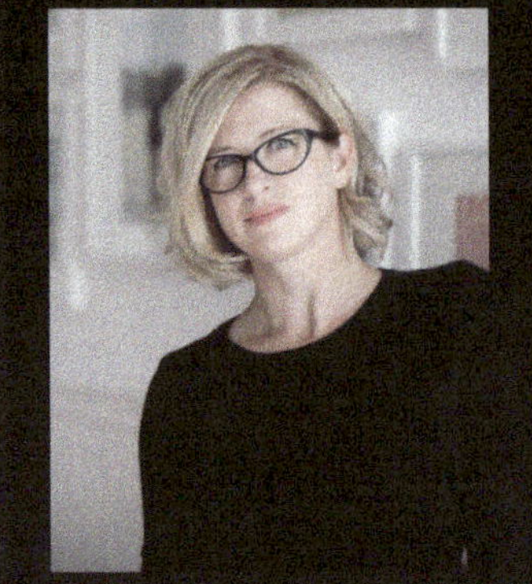

CURATOR 

THE JEALOUS CURATOR
Canada

Danielle Krysa: BFA in Visual Arts & post-grad in graphic design. Danielle is known as The Jealous Curator. TEDx speaker & author of "Creative Block", "Collage", "Your Inner Critic Is A Big Jerk" & "A Big Important Art Book – Now with Women".

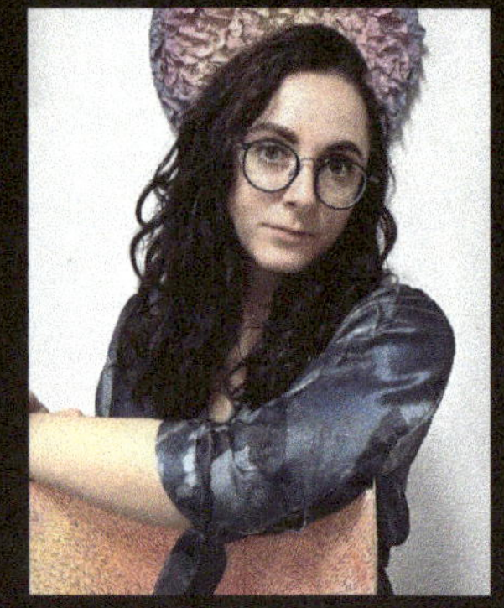

PAINTER 

ANNA COLLEVECCHIO
Russia

Born & raised in St. Petersburg, Russia, I'm a graphic artist with a passion for fine art. Using watercolors, stucco & gesso mixtures, I create paintings with a matte effect & finish them with gold leaf for a glowing halo effect.

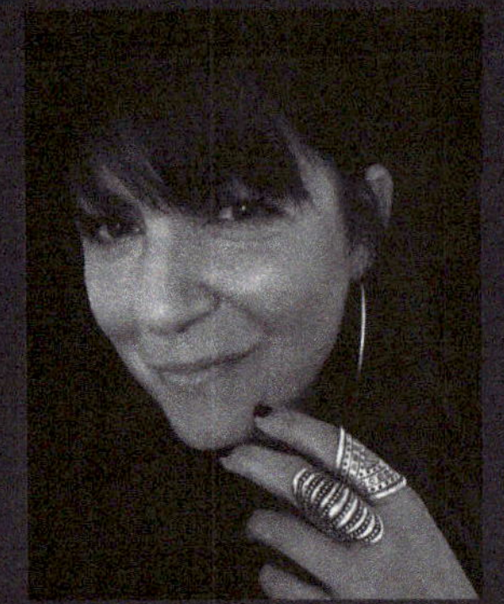

ARTIST 

SARA DE PASQUALE
Switzerland

Sara De Pasquale: visionary artist from Zurich. My art captures urban life's energy, blending ceramics with empowerment, love, and acceptance. Join my visual journey celebrating the beauty of the present moment.

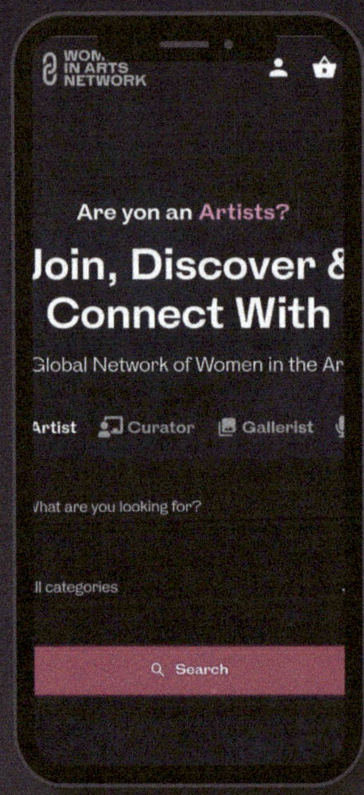

BECOME A MEMBER TODAY!

WWW.WOMENINARTSNETWORK.COM

Learn More

Get Published
In next issue

Submit your artwork for the next issue of Arts to Hearts Magazines. Join the wait-list or submit now.

For More Opportunities

Submit to Call for Art
Showcase your Artwork
Get Global Exposure

Join the Waitlist

Get published in next issue
Show your latest Artwork
Get Recognised

Arts To Hearts Quest

A 90-Day Journey To Find Your Artist Soul" is the ultimate guide for artists exploring their creative potential and connecting with their true selves.

Shop Now

Scan to get access

MASTER
ARTIST INVENTORY
Management system

Our Inventory Management Master Sheet is designed to empower artists like you, helping you increase productivity, gain valuable insights into your artwork's whereabouts and sales, and make informed decisions to maximize your earnings.

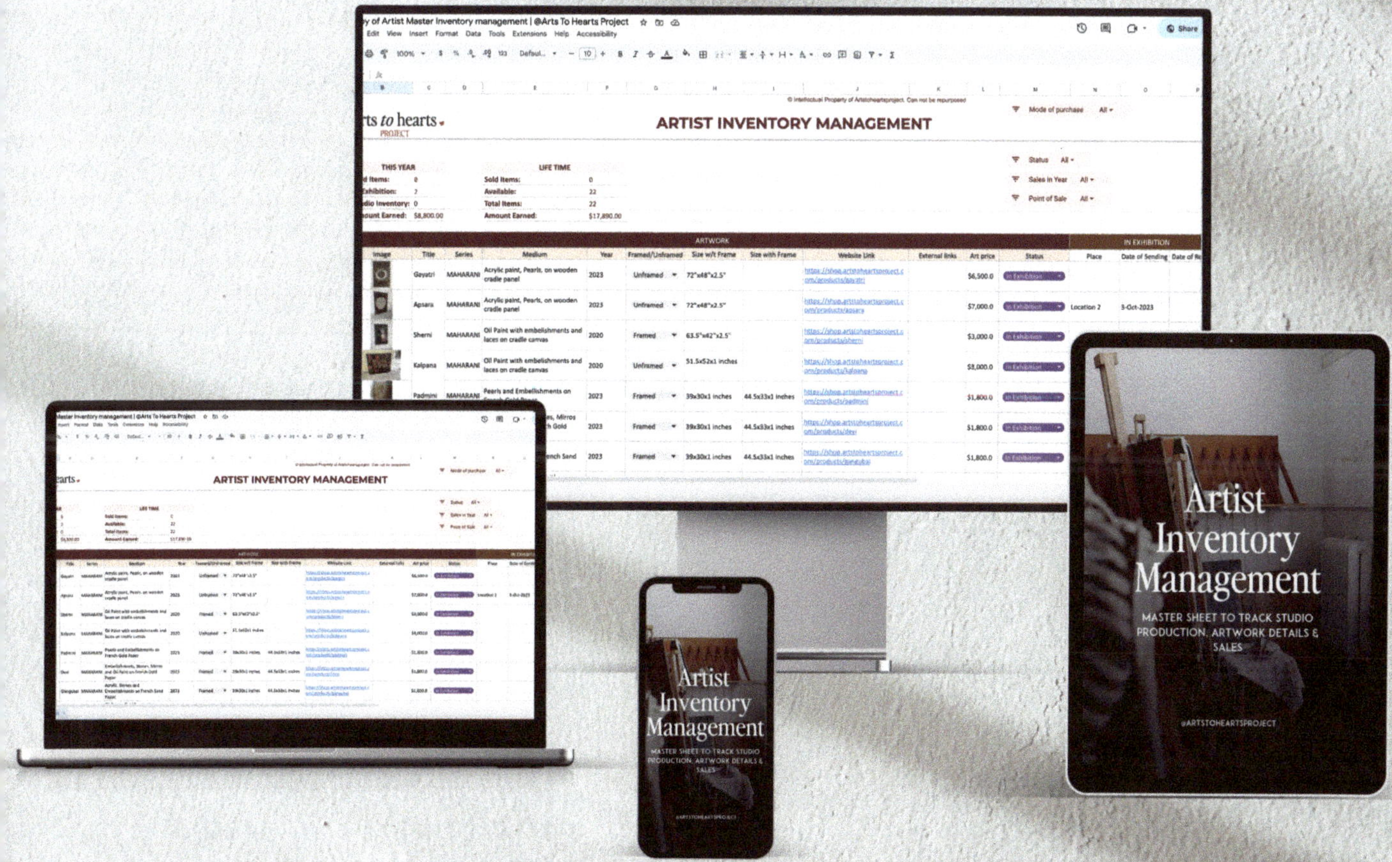

ACCESS NOW

WWW.ARTSTOHEARTSPROJECT.COM

arts to hearts

MAGAZINE

We are a contemporary
Art publication on a mission to
Discover, connect, and engage with
Contemporary & emerging
Women artists from around the world.

A Product of

ARTS TO HEARTS PROJECT

We are a global creative community uniting contemporary & emerging women Artists
to build successful, fulfilling, and money-making careers via collaboration, learning,
community, networking, and peer-to-peer learning.

SUBMIT YOUR WORK

We have several opportunities throughout the year for people
interested in the global arts. From open calls to grants to exhibits,
you can stay on top of all our upcoming and ongoing opportunities
by subscribing to our newsletter on our website.

COVER ART
Vintage Valentine
2023
29.7 x 21cm

VISIT OUR WEBSITE
www.artstoheartsproject.com

FOLLOW US ON INSTAGRAM
@artstoheartsproject

ISBN CODES
E-book reader: 978-81-968407-1-6

Paperback / Softback: 978-81-968407-5-4

JOIN ARTS TO HEARTS CLUB
http://www.artstoheartsproject.com/athclub

EMAIL info@artstoheartsproject.com

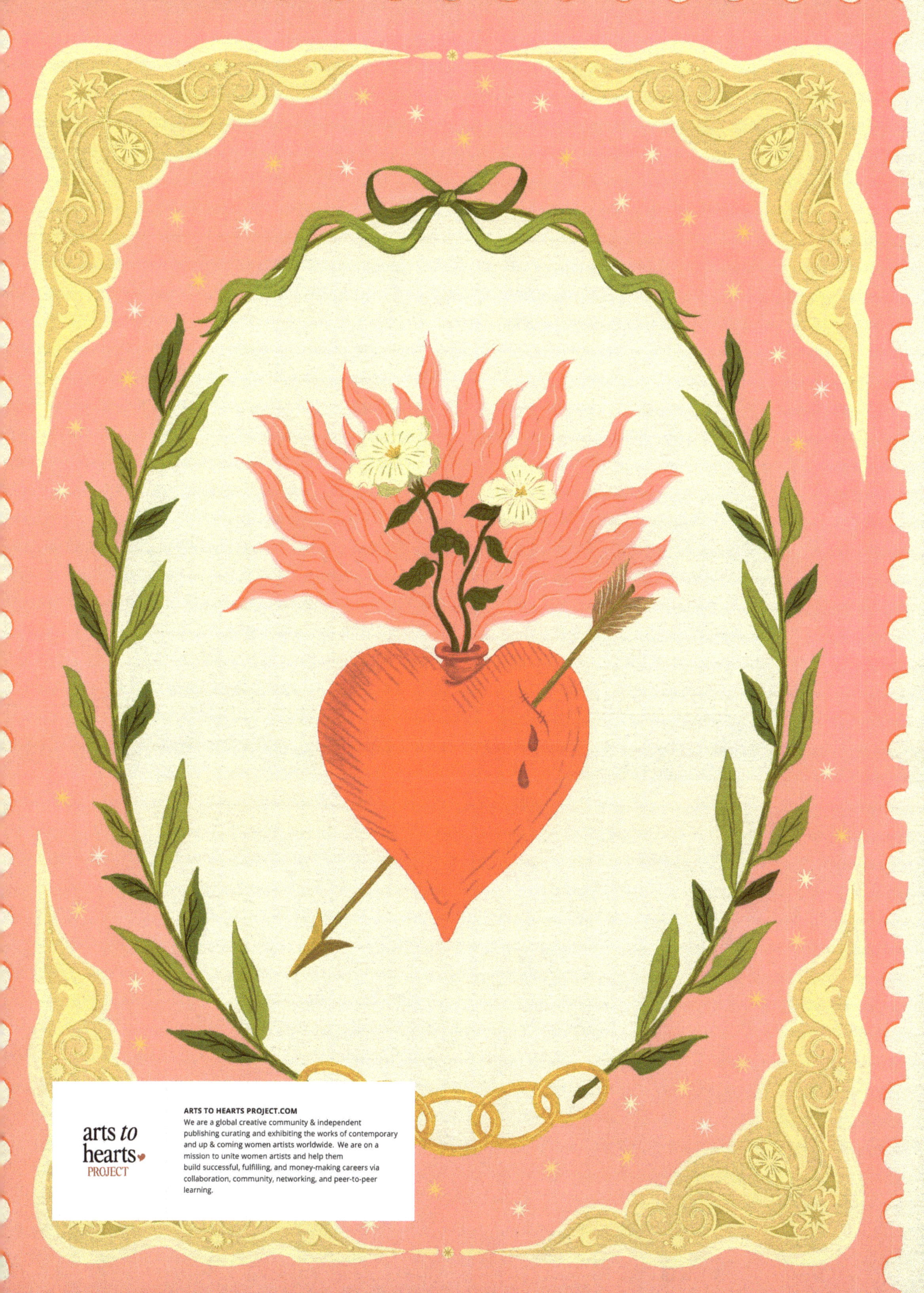
arts to hearts PROJECT

www.ingramcontent.com/pod-product-compliance
Lightning Source LLC
Chambersburg PA
CBHW060941310326
42107CB00056B/1878